T0270072

"Once again, Tom lets readers tap into his incredible network of energy thought leaders to see that Thomas Edison's spirit of innovation is alive and well."

—**Tom Kuhn,** President, Edison Electric Institute

"Tom has assembled decades of strategic advice and insight on innovation and our clean energy transition into a single, highly readable volume, which will become required reading for executives, investors, and policymakers in our sector."

—**Richard McMahon,** Senior Vice President of Energy Supply and Finance, Edison Electric Institute

"*Bright Moves* delivers a strategy primer on why utilities are at an inflection point between 120 years of operational excellence and a digital age promising better, faster, cheaper innovation. Tom takes us from the operating floor to the C-suite to share innovation best practices to create value through commercialization."

—**Bob Irvin,** Executive Director, Joules

"The electric and gas utility industries have innovated for years to meet rising customer needs and expectations. As *Bright Moves* describes, innovation will play an even greater role as the industry continues to execute its robust clean energy transition plans reliably and affordably."

—**Warner Baxter,** Executive Chairman, Ameren

"*Bright Moves* chronicles how the utility industry has effectively managed change and brought benefits to customers through innovative projects in generation, the grid, and customer experience. We will continue to make advances in innovation by encouraging customer engagement in driving decarbonization and battling climate change."

—**Mark Fronmuller,** Senior Vice President of Strategy, Sustainability, Innovation, and Risk Management, Ameren

"*Bright Moves* artfully captures the innovation journey the utilities industry has traveled, the challenges and accomplishments along the way, and the vital role innovation plays in charting our transition to clean energy."

—**Scott Morris,** Chairman of the Board, Avista

"A deep dive into the utility industry's history of innovation is long overdue. You don't have to be an industry insider to find *Bright Moves* a compelling read. Innovation is the lifeblood of our industry, and Tom captures both its importance and its value to our companies, our customers, and the future of the energy industry."

—**Dennis Vermillion,** President and CEO, Avista

"*Bright Moves* provides an in-depth look at how U.S. utilities are leveraging our innovation capacity to both strengthen our core business and position our companies as vital partners in achieving the cleantech transition."

—**Lynn Good,** Chair, President, and CEO, Duke Energy

"Innovation in the utility industry has been taken for granted for some time. Tom's book highlights the work the industry is doing in this area in a very meaningful way."

—**Brian Savoy,** Executive Vice President and CFO, Duke Energy

"With over four decades of experience, Tom has helped many companies find and pursue key opportunities to innovate, shorten the learning curve, and challenge us to be better at what we do, which is deliver for our customers a clean, affordable, resilient, and more equitable energy future."

—**Steve Woerner,** President, New England, National Grid

"Innovation in the energy sector has traditionally been slower than in other sectors. We need to marshal forces in almost a moonshot-like fervor to create the innovation that will be required for an efficient transition to a clean energy future. Brought together by our common goal to provide clean, safe, reliable, and affordable energy, Tom and I have worked for decades to discover innovative energy solutions for customers."

—**Tom Fanning,** Chairman and CEO, Southern Company

"Innovation across the entire enterprise is now a required element of strategy for electric and gas utilities. Fail to recognize and master this, and you may find your company in the rearview mirror of your peers and competitors. *Bright Moves* provides an opportunity to see how several leading utilities have made innovation a core part of their corporate strategy. Tom's experience in advising and helping these companies shape and stand up these efforts offers a worthwhile time investment for anyone desiring to improve their innovation game."

—**Mark Lantrip,** former President, Southern Company Services

"As you turn the pages, you will begin to see innovation in a new light. This book is chock-full of real-world examples that will broaden your view of how innovation and progress go hand in hand. Some see innovation as the province of the high-tech world. *Bright Moves* shatters that myth and illustrates that innovation is at the core of how utilities think about our business."

—**Gale Klappa,** Executive Chairman, WEC Energy

"Tom has established himself over decades as one of the most respected—and results-oriented—strategic consultants in the utilities industry. Utilities constantly innovate without much notice. This book provides the history of some of the leading innovators, with insights on the most recent success stories."

—**Dan Krueger,** Executive Vice President of Infrastructure and Generation Planning, WEC Energy

"Is there anyone in the utilities industry who has accelerated the innovation movement as much as the author of this book? Though there are several other laudable innovation leaders, I think not."

—**Steve Mitnick,** Executive Editor, *Public Utilities Fortnightly*

BRIGHT MOVES

HOW U.S. UTILITY INNOVATION
IS DRIVING THE
CLEANTECH TRANSITION

Thomas J. Flaherty

GREENLEAF
BOOK GROUP PRESS

This publication is designed to provide accurate and authoritative information in regard to the subject matter covered. It is sold with the understanding that the publisher and author are not engaged in rendering legal, accounting, or other professional services. Nothing herein shall create an attorney-client relationship, and nothing herein shall constitute legal advice or a solicitation to offer legal advice. If legal advice or other expert assistance is required, the services of a competent professional should be sought.

Published by Greenleaf Book Group Press
Austin, Texas
www.gbgpress.com

Copyright © 2023 Thomas J. Flaherty

All rights reserved.

Thank you for purchasing an authorized edition of this book and for complying with copyright law. No part of this book may be reproduced, stored in a retrieval system, or transmitted by any means, electronic, mechanical, photocopying, recording, or otherwise, without written permission from the copyright holder.

Distributed by Greenleaf Book Group

For ordering information or special discounts for bulk purchases, please contact Greenleaf Book Group at PO Box 91869, Austin, TX 78709, 512.891.6100.

Design and composition by Greenleaf Book Group and Lindsay Starr
Cover design by Greenleaf Book Group and Lindsay Starr

Publisher's Cataloging-in-Publication data is available.

Print ISBN: 979-8-88645-061-3

eBook ISBN: 979-8-88645-062-0

To offset the number of trees consumed in the printing of our books, Greenleaf donates a portion of the proceeds from each printing to the Arbor Day Foundation. Greenleaf Book Group has replaced over 50,000 trees since 2007.

Printed in the United States of America on acid-free paper

23 24 25 26 27 28 29 30   10 9 8 7 6 5 4 3 2 1

First Edition

*To my former clients, who consistently demonstrated
just how powerful innovative thinking could be*

Contents

Acknowledgments

THE U.S. utilities industry has experienced many inflection points over its last 50 years. Just between the 1970s and 1990s, it saw the introduction of nuclear power, an oil embargo, passage of Public Utility Regulatory Policies Act legislation to introduce fuel diversity, extended prohibition on natural gas use in new generating facilities, heightened interest in energy efficiency, sentiment against fossil fuel generation, and the renewal and expansion of natural gas generation. But momentous shifts in the U.S. utilities sector did not end then. The significant consolidation of companies, proliferation and demise of nonphysical trading and marketing books, return to basics in strategy, multiple pieces of environmental legislation, burgeoning interest in renewables development, accelerated replacement of cast-iron pipes, rapid coal generation displacement, early retirement of nuclear generation, global sentiment for decarbonization, and several recessions and wars along the way made for a constantly shifting market and an uncertain industry model that continues to today.

As utilities consider what the remainder of the 2020s and early 2030s may bring for them, the nature and pace of change are not about singular utility impacts but about how the entire industry will be affected. More importantly, it will be about how the industry positions itself to meet future challenges and thrive in a market environment where digital mastery and strategic agility will make the difference.

Starting in 2013, I was fortunate to work with several clients on advancing their readiness for the cleantech transition, contributing to understanding the future and its implications for these companies. But the story of these upcoming years will be written by current and succeeding leaders of U.S. utilities, many of which have been at the forefront of experiencing this tumultuous past and will now be shaping its evolution. Their points of view, motivations, responses, and actions provide clear insight into their thinking, priorities, and objectives. They represent a view from the front lines of industry evolution—both challenges and opportunities.

Numerous executives from the government, venture capital, technology research, and utility communities made themselves available to me to provide their perspectives and insights into how they have responded to a range of disruptive influences and, more importantly, how they are preparing to capitalize on the opportunities they see available.

These individuals are highly regarded in their natural sectors, as well as across adjacent sectors that compose the innovation ecosystem. I am appreciative of the willingness of these executives and their staffs to share their time and aid me in telling the stories of their companies, while subsequently informing some of my own perspectives. These are seasoned individuals with a wealth of experience and knowledge to offer utilities, as well as those sectors affected by events of the cleantech transition.

Specific thanks go to the following utility executive chairs, chief executive officers (CEOs), and senior executives who actively participated in the development of this book: Warner Baxter and Mark Fronmuller at Ameren, Dennis Vermillion and Scott Morris at Avista, Lynn Good and Brian Savoy at Duke Energy, John Pettigrew and Ben Wilson at National Grid, Tom Fanning and Mark Lantrip at Southern Company, and Gale Klappa and Dan Krueger at WEC Energy. Also, other officers and staff at each of these companies were vital to providing relevant internal information, perspective, and clarity on their achievements.

Many thanks are also due to CEOs and senior executives at the entities that tirelessly serve and support the utilities industry: Paul Dabbar and Lane Genatowski, both recently with the Department of Energy and the Advanced Research Projects Agency–Energy; Arshad Mansoor at EPRI; Tom Kuhn and Richard McMahon at the Edison Electric Institute; Hans Kobler and Kevin Fitzgerald at Energy Impact Partners; and Bob Irvin and Ryan Rutledge at Joules Accelerator.

Many other CEOs, executives, and professionals from throughout the utilities industry contributed to the body of innovation knowledge I accumulated over my years involved with the sector, shaping my perspectives and enabling this book to be written. All these individuals deserve recognition for the many collaborations we had and their contribution to the utilities industry, particularly related to innovation.

And it goes without saying that the many projects I performed for utilities—and insights gained related to the cleantech transition and innovation strategy and execution—would not have been possible without the many contributions of my consulting colleagues over my long years of involvement with the sector, particularly from the era of innovation starting 10 years ago.

Introduction

THE U.S. utilities industry has enjoyed more than 200 years of development, evolution, and operation in fulfillment of its charter to provide and deliver power and gas to its customers. Across multiple cycles of change in this extended time window, the industry has been subject to gradual, accelerated, and instant change in how it has produced its commodity products and performed its delivery businesses.

Over most of this period, the utilities sector has enjoyed relative obscurity, although when its formation became highly visible as a critical piece of the industrial revolution, the technologies it relied on became more concentrated, novel, or economic. As public sentiment centered on the industry's structure, costs, and performance, it became highly visible in a manner, challenging long-held precepts of purpose and public interest.

Within just the last 20 years, the fundamentals of the business—supply, environment, delivery, consumption, and risk—have been under siege and affected by a public desire to seek something different from the existing model of fossil fuel reliance, subregional decision-making, traditional markets, captive customers, and increasing rates.

Around the year 2000, attention shifted from business as usual to a new paradigm for the industry's role and structure, a move that continues and expands today. A model based on centralized generation (large assets), analog technology (one-way communication), and standardized offerings (utility-designed) has been replaced by one relying on decentralized assets (closer to load), digitalization (binary exchange and conversion), and tailored products and services (customer centricity). Inherently, this translates to broadened supply choices, expanded technology application, and meaningful customer choice.

While many in the industry describe the upheaval in progress as the *energy transition* (i.e., a move away from fossil-fuel-based generation), in reality, it is a much broader and concerted shift to adoption of breakthrough technologies designed to support decarbonization of utilities—the *cleantech transition*—and create valuable technology- and knowledge-based products. Cleantech is the enabler for the larger energy transition, and technology is the fundamental driver of that shift.

The cleantech transition underway is causing the utilities industry to rethink its capital deployment, accelerate technology adoption, and redefine its customer purpose. Although the transition end date is not consistently communicated, many policy makers and utility executives speak in terms of 2035–2050 as the culmination of a multigenerational shift from less fossil fuel to more clean energy, larger- to smaller-scale supply sources, dispersed to localized supply deployment, and cautious to accelerated technology adoption.

The utilities sector is facing challenges that extend well beyond its legacy history. Utilities recognize that successfully navigating the cleantech transition requires unconventional actions to ensure both readiness for the transition and capabilities advancement to see their way through this transition. This recognition leads the industry to the realization that it will need to become far more innovative than it has been in the past.

Cleantech transition readiness requires the utilities sector to think more like the competitive companies it will interface with and rely on, as well as anticipate the future needs of its customers, particularly larger commercial and industrial entities, which are already demanding greater consideration of their needs and have access to alternative providers.

The number of articles, studies, and books published about innovation on the global and domestic business stages continues to grow each year. Whether written by consultants, academics, scientists, executives, or policy makers, they all provide a glimpse into the state of innovation and the direction of travel it is taking—that is, its evolving importance, scope, and sources.

These publications tend to talk about innovation across industries and as a fundamental element of business acumen, rather than take a more vertical look into specific sectors, particularly utilities. In fact, an interested reader is hard-pressed to find material directed to utilities. Certainly, much has been written about the cleantech transition and what the future could look like, but little has been directed to the discrete innovation paths being followed by industry participants or the challenges to stand up, embed, and sustain innovation as a strategy and market-positioning tool.

When innovation is discussed with respect to the cleantech transition, it is typically picked up from a capital investment and asset substitution perspective, rather than from an integrated strategy and platform creation point of view, or a ubiquitous way of thinking within utilities. Thus, there is a gap between external expectations to innovate (to displace) and the internal innovation motivations and approaches adopted by companies (to deliver outcomes).

While a number of utilities have undertaken formal efforts to pursue and instill a culture of innovation, their approaches have usually been bespoke and seldom publicly shared. Smart companies believe innovation provides a competitive advantage and seek to protect their intellectual capital regarding innovation strategy and execution—even the fundamental choices they make and processes they follow. Yet a minority of companies believe that market communication is a necessary predicate for advancing the underlying objective of innovation—positioning their enterprise as an innovator with investors, vendors, regulators, and customers.

The more prevalent case is that many utilities have taken informal approaches to innovation and, while championing its purpose and importance internally, are in nascent stages of adoption and alignment to business strategy, development and deployment of technologies, and design and commercialization of customer offerings. These companies often believe they have an extended time frame to address the cleantech transition, with market evolution moving at a manageable pace against future conditions. They are also concerned that they may lack the scale to succeed in a more competitive market and hope to create advantages that cannot be easily minimized or circumvented.

This book focuses on addressing the awareness gap between *what* utilities are strategically and operationally changing to respond to the cleantech transition and *how* they are conceiving innovation as a means to—and beyond—that end. It reflects my more than 45-year consulting history and the observation and design of a variety of business models, market strategies, and go-to-market models of clients and competitive entities. More specifically, it incorporates direct experience in assisting multiple utilities with assessment of critical innovation priorities, expectations and outcomes, alternative innovation approaches, methods of execution, and definitions of success.

It would have been easier to simply provide a conceptual overview and discussion about innovation in this book, but this would have been a limiter to the value intended from its message. For readers to obtain full value from an innovation-centered book, the discussion needs to extend beyond an abstract presentation about innovation concepts to a more tangible demonstration of how entities and companies are engaged in the practice of innovation for strategic and customer benefit.

Importantly, the relevant innovation community extends beyond core innovation adopters (utilities) to innovation catalysts (external support organizations) that provide fundamental services, advice, or capital to companies and the industry. To enrich this book, it was crucial to provide insight into how government, trade associations, research entities, incubators, and investor groups, which are critical parties to end-to-end innovation processes and outcomes, contribute to the realization of both company and industry objectives. The direct involvement of leaders of these organizations provides external perspective on how they see the purpose of their innovation pursuit, collaborate with companies in and outside the sector, view current industry innovation progress, and anticipate how their roles in innovation engagement and partnering could change in the near- and long-term future.

Several key organizations consented to be profiled, including the Department of Energy Advanced Research Projects Agency–Energy (funding and research and development center), EPRI (research and development center), Edison Electric Institute (trade organization), Energy Impact Partners (investor and advisor), and Joules Accelerator (accelerator). Their insights about innovation success and sustainability and about industry positioning and engagement are invaluable to utility executives and start-ups, respectively.

Of course, any discussion of utilities innovation is diminished without providing direct insight into utilities sector approaches to innovation to date and *where* and *how* these efforts were conducted. Six executive chairs or CEOs and their senior executives responsible for innovation stand-up and/or oversight provided critical perspectives into how they considered the need to pursue innovation, initiated their innovation efforts, developed their priorities and expected outcomes, conducted their assessment and development activities, created grid or customer-directed outcomes, engaged with third parties, and deployed technologies and business models. These experiences yield priceless insights and examples for peer companies to understand and consider and are the centerpiece of this book.

These perspectives, insights, and, most importantly, foresights complemented my own views on utilities innovation developed from hands-on involvement with a wide range of clients in innovation platform conceptualization and stand-up, as well as on market evaluation, technology assessment, partnering models, deployment considerations, and commercialization readiness. The book's structure moves naturally from *why* there is a need for innovation, to *what* companies specifically have done, to *how* innovation success can be achieved.

"Innovation in Perspective" (Chapter 1) describes how research and development (R&D) and innovation have become critical elements of successful company strategies across the U.S. economy. The chapter defines attributes that typify robust innovation capabilities among companies and how the utilities sector is recognizing that market success depends on aggressive thinking and robust market-based systems.

"Disruptive Influences" (Chapter 2) addresses the changing nature of external policies and technologies affecting R&D and innovation activities across the utilities industry. It also identifies how these legislative and regulatory policies and subsequent market-based stimuli are shaping the nature of utilities' responses to these expectations, requirements, and priorities.

"Global Innovators" (Chapter 3) reviews the history of innovation within different sectors of the global economy and how those sectors have responded to external market shifts, particularly with absolute and relative levels of spend. Additional discussion is directed at the composition of the most-admired innovators in the world and what distinguishes them from their peers.

"Utility Investment" (Chapter 4) highlights the focus, nature, and level of historical expended capital and expenditures by the U.S. utilities sector and its companies in recent periods. The absolute and relative scale of this spend, particularly compared to leading European utilities, provides a view into how U.S. companies are positioned relative to select international peers.

"Profiles in Innovation: The Enablers" (Chapter 5) portrays the range of entities that participate in or complement utility R&D and innovation and interface with the sector. It discusses the government, research, trade association, accelerator, and investor entities that enable utilities or start-up companies to achieve targeted objectives of technology, product, and business innovation.

"Profiles in Innovation: The Innovators" (Chapter 6) explores how select utilities have pursued innovation agendas and related strategies, challenges, and accomplishments. It reviews the specific priorities and objectives, stand-up, execution, and achievements of six specific U.S. utilities that have been successful with many elements of R&D and innovation.

"Platform Stand-Up" (Chapter 7) provides insight into how utilities have wrestled with the formative questions of establishing a robust innovation system within their unique environments. It directly assesses the elements and options of embedding a successful platform, including philosophy, governance, strategy, structure, alignment, management, messaging, execution, and measurement.

"Achieving Success" (Chapter 8) analyzes the range of potential external and internal impediments to successful innovation within utilities. The industry's experiences in successfully positioning and sustaining innovation platforms, and the nature of potential responses to adoption challenges, provide insights into how to enhance attainment of intended enterprise objectives.

"Operationalization to Commercialization" (Chapter 9) recognizes that the utilities sector has historically focused on deploying new technologies or capabilities into operations to enhance performance and reliability. This discussion addresses that now is the time for these companies to expand their vision into how to adopt a broader commercial mindset with customers.

"Innovation Strategies" (Chapter 10) describes what companies need to consider in defining, articulating, and messaging their future priorities, emphases on innovation, and channels to optimize spend and focus. It defines the challenges of aligning strategy with innovation and establishes the range of key innovation success enhancers that executives can leverage to advance their objectives.

"Refreshing the Agenda" (Chapter 11) looks over the horizon to how current innovation platforms may evolve and how companies can distinguish themselves from their peers. The chapter also addresses what the next level of innovation could look like and whether utilities can enhance their value with investors and customers as they become more adept in advancing their own innovation platforms.

Innovation is a more qualitative than quantitative topic given the broad range of its interpretation by pundits and practitioners. Consequently, much of the discussion in this book relates to the *what*, *where*, and *how* about innovation, rather than the *how much* spend. Nonetheless, several empirical measures are available and referenced in specific areas of this book to provide a glimpse into the level and direction of spend of both utilities and venture capital.

For companies that have already been on a multiyear innovation journey, readers will remember some of these growing pains and the challenges faced and overcome. Like their peers, they will also recognize similar decisive moments and the available options and considerations at the time that went into ultimate strategy definition, innovation stand-up, and early and ongoing execution. While the innovation process can be choppy and uneven at times, most companies will say any missteps were necessary and that they capitalized on the lessons learned from them.

Far more companies than the group of peers above have yet to formalize how they think about innovation, as many have only been active for a limited number of years. These companies may be considering a future path to potentially pursue or elevate internal innovation, jump-starting a directed effort to meet new market direction, or course-correcting a current effort to regain momentum on the innovation journey. In these cases, lessons learned from earlier starting points and the more active history of their peers can help these companies accelerate their own efforts and avoid this learning curve. These utilities will gain a broader understanding of what can make innovation actions successful and outcomes more attainable.

Non-utilities readers may have less appreciation about how the utilities sector has been approaching innovation, what results have been achieved, and how those results will manifest in a manner visible to them as customers. But this book will enable them to think about how different the utility business may look to them in the future.

The U.S. utilities sector (as opposed to individual companies) has had an active history of R&D conducted internally at the company level, as well as through a population of supportive third parties. While much of this research has been more asset targeted than overly broad in its intent, it has created a rich history for the industry to build on. And with the acceleration of the cleantech transition, the sector has elevated its emphasis on readiness for a future landscape that is still unclear.

This readiness journey to decarbonization and digitalization has taken almost a decade to date and will continue for several more to come. The utilities industry anticipates that innovation expenditures will continue as a normal part of its business spend pattern. What will be different is where this spend will be targeted and how the go-to-market models for each company will incorporate the results of this innovation.

At present, the U.S. utilities industry's level of innovation spend does not even remotely parallel that of other traditionally competitive industries. In fact, it substantially trails that of its larger international peers, which is also quite modest relative to other sectors and has not been appreciably increasing over time.

There is no reason, however, why the nature of innovation imagination, and thus the level of related spend, should remain so constrained. It is possible that a *push* from state regulators and a *pull* from customers could be a catalyst to incent utilities to expand their commitment to innovation and absolute level of spend. Additionally, the utilities sector is a highly technical sector that is heavily dependent on technology for the supply, transportation, and delivery of its commodities. Consequently, well-funded and global original equipment manufacturers are embedded providers and constantly engaged with their utility customers. These entities—whether simple providers or active competitors—could act as a further catalyst to the level of necessary innovation spend.

With the clean energy transition directionally correct but consequentially uncertain, the U.S. utilities industry will remain in flux for the next several decades. The sector will look substantially different by 2035, even if some of its core tenets remain intact regarding safety, reliability, quality, and affordability. Innovation will be a centerpiece of utility strategies and a focal point for utilities' internal organization as well as their external customers. The shape of innovation in this dynamic environment will further emerge over the course of the next five to seven years, but more time will be needed to sharpen its future contours as the ultimate selection of priorities is yet to be fully visible.

CHAPTER 1

Innovation in Perspective

G ROWTH and prosperity in the U.S. economy over the 20th and 21st centuries have been jointly stimulated by directed federal policy, continuous technology evolution, aggressive market strategies, and intelligent company management. But less visible and more essential catalysts for these outcomes have been underlying executive attitudes and commitments to relentless advancement of their fundamental businesses, core technologies, and product offerings inherent to their current and prospective customers.

These catalysts stimulate continuous business expansion through emphasis on two fundamental strategic activities undertaken by executive leadership of successful companies—pioneering R&D and revolutionary innovation. R&D has been a staple of many industries since the first and second industrial revolution eras of the 1700s, 1800s, and early 1900s.

But later in the 20th century, after these two initial industrial revolutions, the third industrial revolution began—the digital revolution—and industries such as manufacturing, pharmaceuticals, aerospace, electronics, and telecommunications rocketed in growth, spurred by incessant R&D and innovation. These two disciplines became table stakes for software-, technology-, services-, and product-oriented companies and aspirations for other sectors.

The focus on R&D has been sustained across these centuries as companies and industries recognize that technologies are not static or irreplaceable. Similarly, market positions are fragile and susceptible to ongoing disruption as competitors seek to solidify or create a formidable competitive position or establish future market distinction. And this R&D—whether basic or applied—has been the impetus and destination for considerable capital investment by companies, universities, laboratories, and the federal government.

However, over the past 20-plus years, traditional R&D discovery, evaluation, testing, advancement, and adoption activities have been supplemented by a more thought-provoking companion—the advent of less capital-intensive and more targeted application directed at strategically propelling a business forward.

An evolution has shifted from an R&D-rich environment, highly compulsory and invaluable to select industries, to one where the quest for innovation is something all companies can pursue at their own scale and intensity. And they can address this opportunity without committing to large and sustained capital spend, where eventual results are generally uncertain and often unfulfilled.

R&D used to be thought of as fundamental business advancement or scientific breakthroughs, occurring over long periods, and dependent on sustained capital commitment. Innovation is now viewed as much more facile and characteristic of targeted commercial application, near-term time horizons, and reliance on internal intellectual capital. And where R&D is conducted at scale among a limited set of qualified entities, innovation operates more fluidly across a mix of software developers, asset designers, solutions providers, and affected customers.

Innovation is a headline word in business vernacular today. It is frequently misunderstood, generally overused, and sometimes misused, but it remains nonetheless at the center of executive dialogue, academic interest, article focus, conference content, and business practice across American industry.

Consequently, innovation can easily become a vague trope used to characterize anything from normal management curiosity or sporadic interest in fundamental business change to deep exploration of business differentiation or reconfiguration of an industry itself. Particularly for utilities, appropriately framing innovation as a fundamental underpinning of a company's strategy will be important to optimizing any efforts expended on adoption and execution.

It is important to frame exactly what innovation means as referred to within this book. Innovation is not a process, project, or program, even though each is an element that is part of creating and enabling the overall fabric of innovation. These dimensions simply imply something that is short term in focus and inconsistent with what innovation should be about.

The goal of utilities—and all companies—should be to define an innovation model that moves an entity from an initial starting point to the establishment of an embedded and expanding platform. The innovation model encompasses the overall framework that leads to a formal platform embedded in the DNA of a utility and reflects a core mindset that permeates *how* the organization thinks about itself and its evolution. The innovation platform is partially a tangible construct that is positioned as the test bed for new ideas and the launchpad for operating and market excellence. But it is also partially intangible as it reflects a conceptual notion of business evolution that leads a company to its next level of maturity and performance.

This suggests that understanding *what* innovation is, and *what it is not*, is fundamental to considering the purpose and nature of actions to be taken. Further, it implies that utility executives need to determine dispassionately and thoroughly what they are attempting to accomplish by investing resources into standing up and sustaining a concerted innovation effort.

Framing Innovation

The term *innovation* is sometimes adopted to include general activities that focus on improving business execution and positioning, while at other times it is reflective of purposeful actions intended to fundamentally alter delivery systems and business models. Thus, the eventual impact can be relatively minor and adaptive or significant and disruptive.

As a generic term, innovation is in the eye of the beholder—what looks like innovation to some may be only business as usual to others, and what looks like disruption may simply be change. Innovation comes in many different flavors depending on the industry space occupied. For brand-driven, technology-dependent, or product-reliant companies, innovation is the differentiating lifeblood of these entities. Without continuous ideation, dedicated resources, rigorous development, sufficient spend, active management, and employee commitment, achieved market stature can be fleeting and fatally erode.

For modern-era companies like Alphabet, Amazon, Apple, Intel, and Microsoft, among others, innovation (often grounded in pure R&D) has been a touchstone of their fundamental enterprise DNA. These companies incessantly think about how to innovate in a manner that preserves and builds market share and brand reputation, as well as creates and captures new markets and untapped revenue sources. In each case, either technology (for applied use) is the competitive backbone, or scientific acumen (for the public interest) is the path to market leadership.

Stepping back from these entities, it is easy to understand why they are renowned for their innovation aptitude. They tend to operate in market sectors where technology is core to business success and dramatically evolves in real time. In addition, these companies tend to operate in highly concentrated industries where customer preference for their market offerings is a distinctive brand advantage. In both cases, sustained innovation at scale is critical to securing existing market position and capturing additional sector advantage.

For these companies, innovation is a competitive prerequisite, not a casual activity. At its core, innovation is a way of life at these companies and a trait nurtured and embedded throughout the enterprise. These companies do not consider innovation optional, as they face a daily challenge of ensuring their innovation focus is centered on the right areas to pursue and prioritize.

When you are already large scale with aggressive competitors—both traditional vendors and market disruptors—who are seeking to either erode existing market advantage or create new market domains, it is easy to rationalize that future brand positioning is closely tied to how well near-term innovation priorities match long-term market direction.

For capital-intensive, technology-reliant, or customer-facing companies—like utilities—innovation is a catalyst for market, operating, and customer performance. Without executive aspiration, strategic commitment, and employee engagement, market position can be disintermediated and easily forfeited. This is the challenge utilities face—understanding the difference in requirements between surviving and thriving and the trade-offs between action and inaction.

Utilities are relative newcomers to innovation emerging as a necessary enterprise capability. This sector has had to address pockets of competitiveness in areas like generation markets, operating role contraction, or original equipment manufacturer (OEM) and start-up disintermediation, but it has not had to face a *technology push–customer pull* environment like the present, where technology availability is forcing companies to adapt, and customers are often savvier about new technology availability and adoption benefits than the legacy utility.

The emphasis on *technology push* starts with OEMs, start-ups, software developers, and solutions providers being commercially incented to bring their new or enhanced offerings to market and convince customers of the merits of adoption and installation. These OEMs and vendors are acutely aware of the sea change occurring in the utilities sector and are determined to both accelerate its occurrence and secure leading market positions from adoption of their technology or software.

As expected, new technology availability leads its actual deployment as customers are slow to make technology changes—significant or minor—until they are confident that the offering to be deployed has been sufficiently field-tested and qualified. As a customer group, utilities are even more risk averse and are generally reluctant to adopt new technologies until market proven and to install new software without market demonstration among respected peers, sometimes taking a decade or more to fully deploy new technology.

In some cases, however, customer awareness of available technology enhancements outpaces the level of utility knowledge of these new offerings. The level of *customer pull* is usually facilitated by OEMs and vendors seeding the market with information and emphasis on demonstration projects intended to address customer concerns over early adoption and performance. In many cases, customers tend to learn more about these technologies and offerings directly from OEMs, vendors, and peers than they do from their utility providers.

When customer awareness and interest are ahead of utility knowledge and confidence, customers hold the transactional high ground, notwithstanding the quality of the preexisting relationship. Customers are aware that the utilities sector is reticent about sudden change and more comfortable with steady migration toward an end, rather than an untested shift away from the proven status quo, particularly when new software is involved.

Several utilities can be identified as R&D veterans, but these prior activities tended to be highly concentrated around their largest and most expensive assets—generation plants—and occurred in a distant past and in an environment unlike that in which they operate today. Several companies, such as Southern Company, American Electric Power, and Duke Energy, have been very successful with their R&D programs and have walls of patents to illustrate their activity and prowess.

But as generation fuel types shifted away from large-scale assets, and micro-technologies were deployed within the grid and networks, the ability to sustain an at-scale R&D effort diminished. Now, third-party reliance on a broader R&D community exists, with utilities centering their innovation efforts on performance improvements, technology displacement, regulatory concepts, business models, and, of course, customer responsiveness.

The challenges above provide the framework for this book and address how far the utilities industry has progressed in its innovation efforts, which impediments are constraining progress or jeopardizing future innovation success, and what the utilities sector can do to ensure future success. But these challenges, and utility actions in response, need to be further underscored by framing how to think about innovation itself and the type of impact anticipated from its pursuit.

Three Models

To put the concept of innovation into context, a simple working definition was adopted to frame a central tenet for this discussion. While more elegant wording and expanded descriptions appear in many theoretical journals and business discussions about innovation, minimal words can best convey what it refers to. In a practical sense, *innovation is simply the sustained development and deployment of new ideas that measurably enhance the value of the business—to both shareholders and customers.*

This definition sets the tone for considering how to think about innovation relative to R&D, which is either basic (discovery) or applied (commercial) and focused on exploration first and application second. In contrast, innovation is centered on improving how a business enhances its business model, go-to-market model, production system, delivery network, offering portfolio, and customer relationships. While R&D travels from the theoretical to the possible, innovation moves from an identified gap to a practical solution and outcome.

Innovation can be thought of as a progression of archetypes, rather than a single model, as different objectives and approaches may apply at different junctures of a business and for different strategic purposes. What distinguishes one archetype from another is the nature of the business, its dependencies on technology evolution or offering attractiveness, and the competitiveness of the sector.

Some sectors, like manufacturing, are constantly seeking production improvement and are eager to make a series of small improvements that adopt radical changes. Other sectors, like electronics, seek to leapfrog competitors and are far more comfortable with step changes in product and service functionality and features. And a few sectors, like services, seek to create a new category and revolutionize the service concept in a much more attractive manner.

Three models can be used to illustrate the spectrum of innovation characteristics: *incremental*, *advanced*, and *breakthrough*—each of which has different characteristics and intents (see Figure 1). *Incremental* best fits when operating performance and relationship strengthening are the focus; *advanced* is apropos when the intent is to substantially alter and enhance underlying business delivery platforms; and a *breakthrough* model aligns with seeking to shatter existing business models and redefine *where* and *how* a company makes money.

Incremental innovation is the initial stage of progression along the spectrum and typically focuses on better, faster, cheaper products and services, as well as small changes to business operating processes and performance. The outcomes of this stage do not usually result in above-average revenue growth and may be typified by product enhancements, next stage add-on products, and operational enhancements. This stage is largely reflective of how the preponderance of companies have historically approached innovation, such as Procter & Gamble and General Motors. Most utilities are at this stage given their relative immaturity and focus on early tangible results. This stage can also be considered *innovation with a lowercase i* and focused on simply making the business better.

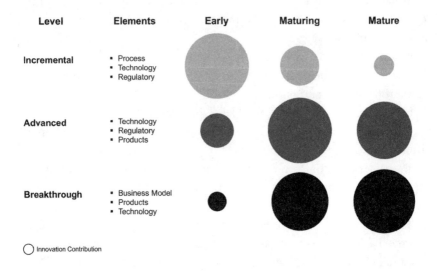

Level	Elements	Early	Maturing	Mature
Incremental	• Process • Technology • Regulatory			
Advanced	• Technology • Regulatory • Products			
Breakthrough	• Business Model • Products • Technology			

○ Innovation Contribution

Figure 1. Innovation archetypes.

The second stage is *advanced* innovation, which is targeted at creating significant change to either technologies deployed or market offerings to drive higher-than-average revenue and margin growth. This stage is typified by completely new and/or sophisticated platforms that enable a step change in the go-to-market model and expansion of market offerings. This stage often focuses on how companies compete and drive economic growth and value—for example, Samsung and Amazon. Utilities have yet to operate in this stage, even the larger entities that have deployed and dedicated significant resources to these platforms, beyond operations-oriented efforts. This stage reflects more attention to business growth and sophistication and can be considered *Innovation with a capital I*.

The third stage is *breakthrough* innovation, which is intended to redesign the basis of competition for the business by defining entirely new markets and offerings, expanding the nature and sources of value to customers, and reshaping how other market players are engaged. This stage is usually the product of serial innovators with consistently superior innovation capabilities or who seize market leadership by inventing novel ways to think about business purpose or delivering customer solutions, such as Tesla and Apple. This stage is still beyond the grasp (but not the reach) of most utilities and reflects the conservative nature of companies and the stage of market and innovation maturity they operate within. This final stage can be considered *INNOVATION in all caps* and reflective of game-changing moves and differentiation.

While the utilities sector is making progress along the innovation learning curve, it lags behind more competitive industries that have had decades to curate their position in new markets where intellectual capital really matters. Utilities are also subject to close regulatory scrutiny, which constrains the degree of freedom of companies and adds hurdles that other sectors do not face in competitive markets.

However, there are no showstopper reasons why utilities cannot expand their conceptual horizons, increase their level of committed funding, or accelerate their pace of actual idea exploration, assessment, and deployment, when it comes to innovation. All it takes is a combination of executive leadership, resource commitment, and thoughtful reimagination. Some of this thinking shift may benefit from adjacent influences, like the board of directors or customers, which would bring critical points of view to utilities wrestling with appropriately defining the right to position innovation in their enterprise.

It has been posited that all companies will be technology companies in the future. They will continuously incorporate fundamental technology elements into their market offerings (for example, telecommunications), be heavily dependent on technology applications from others for performance within their core offerings (such as aerospace), or develop and share technology advances across industries (as in electronics).

If the above premise is accurate, then most companies will need to become serious innovators, as the pace of change in technology evolution is rapidly accelerating and either creating market disruption to be addressed or providing market opportunity to be captured or foregone forever.

Even if this premise is only partially correct, these circumstances reinforce that companies absolutely need to become adept innovators and view these capabilities as both table stakes and differentiators to those companies that do not recognize these external market shifts and related requirements. As is further addressed in a subsequent chapter, the largest and most successful companies in the world are typified by a culture of innovation that reflects creating internal value from *advanced* or *breakthrough* thinking as a way of life in a market where companies either innovate or die.

Innovation Intensity

Simply expending prolific amounts of cash is not indicative of either market success or value creation. Expenditures are simply a barometer for innovation intensity, not the societal or financial value derived from its execution. But for the types of companies mentioned earlier, it is instructive to recognize that high levels of expenditures are usually linked to sectors that are rapidly evolving, intensely competitive, and uniquely differentiated.

As previously indicated, industries like manufacturing, pharmaceuticals, aerospace, electronics, and telecommunications are prodigiously innovation-oriented because their sectors are highly competitive, always evolving, and built on perfecting smart and needle-moving ideas into marketable solutions.

For example, manufacturers are always seeking more efficient production methods or equipment because large impacts to fixed and marginal costs and time to market can occur. Pharmaceutical companies constantly search for new cures and medicines to address known or unserved public health issues, solve long-standing population maladies, and enhance the effectiveness of existing treatments. Aerospace companies episodically invest in asset safety, as well as large-scale product modernization in functionality, features, and efficiency because of high individual unit costs, and pursue next-generation and futuristic assets.

Other companies that rely less on hardware and more on software, like electronics and telecommunications, tend to focus on improvements that facilitate power, speed, resilience, and information dynamics that enhance product functionality and lead to feature proliferation. These companies hold a pivotal position in world economies, as they tend to possess massive scale, global reach, and ubiquitous presence.

Most industries that preceded the digital revolution are now heavily reliant on these technology-based innovators, and those that were created in or after the 20th century are closely linked by, or to, the products these new technologists conceive.

Other sectors have their own technology and competitive drivers that compel high innovation commitment and drive companies to pursue continuous market advancement and offering distinction, whether in a product, service, or solution. Thus, the nature of industry evolution has created an unseen integration among technology creators, providers, and users.

Specific attention is provided to the innovation experience of global countries, sectors, and players in a subsequent chapter. But insight into the absolute and relative scales of R&D and innovation furnishes initial context for understanding the commitment that large and successful companies make to ensure future competitiveness and strategic positioning.

In 1995, Booz Allen Hamilton (later Booz & Company), which subsequently became Strategy& when acquired by PricewaterhouseCoopers, launched the *strategy+business* magazine (a quarterly strategy-oriented journal) directed at a global audience of senior executives. This journal captures thoughtful essays, articles, and studies from a range of authors and sources.

An annual feature of this journal has been the *Global Innovation 1000 Report* (GI 1000), a study of how key competitors across the globe were pursuing innovation; the level of country, sector, and company R&D and innovation spend; the identification of the world's most-admired innovators; and insights into various strategic topics driving or underlying innovation exploration, like how innovators reach market success.

The most recent study was the 2018–2019 release, not yet updated after the COVID-19 pandemic, which affected company access and data availability. This study addressed the factors identified above, with a key issue as a centerpiece of related survey and data analysis: "What the Top Innovators Get Right."[1]

As usual, the most recent study compiled the absolute level of spend for an extended time (in this study from 2005 to 2018). From a starting point of approximately $425 billion in 2005, R&D and innovation spend had almost doubled over the period, increasing at an approximate 5 percent annual rate of growth. Across the survey, respondents were investing approximately 4.5 percent of revenues in R&D and innovation, with some companies in the pharmaceutical sector investing 15 percent to 25 percent of their top line.[2]

As mentioned earlier, *how much* is spent matters far less than *how well* it is spent and much more on *what is achieved*. How companies move from absolute spend to the much loftier position of most admired is addressed later in this book, but understanding what drives innovation success over innovation intensity is more illuminating.

To achieve innovation success, six factors were identified as success elements for the best-performing members of the GI 1000. These factors reflect several themes already introduced above and recognized in a later section of this book.[3]

- *Innovation and business strategy are closely aligned.* A critical underpinning of innovation success is ensuring that the core strategies of the business are reflected in the targeted strategies underlying the scope and emphasis of all innovation efforts. This ensures there are no disconnects between enterprise aspirations and investment priorities.

- *Company-wide cultural support for innovation exists.* Successful innovation starts with how well the employee base understands and embraces the intent and requirements of innovation. Embedding innovation in a company's DNA requires constant nurturing and consistent messaging and action, particularly incentives and risk alignment.

- *Senior leadership is highly involved.* The most successful innovation models start with executive sponsorship and stewardship of the enterprise effort from conception of its vision through its sustained execution. Employees look for commitment at the executive level, which is typically demonstrated through active product or technology reviews and team engagement.

- *End users provide direct insight into innovation thinking.* Most innovation efforts start market back—that is, through the lens of market gap and customer need identification. The voice of the customer is a needed element of developing the innovation emphasis to ensure perceived gaps are real and expected outcomes can make a meaningful difference.

- *Rigorous control of project selection occurs early.* The risk of an innovation effort becoming insular and wandering offtrack is high without hands-on oversight to challenge the problem-and-solution fit. Once problems are selected and prioritized, and product scopes and designs are determined, active management is responsible for holding execution to targets and outcomes.

- *A holistic approach is taken to integrating these attributes.* The secret sauce of innovation success is the ability to excel at each of the above factors and to be able to integrate the combined model into a seamless whole. Thinking of innovation as an end-to-end model, where each element works in tandem with another, strengthens the ability to achieve expectations.

More discussion of innovation success strategies is provided in a later chapter, but it is clear that thinking of innovation as a platform and system, rather than a program and process, is critical to determining how to align and embed it within a company.

The above takeaways are not radical concepts to embrace; rather, they signify that innovation needs to first be thought of strategically but then visibly enabled by a strong culture with a common view of purpose and direction. For companies that have been committed to innovation for an extended period, these factors have become embedded in their mindset and DNA, while for companies that are novices in this domain, the challenge remains to fully align the market, enterprise, and employee dimensions critical to conceiving, executing, and accomplishing successful outcomes.

Capabilities Prowess

As companies grapple with how to enhance the purpose and intensity of their innovation efforts, they recognize a change is required to the internal mentality of how the company collectively embraces the challenge and employees cohesively execute it. They also realize that to match the efforts of their natural competitors and unconventional market entrants, never mind evolve to a leading innovator role in the markets in which they operate, they need to tackle innovation from a different perspective and with increased vitality.

As referenced earlier, innovation is neither a cavalier nor an intermittent activity. Rather, it needs to be a concerted enterprise-wide effort and fundamental to a company's purpose and market strategy. And like other critical undertakings, innovation is not just a single system; it is itself an integrated value chain composed of sequential stages and activities.

This closed-loop value chain is end to end and converts exploration into outcomes, which is the fundamental precept underlying innovation (see Figure 2). If innovation is viewed only as a series of actions, then it is likely to fall short of expectations. More appropriately, it should be considered a critical capability—with multiple logical stages—that is targeted at producing sustained, meaningful, and tangible impact to a business, such as first-of-a-kind (FOAK) technology, next-generation equipment, smart technologies, product gaps, integrated platforms, pricing concepts, or new business models. Innovation is not a process to be followed; it is a table-stakes tenet of the success formula of a business.

The innovation value chain can be viewed as consisting of seven key activities that allow companies to identify, conceive, assess, develop, learn, adopt, and monetize the fruits of their labor across a timeline from scanning to commercialization.

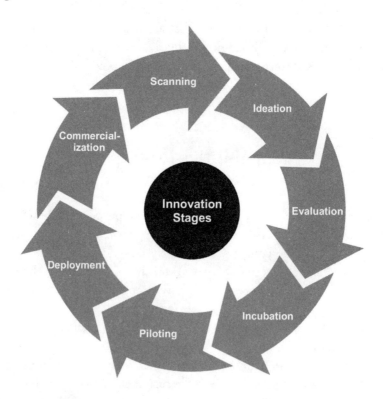

Figure 2. Innovation value chain.

These seven activities reflect how a company can think sequentially about analytical progress and end use application as it moves from stage to stage. Several of these activities naturally also preserve an off-ramp to a company when its initial hypotheses of need, fit, and value do not prove themselves out.

Each of the end-to-end activities within the innovation value chain are described below:

- *Scanning:* This activity provides a view into drivers affecting direction, customer positioning, company risks, and market opportunities. This early-stage activity presents an outside-in picture of how the future could unfold and affect the current business and market positioning.

- *Ideation:* Creating a foundation for innovation incorporates the kind of free thinking that encourages identification of high-potential concepts for exploration. This open-seas approach creates the portfolio of fresh ideas to be assessed for consistency with enterprise priorities.

- *Evaluation:* A detailed screening activity follows to allow the funneling of ideas through a series of qualifying criteria designed to filter through many options to the best ideas. This activity ensures objectivity is maintained and enables logical and empirical selection and prioritization.

- *Incubation:* Targeted, high-potential ideas are subsequently selected for further nurturing, development, investment, and perfecting within the business. This activity scrutinizes idea application and readiness for adoption and allows for continuing proof of concept.

- *Piloting:* As ideas progress from concept to application, companies continue to refine their development work and fit-for-purpose adoption. Companies use this stage to challenge readiness and whether adoption expectations are consistent with market realities.

- *Deployment:* As ideas mature to market-ready status, companies then frame how they are to be rolled out within the business or market. This activity focuses on operationalizing within a business and defining the model for realizing ubiquitous adoption.

- *Commercialization:* For new products and services directed at external customers, this go-to-market activity is critical to realizing tangible market impacts. Converting market-based ideas into expected revenues distinguishes simply good ideas from high-value market offerings.

Companies need to be adept at navigating the various activities in the innovation value chain. Successfully moving through this activity continuum is critical to optimizing innovation outcomes and creating excitement within external markets and the internal employee base. A well-conceived innovation model positions companies to achieve outcomes not otherwise considered attainable under a business-as-usual approach.

Innovation for improved internal operating performance is often a common objective of a business—and this is an acceptable outcome of its own. But the revenue side of the business equation is even more valuable when new markets, offering extension, market share, margin enhancement, and portfolio expansion are available to capture. Growth-oriented companies are well aware of these opportunities, but less traditional sectors, like utilities, lag behind their cross-industry counterparts in thinking about leveraging innovation to propel a significant advance in business vitality and positioning.

Utilities Transition

Most industrial and consumer companies are subject to many of the same externalities and trends, regardless of the sector. Externalities such as fiscal policy, legislative enactments, capital markets, geopolitical risks, and a supply chain hindered by COVID-19 all affect the views of companies regarding the strength of the economy, general consumer attitudes, and viability of current strategies.

At any moment in time, specific externalities may appear to be a dominant influence on the economy, but all those referenced above continue to have significant impact on management decision-making and strategic direction. But the significance of some directional trends can have an out-sized impact across all sectors when factors affecting broad societal themes, like climate change, are involved.

A particular influence on traditional oil and gas and utilities sectors is the sharp and accelerating requirements of the cleantech transition, specifically the emphasis on reducing—and attempting to eliminate—carbon emissions. This path to net-zero is at the crux of the global shift toward the adoption of clean technologies to enhance the quality and cleanliness of air and water.

In addition to fundamentally changing the nature of commodity supply sources, this shift is also manifesting itself in capital markets as financial institutions are embracing the tenets of net-zero emissions and applying new standards, disclosures, and divestment requirements on borrowers, with the stated intent to withhold capital to those companies that do not embrace and act on net-zero commitments. At present, net-zero standards, goals, and commitments are a core driver of utility strategies, capital allocation, asset ownership, and system operating choices, with the likelihood that future mandates and requirements will escalate in scope and significance.

But the utilities industry has been dramatically affected by sectoral policy and regulatory actions before. In the mid-1990s, the utilities sector was rocked by the adoption by several states of competitive energy supply policies that led to business restructuring, business or asset divestment, and role realignment. Power supply businesses were separated from their integrated structures, and responsibilities for commodity acquisition for customers was also divested for customers in these states, with retail suppliers created or separated from the legacy business.

These business-segment-unbundling policies initiated in the United Kingdom but took little time to spread to other European countries, Australasia, and Latin America. And like other governmentally created energy policies over time, they were designed in the spirit of increasing sector competition. This internationally developed mandate was initially embraced by the California Public Utilities Commission and then spread to other activist state governments and regulatory commissions on the East Coast and other large or populist states.

Significant policy shifts have also been directed at the utilities industry with respect to the role of nuclear power and renewables as energy sources, asset hardening and resilience to protection against natural catastrophes, and elimination of new natural gas connections. These shifts are in line with general policy and regulatory trends toward net-zero emissions. More specifics on these disruptive influences on utilities are discussed in the next chapter.

In the past, unlike their competitive sector peers, utilities seldom placed innovation as a front-of-mind objective or strategy. Utilities were generally late to embrace innovation as a critical capability and at the level necessary to achieve the readiness to meet the disruptive challenges that presently exist and will emerge—a position they are in the midst of changing. While the window for cleantech transition readiness will remain open for decades, it takes time for adequate preparation to determine the most advantageous responses, implement appropriate response actions, and position the business to optimize available value from path selection.

In this environment, the role of innovation becomes even more important to enabling the industry to take advantage of available market opportunities or to find a path on which to successfully compete. And when technology evolution is moving at an accelerated pace, it further places the utilities sector at a disadvantage against more agile and attuned competitors that disintermediate markets and existing companies, without the same type of regulatory overhang. Thus, at a time when the business and operating models of utilities are under continued stress, the need for heightened innovation commitment dramatically grows, particularly as the utilities industry finds itself positioned for the next stage of its structural evolution.

To match the speed of market reshaping and competitive challenge, utilities need to recognize the impact that disruptive technology can have on them as both traditional market participants and emergent competitors. New technology offerings by vendors, awareness by customers, and adoption by utilities will create a challenge of carving out the right role for legacy providers to play while meeting burgeoning needs of end users and fending off pervasive competitors for customer attention.

Thinking through how innovation can enhance market position in an evolving marketplace can enable utilities to shift from conservative and cautious market observers to highly engaged technology advocates and adopters focused on creating value for themselves and customers.

CHAPTER 2

Disruptive Influences

TRADITIONAL industries are subject to continuous disruption from a confluence of market, consumer, technology, regulatory, and policy stimuli. All sectors are subject to the same types of factors, though not all affect each industry simultaneously, even when several converge on a specific sector at the same moment.

Utilities make up an industry that is highly dependent on the adoption and deployment of technologies throughout the business. From energy supply through transmission and distribution and on to customer service, all functions within an electric or gas utility rely on technology as a foundation for functional performance.

And this technology does not just relate to large, visible assets like power plants, control centers, pipelines, transmission lines, substations, or call centers. Technology is ubiquitous throughout the operations of a utility, and it involves microscale elements like sensors, controllers, breakers, gauges, and a host of similar small components embedded throughout an operating system or network.

Over its history, the power supply segment has seen itself disrupted by the evolution of technology (e.g., from fossil fuel to nuclear, renewables, and storage). It has also seen an evolution in the wires side of its business, moving from lower voltage transmission lines of less than 220 kilovolts to large-scale lines of 500 kilovolts to 765 kilovolts, and the distribution network moving from analog voltage management and passive systems to digital microcontrollers and smart grids.

The natural gas sector has also evolved from simple intrastate pipelines for local supply to liquified natural gas (LNG) to support global markets, and from flow monitoring to dynamic, real-time modeling. Local distribution companies (LDCs) have similarly evolved from cast-iron and steel pipes to plastic and corrugated stainless steel, and to adoption of advanced materials for manufacturing and coating.

For both electric utilities and LDCs, even the customer service function has benefited from new technologies and evolved from handheld meters to automated meters and from one-way to two-way communications.

All facets of utility operations are dependent on technology for aspects of fundamental system design, construction, installation, maintenance, measurement, and monitoring processes. These underlying technologies are often fundamental to system operations, asset availability, equipment protection, performance monitoring, work productivity, or consumption control, among other purposes. And these underlying technologies are in constant stages of evolution, either next stage maturity or outright replacement with emerging advancements.

OEMs and vendors are dedicated to elevating their own innovation models to continually upgrade their offerings to utilities and to their direct customers. These manufacturers are committed to developing advanced technologies that make their assets or equipment more impactful to utilities and customers and provide differentiation to alternatives in the market.

Utilities are continually assessing how technologies are evolving and improving in functionality, durability, and performance. Utilities face a constant adoption challenge, however, as they are often slow to upgrade or adopt new technologies until proven through bench testing, pilots, or deployment elsewhere. As an industry, utilities are a large market for technology acquisition, even though they are risk averse to being an early adopter.

Why are utilities so reluctant to be on the front edge of new technology adoption and deployment? Part of the reason is they simply do not want to be wrong about technology selection. They are well aware technology options are proliferating every year, and what looks to be a perfect choice in one year may be replaced by a better option the next year. The other part of the rationale for slow adoption is they see no real upside and far more downside to moving fast from a regulatory perspective if the wrong choice is made or the deployment is unsuccessful.

Somewhat muted in both parts of this thinking, however, is the impact slow decision-making and adoption have on customer perspectives about incumbent consideration of their concerns and requirements. It is not a tenable practice for utilities to "slow play" advanced technology adoption and deployment when customers are as savvy as they are today about energy management and as aware as they are about technology evolution to support this objective.

For many technologies, such as automatic generation control, system operations computers, advanced gas turbines, digital relay, high-voltage direct current (HVDC) lines, last-mile communications, and advanced metering infrastructure, the time from availability to ubiquitous adoption could range between 15 and 25 years from when a technology was first offered.

Admittedly, some of these technologies came to market between 1960 and 2000, when utilities were particularly circumspect about new technology adoption and the incurrence of unnecessary risks to the business. But some of these reflect technologies, like digital communications and advanced meters, which have been developed within the last 20 years and still experience slow adoption. For example, smart meters were introduced around 2005 but still only enjoy about 80 percent penetration within the industry after more than 15 years.[1]

Of course, the development of new technologies is also driven by expectations of customers for some enhanced combination of choice, control, convenience, comfort, and/or communications regarding the options available from their utility provider. The level of regulatory interest in the outcomes from technology adoption, particularly in enabling public policy to be advanced, is also an important consideration driving technology evolution and adoption.

Cleantech Transition

Besides new technologies being a continuously disruptive influence, policy development has also affected utilities and been a contributor to the types of operating evolution described above. For example, the United States made a conscious decision to develop nuclear power because of its lower cost potential, and it was driven by a governmental emphasis on making nuclear a significant element of the power supply. Similarly, the high cost of inefficient fossil fuel plant types drove regulators to encourage utilities and OEMs to design more efficient boilers and turbines.

More recently, climate change policy precipitated federal tax policy to create tax credits and subsidies to encourage renewables installation, even though the economics were—and still are—not overly compelling. Recent climate change policy shifts have also resulted in a more concerted effort to detect methane emissions from LDC systems through measurement devices, moving from infrared cameras to laser detection.

The move from a fossil-fuel-based power supply system to one that is "green and clean" is the focus of the cleantech transition. The intent is to permanently move away from fossil fuel sources and replace them with renewables, storage, and future clean technologies to reduce energy-related carbon emissions to zero by 2050, if not sooner. This goal of carbon emission reduction reflects a net-zero focus (i.e., emissions added to the atmosphere are fully offset by the amount removed by other actions).

Within the United States, 24 states, plus the District of Columbia, have established mandates for net-zero outcomes, with target dates ranging between 2032 and 2050. Many utilities have also individually established similar outcomes within a consistent time window, with interim goals intended to show significant progress by 2035.[2]

The advent of the cleantech transition is often debated about when it initially began. Some would say that it began in the mid-1990s as global attention to climate change became a topic of high interest at the governmental level. Others would mark the beginning of this transition as the turn of the century and the early 2000s, when wind generation started to be deployed, albeit in small amounts and in only a few states. For purposes of this discussion, the cleantech transition is assumed to truly start in earnest in 2005, when the amount of wind generation installed began to consistently grow by meaningful measures. This period reflects the passage of the Energy Policy Act (EPACT) of 2005, which for the first time established renewable fuel standards and provided tax incentives to encourage construction of these assets.

EPACT contained several specific actions that served to set a tone for future climate change direction and jump-start the focus on renewables, as well as enhance the focus on energy efficiency, natural gas, and carbon sequestration:[3]

- Authorized tax credits for wind and alternative energy producers

- Included wave and tidal power as renewable technologies

- Authorized $50 million annually for biomass grants

- Authorized loan guarantees for innovative technologies that avoid greenhouse gases

- Authorized $200 million annually for clean coal initiatives

- Authorized $2.95 billion for R&D and building an advanced hydrogen cogeneration reactor

- Extended the 30 percent solar investment tax credits, also qualifying wind for receipt

- Accelerated depreciation from 20 years to 10 years

- Offered a tax deduction for energy-efficient property installed in commercial buildings

- Offered tax breaks for energy-conservation home improvements

- Required all public utilities to offer net metering on request

But the focus of the cleantech transition is not simply the movement away from fossil fuel to renewables; it also includes the emergence of new technologies that move beyond renewables into new spaces in the distribution system and behind-the-meter with customers, signaling shifts in utility operating strategies and in customer expectations and attitudes toward incumbent providers.

These types of technologies were still early in their development in the mid-2000s and would not begin to approach commerciality until the front years preceding 2020. This time frame also coincided with the emergence of venture capital, which began to seriously invest in start-ups that were the progenitors of these emerging technologies.

The value of the cleantech transition movement is that it awakened the utilities industry from its traditional thinking about the value chain and business model and opened its eyes to what a different future could look like. Once the transition was perceived to be a reality, utilities started thinking about *where* they fit in this future and *how* they would need to transform their companies to meet a new set of policy, environmental, technology, market, customer, and regulatory challenges that were unleashed.

The cleantech transition has affected more than just how utilities are decarbonizing their generation fleet and overall business. It has created derivative impacts on competitors, OEMs and vendors, customers, regulators, and even Wall Street, as all these parties seek to enhance their own climate change outcomes or position themselves to further influence how utilities respond to external policies and mandates.

Competitors to utilities, like renewables developers, electric charging station owners, compressed natural gas station operators, and smart device retailers, all offer an alternative to the incumbent for selected value chain investment and services. Under the right circumstances, they can easily disintermediate the natural rights of a utility in serving its customers.

OEMs and vendors are similar to competitors in that they have the ability to offer services to customers—particularly large commercial and industrial ones—that also displace the traditional relationship a utility maintains with its customers. If utilities are not offering solutions to meet the needs of customers, like energy management, demand response, energy efficiency, equipment monitoring, micro-generation, and shared or transactive energy, then these entities will step in to fill that gap.

A range of solutions providers—hardware and software entities that can offer technology to support provision of energy- or data-related services to customers—is also focused on the cleantech sector. These companies can offer point or integrated solutions to customers in enabling resource integration and management, asset and device interconnection, energy control, data analytics, building and facilities management, equipment performance enhancement, and smart grid design and operations, among a range of other services. The power in these solutions providers is not just *what* they can provide but *how* they can integrate multiple solutions to create a broader platform for further advantage and value.

The expectations and attitudes of customers across all classes are also shifting as they become more aware of the significance of decarbonization on their own businesses, the nature of technology availability that can support their operating and information needs, and the expectations that third parties have for progress against net-zero goals. While these considerations are more important to large commercial and industrial customers, residential customers are also interested in home energy management, green power supply options, and increased engagement value with their incumbent providers.

Venture capital quickly found opportunities as a result of the cleantech transition to carve out a niche for its own capital deployment purposes. Several venture capital firms specialize in the cleantech space and have put their capital to work with start-ups, as well as with utilities that seek to utilize a well-capitalized specialist in this area to mitigate their own risks. In some cases, these venture capital firms, like Energy Impact Partners (EIP), have created "club" arrangements across multiple utilities and with participation from oil and gas and other commercial enterprise businesses that align against aspects of the utility value chain (e.g., in electric mobility).

Since the cleantech transition has its roots in policy—both federal and state—it is no surprise that regulatory agencies at these levels are also front and center in enabling the market shift to occur or affecting its direction and timing. These agencies have a direct hand in the standards that are established, the recovery of costs, the permissions for market participation, and the rules of market operations that utilities contend with.

As one would expect, Wall Street is particularly interested in the purpose and outcomes of the transition. Aside from the financing opportunities and challenges that follow a shift in capital allocation and embedded generation mix, Wall Street is finely attuned to how the cleantech transition will align with the emphasis on environmental, social, and governance (ESG) principles that have been established to respond to the global pursuit of decarbonization. As a practical matter, Wall Street has an expectation that utilities will work toward all matters of carbon reduction, and new technologies enabled by the cleantech transition will be a fundamental element of how decarbonization is accelerated.

Finally, just as the strategies and actions of utilities are directly affected by the cleantech transition in terms of opportunity identification and market positioning, so too is capital allocation. Historically, utilities made large capital investments in large-scale centralized generating plants. The cleantech transition has short-circuited these types of investments, as renewables investment (with or without battery storage) is far less intense.

While more capital investment is now being spent in the distribution segment today than in generation, smaller increments of capital relate to renewables and the network compared to traditional generation. The same situation is true for LDCs, where pipeline expenditures are out of favor and reduce total capital expenditures, notwithstanding the significant level of investment directed at main replacement. If total capital is not maintained at high levels in the future from the cleantech transition, the earnings power of utilities could be adversely affected.

The cleantech transition is a game changer for utilities. It substantially shifts the focus of utility investment away from traditional spend categories to new, and sometimes less, conventional destinations for deployment. It also opens the aperture for expanded "ways to play" for utilities in the transition, whether in investment substitution, technology adoption, market entry, or customer relationships. Utilities have the potential to be great beneficiaries of the cleantech transition if they are open-minded about its implications and aggressive in pursuit of the range of new opportunities that are emerging from this sea change event.

Technology Evolution

The U.S. utilities industry has always been active with R&D, either on its own for the largest companies in the industry or through sponsored industry groups like the EPRI and the Gas Technology Institute (GTI, formerly the Gas Research Institute), as well as federal agencies with various research laboratories missioned to advance energy-related research. In addition, there have always been a broad number of universities with focused energy-related R&D, as well as a deep OEM and vendor community whose business purpose is bringing new technology and innovation to its customers.

To be expected, the nature of R&D and innovation focus changes in cycles over time. In earlier decades, the focus in power was largely about a shift from coal-fired generation to nuclear, followed by a further shift from coal to gas-fired generation. Starting in the 2000s, the shift away from coal intensified with a continued emphasis on gas, but attention was then directed toward renewables as supply sources, and the industry was actively pursuing carbon capture and sequestration (CCS) as a means to clean coal as a fossil fuel source. And before 2020, renewables were common to the generation stack, but they were complemented by battery storage (see Figure 3).

By 2020, electrification was attracting more attention as a substitute for oil, diesel, propane, and natural gas throughout certain elements of the

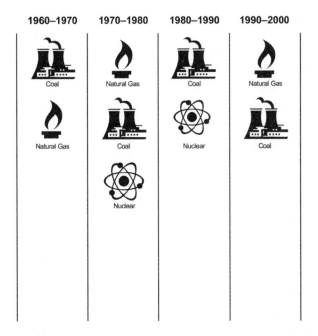

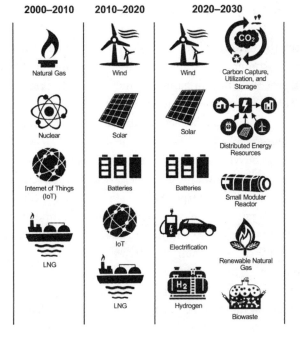

Figure 3. Technology evolution.

economy, like transport. The industry began to focus on distributed energy resource management (DERMS) as software was developed to enable utilities to leverage new technology to monitor, integrate, and operate multiple interconnected assets and devices. And most recently, significant attention has been generated across multiple industries, including utilities, on the prospects for hydrogen as a clean fuel.

On the natural gas side, R&D and innovation have long been focused on pipeline integrity and gas storage, with natural gas as the bridge between fossil fuel and a cleantech-based power supply. In the 1990s, compressed natural gas (CNG) vehicles became available as an alternative to conventional gasoline.

By 2010, the shale gas revolution was underway, substantially changing the economics of production and commodity and reflecting an innovative approach to conventional drilling methods, which affected LDC supply strategies. In this same time frame, LNG was becoming extremely popular as a means to convert traditional natural gas into an exportable liquid state, and the first exports occurred in 2016. By 2020, attention had accelerated on renewable natural gas and the reduction of methane emissions from biowaste and other sources. As with the power sector, hydrogen is also relevant to the natural gas sector as pipelines, once upgraded, are a natural transport mode.

Of course, the Internet of Things (IoT) pervades how American industry and consumers communicate, share data, and enable control of technologies, processes, buildings, and homes. The IoT is not a direct focus of utility R&D and innovation, but it is a fundamental pathway to how innovative technologies can be activated and provided, particularly in a data-driven economy.

To be sure, the heaviest emphasis of the utilities industry is clearly on cleantech, as policies, technologies, and behaviors are converging to enable these offerings to be fit-for-purpose to its specific needs. Cleantech is not entirely displacing traditional R&D and innovation, as operating needs for functionality and performance will never dissipate, but the externalities of climate change are an overwhelming driver of executive, regulatory, and customer attention.

Beyond the cleantech emphasis on decarbonization, the factors of decentralization, digitalization, democratization, and disintermediation are all also contributing to the observed explosion of new technologies. Each of these drivers has a unique influence on technology evolution, but all derive their impacts from the central theme of decarbonization, which is foundational to the cleantech transition:

- *Decarbonization:* The movement to get to net-zero is the central theme underlying the utilities industry and has been for several years. The drive to deemphasize coal—and to some extent natural gas—is the centerpiece of policy and has now become a principle of the investment and financing communities. Many areas of utility operations (e.g., power supply, fuel supply, distribution operations, and fleet management, among others) have focused R&D and innovation efforts around identifying and deploying technologies to reduce carbon.

- *Decentralization:* As climate policy affects the type of generation sources relied on, it also has an impact on the nature and location of power supply and transmission and related technologies. Moving from coal and gas to renewables and storage reduces the scale of an individual generation source (affecting earnings) and results in a different mix of remote versus localized assets. The transmission grid and distribution network may need to be reconfigured to accommodate retired plants and may result in localized batteries, as well as DERMS technologies.

- *Digitalization:* The move from analog to digital technology and the proliferation of the IoT have changed how utilities construct their internal platforms to execute the business and leverage their networks and communications environments to support individual customer and business needs. These backbone technologies and performance models further enable other technologies to be adopted and operations, buildings, or premises to integrate across multiple platforms to enhance the value of the current infrastructure and future platforms.

- *Democratization:* The move toward cleantech also changes the way customers look at their utility as a source of more than just energy. Customers are increasing their expectations for added value from their provider. These customers want to know more about energy consumption and be empowered with more of its control. With these behavioral shifts, customers are looking for utilities to be more communicative with them and are willing to leverage new technologies (e.g., smart homes) to advance their energy management goals.

- *Disintermediation:* With changes in market policies and burgeoning technology availability and adoption, the potential for new competitors to step into traditional utility roles increases. OEMs and vendors can play several roles with utilities—sometimes partners, generally providers, occasionally competitors, and always customers. As providers of equipment or technology, they have the capability to extend their role with customers and move beyond only hard goods to where they displace the incumbent with monitoring or control services available from a utility.

While these five influences have an outsized impact on technology advancement and adoption, they are not the only influences that affect the technology environment. OEMs and vendors are in the business of anticipating customer needs and bringing technologies to the market that enhance customer business performance and the current customer relationship. Product or service evolution—whether technology-based or not—is a core element of how these entities secure and expand market share, as well as increase the value of their brand to customers.

Since the value of technology to customers is increased when a provider can bring something new to its business proposition, there is an incentive for OEMs and vendors to continually advance this value to large commercial and industrial customers. There is even greater incentive for start-ups to seize market and technology gaps to provide technology offerings to satisfy unmet needs, and more importantly, to create needs and use value a customer may not realize they can benefit from.

The current internal utility environment is often thought of as an amalgam of technologies supporting operations execution and customer interfaces. The technologies are provided by a range of OEMs and vendors and create a portfolio of bespoke products that do not always easily align and fall far short of an integrated platform.

These technologies relate to every aspect of the utility value chain and reflect various vintages of design and installation. While many existing technology applications reflect a narrow purpose and utilization, some for plant or pipeline system control, distribution management, or call centers have multiple tasks to handle. These technologies need to be particularly versatile and scalable to meet the growing needs and customers of their host companies.

Technologies are often thought of as specific applications and fit-for-purpose within the utility business. However, they can more practically be thought of as families of technology since multiple providers and technologies usually exist in any single operational area. It is more appropriate to think of the technology environment as an ecosystem where business domains can be narrow or broad, and individual elements may stand alone or align with other elements within this network.

The potential families of technology can include a range of specific types and applications for use in the utilities industry for traditional value chain areas and now for emerging businesses, new functions, and innovative use cases. Some elements of these families may result in load or throughput building, while others may offer enhanced load or throughput management, and still others may lead to load or throughput curtailment.

The identified families reflect traditional utility categories and elements, as well as frontier areas where future development and deployment may still have years to run (see Figure 4). Each of these families has an ecosystem to itself, as well as crossover adjacency with other areas:

- *Conventional generation:* Primary generation sources like nuclear, coal, gas, and hydro all continue to pursue innovation in design, functionality, and performance to drive lower unit costs or improved output. These sources have expanded to include carbon capture, utilization, and storage (CCUS) for coal, as well as general net-zero emission technology deployment. New technologies are being pursued across every dimension of conventional generation.

- *Alternative generation:* Utility-scale wind and solar generation are typically thought of as primary renewables generation sources, at least for those that have achieved a level of scale. But new or expanded sources, like bioenergy, geothermal, wave and tidal, rooftop solar, micro-turbines, battery storage, and fuel cells are now receiving significant attention as sources for new investment and technology evolution and market readiness.

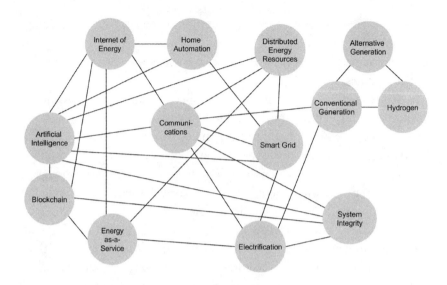

Figure 4. Technology family alignment.

- *Mobility and electrification:* Substantial effort has occurred to drive passenger and light-, medium-, and heavy-duty electric vehicle (EV) adoption across a range of vehicle and equipment types, as well as financing, charging, vehicle-to-grid, energy services, and fleet conversion analytics for vehicles. The pursuit of vehicle and equipment electrification related to ports and buildings is also creating new technology development.

- *Distributed energy resource management (DERMS):* The recent focus on microtechnologies has created the opportunity for multiple small-scale devices (e.g., sensors, monitors, and controllers), supply sources like micro-generation, and sophisticated hardware and software to support network interconnection and integration to achieve deployment and adoption. This area may be attracting the broadest set of new technology innovation.

- *Communications:* The focus of the industry on the nexus between utilities and telecommunications has generally been limited, except where individual companies owned private networks or assets. The expansion of fiber, growth in broadband, availability of new spectrum, and increasing value from private broadband networks are now heightening the level of utility interest in the search for solutions to their network resiliency and security needs.

- *Home automation:* The customer premise is a fast riser in technology inquiry, adaptation, and deployment and offers great promise when products, services, and solutions can be available to customers. Smart technologies addressing thermostats, appliances, lighting, micro-turbines, battery storage, energy management, and the IoT offer valuable services to customers. In addition, these services offer the opportunity for new revenues for providers when bundled.

- *Smart grid:* Adverse weather events have precipitated an interest in greater resiliency through development of self-contained microgrids composed of micro-generation, resilient networks, connected battery storage, and intelligent meters. The new technologies underlying smart grids are not limited to resilience application but extend to intelligent devices placed in the system for fault analysis, leak detection, predictive analytics, and corrosion control.

- *System asset integrity:* Both the electric and natural gas sectors provide continuous attention to protecting the operating system assets they maintain for transmission lines, pipelines, and network delivery. R&D and innovation efforts related to materials integrity, such as pipelines and the deployment of improved coatings, remote testing, and robotic inspection, as well as failure detection across an electric network system, offer potential for new technology.

- *Energy-as-a-service (EaaS):* The explosion of DERMS offers utilities the opportunity to leverage these technologies and convert them into services that can be provided to customers to complement pure commodity supply. The ability to enable customer access to other non-owned assets changes the traditional relationship to now enable utilities to aggregate energy for sale to the grid, as well as optimize various energy efficiency opportunities for consumption management.

- *Hydrogen:* The interest in hydrogen as a new fuel substitute is now a global phenomenon, since it cuts across industries beyond utilities. Hydrogen comes in various forms, such as gray (from reforming natural gas), brown (from coal), blue (from natural gas with CO_2 storage), and green (from renewables with electrolysis), along with new emerging sources. All have an application in converting hydrogen into a fuel and can also be utilized in vehicles through a fuel cell.

- *Blockchain:* This technology is less utility-focused and has its roots in multi-entity transactions that can occur across industries wherever large amounts of stakeholders exist. In energy, blockchain has the potential to align multiple parties, like suppliers, grid or network operators, metering operators, financial services providers, or traders and marketers. This technology enables enhanced security to transactions through a managed network for multiple parties.

- *Artificial intelligence (AI):* Machine learning and natural language processing have led to the utilization of AI as a means to perform tasks that normally require human intelligence. The use of algorithms allows deep statistical analysis to identify and remember behavior patterns that can be applied to demand forecasting, asset efficiency, demand management, predictive maintenance, and customer engagement.

- *Internet of energy (IoE):* An underlying catalyst for energy-system-driven innovation and enhanced planning, decision-making, and execution is IoE, which enables the utilities industry to seamlessly engage with multiple parties in an ecosystem, like developers, financiers, and traders for the purpose of communicating, optimizing, and increasing the efficiency of the energy system. IoE frequently incorporates AI as an engine for identifying opportunities.

These technology families provide a comprehensive view of the key categories where investment is being made to follow market trends and prepare the utilities industry for a different future. Each of these families comprises a range of related technology applications that currently exist (or may in the future) and lead to evolution of the business.

As the figure illustrates, an overall ecosystem exists within the utility technology environment (excluding corporate applications) that includes direct application for each of the families, and for elements like storage, AI, EaaS, communications, and DERMS that cut across several of these categories. This ecosystem is continually shifting as new technologies or use cases emerge.

Some of the technology families are already robust in their adoption and deployment, while others are still nascent, and others are even more embryonic. Historically, conventional generation—and its underlying fuel types—has been very mature in its development, although continuous effort is expended on ultraefficient gas turbines, CCUS, and nuclear equipment performance. Technology in the electric and natural gas networks is also mature in many aspects, but the sheer scale of investment and the nature of operating challenges are attracting substantial new technology investment for expanded purposes.

Certain technologies in power supply, like batteries and fuel cells, are still coming of age, even though they have been deployed for several years, or in the case of fuel cells, for decades. But other areas, like alternative generation, mobility, and DERMS, are still in an early stage of development and adoption, and even customer acceptance. And broadband is emerging as a valuable technology to enhance, protect, and add value to the grid.

Most of the technology families remain embryonic and are in an early readiness and adoption stage. Technical areas like IoE and blockchain are not yet ubiquitous, while home automation, hydrogen, AI, higher-spectrum private broadband, and EaaS are just finding their footing.

The future evolution of technology is hard to predict, particularly since adoption timetables can take decades, as opposed to years. One way to peer over the horizon is to construct a technology landscape that arrays the possible availability of emerging technologies across periods. This is illustrated in a later chapter, but Figure 3, earlier in this chapter, illustrates both the historical introduction of technologies, as well as the potential timing of some of these applications or capabilities referenced above. The electric and natural gas sectors can be confident that the pipeline of emerging technologies is robust, and what can be observed today will likely quickly change because of acceleration, displacement, or new discovery.

Technology availability generally faces several impediments to adoption. The first is utility imagination about utilizing new technology to mitigate operating challenges within the business. Second, even if the level of imagination is supportive, utilities are risk averse and not eager to be early adopters. Third, the requisite level of funding may not be sufficient to support the pursuit of technology innovation and application on a consistent basis. Finally, the ability of utilities to stay ahead of the technology curve is difficult, as they are not as plugged in to external R&D and innovation as more competitive peers are, because of other priorities of the business.

Fortunately, there is a proliferation of start-ups in the business of changing utility mindsets about technologies and the value of adoption. These start-ups offer insights into technology direction, critical features of assets, equipment, hardware, and software, and can—if leveraged—accelerate utility awareness and appreciation for *where* and *how* technology can enhance utility operations or market positioning. While there are thousands of start-ups in various stages of maturity, everyone knows not all will survive. The vexing problem, however, is no one really knows *which* ones will survive and thrive, leaving utilities to ponder the decision options before them—adopt now, adopt later, or stay on the sidelines.

Customer Preferences

The cleantech transition is not just about technology disruption and evolution; it also reflects a shift in customer perspectives and prerogatives among all classes. The groundswell in governmental, business, and public sentiment for some level of climate action has affected corporate decision-making and individual choices.

For large commercial and industrial customers, federal policy sets a tone for company decisions about net-zero emission attainment. This proscriptive tone colors board of director attitudes and executive decision options. Even as these customers become more and more supportive of climate action, the ESG movement is compelling companies to be even more committed to net-zero emissions. The financial community at large has aligned itself with stringent environmental constraints to drive company decisions and caused concern among borrowers about access to financing if their progress toward net-zero emissions is considered inadequate by Wall Street.

For example, the Net-Zero Asset Owner Alliance, which is an international 69-member group of banks and asset managers with more than $10 trillion assets under management, has targeted the 14 highest carbon emitters—energy, transport, and steel—to reduce carbon emissions among their portfolio clients. They intend to reduce carbon emissions from portfolio companies by 49 percent to 65 percent by 2030, and 100 percent by 2050, while seeking to have the utility and energy sector assets they manage eliminate 75 percent of coal plants by 2030 as well.[4]

Another group—the Climate Action 100+—is even larger, with more than 600 signatories and $65 trillion in assets under management. This group is working directly with 167 of the world's largest corporate carbon emitters to drive faster climate action to achieve net-zero emissions by 2050. The Climate Action 100+ initiatives moved past awareness and collaboration campaigns to specific comparisons using its "Net Zero Company Benchmark" in 2021, with further emphasis on shareholder climate action; short-, medium-, and long-term emissions targets; and board climate competence.[5]

But a larger concern is the enthusiasm and potency of activist investors who are aggressive in presenting proposals to boards to force environmental action. For companies seeking orderly retreat from carbon-related activities, these "uninvited guests" can create havoc with existing strategies and their timing. Particularly at annual shareholder meetings, activist investors and environmentalists are passionate about their intentions and increasingly effective in gathering support for their proposed restrictions or actions.

Large commercial and industrial customers are significant energy consumers with substantial energy bills. They have been ardent energy managers for decades, given their energy intensity, and have the means to pursue alternative energy sourcing. With this external backdrop of institutional verve for carbon reduction, many companies have already been active in procuring renewables energy through purchase power agreements (PPAs). In 2021 global companies purchased more than 30 gigawatts of clean energy through PPAs, which increased by approximately 24 percent over the previous year's record, with 65 percent (more than 20 gigawatts of these purchases) occurring in the United States. High-tech companies, like Amazon, Meta, and Microsoft, dominated among more than 137 companies in 32 countries.[6]

These large energy consumers are motivated to comply with net-zero emission objectives, reduce energy consumption, and lower total energy bills through a combination of new technology adoption, increased energy efficiency, and demand management methods. For these types and scales of energy consumers, compliance is viewed as good business and a part of community presence and stewardship.

With respect to energy consumption, these large commercial and industrial customers are increasingly active in adopting new technologies that can enable them to proactively monitor equipment performance, utilize devices for controlling energy utilization patterns, and enable demand response to be adopted to curtail consumption during periods of disruption or high prices. The emergence of new technologies that provide increased energy consumption insight and enhance company energy management is a particularly welcome occurrence for these customers to enable them to balance enterprise profitability with environmental and social responsibility.

Conversely, the circumstances regarding net-zero attainment are very different for residential customers, as they have far less consumption control and market clout, with respect to carbon emission reduction, than larger energy consumers. Residential customers are not entirely without means to support climate action, but these efforts are not as robust as those available to larger customers with broad footprints and multiple locations.

Residential customers tend to have more basic issues—for example, how to gain more options for energy sourcing and how to reduce their consumption and related bills. For the full year 2021, the National Bureau of Economic Research reported utility bills were approximately 1.3 percent of disposable personal income, a number that only modestly fluctuated higher at other times during the year. Essentially, even though inflation was raising the costs of other goods and services above wages, the effect on utility bills was negligible. However, with inflation running at significant levels through 2022, this prior relative relationship has diminished, and utility bills are running well above this prior level.[7] In September 2022, electricity prices within the Consumer Price Index were up 15.5 percent over September 2021, and gas prices were up 33.1 percent for the same year-to-year period.[8]

This relative pricing outcome is good news for customers, but it does not deter them from focusing on several other energy-related objectives—namely improving their overall energy position. Residential customers largely consist of digital adopters, or those over 40 years old who are less technologically savvy than their younger counterparts, who are digital natives under 40 years old and grew up with the internet and technology.

But although digital adopters are less technologically savvy, they are still focused on several attributes that are important to them: choice, control, comfort, convenience, and communications. All these attributes are indicative of customer wants and important determinants of customer satisfaction with their utilities.

Yet customers have not been active seekers or adopters of new technology—whether digital natives or adopters—and this is partially explained by the low relative share of disposable personal income that relates to utility bills. The other explanation is that customers are simply not as interested in electricity or natural gas as commodities as they are in communications and infotainment.

Nonetheless, the right kinds of technology can deliver high value to customers. Smart thermostats (e.g., the Nest product) are simple to use and offer a set-and-forget device to enable better energy temperature stability and reduced consumption. While home charging for EVs is a necessity for owners, it is a topical and visual reminder of how technology is enabling alternatives to internal combustion engines and providing a means to contribute to lower carbon emissions.

The same is true for rooftop solar, which offers a source of clean energy and displacement of fossil fuel generation. And these technologies offer the ability for customers to become "prosumers" and enable two-way engagement with the grid and sale of available kilowatts when the grid is in need.

Other technologies like micro-turbines, home hubs, and domotics (domestic robots) are also available and can further enable energy management, but these do not enjoy the same level of awareness and appreciation at this point in their maturity. In addition, the costs of related equipment versus the value of their acquisition and adoption have yet to attract customers.

The growing availability of premise-oriented technologies offers the opportunity to address the identified attributes above in the near future, but utilities will need to paint a more attractive and compelling value proposition to enhance customer adoption.

Herein lies an opportunity for utilities to use the availability and adoption of these technologies to demonstrate their positive impacts on energy consumption and home energy management. The availability of these technologies offers opportunities for solidifying the current customer relationship and high-grading the perceived role of the utility from a simple provider to a value-oriented partner. This outcome has the additional benefit of creating new sources of revenue for a utility, whether from increased load (EVs), reduction in demand (home automation), avoided new supply (micro-generation), or system optimization (transactive energy).

OEMs and vendors can offer several of these products or services that create disintermediation potential and both foregone revenues and relationships. This outcome is not what a utility should allow to happen when opportunities currently exist to help customers of all classes find solutions to their energy challenges and avoid diminishing their incumbent value proposition.

The general evolution of existing technologies and the proliferation of new offerings position utilities to enhance their internal operations and improve reliability, resilience, and environmental commitment. These technologies can also deliver new types of value to customers based on capabilities for which incumbents are recognized—energy management, equipment performance, system analytics, and carbon emissions management.

With the growth in technology availability, the need for R&D and innovation is heightened, and the value from its deployment is enhanced. The utilities industry needs to be acutely aware of developments in new technology and, more importantly, how to translate these advances into tangible and practical applications to their business to serve the needs of their customers and avoid inviting competitors into the customer domain.

CHAPTER 3

Global Innovators

R&D and innovation have been recurrent activities for countries, sectors, companies, institutions, and entrepreneurs since the first industrial revolution began in the mid-1700s. Many researchers cite the beginnings of this first industrial revolution and R&D occurring in the United Kingdom, with the resulting steam engine a primary invention to support the shift from an output (labor-based) to a factory (machine-based) system of production. With the move from rural to city locations, a resulting growth in population, and a need to provide products that meet related demand, industries like textiles became early movers in advancing production technology, as in the advent of the industrial revolution in the United States in the late 1700s.[1]

This first industrial revolution subsequently expanded across countries and framed the continued development of more effective and efficient means of production. By the late 1800s, the second industrial revolution had begun, with emphasis on scientific exploration and application (e.g., electricity and the internal combustion engine) to further accelerate and expand manufacturing. The advent of both natural gas and electricity production and utilization during the 19th century provided new means to address challenges experienced by cities and companies, and it harkened the arrival and acceleration of public services and business productivity, as well as game-changing inventions like the telephone and automobiles.[2]

The second industrial revolution lasted through the mid-1900s before giving way to a third industrial cycle—the digital revolution—that itself has extended over 30 years. This revolution produced the evolution and application of electronics, telecommunications, nuclear energy, robotics, biotechnology, and, of course, computers to increase the productive power of all sectors and to bring global connectivity to individuals and businesses alike. In this era, functionality, simplification, speed, and miniaturization have all heightened productivity and enabled knowledge to be more effectively and widely shared, as well as increasing the value of information.[3]

A new revolution was initiated after 2015 with the widespread ubiquity of the internet and the ability to collect, store, and move large amounts of data. But the internet is only one dimension of the fourth industrial revolution—Industry 4.0. This current industrial cycle is characterized by adoption and adaptation of AI, nanotechnology, advanced robotics, cloud computing, and the IoT, among other areas of advancement. This fourth revolution is still in its ascendancy but beginning to be even more pervasive in new technology development and deployment and application to the simplest common denominators—for example, the way we visualize, communicate, experience, and work.[4]

In a pure sense, all four revolutions have been initiated and invigorated by the level, ubiquity, quality, and sustainability of the R&D underlying their formation and perpetuation. This is not surprising given the fundamental nature of the U.S. economy—heavy manufacturing to mass manufacturing to smart manufacturing to collaborative manufacturing throughout the 270-plus years of evolution across these industrial revolutions. Across this entire period, R&D has been a foundational element of sustained productivity and profitability.

The history of R&D and innovation obviously has its roots in basic manufacturing processes—machining, molding, joining, and forming—to fulfill industrial company needs to create equipment to enable production activities. Given the nature of economies throughout the duration of the early industrial revolutions highlighted above, this focus on core manufacturing was fundamental to the development of both nations and companies.

But all innovation is not R&D-based, and as the decades progressed, intellectual capital became available and applicable in other ways than simply toward tangible assets and production processes. With the availability of the internet, economies and companies were able to capitalize on global connectivity and an explosion of information that increased awareness and access, abbreviated timelines and turnarounds, expanded products and services, opened new relationships and markets, and elevated value creation and capture.

While global economies have not abandoned their historical roots, the nature and direction of innovation have catapulted countries and companies into a digital age that has shattered the prevailing boundaries of imagination. And the frontiers for innovation continue to be pushed further because there are no limitations to ideation—ideas have no barriers to creation or application; nor do they expire by a certain date.

This evolution in innovation since the start of the 21st century has now put companies into a space where there is not just an incentive but a mandate to be aggressive and imaginative in the development and execution of a sophisticated innovation model. Further, once the market has moved in a specific direction, any window of opportunity does not stay open indefinitely. Stated another way, time is a perishable commodity; a lost opportunity to differentiate oneself from market peers through innovation is foregone forever.

Innovation Mindset

One of the more iconic entities for R&D was initially named Bell Telephone Laboratories, then AT&T Bell Laboratories, and then Bell Labs Innovations (while part of AT&T). It is now known as Nokia Bell Labs (Bell Labs) and has an illustrious history rich in development of some of the most fundamental technologies to the global economy (e.g., the transistor, the laser, the photovoltaic cell, the Unix operating system, and information theory, among many other key accomplishments).[5]

While Bell Labs started with a focus on telephony, it quickly evolved to not just a communications orientation but one where basic research for the advancement of science and the public good was also a critical underpinning of its charter. Hence, its contributions have been widely recognized as beneficial to the government, the military, the business world, and consumers, and yielded numerous Nobel Prizes and patents.

Where R&D has typically been more centered on multiyear investment to achieve breakthroughs in asset technologies and scientific discovery for application, innovation offers a more knowledge-based approach to business evolution and a means to integrate intellectual capabilities within a business.

Since innovation is about creating something new that adds value to an existing enterprise, it does not always have to be accompanied by significant investment to achieve its ends. Remember, the first stage of innovation is *incremental*, where simple improvements to the business are sufficient and often the principal goal. They do not have to revolve around hard assets but can be valuable when directed at an operational execution or customer interaction.

What is important is that the value of R&D and innovation lies in recognizing its purpose in meeting the needs and opportunities of the market, and in improving competitive positioning, whether strategic, financial, or operational.

The largest and most-admired enterprises in the world are avid devotees of sustained R&D and innovation. They have long histories of dedicated R&D exploration and discovery spend, coupled with prodigious spending on market needs identification and evaluation, and product development and deployment.

Many of these companies reside in the most populous countries of the world, but many are located in small countries as well. Many of these companies are widely renowned brands, while others are more recent disruptors to the competitive playing field. Many of these entities represent established industries, while others come from health care or the software and technology sectors.

A review of where R&D and innovation exist and thrive, as well as which companies tend to prevail in this environment, is instructive to understanding how U.S. utilities could think about positioning themselves to meet the emergent demand of their marketplace. This background perspective also provides insights into how different countries have approached their R&D and innovation actions and exhibit different spend profiles and trends, as well as how different sectors and companies compare against their peers in historical patterns and trends.

Global Innovation Index

An emphasis on R&D and innovation has been a mainstay of the largest global countries for decades, particularly those that have national champion companies, like Korea, Japan, France, and Germany, or acknowledged market icons, like the United States, and are also *technology-based* and/or *product-centered*. These countries, and many others both large and small, combine a national (government-supported) and company (business-led) model where funding is a national priority and a means to ensure local gross domestic product (GDP) and individual entity growth.

The World Intellectual Property Organization (WIPO) in Geneva recently released its 14th annual study on global innovation titled "Global Innovation Index 2021: Tracking Innovation through the COVID-19 Crisis." These studies follow the nature, level, and proclivity of innovation across the globe, including 132 countries in the 2021 analysis. WIPO has developed an index-based comparison utilizing 81 indicators under seven key pillars. These pillars address a range of critical areas for assessment and comparison, with some of the indicators referenced below as well:[6]

- *Institutions:* This initial pillar covers the political, regulatory, and business environments prevailing in the country, and issues like stability, transparency, redundancy, and insolvency, which are critical to capital formation, legal models, and ease of doing business.

- *Human capital and research:* The second pillar addresses local conditions related to education, research, funding, and rankings, and areas like learning levels, university quality, teaching ratios, math and engineering graduates, R&D spend, and investor quantity.

- *Infrastructure:* The third pillar explores the level of information and communications access, logistics performance, capital formation, and environmental performance to understand about online adoption, electricity output, and ISO certification.

- *Market sophistication:* This fourth pillar assesses credit markets, local investment, and trade diversification, and further evaluates areas such as access to capital, minority investor protection, local business and market scale, and industry diversification.

- *Business sophistication:* The fifth pillar includes analyses of knowledge intensity and distribution, innovation linkages, and knowledge distribution, with a focus on training, R&D conduct, collaboration, and spend, imports, and deal activity related to the country's market positioning.

- *Knowledge and technology outputs:* The sixth pillar encompasses knowledge creation, scientific contribution, labor productivity, and knowledge diffusion, with attention given to patent filings, scientific and technical contributions, new businesses, and software spending.

- *Creative outputs:* The final pillar measures intangible assets, creative goods and services, and online creativity, as well as issues like global brand value, creative exports, select industry intensity, information access, and application development that create a picture of R&D robustness.

The Global Innovation Index 2021 (GII 2021) employs a robust methodology to identify and collect relevant data, assemble and categorize data into tranches, evaluate and measure data absolutes and trends, and interpret and compare data meaning and positioning. WIPO utilizes several advisory boards, review panels, and industry partners for study guidance and methodology review. It spends considerable effort ensuring data quality and addressing anomaly and normalization adjustments.

Like every R&D- and innovation-focused organization or analysis, GII 2021 has developed its own definition of innovation that it adopts to communicate about purpose and intent. The WIPO definition is a bit narrower than the one I have adopted for this book and tends to focus on an offering orientation:

An innovation is a new or improved product or process (or combination thereof) that differs significantly from the unit's previous products or processes and that has been made available to potential users (product) or brought into use by the unit (process).[7]

Regardless of the innovation definition utilized by GII 2021—and those adopted by other organizations profiled later in this book—the essence of the delineation is the creation of something new that can be offered to customers for their benefit. Presumably, that is what any company should be attempting to accomplish—please its customers and add value to its business.

The GII 2021 study had a specific topical interest in the impact of COVID-19 on the level of innovation occurring during 2020. While the full story of COVID-19 impacts on economies, companies, and innovation won't be ascertained until late in 2022 or 2023, it does provide a glimpse into first-year impacts.

From a global perspective, the level of innovation spend between 2019 and 2020 (the last year for which data was available) grew by about 10 percent year over year (also about 10 percent in the United States). In addition to the level of spend, the number of scientific articles grew 7.6 percent worldwide, international patent filings reached an all-time high in 2020 and grew by 3.5 percent, and venture capital deals grew by 5.8 percent in 2020, with strong growth experienced in the Asia-Pacific region, while declines occurred in the United States and Europe.[8]

Given this data, it does not appear that the pandemic slowed the pace of innovation across the globe. Rather, COVID-19 may have been a catalyst for countries to pursue health-care medicine and treatment opportunities, as well as seek to ameliorate market downturns while strengthening the competitiveness of economies, industries, and companies. According to GII 2021, the software information and communications technology (ICT), related hardware and electrical equipment, and pharmaceuticals and biotechnology sectors were the strongest investors in 2020, which fits the narrative that companies focused on business connectivity, information dissemination, and consumer entertainment were actively attempting to seize competitive advantage where it existed.[9]

A more telling result from the GII 2021 study was the country rankings that were produced across the 132 economies analyzed (see Figure 5). The top 20 countries would likely not surprise an experienced observer, but the rank order of these countries could provide more of a surprise. Remember, these rankings are not purely about innovation investment scale, innovation success, or relative peer admiration. These rankings are based on the seven key pillars previously defined and the 81 related indicators that compose these pillars.[10]

	Economy	Score		Economy	Score
1	Switzerland	65.5	11	France	55.0
2	Sweden	63.1	12	China	54.8
3	United States	61.3	13	Japan	54.5
4	United Kingdom	59.8	14	Hong Kong	53.7
5	Republic of Korea	59.3	15	Israel	53.4
6	Netherlands	58.6	16	Canada	53.1
7	Finland	58.4	17	Iceland	51.8
8	Singapore	57.8	18	Austria	50.9
9	Denmark	57.3	19	Ireland	50.7
10	Germany	57.3	20	Norway	50.4

Figure 5. Innovation index, 2021.

(Source: Data from World Intellectual Property Organization, *Global Innovation Index 2021: Tracking Innovation through the COVID-19 Crisis* [Geneva, Switzerland: WIPO, 2021].)

The country economy rankings in the figure reflect an index-based comparison based on analysis of all 81 factors and unique weightings to the identified factors. This approach moves beyond pure numeric or scale-based ratings to leverage a well-developed scoring model that reflects the underlying environment for innovation in countries (inputs), as well as the extent to which innovation achievements have been produced (outputs). The message here is that the GII 2021 methodology values the adequacy of the starting point—the institutions, infrastructure, market dynamics, and financial stability—as much as the history of overall achievement, specific accomplishments, and market reputation when evaluating the positioning of innovation in a country.

Among the top 20 innovation leaders in the GII 2021 study, the inclusion of the United States, United Kingdom, Korea, Germany, France, China, and Japan would appear as no surprise. However, the presence of Sweden and Switzerland as the two highest-ranked countries for innovation—for both the local environment and actual accomplishment—would be surprising, particularly given the scale at which innovation spend would occur given the size of these respective economies. However, the fact that both Sweden and Switzerland are the only two economies that have consistently remained in the top three over the last decade, and along with the United States and United Kingdom have consistently been in the top five for the last three years, suggests that the productivity of their innovation has excelled relative to many of their larger peers.[11]

Within the top 20 country economies, there is a heavy European, Asia-Pacific, and North American representation. Yet several smaller or less densely populated countries—Finland, Netherlands, Singapore, Denmark, Israel, Iceland, Austria, Ireland, and Norway—are also part of this top 20 group. Again, this ranking reflects not just what they do to produce the level of innovation occurring but, more importantly, the underlying conditions they start with and what they achieve through their innovation efforts.[12]

While the GII 2021 study is structured at the country and sector level as opposed to covering specific companies, the information provided illustrates that innovation activity, at least as represented by investment, has been highly resilient. More importantly, it illustrates that innovation activity is not localized in only the largest industrialized countries. Many small to midsize countries have demonstrated their prowess at innovation and can proudly consider themselves more productive than their peers, even as starting points can widely differ.

Global Innovation 1000

The assessment of innovation positioning across 132 economies provides insight into how outside observers view the level of country emphasis on advancing their economic futures and fortunes. This type of assessment enables pundits, researchers, and interested parties to understand exactly which countries are leaders in innovation and how they fare across a wide range of indicators. But reviewing commitment and contribution at the country level has its limitations and does not address another critical dimension of innovation activity—how individual companies perform.

Earlier in the book, I introduce the GI 1000—an annual study performed by Strategy& and published in *strategy+business* magazine—which analyzed the innovation spend and outcomes of the top 1,000 companies in the world. While also consistently analyzing the level of innovation spend and the comparative financial results it produced, the study also addressed topical issues such as impacts from cross-border collaboration, digitalization, ideation, culture, innovator success, and customer connection, among others.

Although the study was not conducted in 2020 (for 2019) or 2021 (for 2020) because of COVID-19 constraints, the most recent study still provides useful insights into the state of innovation play around the globe among the largest companies in the world.

A useful indicator in assessing innovation spend is determining just how much actual investment GI 1000 companies apply each year on an absolute and relative scale. For 2018, the GI 1000 spent almost $800 million, which was an 11 percent increase to the prior year and four times the level in earlier front years. On an overall basis, GI 1000 companies continued to spend about 4.5 percent of revenues on innovation, even as revenues increased at the same pace as innovation spend.[13]

Of more interest is *how well* innovation spenders perform in their markets. For those GI 1000 companies known as leveraged innovators (high financial performance with lower relative innovation spend), the 88 companies that earned this distinction had five-year sales growth at 2.6 times the sales growth of the full GI 1000, market capitalization growth at 2.9 times the peer group, and the level of innovation intensity at less than the median of the full peer group.[14]

Thus, the empirical data across the GI 1000 suggests that pure investment levels do not necessarily lead to superior financial results, but that smart innovation investment, coupled with adroit management, can catapult a company into differentiated results. This provides the sweet spot for companies to capture—that is, finding the *right targets* for spending, the *right level* of spending, the *right balance* of spending, and the *right execution* of spending—to lead to elevated market and financial outcomes against peers.

Analysis was also made of the relative innovation positioning of multiple sectors of the economy to provide insight into cross-industry investment. These seven sectors—health care, computing and electronics, software and internet, automotive, industrials, chemicals and energy, and aerospace and defense—compare the level of innovation spending made over time.

The GI 1000 study covered the spending pattern of each industry beginning in 2005 and illustrates changes in spending levels *by* sector and relative positioning *across* sectors. Only two sectors—aerospace and defense and chemicals and energy—did not increase spending in recent years (see Figure 6). All sectors exhibited a general increase to their innovation spend over time, although in several sectors, the trajectory of spend has shifted, with health care and software and internet dramatically growing—even before the pandemic.[15]

Although the focus of the GI 1000 study has been on companies, the context in which sectors and enterprises invest in innovation is important to note. The study addressed innovation spend on a global basis, using a mix of regions and selected stand-out countries. Companies in North America still maintain a large lead over the next-closest region (Europe) in spend levels, and innovation spend's long-term relative growth curve remains strong. Of note is the high growth rate of recent innovation spend in China as it continues to align country goals with its industrial capabilities, and the flattening of Japan's growth despite its early relative positioning.[16]

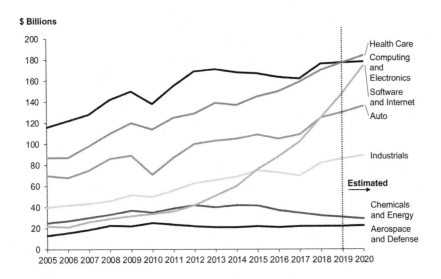

Figure 6. R&D spending by sector.

(Source: Barry Jaruzelski, Robert Chwalik, and Brad Goehle, "The Global Innovation 1000: What the Top Innovators Get Right," *strategy+business*, October 30, 2018, https://www.strategy-business.com/feature/What-the-Top-Innovators-Get-Right.)

With respect to where these countries center their innovation spend, North America dominates in aerospace and defense, software and internet, and health care; Europe emphasizes spend in the aerospace and defense and chemicals and energy sectors; and Japan's focus is in automotive and chemicals and energy. China's most dominant spend focus relates to industrials, which, in part, reflects how much of global economy purchases have been outsourced over time to the Middle Kingdom.

A much-awaited element of the GI 1000 study is just how companies within the Global Innovation 1000 peer set are ranked relative to their innovation spend. Even as innovation investment has been consistently growing globally and across many sectors and companies, it appears more companies are finding that spend quality is far more valuable than spend level. This is proven out in the earlier-referenced comparison of the highly leveraged innovators to the full peer group.

To start with, the top 20 innovators compose less than 30 percent of the total annual spend in the most recent GI 1000. Year to year, the top end of the top 20 spenders do not widely vary and sustain a high position across periods, even though any single year may vary a couple of ranking points depending on the level of investment variability.

Several of the top 20 innovators (e.g., Alphabet, Amazon, Apple, Facebook, Microsoft, and Netflix) are typically considered to be digital companies, with the remaining entities split among the health care, computing and electronics, industrials, and automotive sectors. The change in year-over-year spend in the most recent GI 1000 study was broad, ranging from declining by 11 percent to increasing by 40 percent. Generally, only six of the top 20 innovation spenders reduced their year-over-year investment.[17]

In addition, the level of innovation intensity is generally above the peer group average of 4.5 percent, with a range between 3.6 percent and 25.4 percent. Only two of the top 20 spenders were below the full GI 1000 peer set average, with health care companies ranging between 14 percent and 25 percent and digital companies between 12 percent and 15 percent, except for Apple, which was just above the full peer set average. While the range of innovation intensity varies widely, even among the largest and best companies, most companies at the top end of the comparative scale are serious about their commitment to innovation and the level of necessary investment required for their purposes.[18]

More importantly, though, is what these companies achieve for their investment and how they are perceived by their peers. While all of them are successful, the reputational value of some companies' innovation results can far outstrip the level of their underlying investments. For example, Apple is the most widely admired company in the world for its innovation, but only spends approximately 5 percent of its revenues to achieve its purposes and is ranked 17 of 20 in the level of spend. Thus, actual spend levels are not a clear arbiter of innovation success.[19]

The 10 most innovative companies as selected by their peers through a survey conducted among the GI 1000 show a high degree of consistency across many of the included entities since 2010. While several global companies, like 3M, Toyota, Procter & Gamble, and IBM started as among the most admired, they have all fallen out of this group, with a couple of them not even among the top 20 spenders at this point.[20]

Again, it is the digital companies that heavily compose this group, along with other automotive and industrial entities. Apple has been the most widely admired innovator since the GI 1000 analysis began in 2010, followed closely by Alphabet. Other top 10 most-admired companies have been slightly more varied in their ranking perception, with some like Amazon moving from off the list to the current number two position.[21]

One reason for the admiration of these companies is what they have accomplished in their markets (i.e., a dominant market role, impressive offerings, and consistently high valuation and growth). But these top performers have also demonstrated superior market results compared to their peers.

When comparing just the top 10 innovators to the top 10 spenders on innovation, the financial results are impressive. The top 10 innovators far outpace the top 10 spenders across revenue, gross margin, and market capitalization growth, generally by wide amounts. Figure 7 illustrates the gap between top innovators and spenders, with the best innovators exceeding the largest spenders by 12 percentage points in revenue growth, 18 percentage points in gross margin growth, and 21 percentage points in market capitalization growth.[22]

For the most-admired innovators in the GI 1000, innovation is a part of the permanent fabric of their business. It is omnipresent within the organization and provides a clear and fundamental linkage to how these companies execute on their strategies. These most-admired innovators also have turned decades of investment, exploration, invention, and commercialization into deeply rooted cultures of innovation within their enterprises.

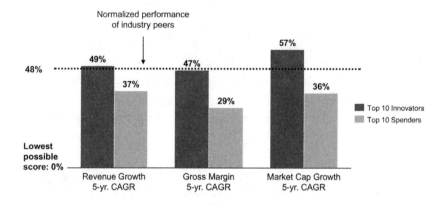

Figure 7. Innovator versus spender performance.

(Source: Barry Jaruzelski, Robert Chwalik, and Brad Goehle, "The Global Innovation 1000: What the Top Innovators Get Right," *strategy+business*, October 30, 2018, https://www.strategy-business.com/feature/What-the-Top-Innovators-Get-Right.)

Companies like Alphabet, Amazon, and Microsoft are software and internet market makers and think about expanding platforms and services on a global scale. Apple and Samsung are computer- and electronics-focused and pursue a continuous stream of new products. Johnson & Johnson, Merck, and Roche are health-care companies that thrive on the creation of new offerings targeted at quality-of-life issues. All these companies seek not just product and platform evolution but the creation of first-to-market and ubiquitous breakthrough offerings available on a global scale.

While all the most-admired companies on the GI 1000 top 20 innovators list are successful in their specific markets, they are successful for several reasons. First, they compete in competitive markets that challenge companies to innovate or die. Most CEOs do not like that equation and prefer to invest in ideas, rather than suffer avoidable consequences. Second, these companies have instilled corporate curiosity into their DNA, and it is now a natural experience for employees at all levels to pursue new ideas and invention. These employees feel they have the necessary freedom and incentives to pursue open thinking without fear of failure and adverse consequences.

Finally, the top 20 innovators have perfected systems of innovation that are embedded, self-sustaining, and continue to mature over time. For many CEOs, these enterprise systems and the accompanying culture couldn't be turned off or abandoned if they hoped to remain competitive.

These companies have been widely recognized and rewarded by the financial markets. In August 2018, Apple became the first publicly listed U.S. company to cross the $1 trillion threshold in market capitalization. And in September of that year, Amazon also passed the $1 trillion threshold.[23] Between 2020 and 2021, U.S.-based companies Alphabet, Meta, Microsoft, and Tesla also crossed the $1 trillion market capitalization barrier, and Alphabet, Apple, and Microsoft burgeoned above the $2 trillion market capitalization level. And in early 2022, Apple's market capitalization crossed the $3 trillion level.[24]

This expansion in enterprise value, coupled with high market receptivity to the products, services, and offerings of these companies, is perhaps the best barometer of the value of sustained innovation. And these companies continue to build enterprise value as they sustain and expand the level of innovation. When Apple's market capitalization increases from $1 trillion in 2018 to more than $3 trillion in a three-year period running into 2022, the ability to continue to deploy a steady 5 percent of revenues into innovation creates its own multiplier impact to year-to-year spend.

With results like the above, it is not difficult to understand why competitive companies are so enamored with the value of innovation. It has proven itself to be fundamental to business growth, integral to strategy execution, important to workplace development, and supportive to the psyche of employees. Innovation is not an activity or a program; it carries far more weight and significance to the value of an enterprise. It is an overall model for how to succeed strategically and a platform for business, technology, product, and solution excellence.

Utilities Positioning

Clearly, the best innovators have developed deep expertise and capabilities around the art of innovation. These capabilities are the result of decades of concentrated effort on building innovation prowess and accomplishment.

The best companies also have a knack for embedding these capabilities within their business and in advancing related skills through continuous enhancement of core processes and concerted attention to evolving their innovation acumen.

A robustly competitive environment is not the world in which the utilities sector has had to contend over its life cycle. While the fully integrated industry model has been broken in many states, much of the legacy model continues in place in more than half of the United States, and it is not likely to further unbundle and become substantially more competitive than it presently is in the power supply and delivery elements of the value chain.

However, in the downstream areas where utilities and customers intersect, the nature of competition is nascent today, but technology is rapidly pushing it to become more open and subject to different rules of engagement. Although commodity supply channels are fairly fixed (at the moment), network interconnection and behind-the-meter applications create a different type of playing field for the future. As OEMs interact more directly with customers, and customers become aware of more options for energy management and control, they will seek out mechanisms—software, smart devices, or base equipment—to exercise more direct involvement with vendors or their utilities.

Clearly, the contours of competition in the utilities sector will be very different from those that exist in most competitive industries. In certain value chain segments, no barriers to competitor entry exist, while in others, utilities essentially exist as sole asset owners and providers of certain critical services. Utilities will need to be comfortable existing in whichever elements of the value chain they participate in.

To meet potential competitors where they seek to disintermediate an incumbent, utilities will need to be comfortable interfacing with nontraditional providers about system interconnection requirements, as well as engaging directly with customers in more and different ways about energy utilization and management than they have had to in the past.

Utilities are equipped from expertise and commitment perspectives to meet these emerging challenges but have proven to be less consistent and adept at moving at the pace of the market (technology, vendors, and customers) that is likely to be required in the future. The gap between market and customer requirements for action and utility capability and capacity to satisfy these requirements poses a critical challenge for the industry.

For utilities, the experience of global competitors can be very instructive as the industry looks forward to a future path very unlike the one it has traversed over its recent past. As the GI 1000 study clearly indicates, absolute and relative innovation spend in the energy sector—whether by legacy oil and gas or utilities companies—has been extremely sparse relative to other sectors.

Utilities can learn much from observing how other sectors have approached innovation on a much larger scale and stage. Utilities can easily recognize that growing revenues organically—beyond simply through price changes, service territory move-ins, and basic customer demand—will require creativity around broadening the purpose and role of the utility, increasing the touchpoints with customers, and expanding the offerings made available to customers.

While for utilities, innovation to date is a reflection of the nature of the sector—its legacy past, risk aversion, and state of regulation—the future for utility innovation will be very different from how the industry has existed over the past 20 years, never mind the 200 years since its inception. A need for expanded innovation focus has already emerged and will continue to heighten. This need will not dissipate and will only grow as synchronization of the relationship between *technology push–customer pull* deepens within the utilities industry.

CHAPTER 4

Utility Investment

R&D and innovation have been constants for American and global industry for hundreds of years. But even though the utilities sector's investment in innovation has historically been modest compared to other types of sectors, that does not mean the utilities industry has not pursued its contributions and benefits over its history. It is the scale of that commitment, not the commitment itself, that is different from its peers.

In a general sense, the utilities industry has had an episodic past with R&D and innovation because it never truly was incented to pursue it—operationally or financially. Certainly, pursuing R&D regarding new technologies for adoption within the business is worthwhile, but to be an *alpha* innovator was inconsistent with the industry persona. The industry has always been risk averse, so why take on new, large, and visible risks? And from a financial perspective, the same return level would always be there when new technology was adopted, so why not just wait and follow the broader industry's lead?

For many decades, there was no upside to pursuing R&D and innovation if it exposed a company to incremental risk, particularly at the regulatory level, even if expenditures were made and reimbursed from customers (if allowed to be undertaken at all), and no visible results could be demonstrated within a reasonable time. Since utility executives are wary of creating additional regulatory scrutiny and second-guessing, there was little incentive for action, at least at significant annual scale. Nonetheless, utilities could not entirely disengage from the need for applied R&D and innovation—the challenge was how to best accomplish it.

The utilities industries, particularly the electric and gas sectors, are highly asset intensive and require significant amounts of capital to enable them to be continuous investors in both large- and small-scale assets. For electric companies, vast amounts of capital have flowed to expensive generation production assets, large-scale, high-voltage transmission lines, and highly dispersed distribution lines. While for gas, local distribution companies (LDCs) have similarly invested in short- and long-distance pipelines, gas storage facilities, and distribution mains and service lines, which, while requiring sustained capital for growth and replacement, have far lower intensity than electrics.

Given the range of fuel supply sources and options, utilities tended to invest first in their most necessary asset opportunities since these capital requirements, earnings contributions, and costs were usually the most defensible, and performance was often influenced by the level of capital deployed to maintain operations. Then they invested in areas where safety, service quality, and reliability were critical, and where operating interruptions and/or outcomes could have attendant adverse consequences. Finally, they invested in growth and asset replacement to meet the continuing needs of the business.

The snapshot of capital deployment above reflects how capital prioritization and allocation were typically determined by management. While a wide range of capital sources has been historically available to the industry, this is not the same thing as capital availability being infinite. Companies still must maintain creditworthiness and demonstrate a return on capital employed to both shareholders and regulators.

Consequently, investment in R&D and innovation was often last in line relative to other internal needs and subject to more considerations and variability than typical capital opportunities. Keep in mind that utilities make their money in three different ways: first, by earning returns on what they invest (their assets); second, through efficient operating performance (their costs); and third, from effectively managing regulation, which has an awful lot to do with the ability to prevail in the first two areas.

Thus, when utilities think about R&D and innovation, *how* to optimize the business weighs heavily on any investment decision. And innovation focus needs to be directed toward where technology adoption can translate into lower unit costs or higher outputs; and thus higher returns and enhanced operational performance; and thus greater earnings or lower financial, operating, or regulatory risk; and thus lower risk premiums, when considering capital investment targeting.

Historical Imperative

Through its long-dated history, electric utilities have typically directed their R&D and innovation focus toward generation assets to achieve increased economies of scale, more efficient equipment, and improved plant performance, where the potential benefits from technology evolution would presumably be the highest. And LDCs typically directed their discretionary capital toward improving gas system operating reliability, where expected benefits would be assumed to occur from lower operating costs and avoided system interruptions.

Historical capital investment in the electric sector was for decades largely dominated by investment in new generation capacity or additional capacity upgrades to existing plants. In a growing economy—leading to increased energy demand—investment in the generation segment was a sure winner because no company or regulator ever wanted to be caught short and face those consequences. Accordingly, the emphasis on meeting a sustained upward demand curve through new capital investment was both logical to explain and easy to demonstrate.

During this period, an emphasis on generating plant technology—primarily coal—existed because of its dominance. Nuclear emerged in the late 1960s to early 1970s, but because of the safety aspects of the technology itself, utilities were not the primary sources for R&D, and the Department of Energy (DOE), universities (sometimes on contract to DOE), and OEMs were the entities where this R&D occurred.

However, public attitudes substantially changed in the late 1980s as prices for energy users continued to increase. At the same time, both individual consumers and commercial and industrial companies became increasingly interested in energy efficiency, which, of course, would flatten or restrain demand growth (hence the need for new power plants). These new attitudes did not completely offset the need for new generation, as existing plants (particularly old coal) were aging, less efficient, and environmentally unfriendly.

The trend toward reduced need for new generation capacity took decades to run its course as demand growth still occurred from new customers, industrial production expanded, and greater energy intensity emerged from more energy-consuming devices in a premise, building, or factory. Eventually, the demand curve did flatten in the 2000s, and the more than 2 percent growth in energy use declined to less than 1 percent. The efforts to increase energy consumption efficiency, the move of large amounts of industrial load offshore through outsourcing, and the occasional recession all contributed to a vastly different market environment than utilities had been accustomed to operating within.

Over time, what these sectoral shifts did was dampen the interest in, and need for, new technologies and revolutionary methods to achieve greater generation plant operating efficiency, thus reducing the enthusiasm for targeted R&D and innovation centered on generation as a segment. Figure 8 illustrates the relationship of generation-related capital investment to all other sources of capital deployment over time.[1]

The decline in generation-related capital investment was continuous and significant on a relative basis to other utility business segments. By 2017, the generation sector was no longer the primary consumer of capital investment. As the need for large, centralized generating stations diminished, the absolute need for new capacity did not disappear; it was rather displaced by the demand for renewables-based generation, which, while more expensive per unit of output and more intermittent in production, was cheaper to build, far more environmentally friendly, and more consistent with the changing public sentiment over generation sources.

In tandem with the decline of generation-related capital investment, other electric business segments both captured more share of the capital portfolio and gathered more interest from utilities as a destination source for investment since these areas were a target of OEMs and software developers for new technologies. And while utilities had often conducted their own internal R&D and innovation for generation, these companies were not experienced—nor did they desire to be—in the software development business.

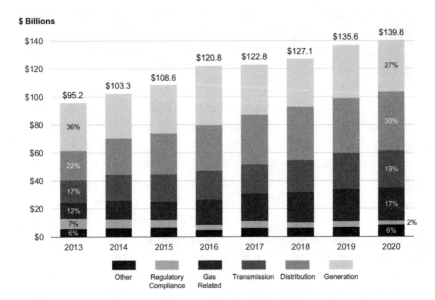

Figure 8. Shift in capital investment.

(Source: Edison Electric Institute, "Industry Capital Expenditures," June 2021, https://www.eei
.org/-/media/Project/EEI/Documents/Issues-and-Policy/Finance-And-Tax/bar_cap_ex.pdf.)

Much of this new capital investment for the distribution segment
reflects several other emerging business drivers—modernizing the existing
network, increasing the level of digitalization, strengthening the network's
resiliency, extending its local reach, and expanding the underlying infrastructure to accommodate new technologies. Utilities managements were
finding that the availability of these technologies in the market provided
new options for adoption and deployment within the network to increase
its optimization.

Current forecasts for electric business capital investment reflect the historical decline in generation segment capital allocation and suggest that it
has been permanently supplanted by investment in the grid and network
segments of the utility value chain. Notwithstanding the decline in generation segment spend, total capital spend for utilities continues to grow and
is simply being reallocated and enhanced to reflect the kinds of new needs
discussed above.

Industry Innovation

It should be recognized that in the early days of utility R&D, this activity was conducted internally by individual companies, as they could direct it toward their specific needs and move at their own pace. While having R&D preserved under management control has its advantages, the larger democratization of it magnifies its value across the industry.

Given coal's predominance as a fuel source for generation for so many decades in the United States and globally, utilities centered their R&D efforts in this area, focusing on production efficiency and operating costs. When electrics were more active in conducting their own internal R&D through dedicated internal organizations, like at Southern Company, American Electric Power, and Duke Energy, they were awarded numerous patents, with most involving generation asset enhancements.

These patents were primarily applicable to coal plants, which dominated the sector for decades, given the massive supply of indigenous coal available. However, as nuclear power emerged as a reliable fuel source, regulators became concerned over rising utility bills, carbon emissions became an environmental problem, natural gas became cheaper, and companies devalued internal R&D, far less attention was formally dedicated in the direction of R&D. LDCs also reduced R&D spend, although these levels were far lower than those of electrics.

Even after 2010, when coal was environmentally out of favor, certain U.S. utilities reoriented their generation R&D to focus on gasification technology to enable coal plants to convert carbon into pressurized gas. This conversion process would essentially enable the largest fuel source in the United States to be utilized but reduce the emissions footprint through transformation of a coal-based facility into a combined cycle gas plant for output. Both Duke Energy and Southern Company spent billions either constructing or converting existing plants to integrated gasification combined cycle (IGCC) technology.

Starting in the 1970s, the electric and gas sectors tended to replace internal R&D spend with externally directed spend toward third-party research entities with more collective support—EPRI and the Gas Technology Institute (GTI)—that gradually supplanted much company-specific R&D in favor of broader industry applicability.

These groups enabled both the electric and gas sectors to expand the contours of R&D conducted, all the while improving the economics of its endeavor. This democratization allows utilities to obtain more bang for their buck and enhance the depth and quality of their targeted R&D. With their track records, both groups have also helped secure regulatory support for R&D as a discretionary expenditure, galvanizing regulatory interest and engagement in its pursuits—a welcome outcome to an industry where regulatory involvement is not always so productive.

EPRI is profiled later in this book, but it has become a widely recognized source for both basic and applied R&D, as well as other technology assessment and testing activities that further support the utilities industry's interest in innovation. EPRI addresses a wide range of value chain segments and technology areas and has become a go-to source to the industry, along with all the other sources available from traditional channels like the federal government, universities, laboratories, OEMs, start-ups, and utilities themselves. The same is true for GTI, which preceded EPRI as an institution.

The utilities industry is fortunate that EPRI for electrics and GTI for natural gas provide an accepted source of R&D support to those sectors' many members. Each sector is well represented within its respective R&D entities by key executives from its members, who help these R&D groups define priorities and near- and long-term areas of interest.

While the utilities industry has been engaged with R&D and innovation for much of the 20th century, it does not resemble how other competitive industries approach these efforts. Companies within the GI 1000 are far more experienced and committed to R&D and innovation, with far more to show for their historical efforts. This is not so surprising when you consider the competitive environments for industrial and consumer companies and that of utilities—the market playing fields are not comparable, and the long-term challenges are not equally foreseeable.

The U.S. utilities industry as a group began to seriously think more about R&D and innovation in the late 1990s, when the Kyoto Protocol was initially signed by a number of nations, particularly in Europe. By that time, the environmental movement had been gaining traction with policy makers globally and in Washington, and with regulators in many states in the United States. The shift in policy perspective among policy makers and regulators was directly influenced by well-funded, vocal, and contentious antagonists in the climate community, which created top-of-mind visibility to environmental issues among large swaths of the population.

Around 2005, U.S. utilities as a sector started to rethink the implications of significant climate change targets that were being established around it. To accomplish the goals inherent in the Kyoto Protocol (developed countries)—and later in the follow-on Paris Agreement (all countries)—U.S. utilities would need to retire and replace a significant amount of its coal-fired generation with new sources (nuclear, gas, or renewables), all of which drive carbon emissions substantially down, although not entirely away.

Thus, the utilities sector, through its governing groups like the Edison Electric Institute (EEI) and the American Gas Association (AGA), began to actively prepare for an environment it had hoped would never materialize and it had been reluctant to completely embrace. Whether by design or default, R&D and innovation became increasingly discussed as a necessary foundation and enabler for making this shift from a fossil fuel fleet to a "carbon-lite" asset portfolio. Industry executives recognized that more investment in identifying, evaluating, and piloting new generation technologies was necessary to support the implicit direction and explicit goals of policy makers.

Industry executives also recognized that while the focus might be on generation, the derivative outcomes of decarbonization would be accompanied by decentralization and enabled by digitalization. Thus, a broader sense of how different the future would look permeated utilities industry thinking and evolved the realization that the industry was about to undergo a sea change in structure and delivery model that would be precipitated and enabled by disruptive technologies.

Hence, a focus on R&D and innovation was not just to be utilized to catch up and prepare for anticipated change but also to provide necessary insight into how different the future could look and what that meant for utility market participation, operational execution, and business model design. While it took a few more years to materialize, by 2015 the utilities sector was starting to actively migrate its strategies and becoming more acutely interested and broadly engaged in innovation than it had ever been. But it would still take several years for intent to translate into action within the industry, and as usual, it would be the monoliths that had already taken steps to emphasize R&D and innovation that would lead the movement.

Spend History

The utilities industry is not a total latecomer to R&D and innovation, but it has been a relatively low absolute and relative spender on these activities, whether internationally or in the United States. There are exceptions to the rule, of course, but few global or domestic utilities are significant R&D and innovation spenders.

R&D and innovation spend within the U.S. utilities sector is a difficult number to capture, despite the level of reporting required by the federal government and state regulatory authorities. It is even more difficult to ascertain for international utilities because of government ownership, cross-ownership, lack of transparency, reporting interpretation, and typical reporting anomalies. And for certain countries, like China, Russia, and India, where large utilities are in place but country norms are hard to overcome, it is even harder, as public information is scarce and difficult to accumulate.

While at Strategy& in 2020, I led a review of R&D and innovation spend for the largest utilities across the globe—the Global Top 40 (GT40)—excluding China, Russia, and India. This study assessed the drivers for R&D and innovation, how the industry was approaching innovation as a model, the absolute and relative levels of spend, the role of venture capital, and how internal corporate funds were being positioned for direct investment.

Recall that the average level of R&D and innovation spend among the top 20 innovators in the GI 1000 was approximately 4.5 percent of annual revenues, with several companies in the mid- to high double digits. For the GT40, the average spend was approximately 0.6 percent of annual revenues (net fuel), which is substantially below what software, health care, electronics, aerospace, automotive, industrial, and consumer companies spend.[2]

Some companies, like Fortum, Électricité de France (EDF), Korea Electric Power Corporation (KEPCO), Iberdrola, and Energias de Portugal (EDP), spend more than 1 percent of their annual revenues (net fuel) on innovation, but that is well below the GI 1000 innovation average. Even more revealing is that the largest relative innovation spender—Fortum—spends only approximately 2 percent of its annual revenues (net fuel) and it is a relatively small entity. This spend level is also after an 8 percent compound annual growth rate over the past five years.[3]

The largest annual spender has been EDF, which invests more than $600 million annually, by far the largest amount in the global utilities industry. And only four other utilities—all from Europe or Korea—spend above $100 million annually, with the total GT40 peer set at approximately 0.7 percent of annual revenues (net fuel).[4]

The range of spend across U.S. GT40 members has an exceptionally wide dispersion, from approximately $60 million to significantly less than $1 million. The largest U.S. utility innovation spender was Southern Company at just under $60 million annually, but the level of investment falls off quickly after Duke Energy and Edison International, which are less than half this amount. In fact, of the GT40, half of this group is composed of U.S. entities, with the majority spending less than $5 million annually, leaving U.S. companies with approximately 0.2 percent of annual revenue (net fuel).

When just U.S. utilities are reviewed, the picture doesn't much change. According to 2021 data from S&P Capital IQ Pro, the average relative spend amount has not changed, as illustrated in Figure 9.[5]

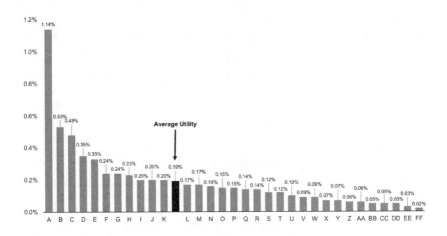

Figure 9. Utility R&D spend percentage.

(Source: Data from Federal Energy Regulatory Commission, Form 1 filings, 2021.)

This outcome of absolutely and relatively low R&D and innovation spend is not surprising given the changes to the utilities industry over the last 40 years. The convergence of regulatory and consumer backlash over perceived high prices, specter of market opening, demand destruction, alternative investment requirements, transition readiness activities, shrinkage of discretionary spending, and higher regulatory scrutiny of business priorities led to a de-emphasis on R&D and innovation and the resulting atrophy of these capabilities internally. But again, these outcomes were all relative (i.e., spending generally declined—sometimes sharply—but it did not entirely dissipate).

The utilities industry's interest in emphasizing R&D and innovation has now been reinvigorated as another wave of disruption moves across the sector, changing its fundamental rubric: big generation sources are out, and small sources are in; analog technology is out, and digital technology is in; scale is out, and miniaturization is in; dumb assets are out, and smart networks are in; standardization is out, and personalization is in; and unitary customer communication is out, and bilateral communication is in. This disruption leaves utilities faced with significant degrees of change in *how* they approach their future business purpose and customer role, with an accelerating pace of these fundamental changes.

To successfully compete in this more competitive market and set of heightened customer demands, utilities will need to substantially improve all aspects of their game regarding this transition—philosophy, aspirations, business model, market positioning, employee engagement, and innovation commitment. If utilities cannot find the internal funding capacity to commit to R&D and innovation, then the sector will need to access external sources to help close gaps in investment.

Venture Capital

Fortunately for utilities, a natural source of new capital has emerged that is focused on investing in the clean energy transition, as well as collaborating with utilities as partners in opportunity identification, assessment, investment, positioning, and monetization.

The entry of dedicated funds to the clean energy transition by external venture capital—whether existing firms or new entrants—has enabled utilities to work with seasoned partners that can extend their market presence and financial reach. Venture capital firms have positioned themselves as co-investors with utilities, although elements of this investor class can also be competitors to the market objectives and options of utilities, as they do not need to partner with utilities to invest for their own planned outcomes.

The nature and pace of change in utilities related to the new energy services transition has not gone unnoticed by venture capital. These firms are well aware of *how* the future utilities sector will need to evolve and *what* utilities need to do and can do to benefit from a disrupted market. Venture capital firms are well equipped to work with start-ups to directly provide funding but more importantly to infuse experienced board members and management expertise (where needed) to guide these embryonic firms. In addition, they serve to allow utilities to hedge their risks and learn about this investment channel with lower exposure.

These venture capital partners typically have a deep pool of available capital that is dedicated to finding, nurturing, and exiting their investments as the start-ups mature and are ready for either outright sale or stand-up as a separate market entity. These funds typically have developed comprehensive data sets of the population of available technology-based entities—software developers, solutions providers, or manufacturers—which offer detailed considerations and assessments of underlying technologies, market assessments, solution attractiveness, offering readiness, and growth potential.

The landscape of emerging entrants into the clean energy transition continually shifts as start-ups are founded, mature, and wither, or monetize in some form in the marketplace as parts of another enterprise or as newly capitalized entities. While everyone knows there are thousands of software firms all working on some technological aspect of the clean energy transition, no one is certain exactly which firms will materialize as the next unicorns. Consequently, these venture capital firms hedge their bets by investing in multiple entities across the utility value chain, technology family, or maturity cycle. This diversification enables these venture capital firms to build a bundle of investments and utilize appropriate risk hedging to optimize the exit value across the entities within the portfolio.

There are dozens of clean energy transition–oriented venture capital firms in the market in the North American, European, and Asia-Pacific regions. As would be expected, capital travels well across borders, so no single entity or capital source has a monopoly on financial investment, and opportunities can exist in any corner of the world. Accordingly, the U.S. utilities sector incumbents have a host of potential partners to choose from, depending on their objectives.

Some venture capital firms have robust portfolios of start-up investments reflecting early and active involvement with the entrepreneur sector and utilities as potential members of their investor group. Others are newer and smaller, with just a few investments and perhaps a different business model or financing approach. Regardless of the venture capital firm market approach, these entities act as force multipliers to utilities for investment identification, funding collaboration, start-up value optimization, and risk mitigation.

Like the levels of R&D and innovation spend referred to earlier, total global venture capital investment is also difficult to ensure that complete data availability is attainable. According to Mercom Capital Group, since 2015, almost 1,000 separate deals have been executed, totaling approximately $40 billion in cumulative investment over the period. The "high water" year was 2021, with approximately $10.6 billion in transactions, more than the total of the previous four years (see Figure 10). These deals have addressed the technology categories of battery storage, energy efficiency, smart grids, and solar, and the average deal size has been around $10 million to $20 million, with few outliers to this value.[6]

While the amount invested per technology category varies by period according to technology maturity and investor interest, for 2021, battery storage was valued at approximately $8.8 billion, smart grid at approximately $1.2 billion, energy efficiency at approximately $122 million, and solar at approximately $490 million, based on Mercom Capital Group research. These invested amounts exclude typical investments in renewables development and associated financing, which have become more about project development or sale than technology basis.[7]

Most of the battery company investment has centered on lithium-ion batteries, since they have been the most market ready because of difficulties in other chemistry performance or cost. Grid optimization has been the most popular destination for smart grid investment, with home and building efficiency the largest recipient of funding in energy efficiency. For solar, thin film has been the choice of funding by venture capital firms. As new technologies mature within each category, it is likely that not only will the technology type evolve, but so will the investment dedication among technology categories.

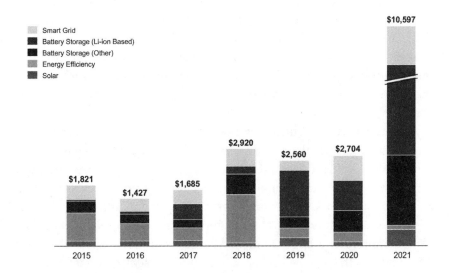

Figure 10. Venture capital sector investing. Note: Solar includes the thin film, balance-of-system, and software segments and excludes project development and financing.

(Source: Data from Mercom, "2019 Q4 and Annual Funding and M&A Report for Battery Storage, Smart Grid, and Efficiency"; Mercom, "2019 Q4 and Annual Solar Funding and M&A Report"; Mercom, "2021 Q4 and Annual Funding and M&A Report for Battery Storage, Smart Grid, and Efficiency"; Mercom, "Annual and Q4 2021 Solar Funding and M&A Report." Reports are available at https://mercomcapital.com/clean-energy-reports.)

Mercom Capital Group indicates that European and North American venture capital surpasses other regions in 2021 at more than \$1 billion each, particularly in battery storage. For the Asia-Pacific region, solar dominates at above \$650 million.[8]

Venture capital firms do not indiscriminately increase their investments in new energy solutions as options expand. They tend to vary the amount of funding and technologies as new options emerge or markets overcrowd. Venture capital is also adept at cycling its investment across multiple stages of technology maturity. Some are inclined to be early-stage investors, while others participate in subsequent funding stages. And some cycle capital across emerging, developing, and close-to-market technologies and time their exits to improving economics and increasing market familiarity with the underlying technology.

How venture capital invests is also an important characteristic, as is *where* it decides to place its capital. Venture capital firms seek to balance their investment opportunities to match their risk profiles and will often coinvest with their peers for risk management. The investment profile of these venture capital firms also reflects a disciplined model for investing that seeks competitive positioning ahead of the relevant technology market curve.

Traditional venture firms are now seeing internal corporate venture funds participate in their traditional market investment opportunities, sometimes as competitors and sometimes as stand-alone investors. These corporate investors are coming not just from utilities but also from oil and gas companies, OEMs, and infrastructure funds. Utilities are creating these internal venture funds to gain more control over investment deployment compared to a larger fund, and because they believe that they have specific needs that can be best dealt with through self-management.

U.S. and other GT40 utilities are already positioning themselves as serial investors by coinvesting with other venture capital funds. But some utilities have stood up separate investing arms to create capabilities for deal origination and enhance attractiveness to start-ups. Several of the GT40 companies have already created internal corporate venture capital groups that engage directly with start-ups in the market or in collaboration with other venture capital funds. These units identify, evaluate, fund, incubate, and monetize new energy solutions start-ups and provide both targeted and expansive investment in the technology community.

These utilities have focused their investments across the breadth of disruptive technology solutions, including battery storage, smart grid, and electric transport. For example, Southern Company provides project funding for Bloom Energy, which produces solid oxide fuel cells. And almost 30 utilities are members of Energy Impact Partners (EIP), which has multiple members across two funds totaling approximately $2.5 billion in new energy businesses.

The oil and gas sector has exhibited interest in the clean energy transition as it recognizes the displacement that will occur to it from climate change policies, ESG restrictions, demand patterns, and price declines. And OEMs see a market opportunity to fund a new technology that may integrate with an existing offering, or that has the potential to establish a new line of business, like hydrogen or carbon capture, utilization, and long-duration storage. These corporate venture capital funds have increased the level of capital availability to start-ups and to the total investment the utilities sector can leverage in these types of investments.

Companies like Chevron, Equinor, Total, Shell, and BP have been active participants from the oil and gas sector, investing in areas like electric vehicle (EV) charging, distributed energy resources, fuel cells, and batteries. OEMs like Schneider Electric, Volkswagen, and BASF have also been active investors in batteries, smart grid solutions, and hydrogen. It should also be noted that global utilities like E.ON, Tokyo Electric, Engie, and Centrica have also been active participants, particularly in the North American market given the plethora of U.S.-based software developers and solutions providers.

How these multiple venture capital providers engage and interact will remain interesting to follow. The venture capital space will become more crowded, and multiple participants in transactions will be increasingly more common. It is likely that the market will see venture capital firms fulfilling multiple roles in their relationships with utilities—signaling market direction and potential, coinvesting as partners, and competing for funding presence and participation.

Presence and Reach

While utilities have expanded their portfolios through a range of strategic participation models, they have also been actively extending their innovation models over the past half dozen years. It would probably be surprising for readers to learn that utilities actively engaged in the pursuit of innovation are not limited to only what they can accomplish within their corporate headquarters. Some companies have expanded their footprint by either establishing off-site facilities to house their innovation labs and resources, or they have created a local presence in innovation hotbeds to enhance their market and technology awareness, positioning, and opportunity access.

Just as innovative technologies are continuing to advance, so are utility approaches to pursuing innovation as a strategic undertaking. The chase for high-value R&D and innovation causes utilities to think differently about how to advance their understanding of evolving market dynamics.

As they have pursued innovation, utilities have recognized where they have shortcomings in areas like technology awareness, use case, market expertise, and deal flow.

Innovators know that creative thinking for new energy solutions occurs everywhere—through government, universities, laboratories, OEMs, start-ups, and venture capital. No single group monopolizes creative thinking, providing a challenge to utilities to hone their intrinsic capabilities and leverage opportunities to source needed capabilities from this robust community of ideas. If new ideas are likely to originate where the problem solvers are located, why not more closely align with these entities where they exist?

Utilities know they need to become active members of the R&D and innovation community to further open the aperture about the art of the possible and shorten the market discovery window. Consequently, they have become open to the notion of utilizing or creating "force extenders" to explore technology boundaries and develop enhanced market-sensing mechanisms.

In addition to creating distinct innovation centers for their own employees to freely collaborate and explore solutions, they are also creating an innovation presence where other innovators reside, co-locating alongside them. Smart companies are also creating preferred relationships with established innovation hubs and labs to leverage the broader knowledge base and avoid replicating these facilities.

A few companies are also establishing discrete scouting centers to extend market presence and using this additional reach to signal market interest, align perspectives and priorities with key market participants, address knowledge gaps through access to expertise, and open more collaborative channels to the community of advanced technology thinking.

Numerous R&D and innovation centers exist beyond Sand Hill Road in Silicon Valley, where start-ups are continually birthed and the mecca of venture capital is considered to reside. While Silicon Valley has a disproportionate number of software developers and design engineers, other technology centers like Boston, Seattle, Toronto, London, Paris, Tel Aviv, Seoul, and Singapore, among other cities, are hotbeds of electric and gas innovation.

Utilities R&D and innovation is a global activity and not limited to the immediate service territory of an incumbent. Innovation happens where ideation occurs, and perfected ideas are fully portable as technologies, hardware, solutions, platforms, and other more tangible outcomes to the broad user community of sponsors, OEMs, utilities, and customers. Although U.S. utilities have been more tourists than pioneers in establishing remote presence through scouting centers, companies like EDF, Engie, RWE, and E.ON have been globally active, including creating a presence in the United States to access or incubate start-ups.

In general, European utilities like Enel, EDF, EDP, Iberdrola, E.ON, and Naturgy are well ahead of U.S. utilities in the art of innovation. They have been at it longer, invested more, established multiple locations for presence, and emphasized innovation more highly as a corporate value.[9]

To be successful, utilities need to embrace innovation as a corporate imperative—continuous, pervasive, and boundaryless. While utilities continue to bring an internal perspective to bear on technology priorities and spending, they should also focus on additional objectives of syndicating R&D and innovation spend and activity among multiple partners. This syndication—and the collaboration it allows—will enable the sector to advance and accelerate its positioning for technology awareness, adoption, and deployment, as well as place it on a path toward securing its competitive position and building value for the business.

Success will also be aided by reassessing the level of capital spend dedicated toward R&D and innovation, and utilities as a sector—particularly U.S. utilities—will be challenged to up its game. The current industry spend level of 0.16 percent simply will not provide the requisite investment capability to attack the clean energy transition across the multiple fronts that are being affected. More discussion on this point occurs later in this book.

CHAPTER 5

Profiles in Innovation: The Enablers

THE utilities industry is a significant element of the U.S. economy and both a prodigious capital investor as well as a sector directly charged with identifying and satisfying customer needs. As a result, it finds itself naturally consumed with the need to anticipate its future challenges and design responsive and creative approaches to securing its strategic and customer positioning.

As an industry, U.S. utilities have a clear stake in how they are competitively positioned, particularly as OEMs, vendors, and solutions providers are seeking ways to disintermediate their domain, and their legacy marketplace is becoming more fragile. With this external environment in mind, the U.S. utilities sector is progressing from a nascent stage of innovation to one where activities are increasingly more purposeful and targeted. However, these companies recognize that the pace of industry disruption, the breadth of this activity, and the scale of its impacts create challenges beyond the existing capabilities of individual companies to adequately address.

On the one hand, technology disruption is pervasive and accelerating, and it is a challenge for utilities to be fully aware of how rapidly some of the efforts to create new software, develop market solutions, and integrate across broader platforms are progressing. In tandem, the sources of competition are expanding, and it is difficult for utilities to identify these entities early and understand their market positioning and intent to pursue the market. Finally, the evolution of the energy production and consumption markets is resulting in sweeping shifts in the roles played by various participants and the accompanying impacts to incumbent utilities.

Fortunately for utilities, there is a preexisting, capable community of potential partners of whom companies can avail themselves. These entities represent a cross section of federal government, research entities, trade associations, incubators, and investors. These types of partners provide a mix of basic and applied R&D expertise, innovative testing and piloting experience, policy advocacy, start-up nurturing, funding capacity, and strategic advisory capabilities. And their capabilities range across the utility value chain and disruptive technologies and solutions platforms.

In this chapter, several enablers, or *champions*, of innovation are profiled. These are entities that contribute to furthering the ability of the U.S. utilities industry to succeed with its R&D and innovation efforts. The profile of each entity addresses the purpose and history of the entity, scope of R&D and innovation activities, engagement with utilities, and examples of direct contribution to the sector. While there is a host of other groups, like universities, private laboratories, OEMs, vendors, and capital sources dedicated to R&D and innovation in some form, the groups profiled provide insight into leaders from multiple points of the innovation community spectrum.

Five specific entities are profiled: the Department of Energy (DOE), including its Advanced Research Projects Agency–Energy (ARPA-E); EPRI; Edison Electric Institute (EEI); Energy Impact Partners (EIP); and Joules Accelerator (Joules). Each entity's profile includes key executives representing the group. Collectively, these entities provide a broad view into the range and nature of the assistance available to U.S. utilities to support their innovation efforts. While there is a broader R&D and innovation community that extends beyond these entities, like numerous universities and laboratories, the profiled entities are the mainstays that enable U.S. utilities to take advantage of knowledge and capabilities outside their companies.

- *DOE ARPA-E:* At the federal government level, two parts of this agency are involved in R&D and innovation that affect the U.S. utilities industry. Within DOE, basic R&D is conducted on several areas involving energy efficiency and renewables. At ARPA-E, applied R&D is conducted across a host of areas intended to advance technologies to a commercial stage.

- *EPRI:* The U.S. utilities industry is a primary funder of applied R&D within this entity on behalf of the overall sector. The R&D program is broad and covers dimensions across the utility value chain, from upstream power supply technologies to downstream customer areas. Utility members can subscribe to the entire R&D program or select areas for participation.

- *EEI:* This is the official trade association for the U.S. utilities sector and represents its interests on Capitol Hill with various federal agencies and before certain state regulatory groups. EEI focuses on helping its members pursue policy alignment at the national level, as well as create opportunities for the advancement of the industry.

- *EIP:* This venture capital entity is the most highly capitalized energy technology fund of its type within the United States and invests in a wide range of technologies relevant to utility operations. Its members are both international and domestic and provide term funding to support a multiyear program of start-up businesses through their enterprise maturity.

- *Joules:* This entity is a nonprofit incubator and accelerator for cleantech start-ups focused on utility-relevant technology development and deployment. The range of technologies addressed is broad, and the focus of this entity is to provide a forum for entrepreneur introduction to potential investors and technology adopters, including utilities.

While U.S. utilities are already actively engaged in R&D and innovation at varying degrees of commitment, the fundamental purpose and intent of these entities is centered on the advancement of the sector and the identification, evaluation, and deployment of technologies and individual start-ups that may emerge as critical contributors to the industry.

While several of these entities have a rich history of supporting the U.S. utilities industry, others are more recent partners to the sector. Each fulfills a particular mission for the industry, and they collectively provide technology assessment, policy shaping, capital access, and business advice to benefit innovators and incumbents as they move through the clean energy transition.

Department of Energy

DOE is a unique agency within the federal government. Through its National Laboratories, the department encompasses a broad scope of scientific research initiatives, including nuclear weapons, high-risk energy R&D, administration of the federal power marketing agencies, energy regulatory programs, central energy data collection and analysis, and energy efficiency and technologies, among others.

DOE was stood up in late 1977 amid a national energy crisis related to the adequacy of the oil supply and a lack of clear direction for energy policy. In addition, the commercial nuclear power sector was burgeoning, but the roles of nuclear licensing and regulation were vastly different from those related to development and production of nuclear power and weapons, which were operating in a Cold War environment. This led to the creation of a new regulatory agency—the Nuclear Regulatory Commission—to focus solely on the commercial nuclear sector, including utility owner-operators.[1]

Key existing agencies at the time, like the Federal Power Commission, the Energy Research and Development Administration, and the Federal Energy Administration, were integrated into DOE, and roles were redefined and realigned.[2]

The role of DOE related to the energy sector changed over time as the needs of the United States evolved. For example, the fuel shortages of the late 1970s led to a role in overseeing the construction of the Trans-Alaska Pipeline System, an 800-mile pipeline from Prudhoe Bay to Valdez, Alaska, which would serve as a transit for crude oil to the lower 48 states. In the 1980s, attention also shifted from unlimited energy consumption to an emphasis on energy efficiency. In the 1990s, a new focus was provided to small-scale supply resources, like geothermal and biofuels, under the Public Utility Regulatory Policies Act (PURPA), which was administered by the Federal Energy Regulatory Commission (FERC).

And in the early 2000s, a renewed emphasis on industry-wide data management and reporting occurred via the Energy Information Administration (EIA). This was followed by a focus on regional transmission operator creation by FERC to ensure a more effective and seamless grid, as well as by the support of emerging technologies, like wind, solar, and biofuels, to address climate concerns, which had been building since the turn of the century. These latter actions had their genesis in the Energy Policy Act (EPACT) of 2005, which was enacted under the George W. Bush administration to address the lack of a robust energy policy over almost 13 years, and which provided stimulus to a new wave of policy and technology development.

Within DOE, responsibility for basic R&D exists within the Office of Science, while applied R&D occurs in other offices throughout the organization. Basic or fundamental research is targeted at discovery and the identification of new frontiers in cutting-edge technology that are not limited to energy, tangible matter, or to the earth itself. This office collaborates with industry, more than 40 Fortune 500 companies, smaller entities utilizing specialized capabilities, and facilities to support topical discovery. The R&D in this office focuses on a range of projects related to nanotechnology, new materials, miniaturization, and quantum physics, among a host of additional areas.[3]

DOE's mission as it relates to utilities focuses on a range of decarbonization initiatives; nuclear, grid, and energy efficiency technologies; and a mix of other responsibilities, like cybersecurity, applied research, and technology incubation and acceleration activities. These programs afford DOE many opportunities to maintain general working relationships with the utilities industry, as well as engage them directly in specific programs of interest and demonstration projects funded by DOE.

Over the course of several decades, DOE and its National Laboratories contributed to a significant amount of energy, science, and defense research and development:[4]

- *The Manhattan Project:* Discoveries driven by project founders Niels Bohr, J. Robert Oppenheimer, Ernest Lawrence, Leó Szilárd, Enrico Fermi, and Glenn Seaborg led to the discovery of fission, plutonium, and the development of the atomic and fusion bombs.

- *Nuclear reactor invention:* The naval reactors program that developed the reactors for submarines and surface ships made critical contributions to the commercial nuclear sector, one of DOE's most valuable programs.

- *Discovery of RNA:* The Oak Ridge National Laboratory started research into potential human cell damage from radiation soon after World War II, with the research leading to the discovery of RNA.

- *Neutrino detection:* The first experiential detection of the neutrino, one of the most abundant particles in the universe, but also one of the hardest to detect, occurred at the Savannah River National Laboratory.

- *Quark detection:* The National Laboratory Stanford Linear Accelerator Center (now named SLAC National Accelerator Laboratory) was the first facility to detect the much-hypothesized quark.

- *High-performance computers:* The National Laboratories were the developers, along with private computing companies such as Intel, IBM, and Cray, of many generations of supercomputers, as well as the first users of the desktop computer in the world.

- *Lithium-ion battery:* DOE funded the science collaboration team that developed the chemistry for the lithium-ion battery, which led to the team receiving a Nobel Prize for the discovery.

- *Hydraulic fracturing drilling:* Through the National Energy Technology Laboratory (NETL), DOE supported hydraulic fracturing testing in its early stages of development, leading to a fundamental breakthrough in natural gas production.

- *Human genome mapping:* The Joint Genome Institute, started by the Lawrence Berkeley, Lawrence Livermore, and Los Alamos National Laboratories, developed the Human Genome Project to start mapping the human genome.

- *Dark energy and dark matter:* High energy physics efforts at several of the National Laboratories helped lead to the development of theories related to the creation of the universe as it is known today.

- *The SunShot Initiative:* DOE efforts to target significant cost reductions lowered solar photovoltaic costs by more than 90 percent, which led to this technology becoming commercially available for the power markets.

- *Gene editing:* Three National Laboratories supported the Nobel Prize–winning discovery that CRISPR-Cas9 can be used to edit genes, leading to a revolution in the ability of the life sciences sector to conduct analysis and editing of genes.

- *National quantum initiative:* The National Laboratories led the world on quantum science experiments, including materials and particle physics, and catapulted the quantum technology revolution through the DOE quantum initiative.

- *COVID-19 vaccine:* High-performance computing and imaging facilities were critical to developing solutions to the COVID-19 pandemic, with several of the National Laboratories quickly imaging the virus, and supercomputing capabilities identifying the most likely vaccines in only three weeks.

When the Biden administration took office in 2021, it made climate change its highest energy priority and worked to enact legislation directed at decarbonization, as well as heightening federal interest in exploring new technologies and sponsoring cleantech demonstrations to jump-start development and deployment. The Bipartisan Infrastructure Framework was announced in June 2021 and was directed at both hard and soft dollar expenditures, with some directed at tangible infrastructure, some at tangentially related infrastructure, and some entirely unrelated.

Of the $1.2 trillion expenditure within the framework, approximately $90 billion directly related to the electric and gas utilities sectors, with commitment to additional environmental expenditures. The most direct framework expenditures related to utilities were targeted to expand EV charging, electrify public transit and school buses, build out the national electric transmission system, increase energy efficiency, improve grid and network resilience, support nuclear power, and sponsor cleantech demonstrations.[5]

The final bill, passed on November 6, 2021, was the Bipartisan Infrastructure Deal (BID), which provided $7.5 billion for EV charging and $65 billion for power infrastructure to upgrade and expand the transmission system and grid, as well as invest in technologies that will reduce greenhouse gas emissions.[6]

DOE subsequently announced that it would set aside $21.5 billion to establish an Office of Clean Energy Demonstrations (OCED) to focus on hydrogen hubs, electrolysis, and carbon capture, with attention also provided to advanced nuclear reactor technology. The focus on hydrogen and carbon capture is intended to be executed across several agencies of government.[7]

While advanced nuclear technology set-asides have typically been the province of the Office of Nuclear Energy (NE), they were included as part of the OCED package, although NE may retain this responsibility for some time. The BID also set aside $6 billion for a nuclear credit program to preserve the existing fleet and avoid premature shutdown. This program exists outside of the zero-emission credit (ZEC) offered by several states in support of nuclear plants in their states.[8]

A subsequent restructuring of DOE to fit its broader set of energy objectives and priorities occurred in early 2022, and various offices were realigned or created. The DOE organization consists of multiple offices, with more than 15 having a direct or indirect relationship to innovation that applies to the utilities industry:[9]

- *AI and technology:* The purpose of this office is to accelerate machine learning and AI capabilities through strategic portfolio alignment and by scaling DOE-wide end use cases that expand policy, partnerships, and innovations.

- *Energy efficiency and renewable energy (EE&RE):* This office advances decarbonization by accelerating research, development, and deployment of cleantech technologies, with a focus on application in electricity, transportation, industrial processes, buildings, and agriculture.

- *Fossil energy and carbon management (FE&CM):* This group's role is to minimize environmental impacts of fossil fuel while working toward net-zero emissions, particularly in the electricity and industrial sectors, with responsibility for economic transition of affected local communities.

- *Nuclear energy:* The primary mission of this office is to advance nuclear power as a resource and support new nuclear technology development and analysis of technical, cost, security, and waste disposal challenges facing the industry.

- *Electricity:* The purpose of this office is to ensure that the nation's critical energy infrastructure is resilient, reliable, and secure, and it oversees federal and state policies that shape electric system planning and market operations.

- *Manufacturing and energy supply chains:* The stand-up of this new office signaled a focus on securing critical supply chains to ensure resiliency in the economy and to modernize the energy infrastructure in support of the clean energy transition.

- *Clean energy demonstration (OCED):* This new office was created to support cleantech development in areas like carbon capture, hydrogen, grid-scale energy storage, and small modular reactors through demonstration of new scale technologies to accelerate deployment.

- *Cybersecurity, energy security, and emergency response:* The purpose of this office is to monitor threats to the nation and protect the flow of energy by improving energy infrastructure security and preparing for the occurrence of natural and man-made threats.

- *Loan programs:* This office finances large-scale, all-of-the-above energy infrastructure projects that may be first-of-a-kind (FOAK) and other high-impact, energy-related ventures without traditional access to debt from private lenders, such as new nuclear, EVs, and large-scale renewables.

- *State and community energy programs:* The purpose of this office is to provide funding and assistance to local communities in enhancing energy security, advancing state energy initiatives, and addressing energy affordability.

- *Indian energy policy and programs:* The mission of this office is to maximize the development and deployment of energy solutions (e.g., electrification, infrastructure, and efficiency) on Native American lands.

- *Technology transitions:* This office focuses on expanding the public impact of DOE's R&D activities by incorporating market pull to achieve the goals of commercialization within the business and industrial sectors.

- *Project management:* This office fulfills a multipurpose role of independent monitoring, assessment, and reporting on project execution, including review of performance baselines in scope, cost, and schedule, as well as general leadership in performance management systems.

- *ARPA-E:* The purpose of this group is to advance high-potential, high-impact technologies that are not yet ready for private sector investment in ways to generate, store, and use energy, but can be meaningfully advanced, with a small amount of funding within a defined period.

- *Advanced Research Projects Agency–Climate (ARPA-C):* This group is charged with developing game-changing technologies, such as small modular reactors and low-energy buildings, but outside the agenda of ARPA-E, to avoid duplication and highlight those technologies still at a stage of affectable development.

- *Science:* This office is the largest sponsor of basic research in physics, material sciences, chemistry, and energy, and over-sees an array of large-scale scientific facilities at the National Laboratories.

DOE has a substantial budget as an agency for its complete scope of responsibility, with significant funding for those matters relevant to the topic of innovation in utilities. The total DOE budget as proposed for fiscal year 2022 exceeds $45 billion, with almost half of this amount ($20 billion) directed at nuclear security programs. DOE has five separate budget line items focused on energy-related areas of particular interest to utilities: EE&RE, FE&CM, ARPA-E, ARPA-C, and OCED. There are other budget line items that are directly relevant to utility innovation, such as cyber- and energy security, technology transitions, AI and technology, and electricity, but these are broader in scope within the DOE budget than utility innovation–focused.[10]

Each of the five primary groups has an indicated mission and budget for 2022 (see Figure 11):[11]

- *EE&RE:* This office focuses on renewables, sustainable trans-portation, and more efficient homes, offices, and buildings that, when further developed, will lead to lower costs and emissions and higher operating performance. Its overall budget request in 2022 is $4.7 billion, compared to $2.9 billion in 2021.

- *FE&CM:* The focus of this office is on point-source carbon capture; carbon capture, conversion, and storage; methane emissions reduction; hydrogen with carbon management; critical mineral production; and CO_2 removal. The requested 2022 budget is almost $900 million, compared to a 2021 budget of $750 million.

- *ARPA-E:* This office emphasizes a mix of focused programs, new programs, and opportunities to scale up existing programs across areas within the electricity generation and delivery, efficiency, and transportation areas. For 2022, its requested budget is $500 million compared to the 2021 amount of $427 million.

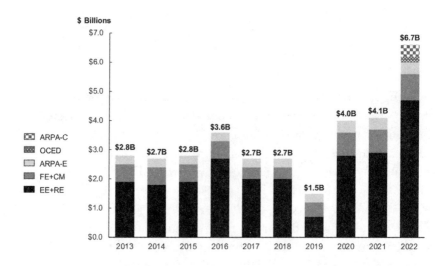

Figure 11. Energy office appropriations, 2013–2022. Note: Numbers reflect budget requests and weren't necessarily enacted.

(Source: Data from U.S. Department of Energy, "Budget Justification" reports, fiscal years 2013–2022, available at https://www.energy.gov/cfo/listings/budget-justification-supporting -documents?page=0.)

- *ARPA-C:* This office focuses on technologies that can dramatically enable the attainment of net-zero emissions from both existing and new technologies, and extends into supply chains, emissions sources, and unconventional methods and techniques to remove CO_2. It was not separately budgeted in 2021 but has a requested amount of $200 million for 2022.

- *OCED:* This office has a new mission within DOE and is responsible for the assessment and development of new technologies that are not commercially ready and in need of obtaining private financing. The office did not exist in prior years but has a requested appropriation of $400 million for 2022.

Over time, DOE has been requesting and Congress has been allocating more budget toward areas where technology innovation can be pursued, as well as sponsoring innovative demonstration projects in a variety of technologies. Over the past 10 years, DOE has increased its budget in the offices above from a 2019 low of $1.5 billion to $6.7 billion, while increasing its inquiry scope across more technologies, expanding laboratory capabilities, providing greater demonstration grants, and targeting major initiatives, like EVs, hydrogen, and battery storage.[12]

This increase in budget allocation reflects a mix of drivers from inside and outside the federal government. Paul Dabbar, retired Under Secretary of Energy for Science within DOE during the Trump administration, commented on how targeted spend for the energy sector was revitalized:

Significant increases in federal government interest and funding for discovery and applied applications have occurred since 2017. The federal budget was capped with the sequester for many years coming out of the 2008 recession. In 2017, when the sequester was lifted, R&D efforts at DOE were determined by Congress to be a key focus area for additional investment. For example, the Office of Science, including its National Laboratories efforts, saw 30 percent increases in funding over the next three years. This allowed a wide array of new, large facilities to be constructed, as well as a significant amount of new technology development efforts, including the Energy Storage Grant Challenge, the National

Quantum Initiative, the Exascale supercomputing program, and the "Industries of the Future" Initiative. This momentum led to the passage of the Energy Act of 2020, the largest energy policy act passed in a generation.[13]

DOE has supplemented its traditional programs by initiating a new effort called Energy Earthshots, which is focused on an "all R&D community" approach, supplemented by inviting universities, businesses, and national laboratories to help accelerate net-zero carbon ambitions. DOE planned on announcing six to eight Earthshots over 2021–2022, with three already announced in 2021—Hydrogen Shot in June, Long Duration Storage Shot in July, and Carbon Negative Shot in November. Three more Earthshots were announced in the fall of 2022—Enhanced Geothermal Shot, Floating Offshore Wind Shot, and Industrial Heat Shot. The Energy Earthshots are viewed as a means to address technical challenges, accelerate breakthroughs, and rapidly advance new technologies to market application by providing a cross-institutional focus.[14]

While much of DOE's efforts are directed at the power sector, funding for natural gas occurs through various office and program initiatives, such as the "Novel Microbial Electrolysis System for Conversion of Biowastes into Low-Cost Renewable Hydrogen" being conducted by Southern Company Gas under the Energy Earthshots program.[15]

A network of 17 National Laboratories is also operated and managed by DOE and covers three primary categories of multipurpose science, multipurpose security, and energy technologies. The three energy-focused labs include NETL, the Idaho National Laboratory (INL), and the National Renewable Energy Laboratory (NREL). Each of these has a different mission:[16]

- *NETL:* As the only government-owned and -operated DOE lab, it focuses on advancing clean technologies, carbon capture, energy infrastructure, and grid reliability and resiliency, and on expanding energy production.

- *INL:* This lab is the center for advanced nuclear reactor and fuel technology analysis, R&D, and innovation, as well as the principal lab for cybersecurity, and supports critical infrastructure protection, including that which is related to energy systems.

- *NREL:* This lab is charged with exploring renewables technologies, sustainable transportation, and energy efficiency to enhance existing and future energy delivery systems.

These labs can be part of or aided by other DOE-wide lab collaborations, such as the Grid Modernization Laboratory Consortium, which encompasses DOE and 14 other National Laboratories. Additionally, the laboratories collaborate on a wide variety of technology challenges and opportunities, such as AI, grid resilience, net-zero carbon, energy storage, battery technology, electrolyzers, fusion technology, critical materials, and earth systems.

The other National Laboratories focus on a variety of matters, including nuclear materials, security, and nonproliferation; basic science related to materials, plasma, particle physics, computing, and chemistry; and attention to national security protection and environmental matters:[17]

- *Ames Laboratory:* This lab focuses on critical material solutions and the discovery, synthesis, analysis, and use of new materials, novel chemistries, and transformational analytical tools.

- *Argonne National Laboratory:* This lab conducts basic research to drive advances in materials science, chemistry, physics, biology, and environmental science.

- *Brookhaven National Laboratory:* This lab stewards research in energy and data science, nuclear science and particle physics, quantitative plant science, and quantum information science.

- *Fermi National Accelerator Laboratory:* This lab acts as the frontier laboratory for particle physics discovery, powering research into the fundamental nature of the universe, including neutrino science.

- *Lawrence Berkeley National Laboratory:* This lab creates useful new materials, advances the frontiers of computing, and develops sustainable energy and environmental solutions.

- *Lawrence Livermore National Laboratory:* This lab confronts dangers ranging from nuclear proliferation and terrorism to energy shortages and climate change that threaten national security.

- *Los Alamos National Laboratory:* This lab addresses nuclear nonproliferation, counter-proliferation, energy security, and responses to chemical, biological, radiological, and explosives threats.

- *Oak Ridge National Laboratory:* This lab manages comprehensive materials programs, two neutron science facilities, fusion and fission energy and science, and isotopes production.

- *Pacific Northwest National Laboratory:* This lab studies ecosystem responses to climate change, power grid modernization, energy storage, cybersecurity, and nonproliferation.

- *Princeton Plasma Physics Laboratory:* This lab develops advanced engineering for fusion, advances nanoscale fabrication, and expands plasma understanding from nanoscales to astrophysical scales.

- *Sandia National Laboratories:* This lab preserves the nuclear stockpile, protects nuclear assets and materials, and addresses nuclear emergency response and nonproliferation.

- *Savannah River National Laboratory:* This lab provides practical, cost-effective solutions to nuclear materials management, national security, environmental stewardship, and energy security.

- *SLAC National Accelerator Laboratory:* This lab researches materials, chemicals, biology, energy, high-energy density, cosmology, particle physics, bioimaging, and technology.

- *Thomas Jefferson National Accelerator Facility:* This lab undertakes studies of the fundamental nature of confined states of quarks and gluons, including protons and neutrons.

These laboratories focus on managing their specific stewardship roles, as well as advancing the contours and depth of applied science and innovation. Each of the National Laboratories has constructed a strategic plan, reflecting the notion that "if we had the money, we would spend it like this," and providing a structured way to think about the prioritization and allocation of potential funding.

All 17 specific DOE laboratories have assigned missions, although some of them are related in their scopes and often apply their unique subject matter skills to complement or extend research conducted in other laboratories. This accumulated level of fundamental and applied expertise provides the backbone of the scientific community in the United States related to military, industrial, commercial, nuclear, energy, and civil areas of application.

In addition, DOE has undertaken incubation and acceleration roles with respect to new technologies emerging in the marketplace. The agency launched the National Incubator Initiative for Clean Energy, which ultimately launched Incubatenergy, the first nationwide network connecting incubators and accelerators.[18]

The incubator program was initiated in 2007 and has funded more than 100 start-ups in areas like photovoltaics, concentrating solar power, grid integration, system integration, and soft costs for products and services. The incubator program has had a focus on de-risking start-ups and enabling them to move toward rapid commercialization by addressing technology issues that investors are unprepared to take on at this stage in a start-up's maturity.[19]

In September 2021, DOE initiated its Inclusive Energy Innovation Prize, for which it solicited ideas from entrepreneurs, nonprofit and nongovernmental organizations, for-profit companies, and academic institutions to make the clean energy ecosystem more accessible to disadvantaged communities. The program is intended to make several million dollars available to support, create, and identify incubation, acceleration, and community-based entrepreneurship activities in support of cleantech. Among five specific goals, the program is intended to foster grassroots innovation, bottoms-up collaboration, and specific solutions for the involved communities.[20]

DOE has also established several accelerator programs to extend its support past the incubation stage of start-ups, such as the Accelerator Stewardship and Development programs for advancement of particle research, the Clean Energy Cybersecurity Accelerator to monitor and secure the energy grid, and the Better Buildings Accelerators to improve all aspects of efficiency in building system design through efforts like the Packaged Combined Heat and Power and Sustainable Wastewater Infrastructure accelerators.

In addition, DOE established the Energy Program for Innovation Clusters (EPIC) to fund selected incubators, accelerators, and sponsors of new technologies. In 2020 the first funding went to 20 incubator, accelerator, or sponsor clusters across the United States to address the building of regional hubs for technologies and entrepreneurs.[21]

A second EPIC funding award went to 10 new and established entities throughout the United States in mid-2021 in the areas of energy storage, hydrogen, hardware, and other start-up technologies, again to drive regional technology clusters in key areas of national interest and need.[22]

In August 2022, the Inflation Reduction Act (IRA) was enacted, containing a range of programs to address deficit reduction, health care, clean energy, and tax issues of various types. Numerous provisions were included to address wind, solar, storage, nuclear, EVs, efficiency, and climate resilience related to the power and utility sectors—in particular, rebates for heat pumps and home appliances and production or investment tax credits for EVs, renewables, nuclear, storage, hydrogen, carbon capture, and advanced manufacturing, along with rebates for energy efficiency.

Although much of the IRA relates to supportive tax policy, the focus of the energy portion of the law is to reduce greenhouse gas emissions through a policy of incentives and enablement of investment. Since the DOE Office of Science oversees multiple technology development initiatives initiated by the BID and previously enacted programs, particularly those related to emissions reduction, its current initiatives will be enhanced by the availability of further policy and financial support.

Advanced Research Projects Agency–Energy

The ARPA-E office was created in 2007 and stood up in 2009, with a focus on applied research across a range of technologies that were still embryonic and in need of support to continue technology development and enable further investor funding as the technology matured. ARPA-E is modeled after the Defense Advanced Research Projects Agency (DARPA); however, a fundamental difference between the two organizations is that DARPA has the defense establishment as a client, which usually has a specific request or need, while ARPA-E has a more diffuse mandate of exploring emerging technologies and advancing them to achieve readiness for commerciality and direct benefit to society.

The focus of ARPA-E is on turning discovery and early-stage technologies into commercial impact, including private company funding, company formation, partnering with other government agencies, and publication of inventions and patents. Since its inception, ARPA-E has enabled multiple projects in categories such as grid-scale batteries, transportation, grid operations, power electronics, energy efficiency, transportation fuels, power generation, building and industrial efficiency, methane and carbon detection and control, energy storage, and bioenergy.

ARPA-E utilizes several criteria in selecting technology projects for funding, including the impact of the proposed technology relative to the state of the art; the overall scientific and technical merit of the proposal; the qualifications, experience, and capabilities of the applicant; and the quality of the proposed management plan for technology development.

Multiple entities have developed ways to assess technology readiness in early-stage and maturing start-ups. The National Aeronautics and Space Agency (NASA) and the Department of Defense (DoD) have developed their own version of Technology Readiness Levels (TRL) that provide a yardstick for assessing how far along a particular technology has matured. This nine-level readiness scale assesses technologies from the nascent to mature stages and has been published and used as a guide by DOE (see Figure 12).[23]

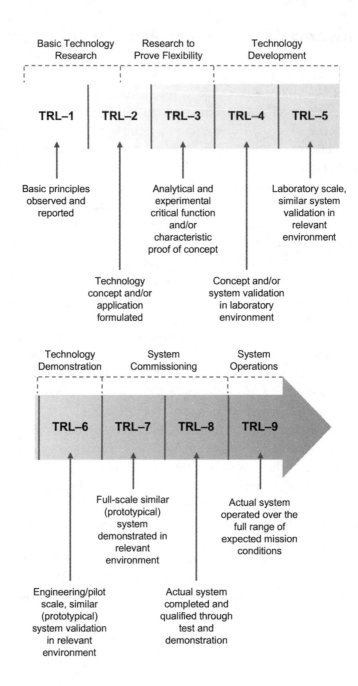

Figure 12. Technology Readiness Levels.

(Source: Data from U.S. Department of Energy, "Technology Readiness Assessment Guide," September 15, 2011, https://www2.lbl.gov/dir/assets/docs/TRL%20guide.pdf.)

Within DOE, various offices focus on different-stage technologies to fit their mission, with the DOE Office of Science working with embryonic technologies where basic research is the focus and scientific discovery is the desired outcome. ARPA-E, on the other hand, is looking at technologies that have passed the proof-of-concept stage but are not yet ready for commercialization and need development and investor funding to proceed to market.

On the nine-point scale, the Office of Science falls along the 0-3 TRL end of the scale (early stage) given its mission, which can include pure discovery where commercialization is often not the intended end result. Conversely, ARPA-E has a more flexible and dynamic mission and is generally focused on the middle of the scale of technologies, where its assistance and funding can provide a significant boost to readiness and scale-up financing. The EE&RE office within DOE also provides support to start-ups, but these are farther progressed in their development. While demarcation lines are not rigid, ARPA-E tends to stand between the Office of Science and the applied office of EE&RE in the development and deployment of energy innovation.

In late 2019, ARPA-E announced a FOAK initiative—the Seeding Critical Advances for Leading Energy technologies with Untapped Potential (SCALEUP). This $100 million program was designed to bring novel technologies quickly to market to enable rapid commercialization in areas like methane emissions, sodium batteries, grid reliability, rooftop-radiating cooling panels, and predictive software capabilities for grid storage and EV adoption to aid in optimizing supply and demand.

SCALEUP is an important and successful new effort in avoiding the valley of death for innovative energy projects and moving innovation from the lab to the loading dock. In SCALEUP 2019, roughly 50 percent of the projects that qualified as SCALEUP finalists secured market-based financing to move them from government-supported projects into the competitive marketplace as products supported by market demand—a very high success rate in comparison to normal venture capital statistics. A major factor contributing to this may be the time and effort supported by the federal government de-risking the particular technologies under consideration.

The intent was to retire underlying technical issues and enable scaling of high-risk and potentially disruptive technologies. Nine finalists were selected for this program: 24M Technologies (lithium-ion-based energy storage systems), AutoGrid Systems (virtual power plant), Bridger

Photonics (airborne emissions detection), Cambridge Electronics (now Finwave Semiconductor; efficient data centers), LongPath Technologies (continuous emissions monitoring), Natron Energy (sodium-ion batteries), Sila Nanotechnologies (high-capacity silicon anodes), SkyCool Systems (refrigeration systems), and Switched Source (grid modernization). After years of scientific work de-risking the technology and a rigorous selection process, it is interesting that roughly one-half of the 22 semifinalists have had a third-party funding event in the year since their selection—enabling these companies to reinforce their business viability and competitive success.[24]

In late 2021, ARPA-E announced the second installment of SCALEUP, which would provide additional funding to previous grantees and require demonstration of widespread deployment, commercial adoption viability, and follow-in private funding. SCALEUP 2021 is providing $100 million to scalable projects where proof-of-concept challenges have been addressed.[25]

ARPA-E tracks numerous indicators regarding its progress, accomplishments, and impacts, and has a rich set of accomplishments it can point to: More than 100 new companies have formed. More than 250 licenses have been issued for ARPA-E technology. More than 260 projects have partnered with another government agency. And more than 180 teams have cumulatively raised more than $7.6 billion in private sector funding to continue to advance technology toward the market.[26]

The agency has invested close to $3 billion in almost 1,300 projects. As of September 2021, it had had 17 exits since its inception in 2009, with market value realized of more than $19 billion from these transactions, confirming that the approach of ARPA-E to technology selection, funding, and development has advanced the level of scientific understanding and resulted in commercialization opportunities for these advanced technologies. Funding is not provided to applicants to whom private funding is readily available, or where the technology is not at a readiness level to secure commercial funding.[27]

The actual budget appropriation for ARPA-E has grown from $180 million in 2009 to a request of $500 million in 2022, with an expectation to continue growth at a rate well above inflation to more than $750 million by 2025 (at the current request level). The amounts appropriated for ARPA-E are separate and distinct within the overall DOE budget. The ARPA-E budget is evenly disaggregated between transportation systems and stationary power systems, and evenly divided between applied R&D and development activities.[28]

Lane Genatowski, former Director of ARPA-E in the Trump administration and an architect of the SCALEUP program, discussed its significance in advancing technologies to market:

> One of our missions at ARPA-E was to help start-up or early-stage companies overcome the valley of death, where their viability could be at risk. These start-ups often had great ideas but an inability to commercialize them due to funding and organizational constraints. Our SCALEUP program was designed to "prime the pump" and bring the forces of capitalism to bear by providing funding to help these companies move their technologies to marketability and downstream customer benefit. Our first SCALEUP was a clear success because it was grounded in providing a multiyear view to support technology maturity that could address anticipated market demand, as well as secure the participation of the private sector in support.[29]

Projects undertaken by ARPA-E—internally and externally—are driven by program managers that can represent internal engineers and scientists, as well as resources from the academic community that may be well versed in the underlying technology. In addition, universities are a significant resource to ARPA-E in project exploration and execution.

ARPA-E maintains multiple avenues for utilities to engage and participate in its programs, but one of the most significant opportunities is the annual Energy Innovation Summit that attracts entrepreneurs, government agencies, researchers, academia, OEMs, vendors, National Laboratory staff, media, and investors.

The Energy Innovation Summit covers a range of topical agenda items dealing with decarbonization, electrification, battery storage, power electronics, and a host of specific technology types and applications that are not currently mainstream. This three-day conference and technology showcase attracts interested parties from around the globe, with specific sessions provided for fast-pitch presentations to panels of financiers, and broader topical sessions held around value chain segments, climate change externalities, and the investment environment.

For the 2022 Energy Innovation Summit, which was the 12th conference and showcase to be held, technologies in the areas of wireless power transmission, terrestrial ecosystems, fusion, critical minerals mining, and industrial vertical farms, among many others, were discussed. The 2021 conference and showcase attracted over 3,000 attendees, with more than 400 technologies exhibited.[30]

Beyond the Energy Innovation Summit, ARPA-E regularly interfaces with utilities and entrepreneurs through various mechanisms, like direct meetings with individual utilities and industrial companies, technical working groups, start-ups, venture capital funds, and universities. These interactions create opportunities to engage in emerging technology viability, existing technology application, industry use case trends, and challenges to energy ecosystem optimization.

ARPA-E has also chartered several initiatives with entrepreneurs to drive innovation, such as its OPEN program that focuses on developing disruptive technologies that strengthen the nation's advanced energy enterprise. For the most recent 2021 program, there were 68 R&D projects in 13 technical areas, involving universities, laboratories, and private companies.[31]

The program earmarked $175 million toward R&D related to EVs, offshore wind, energy storage, and nuclear recycling, and works toward breakthroughs in commercializing a variety of energy solutions that can revolutionize the development and deployment of various technologies. Most projects are supported through existing funded programs like ATLANTIS for deep water wind turbines, BREAKERS for medium voltage direct current circuit breakers, and GEMINA for next-generation nuclear reactors.[32]

Both DOE as an agency and ARPA-E as a unique office within the agency have made substantial contributions to American industry, specifically the energy and utilities sectors over time, through a range of scientific contribution, applied R&D, and targeted innovation programs.

The R&D accomplishments of DOE and ARPA-E have provided vital technical insights and application knowledge to the user community, and the focus on advancing emerging technology has resulted in market readiness acceleration and utility company deployment. As utilities prepare to respond to and thrive in the cleantech transition, the capabilities of DOE and ARPA-E are positioned to further accelerate technology market readiness to enhance broader adoption and enhanced economic performance.

EPRI

EPRI was established in part as a response to the Great Northeast Blackout that occurred in New York City and New England in 1965, and in part to a recognized need for greater energy-directed R&D for the industry and the country. In 1972, two years after the Environmental Protection Agency (EPA) was founded and five years before DOE was created, Congress, state governments, and public and private utilities came together to create an independent, collaborative R&D organization to address significant electricity challenges: EPRI. It is a 501(c)(3) organization with main offices and laboratories in the United States—including Charlotte, North Carolina; Palo Alto, California; Knoxville, Tennessee; Washington, D.C.; Lenox, Massachusetts; and Dallas, Texas—and offices globally in Ireland, Japan, Poland, Singapore, Switzerland, South Korea, and the United Arab Emirates.[33]

Since its inception, EPRI has evolved into the world's preeminent independent nonprofit energy R&D organization, with offices around the world in a collaboration network covering 45 countries and more than 450 companies. It carries a $440 million budget to support its work across 66 programs, with U.S. ($255 million) and international ($130 million) members funding the majority of costs, and the remainder funded by approximately $55 million provided by government branches and other sources. With few exceptions, this funding level has been increasing annually, particularly as the focus on decarbonization broadens and actionable intensity increases.[34]

While EPRI received no funding from international entities or companies when it was launched, it has substantially grown its global engagement over its entire existence. International companies now provide approximately 30 percent of total funding and approximately 50 percent of funding in the nuclear area.[35]

EPRI focuses on driving innovation across the power sector, providing critical value to society through robust collaboration with energy providers and suppliers, vendors, and technology companies. Insights from the institute's energy R&D inform decision-making by government agencies, regulatory bodies, and other stakeholders.

It has a broad charter with respect to its R&D agenda, addressing generating plant enhancements, advancing new energy systems technologies, environmental challenges, infrastructure advancements, energy efficiency, customer solutions, AI, cybersecurity, digital technologies, and electrification. As a result, EPRI is a prolific patent awardee, with thousands of patents to its credit since it was founded.

However, focusing on the pursuit of patents is not an emphasis of EPRI, and the number of awards is not necessarily a reflection of commercial success. Rather, EPRI is focused on providing societal, customer, and member benefits through its R&D, thought leadership, and applied R&D.

Beyond addressing current challenges, EPRI's research portfolio reflects three key themes affecting the utilities industry into the future: Climate patterns are changing. The current energy delivery system is evolving as policies shift and technologies emerge. And clean energy resources such as electrification and low-carbon fuels are expanding in response to both of the items above.

EPRI provides objective, science-based R&D for the advancement and security of the electric sector and acts in a scanning capacity for new technologies applicable to the energy community. EPRI is also focused on minimizing risks associated with new technology or product development (i.e., avoiding or mitigating unproductive and carry-over technical development costs and friction associated with previous programs or projects that can linger for years).

The sweet spot for EPRI's research effort is to accelerate evaluations of early- and mid-stage technologies and provide guidance on methodologies and deployment to help them to scale. Essentially, EPRI's role involves bringing emerging, relevant technology to life and de-risking achievement of large-scale development and deployment. Much of its research focuses on applying its expertise in rigorous testing and simulation to increase the likelihood of deployment on the grid.

Although EPRI conducts both basic and applied research, approximately 12 percent of its budget is directed at exploratory evaluation for the Technology Innovation Program (e.g., in nanotechnologies), with the remainder of its effort focused on getting technologies ready for commercialization. Thus, most of EPRI's research agenda is directed at enabling technologies to be brought to market and deployed for operational, customer, and societal benefit.[36]

EPRI collaborates with domestic and international R&D entities, like

EDF and KEPCO, to share information, conduct targeted research, and advance the energy supply and delivery capabilities of utilities throughout the world. It has collaborated with R&D organizations, universities, and other country institutions across the globe.

EPRI has modified its membership model over the course of its existence to enhance the member and societal value of collaborative R&D. Membership in EPRI provides companies with access to a full range of recurring R&D and periodic study outcomes over the course of each year of involvement. EPRI offers an overall annual membership package that reflects an agenda of research topics (the annual research portfolio) agreed on by its board and advisor groups.

In addition, EPRI offers supplemental add-ons, where members can elect to participate in additional research efforts that may fit particular needs, depending on the type of entity (e.g., integrated, supply, grid, or network). The nature of the R&D supports the individual companies beyond the elements in a program or full membership. EPRI also provides a nuclear program for those who own and operate plants and maintain interests in either existing or emerging advanced technologies.

R&D ERAS

The stand-up and maturation of EPRI has followed a logical path over the 50 years of its existence. Creating the underlying infrastructure and attracting the breadth and depth of required technical resources—that is, shaping the organization—is a necessary first step. This establishes the structure and collaborative format involved with working with its industry and other entity members, and, along with formative R&D and value-based activities with these members, occupied a portion of EPRI's first 10 years.[37]

In the 1980s, still early in its existence, EPRI was described as addressing industry needs, as it directed R&D and other studies into high-visibility areas in that time window, covering nuclear, coal, transmission, materials, and gas. These areas for R&D reflected pent-up and emerging topical issues affecting air quality, technology advancement, and testing capabilities, among many other areas. Even in these early days, EPRI made substantial contributions to the industry, as discussed above related to patents, FOAK achievements, and physical facility stand-up.[38]

In the 1990s, EPRI expanded its exploration of new technologies, broadening its scope of inquiry and focusing attention on specific issues that were beginning to receive increasing external scrutiny, such as advancing environmental R&D amid evolving regulation. Additional attention was directed at developing modeling capabilities for deep analysis of issues and assessment of alternative inputs and outcomes. EPRI continued to make significant contributions to address industry challenges with more patents and FOAK demonstrations, installations, or releases.[39]

EPRI President and CEO Arshad Mansoor commented on the key drivers that influenced the agenda of EPRI in the early 2000s and set a road map for the next decade:

> Five significant external factors affected our research focus and priorities in this time frame: first, shale gas was changing both natural gas production, generation, and prices; second, the significant drop in solar and wind costs due to improving technology economics; third, the advent of the early digital age; fourth, the focus on the smart grid which changed the network infrastructure; and fifth, the impact of technology advancements such as the creation of the iPhone on cloud computing ubiquity and data analytics. These were soon followed by the continuing evolution of artificial intelligence and machine learning, which further enhanced computational capabilities and the power of analytics.[40]

By the early 2000s, EPRI had further evolved into an era where it was "navigating a new century" and emphasizing advancement of existing technologies and directing more attention to over-the-horizon opportunities. These efforts were targeted to address emerging technologies (e.g., EVs, reliable grid integration with renewables and changing demand, smart green and home efficiency technologies), the evolution of topics such as the intelligent network and the "coal plant for tomorrow," and the expansion of global and domestic collaboration.[41]

In the 2010s, a focus emerged on developing integrated energy networks, which introduced new issues like carbon capture, modular nuclear plants, smart grids, electrification, and cybersecurity, as well as issues like ergonomics and long-term nuclear fuel storage. These topics signaled that EPRI's agenda would not only remain robust but continue to expand to meet the needs of the power sector in a time when disruptive technologies were rapidly growing.[42]

Finally, in the 2020s, EPRI evolved its focus on guidance, tools, and solutions to support a net-zero future, as well as new technologies. Formal initiatives on decarbonization were announced, and topics like artificial intelligence, electromagnetic pulses, and advanced nuclear were added to the R&D agenda. A multi-decade game plan was also created to provide a glimpse into EPRI's future R&D and priorities. These longer-term initiatives are discussed further below.[43]

As a renowned energy research organization, EPRI has a reputation for leading-edge R&D and innovation. Over the years, it has conducted critical research in key areas related to a variety of value chain business areas. Since its founding, it has been involved in continuous R&D and meeting the evolving challenges of the industry cycle by cycle, achieving several FOAK breakthroughs:[44]

- *Control center communication:* This work established the Inter-Control Center Communication Protocol, which became the technical basis for subsequent standards established by organizations such as the Institute of Electrical and Electronics Engineers.

- *Three Mile Island analysis:* This project conducted root cause research for the Three Mile Island "loss of coolant accident," which led to the development of thermal hydraulic analysis tools, real-world simulation environments, and a range of risk mitigation approaches.

- *Nuclear utility requirements document:* An early contribution was the development in 1990 of the utility requirements document, creating a single integrated source of operating protocols for new nuclear plants, which has been updated numerous times to include specific application to small modular reactor (SMR) technologies.

- *Electric vehicles:* As early as the mid-1980s, R&D efforts had resulted in the development of a first-generation EV prototype that proved out the technical viability of the technology and the requirements for further economic and commercial adaptation.

- *Gasification-combined cycle technology:* This 100-megawatt IGCC project in 1984 represented the first commercial-scale integrated gasification plant, which was joined by General Electric, Southern California Edison, Bechtel, and Texaco, with substantial reductions in sulfur and nitrogen oxide.

- *Utility-scale fluidized-bed combustion demonstrations:* This project provided the foundation for commercialization of this technology, leading to significant environmental reductions in sulfur and nitrogen dioxide with an ability to utilize several fuels, such as coal waste products and petroleum coke.

- *Predictive maintenance system:* This project created the world's most advanced utility diagnostic and monitoring system and launched the movement toward comprehensive diagnostic systems.

- *Magnetic field recorder:* This FOAK field instrument became commercially available as a result of EPRI's technology development program and enabled the generation of maps of magnetic field flux density.

- *Compressed air energy storage:* This 110-megawatt-capacity plant was the first commercial unit in the United States in over 50 years that provided a new storage facility to be installed on a utility system, enabling long-duration energy storage to be recognized as a viable technology for adoption at scale.

- *Electromagnetic fields:* EPRI established the world's largest program to investigate electromagnetic field health effects, developing several state-of-the-art instruments to measure and analyze magnetic field exposure, leading to the adoption of a pocket-sized measurement device used globally.

- *Nitrogen oxide control:* EPRI sponsored demonstrations of various combustion-based nitrogen oxide emissions technologies that evaluated the cost and technical and reliability performance of various options to address acid rain through plant retrofits.

- *Clean air compliance:* This project pioneered the Sulfate Regional Experiment that assessed how sulfur dioxide emissions behave and migrate in the atmosphere, leading to the development of specific models designed to enable decision-making around utility system modification.

- *Silicon cell efficiency:* This project established a world record for sunlight-to-electricity conversion in silicon and expanded the technological capacity of the industry to understand how high-concentration photovoltaic cells can enable lower-cost electric prices.

- *Plasma-fired cupola:* The ability to convert steel into scrap iron was accomplished by using a full-scale plasma-fired cupola technology (a fossil-fuel-based technology) for electrification to improve production efficiency, lower costs, and reduce emissions.

- *High-temperature superconducting motor:* This program was conducted with DOE's Argonne National Laboratory and Reliance Electric and focused on producing and testing a small direct current machine.

- *Electronics-controlled, variable speed wind turbine:* This program was commercialized through a partnership with Kenetech/U.S. Windpower, Pacific Gas and Electric, and Niagara Mohawk and allows a turbine's ability to operate at relatively low wind speeds.

- *Power quality system:* The first commercial installation of a system to enable ride-through power at public and industrial facilities was supported by AC Battery Corporation and General Motors and enables rapid provision of energy when interruptions could occur.

- *Static synchronous compensator:* The first commercial prototype was developed in conjunction with Westinghouse as part of a larger transmission system program and provides voltage support for these systems.

- *Dynamic voltage restorer:* This project was conducted in conjunction with Duke Energy and Westinghouse and led to the development of the most advanced electronic power controller for serving commercial and industrial customers.

- *Fukushima cleanup:* Immediately following the earthquake, tsunami, and resulting plant accident in Fukushima, Japan, in 2011, EPRI developed an entirely new and historic contaminated water cleanup system for use by worldwide utilities, as well as new procedures and seismic walk-down guidance.

With this history of FOAK accomplishments in mind, in 2018 EPRI recognized that traditional utility resource planning focused on least-cost supply sources would not suffice for a future that would be characterized by rapid deployment of large-scale variable resources; dramatic advances in digital energy and communications technologies; persistently low natural gas prices; increased awareness of potential high-impact, low-frequency events; and growing awareness of the role of the electric sector in achieving environmental and societal goals. Together, these challenges were providing the parameters for the new digital utility that was more adaptable to identified constraints (see Figure 13).[45]

EPRI identified 10 specific resource planning challenges that needed to be confronted, generally related to planning model granularity, business segment integration, analysis boundaries and uncertainties, modeling robustness, expanded planning objectives, and market evolution, among other areas.[46]

As a result of this assessment, EPRI defined six key areas that compose its view of an Integrated Energy Network (IEN) for enhanced supply and network planning. These elements reflected key areas for R&D for the digital utility and identified multiple areas of interconnection, integration, and enablement:[47]

Figure 13. The digital utility.

(Source: Data from Anda Ray, "Eyes Wide Open: The Digital Utility," presentation at the Western Area NARUC Conference, May 23, 2017.)

- *Integrating advances in ICT:* Digital-enabling technologies for transformation utilize advances to address business challenges and attain sustainable benefits.

- *Enabling flexibility and commercial operation:* A ubiquitous network across the system is scalable and can support multiple applications.

- *Enabling efficient asset performance:* Open standards utilize a smart sensor network, data integration, and analytics for asset management and grid operations.

- *Enabling customer and delivery services:* Network planning and optimization with a "digital twin" support customer-responsive, model-based planning.

- *Enabling a safe and efficient workforce:* Leveraging augmented reality and cognitive analytics tools supports a digital workforce.

- *Enabling protection and privacy of data:* Cybersecurity-focused strategies protect, detect, respond, and recover.

These six elements framed a key part of the EPRI planning focus and the R&D agenda to enable and support the digital utility of the future. This framework provides the fundamentals for part of the future technology road map of EPRI.

R&D COMMUNITY

EPRI focuses on collaborating with existing research facilities across the world, assuming they meet its topical and capability needs, though it may seek to stand up unique facilities if it believes it is more appropriate. Thus, EPRI has created or been a part of a range of collaborations or consortia between utilities, government agencies, scientific organizations, OEMs, regulatory agencies, and technical working groups. These collaborations have resulted in the creation of a variety of technical centers, demonstration centers, research facilities, and commercial partnerships to drive and/or support technology development.

Facilities in the past have been stood up for nondestructive evaluation, battery storage, coal cleaning, maintenance and diagnostics, transmission line mechanical research, materials fabrication, materials production, and power electronics applications to provide dedicated concentration on topical areas where R&D conduct can provide accelerated payoff in technology market readiness or breakthrough.[48]

EPRI's labs today focus on several issues: high voltage testing, transmission and distribution (T&D) component aging, full-scale distribution testing, stray voltage detection and mitigation, manhole events, nondestructive evaluation, welding technologies, materials testing and characterization, T&D sensor development, electromagnetic pulse and cyber energy efficiency, distributed energy resources evaluation, ICT integration, lighting, appliance, HVAC, device testing and evaluation, environmental chamber testing, and EV charging.[49]

In addition to these technology R&D centers, EPRI has also partnered with key industry companies in various combinations, like General Motors, Carrier Corporation, Reliance Electric, the U.S. Advanced Battery Consortium, Precise Power Corporation, Oracle, Sure-Tech LLC, and SEMATECH, among many others. These interactions have resulted in several of the FOAK technology developments referenced above.[50]

Besides the number of patents that have been awarded, EPRI has been able to convert its core R&D and membership model into value for its members, and ultimately society. With respect to collaboration, the membership of EPRI is actively involved with the organization with regular one-to-one company briefings, regular board of directors meetings, research advisory group meetings at various levels, program technical working and user group meetings, current and past studies, and reports generated over time and within the current budget year.

EPRI also coordinates the Incubatenergy Network, which supports more than 1,000 start-up companies from across the globe, with more than a dozen incubators and accelerators involved in working with and funding some of these emerging start-ups. This network also helps feed start-ups into the annual Incubatenergy Labs program, which brings together a collaboration of utilities with selected start-ups to address a handful of carefully selected energy system challenges through the application of their respective products and services in accelerated, paid, real-world demonstration projects.[51]

Built to facilitate rapid assessment of start-up innovations in decarbonization, electrification, grid modernization, and resilience, EPRI's Incubatenergy Labs includes 17 utilities representing 58 operating companies and more than 180 million end customers. For the 2021 program, 150 subject matter experts from across these organizations narrowed a field of more than 220 start-ups to select 20 for rapid demonstration. The pace of the program allows projects to be completed in six months or less, and the collaborative nature of the engagements allows 70 percent of start-ups to secure follow-on engagements with participating utilities each year.[52]

A particularly important current undertaking is global collaboration with GTI Energy on the Low-Carbon Resources Initiative (LCRI). This $135 million effort, with more than 50 members, is focused on R&D to identify, assess, and accelerate low-carbon generation and carrier technologies.[53]

This joint program was announced in August 2020, with a five-year prioritized agenda to address eight focus areas: renewables, hydrocarbon-based processes, electrolytic processes, delivery and storage, power generation, end use of low-carbon resources, safety and environmental aspects, and integrated energy system analysis. These were selected as the greatest opportunities to help decarbonize the electric and gas industries, along with other sectors, by commercializing and deploying low-carbon energy carriers and fuels, as well as crosscutting technologies to support their production, transport, storage, and adoption.[54]

Arshad Mansoor discussed just how important this initiative is in contributing to the move toward smarter use of electricity and creation of new natural gas markets:

> LCRI is vital to enabling new technologies to support a decarbonized energy system. While the power and natural gas sectors are already intertwined, we anticipate the level of engagement and integration to far more closely align in the future, so bringing these industries together to collaborate in the research and development space is of utmost importance. We need to accelerate new technologies and scale current technologies over the next two decades to deploy them by the 2040s and reach net-zero by 2050.[55]

Related to LCRI, EPRI has delivered a formal study titled "Strategies and Actions for Achieving a 50% Reduction in U.S. Greenhouse Gas Emissions by 2030." This study reflects deep modeling using EPRI's REGEN (Regional Economy, Greenhouse Gas, and Energy) economy model, which develops, analyzes, and integrates detailed representation of electric and end use sectors, with hourly simulations to capture renewables and energy load and storage variability.[56]

The study captured certain high-level findings and set forth recommendations and guidelines for how the industry could proceed to achieve intended outcomes. It reports that achieving a 2030 goal of 50 percent carbon reduction requires a tripling of the recent pace of decarbonization. The projected 16 percent to 23 percent growth in electricity demand by 2030, driven by economic growth and electrification, would be substantially higher but for efficiency-driven reductions in demands for lighting, cooling, and other traditional electric services. The report also states that a cleaner electric system will require adding as much new generation each year as the United States has added in any prior year, and it would need 500 gigawatts of new capacity, which is one-half of current generating capacity.[57]

FUTURE AGENDA

In 2020 EPRI released its "Technology Innovation Prospectus, 2020–21: Pathways to a Decarbonized Future," which addresses multiple time frames (2020–2030 and 2030–2050) and builds on a series of accomplishments between 2005 and 2020 that set the stage related to producing cleaner electricity and increasing energy efficiency. In this earlier period, work was done to assess climate change issues, with a contingency plan developed to guide future R&D and quantify the value of a broad portfolio of energy supply and emission reduction options. This work on critical topics, still early-stage at the time, provided a foundation for the focus of the TI Prospectus that was developed for the succeeding 40 years.[58]

Arshad Mansoor commented on why the TI Prospectus was developed to refine EPRI's future priorities and focus:

> By this time frame, battery and other technology costs had fallen dramatically and policy and markets had further evolved. Several areas were positioning to be "the next big thing" in energy: hydrogen as the next energy carrier; advanced nuclear emerging as a potentially viable alternative; artificial intelligence continually advancing in power and speed; coal retirements resetting the generation landscape; and a collective message on decarbonization. It

was becoming increasingly clear that electrification would be the tip of the clean energy spear. Our focus needed to reflect this sea change taking place and how the grid, buildings, and industry could provide the necessary flexibility in the making, moving, and using of energy.[59]

The TI Prospectus is partially informed by the work conducted by EPRI that resulted in its landmark paper addressing the IEN, which provides a view into the future regarding *how* the network could be configured, *how* it would need to enable interconnection and integration, and *how* it would provide a path to the future.

The focus areas for the 2020–2030 period in the TI Prospectus pick up with preexisting primary areas of cleantech and EVs but are expanded to include modernizing grid infrastructure (enabling the integrated grid, ensuring IoT interoperability, and integrating DERMS), producing cleaner electricity (expanding offshore horizons, increasing fossil fuel plant efficiency, and digitizing nuclear assets), integrating flexible resources (optimizing battery value), electrifying transportation (mainstreaming EV charging), and electrifying buildings (valuing efficient electrification and driving heat pump innovation).[60]

These topics are important today and have been for several years. But the expanded focus on these topics—and emerging ones—is still early in the level of R&D conducted and still working to reach breakthrough levels. As was observed between 2005 and 2020, technology evolution is continuing, as are the policy and industry externalities that drive the need and create opportunities that inure from these developments.

EPRI's third time frame within the TI Prospectus road map for technology evaluation and development covers the period of 2030–2050 and addresses the continued advancement of existing technologies and the consideration of over-the-horizon technology that is still early-stage. Some of these technologies offer the promise of breakthrough innovation and the advancement of utility (and other entities') market positioning, as well as substantially improving the nation's ability to pursue and accelerate decarbonization.[61]

For the 2030–2050 period, the TI Prospectus sets forth a focus on developing integrated networks (planning across infrastructures and operating at 100 percent renewable energy), producing low-carbon electricity (expanding solar with bulk storage, developing next-generation reactors, and pursuing capture breakthroughs), supplying low-carbon resources (driving indirect electrification and leveraging gas infrastructure), and using low-carbon resources (advancing hydrogen turbines and building net-zero foundations) (see Figure 14).[62]

These topics have a high concentration on moving to a net-zero emissions position, as well as advancing new technologies that offer the opportunity to drive new sources of energy and optimize delivery systems. For example, substantial attention is directed at the development and refinement of existing technologies (low-carbon), advancement of emerging delivery systems (hydrogen), and exploration of next-stage, high-impact technologies (high-precision manufacturing). The TI Prospectus calls for concentration on integrated networks that can provide alternative energy carriers from hydrogen, ammonia, biofuels, and synthetic gas. It also focused on broad electrification in industrial processes, long-haul trucking, aviation, and marine shipping.[63]

EPRI also creates a formal annual agenda to guide its R&D activities each year, covering most value chain operating areas, as well as related topical matters, such as decarbonization, electrification, and sustainability. For 2022, EPRI's Research Portfolio, *Driving Toward a Clean Energy Future*,

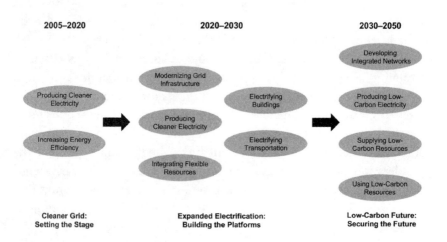

Figure 14. Future technology focus.

(Source: Data from EPRI, "Technology Innovation Prospectus, 2020–21: Pathways to a Decarbonized Future," August 13, 2020, https://www.epri.com/research/products/000000003002019513.)

provides a robust mix of more than 25 specific study areas, with more than 125 subareas across the nuclear, fuel, renewable, fossil, grid, network, and other category offerings for electrification, customer solutions, sustainability, and workplace safety.[64]

A view of the future was also provided by Arshad Mansoor:

> The 2020s will be the decade of electrification, and we all recognize that the energy transition will need to be accomplished in a manner that achieves affordability and security. But for that to happen, carbon capture utilization and storage is critical. And hydrogen as an energy carrier needs to rapidly emerge to drive energy affordability, security, and diversity. Forward-thinking utilities can help create energy flexibility by extending investment beyond networks for resiliency and modernization and toward customers to capitalize on the numerous small devices that exist at buildings and premises to provide additional energy sharing beyond storage. This would reduce costs over time from actions such as increasing management of EV charging periods and water heater utilization for greater energy flexibility.[65]

This research portfolio is a primary focal point for EPRI, but it utilizes several other key mechanisms to drive overall strategic direction, thought leadership, and member communication. For example, EPRI publishes a series of strategic insights in the form of models and white papers to align scouting technologies and R&D with high-impact gaps and opportunities. It also provides thought leadership on topics like integrated grid, integrated energy network, and decarbonization.

Further, EPRI maintains a TechPortal that integrates information on more than 1,500 new technologies, as well as from the LCRI and Incubatenergy program regarding promising concepts to commercial solutions. The hub also organizes and conducts a range of networking forums to exchange information among utility executives and various technology working groups.[66]

Approximately 75 percent of EPRI's technology innovation portfolio focuses on identifying early-stage R&D, including multiyear, multi-project programs, to develop foundational knowledge and nurture innovations from validated concept to pilot demonstration, with specific studies exploring new ideas and novel applications.[67]

EPRI's Research Portfolio is structured around the following major value chain areas, along with subsegment and/or crosscutting topics:[68]

- *Nuclear:* This component leverages a range of plant operating and research experience to reduce risks associated with implementing new technologies, processes, and plants. In this area, strategic initiatives like advanced nuclear technology and plant modernization, and elements such as plant performance, fuels and chemistry, supply management, and other initiatives are addressed.

- *Generation and low-carbon resources:* A range of R&D areas are addressed here, such as non-nuclear and advanced generation, component reliability, asset management and optimization, environmental controls, air quality, water management, coal combustion, renewable technologies, and enabling technologies as part of the overall technology assessment, exploration, and development program.

- *Power delivery and utilization:* This element covers a broad range of technologies, planning, and operations areas like transmission and substations, T&D environmental impacts, and operations and planning; distribution areas like resources, systems, information, communications cybersecurity, energy systems, and climate analysis; and electrification and customer solutions, sustainability and economic stewardship, and worker and community health and safety.

The Research Portfolio—and its related priorities and coverage breadth—changes to reflect changing power sector challenges and impacts to broader policy matters and customer needs.

EPRI's unique niche contributions of unbiased data- and science-driven R&D to the power sector over the past 50 years have been continuous, far-reaching, innovative, and impactful. As it celebrates its 50th anniversary in 2022, the institute is positioned to further advance existing (and enable and accelerate new) technologies that offer promise to meet the challenges of decarbonization, digitalization, and decentralization that form the impetus and basis for industry innovation.

Edison Electric Institute

As the trade association for U.S. electric companies, EEI represents all investor-owned companies in the industry. It also has more than 65 international members and hundreds of OEMs, professional service firms, and other organizations as associate members. EEI was organized in 1933, although an industry trade association had existed in other forms and under other names going back into the late 19th century. The association has responsibility for providing public policy leadership, strategic business intelligence, and industry-centered conferences and forums.[69]

A principal dimension of EEI's charter is to monitor trends in industry technology, customers, and finances that could affect the U.S. electric power industry and lead to potential legislation that would affect its collective membership and their customers. Consequently, EEI maintains active outreach to the U.S. government on Capitol Hill, Pennsylvania Avenue, and various agencies across Washington, D.C. It also engages with other trade associations that represent their own targeted constituencies—for example, regulatory, wind, solar, storage, competitive supply, natural gas, mobility, and climate-related organizations—in dialogue about relevant issues and coordinates responses to overlapping considerations. EEI also actively engages with regulators, policy makers, and other key stakeholders at the state level.

As a trade association, EEI is not an asset owner or operator—but all of its full members are. And the concerns of these members related to the future direction of the power sector are a driving force for EEI's policy agenda. EEI uses this stakeholder-driven process as it works to advance issues based on the dynamic and constantly evolving technology and business environments. Consequently, while it does not directly drive innovation within the industry, it does work to directly advance the position of the sector in preparing for innovation and new policy directions.

Thus, its innovation objective is to support the electric power industry with its technology and policy initiatives by creating more visibility to the legislative, financial, and regulatory communities about the current and emerging challenges, while also enabling the sector to create and bring solutions to market for the benefit of society, communities, and customers.

Tom Kuhn, President of EEI, addressed how the trade association is advancing its member companies' vision for a resilient clean energy future and the innovation this vision requires:

> The innovative spirit of Thomas Edison continues to guide EEI's member companies as they work to deliver America's resilient clean energy. No one in Edison's time, not even Edison himself, could have predicted our world's extraordinary progress in every realm of human endeavor. Yet electricity has powered all of them. And safe, reliable, affordable, clean electricity is the energy that will power even more improvement and innovation for our customers in the decades to come. Our industry's story is one of constant innovation. At every step, we have achieved this progress expressly to serve our customers better and to meet their ever-growing expectations. This is a formidable challenge and an awesome responsibility. It also is a continuous opportunity to grow and to deliver benefits to our customers, communities, workers, and shareholders.[70]

ENVIRONMENTAL REPORTING

In 2018 EEI created a FOAK voluntary, industry-wide reporting model for environmental, social, governance, and sustainability matters undertaken by its members. The ESG/sustainability reporting template is a model that enables transparent, cogent, standardized, and insightful reporting of company progress in addressing clean energy, climate issues and actions, governance matters, and overall sustainability strategies. This reporting model also was adopted by the AGA, and in 2021, EEI and AGA released an updated version of the reporting template.[71]

The template contains both qualitative and quantitative components and was developed to be responsive to the stated needs of the investor community and the impact of reporting on the electric and natural gas sectors (see Figure 15). The template is not intended to supersede ongoing Securities and Exchange Commission reporting by the member companies, and it was developed with flexibility so companies can incorporate the relevant elements into their ESG reporting—that is, there may be some elements defined for use by individual companies that may not be applicable and therefore may be excluded.

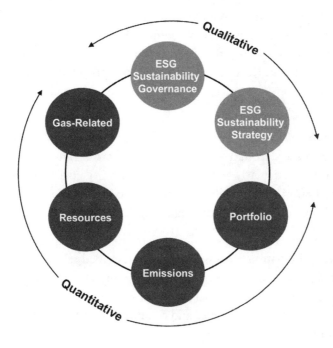

Figure 15. ESG reporting template elements.

(Source: Data from Edison Electric Institute and American Gas Association, "EG/Sustainability Template, Version 3," 2021, https://www.eei.org/en/issues-and-policy/esg-sustainability.)

The template reflects the desire to respond to external expectations for information, as well as enable companies to use a common approach that provides accountability, content, timing, and presentation on a consistent basis across the sectors. Companies are encouraged to address a range of topics that describe the strategies and approaches that are being adopted, including the following qualitative information related to governance and strategy:[72]

- *Adapting to the changing business environment:* This section describes the regional factors and challenges that could affect the business model and responding strategies, including natural resources, economic health, renewables potential, and federal and state commission policy considerations and processes.

- *Managing and adapting to future ESG/sustainability risk and opportunities:* Risks are defined (e.g., climate change, demand growth, stranded assets, environmental compliance, and weather) along with opportunities for hardening and resilience, energy efficiency, and R&D, and plans are developed to address social risks and opportunities, like health, safety, affordability, and business impact.

- *Sustainability plans and progress:* This section identifies innovative practices and initiatives designed to support a transition to lower carbon, particularly climate and sustainability goals related to lower emissions, as well as the way the company plans to engage with its local communities regarding ESG.

- *Natural gas safety and emissions reduction:* Management, oversight, and participation processes are to be described related to pipeline safety, system methane reduction programs, and avoiding reputational risk, with additional attention on emissions and intensity disclosure from all sources and a commitment to a culture of safety and continuous improvement.

Companies are encouraged to provide information about the formal governance and oversight of the ESG process, including the management hierarchy and committee structure, as well as descriptions of climate risk and opportunity identification, risk mitigation, public policy engagement, physical security and cybersecurity, business continuity, and industry coordinating practices.

From a quantitative perspective, a metrics-based model was defined that would capture and organize current, historical, and forward-looking information related to power generation data by resource, electric greenhouse gas emissions and criteria emissions, electric company human and natural resources, and gas company emissions and system infrastructure data.

The ability to provide consistent information to investors is a worthwhile undertaking and puts the electric and natural gas sectors into a leadership role in meeting increasingly stringent ESG requirements. To create the reporting template, EEI and AGA brought together an industry steering committee and an investor group representing institutional investors.

These groups sometimes reflect conflicting points of view, but they have coalesced around the notion that climate change necessitates new ways to think about its implications, along with additional requirements to enable investors to adequately assess the extent of individual company positions and impacts. The clarity provided in the reporting template offers an additional tool to provide information immediately, as well as to provide a foundation for expanded reporting requirements, should that occur in the future.

JOINT COLLABORATION

As an example of leadership with respect to critical issues facing the U.S. electric power industry, EEI brought together industry and environmental leaders to establish the Carbon-Free Technology Initiative (CFTI) in 2021, which involves multiple entities concerned with decarbonization activities, including the Bipartisan Policy Center, Center for Climate and Energy Solutions, Clean Air Task Force, ClearPath, Great Plains Institute, Information Technology & Innovation Foundation, Nuclear Energy Institute (NEI), and Third Way.[73]

The intent of the CFTI is to achieve net-zero emissions in the U.S. electric sector by promoting policies to ensure the commercial availability of affordable, carbon-free, 24/7 power technologies by the early 2030s. The CFTI focuses on policy recommendations to advance key technology areas. Six technologies are the current focus of this initiative: advanced wind and solar energy systems; long-duration storage and advanced demand efficiency; advanced, dispatchable, and renewable superhot rock deep geothermal; zero-carbon fuels, such as ammonia and hydrogen; advanced nuclear energy (both fusion and fission); and carbon capture, utilization, and storage (CCUS).[74]

The CFTI has organized its efforts along four principal activities, including research, development, demonstration, and deployment (RDD&D) and commercial ecosystem issues that can have an impact on technology costs and performance. The CFTI focuses attention on a range of recommended actions, such as enhanced technology demonstration, open-knowledge sharing, cost sharing, FOAK acceleration, financial incentives, tax credits, loan guarantees, price mitigation, technology incubation, removal of entry barriers, reforming of siting and permitting, and creation of collaborative consortia. Through its research and analyses, the CFTI identified the need for Congress to significantly increase DOE's budget focused on RDD&D. Through the joint advocacy of the CFTI's partners, the bipartisan Infrastructure Investment and Jobs Act nearly accomplished that goal.[75]

A significant current undertaking within the U.S. energy industry is the LCRI, jointly engaging both the electric and the natural gas sectors. This initiative was stood up in 2021 and focuses on joint EPRI and GTI efforts to accelerate the deployment of technologies that can directly address and enhance progress toward decarbonization (see Figure 16). While EEI is not directly leading this initiative, it is engaged with both industry research organizations, since its scope—low-carbon energy carriers like hydrogen, ammonia, synthetic fuels, and biofuels—parallels elements of the CFTI, with many of its members as cosponsors.

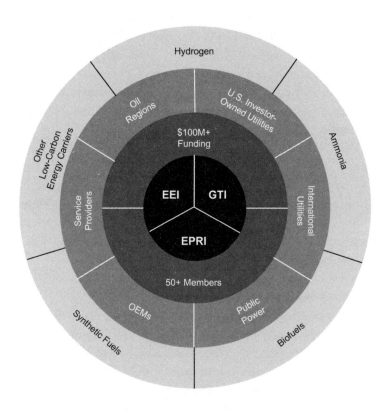

Figure 16. Low-carbon resource initiative.

The LCRI's intent is to expand production, distribution, and application of these alternative energy carriers and enable the integration of these technologies at scale. These energy carriers are needed to enable affordable pathways to achieve deep carbon reductions across the U.S. economy. The LCRI is focused on technologies that can be developed and deployed beyond 2030 to support the achievement of a net-zero emission economy by 2050.[76]

Potential solutions for a net-zero future currently can be prohibitively expensive because of technology maturity, materials availability, and installation and operating costs. In some cases, no known technical solutions exist. In certain cases, technologies to decarbonize the energy grid and the land-based passenger transportation sector have largely already been identified and are being scaled because of the significance of their emissions contribution, although a notable exception to decarbonization is the lack of long-duration storage. Long-haul transportation—whether by road, sea, or air—and numerous industrial processes generally lack proven solutions for decarbonization, or the solutions that exist are expensive relative to the existing, carbon-emitting options.[77]

EEI also supports the Institute for Electric Innovation (IEI) through the Edison Foundation, which focuses on accelerating the adoption of technologies that will foster the continued strengthening and advancement of the energy grid. The IEI promotes information, ideas, and experience sharing across the industry and among policy makers, regulators, OEMs, and technology partners, and seeks out policies that support the business cases for new technologies.

Many electric company CEOs from across the EEI membership compose the Management Committee of IEI, which also convenes a technology roundtable that consists of several technology OEMs focused on building and contributing new technologies that will enhance the future energy grid. Companies like Anterix, Google, Itron, Powerley, and Sensus convene with electric company executives to discuss trends, share ideas, and collaborate on methods and technologies that can solve real-world grid issues. The IEI also develops and releases various reports on selected electric company matters, like smart meter adoption and carbon-free initiatives. The IEI also engages with its members in topical dialogue, and it helps connect technology OEMs or solutions developers with EEI members.[78]

EEI has a long history of representing the electric power industry with various stakeholders—Capitol Hill, Wall Street, and the National Association of Regulatory Utility Commissioners, among others—regarding critical issues that affect the sector and its customers. While relevant policies have always been at the forefront of its focus, EEI has expended considerable effort in recent years on enabling closer engagement among the financial community, technical organizations, OEMs, and its member companies on the nature, impact, and potential of disruptive technologies.

To reinforce the significance of the CFTI, the EEI, in conjunction with EPRI, GTI, and NEI, organized a multi-sector, multi-topical conference called the "Clean Energy Transition Forum: Emerging Technologies to Bridge the Gap to Net Zero," which brought together senior electric, financial, research, and alternative supply source executives to address the challenges of decarbonization, as well as paths to new technology development and adoption. This October 2021 meeting was used to obtain different perspectives from among the government agencies, investment bankers, financial lenders, electric companies, technology and solutions providers, and other trade associations in attendance about technology evolution and its implications for the future related to reducing carbon emissions and bridging the technology gap.[79]

The agenda focused on several key technologies that can have significant impacts on the electric power industry and the country, including advanced SMRs, long-duration energy storage, hydrogen, and CCUS. These technologies are highly topical to all of EEI's members and were first structured into a formal collaborative effort in 2021 through the CFTI, which included the above technologies, plus advanced wind and solar energy and advanced, dispatchable, and renewable superhot rock deep geothermal. With this effort, EEI was seeking to identify specific technologies where its policy advocacy could lead to commercial solutions for promising options related to industry net-zero attainment.

The tenor of this meeting was technology readiness and implications for decarbonization efforts in the United States, as well as recognition of the challenges and needs of the sector and its suppliers to accelerate the maturity and commerciality of these technologies. While each of the represented stakeholders was pursuing the four featured technologies in their own manner, this forum brought together a full range of views but, more importantly, created a mutual dialogue involving challenges, responses, actions, and benefits.[80]

Richard McMahon, Senior Vice President of Energy Supply and Finance, further explained how EEI sought to advance the interests of its members:

> Through our advocacy, as well as fostering collaboration with key stakeholders, EEI supports our members in needed innovation to address the twin challenges of leading the transition to a low carbon energy economy while ensuring a resilient grid. Examples of this collaborative innovation include EEI's design and implementation of an industry-first ESG reporting template developed with the industry's largest investors and other key stakeholders. The CFTI also exists to ensure supportive public policy in the clean energy transition. In addition, EEI sponsors breakthrough technology forums with investors, policy makers, and members focused on SMRs, hydrogen, CCUS, and LDES [long-duration energy storage].[81]

The second forum focused on emerging technologies related to advanced SMRs and was hosted by Guggenheim Securities in April 2022. The forum was cosponsored by several other entities, including EEI, EPRI, DOE, NEI, and the Nuclear Innovation Alliance, and was titled "Investing in Advanced Nuclear: A Catalyst for Our Clean Energy Future." A range of speakers from the federal and state government levels, OEMs, electric companies, regulators, labor, and the above sponsoring organizations provided their views on the benefits of new nuclear power sources—decarbonization, energy security, national security, reliability, resilience, and jobs.[82]

SMRs offer the potential of reducing capital investment requirements to become more affordable, deployable, and achievable, as well as to reduce planning and construction risk and provide greater comfort about the ability to enter operation.

These forums provide a unique way for EEI to support innovation in a manner that complements those of its members. While electric companies are on the front lines of carbon management and reduction, technology evaluation and adoption, capital appropriation and allocation, system integration and optimization, and customer affordability and commercialization, EEI is leveraging its platform for the benefit of the overall industry.

EEI is using both its natural "voice" and reputation in Washington and on Wall Street to create a strong nexus among the objectives and means of decarbonization, the availability and performance of emerging technology, and the capacity and sentiment of the financial community. It has carved out a broad space where it is valuable to its members and to the range of relevant stakeholders. While pursuit of traditional innovation is associated with the five areas of process, regulatory, technology, products and services, and business models, EEI is adopting a fulsome approach to all relevant elements that affect innovation deployment by the electric sector: awareness, relevance, policy, technology, economics, financing, impacts, and commerciality.

MEMBER VALUE

EEI has a wide scope of interest in pursuit of its mission and members, leading to a range of means to deliver value to its members and their customers. These include policy monitoring and advocacy in and beyond Washington; financial and tax engagement with Wall Street and Congress; facilitating public service programs related to storm response and recovery, grid security, veteran hiring, and wildfire mitigation; technical programs in energy efficiency, customer centricity, and system resilience; and clean energy initiative leadership, support, and contribution.

As would be expected, the EEI agenda parallels, and often leads, that of its members across the above areas. EEI has demonstrated leadership in innovation through its programmatic activities, like in electrification and decarbonization, and in particular initiatives that focus on cybersecurity, transmission, and broadband. The purpose of EEI's leadership here is not to drive specific technology innovation at a company level, but to enable and accelerate maturity and commerciality for the industry.

Tom Kuhn believes that EEI's role in advancing the positioning of the industry in and beyond Washington will have many parts:

> Our "North Star" as an industry and an association remains our customers. We continue to center our efforts on maintaining the steady and strong transition to clean energy; modernizing the energy grid to make it more dynamic, more resilient, and more secure; and developing the innovative solutions our customers expect and deserve. As always, our goal is to advance favorable public policy. While impacting the legislative and regulatory process both in Washington and in

the states is never easy, we must—and we will—demonstrate "power by association," making our unified voice heard on the key issues affecting our customers and our nation's energy future.[83]

In 2021 alone, EEI addressed a host of industry-related issues but specifically acted on key areas of innovation that were top of mind for the industry. For example, EEI promoted innovation related to middle-mile broadband infrastructure, fleet electrification, electric charging, building efficiency, and other areas. The efforts expended by EEI help drive innovation in the electric sector, and this includes identifying and socializing workable approaches of other members, technical analytics and technology performance use cases, and technology economics and trends, all of which can help advance how a particular member is positioned.[84]

Throughout 2022, EEI and its members were actively involved in supporting the framing of what became the IRA legislation being pursued on Capitol Hill. The final law provides for a range of financing sources, tax incentives, community grants, climate provisions, and manufacturing support, among other areas relevant to utilities and other energy providers or users. In combination, these elements accelerate deployment of clean energy sources and also enable reduction in future carbon emissions.

EEI was instrumental in shaping many aspects of the IRA, particularly those dealing with production and investment tax credits, as well as other sections targeting clean energy sourcing or emissions reduction. Now EEI is leading in the implementation of the law at the Department of the Treasury and the Internal Revenue Service. The involvement of EEI typifies its focus on enabling policy advancement and continuing innovation among its members.

These types of activities illustrate that EEI is a valuable partner for its members as they pursue innovation, even if it is not a direct technology innovator itself. The ability to leverage its position to define and promote policies and develop programs and materials that aid its members in furthering their strategic and market objectives is a valuable role for it to fulfill.

Through the years, EEI has been enhancing its value to its members, whether through expanded presence, extended outreach, or technical guidance, or through creating a "pull" for other key stakeholders, including the legislative, financial, and regulatory communities. These efforts create enhanced recognition and value to itself and its collective members, helping fulfill the needs of the sector to position for the cleantech transition.

Energy Impact Partners

EIP is a widely recognized venture capital and investment firm focused on investing in energy transition and climate-focused businesses in the utility, industrial, mobility, and cyber and software development sectors. The firm was founded before the cleantech transition velocity was accelerating, with a business philosophy of collaborating with its network corporate partners (strategic investors) to drive deep decarbonization, ultimately transitioning to a net-zero carbon economy. The New York–based firm now manages global assets of more than $3 billion, operating from six additional locations: Washington, D.C.; San Francisco; Palm Beach, Florida; London; Cologne; and Oslo.[85]

EIP's entry into the cleantech venture capital and investment space can be characterized as occurring at the right place and at the right time, as it coincided with the emergence of disruptive technologies and a burgeoning interest from utilities in exploring the parameters and implications of this transition, as well as providing a platform that could be leveraged for market learning, opportunity and threat identification, technology awareness, business application and deployment, core business health, customer engagement, revenue expansion, investment targeting, risk management, financial contribution, and innovation targeting.

Although the utilities sector has always been uneven within its population about market shift awareness and preparedness, in the 2013–2015 period, certain large companies in the utilities sector were coming around to the realization that a sea change in market structure and potential encroachment was upon them, the pace of change was accelerating, and readiness for the future was unsatisfactory.

FUND LAUNCH

This market realization was well known to many utilities sector observers, and in 2015, EIP was founded by an industry veteran and pioneer of corporate venture capital, Hans Kobler, and several of his former team members. At General Electric, Kobler led the Energy Technology Investment Group. He was joined at EIP in 2016 by another industry veteran, Kevin Fitzgerald, as the Chief Utility Officer (formerly Executive

Vice President and General Counsel at Pepco Holdings), who leads commercialization and innovation efforts.[86]

EIP was not the first venture capital and investment firm to take an active interest in the cleantech transition but was among the first to deploy a collaborative corporate venture capital model across the utilities industry and other industry verticals. Several companies in Silicon Valley that were also involved and experienced in broad industry sectors were early entrants to this space. However, the early timing of the entry of these firms was at the front end of many start-up company development activities, and their investments were generally small initial seed money and/or Series A funding.

Hans Kobler provided insight into his thinking about what the fund could accomplish:

> We created EIP because we believed the energy transition was at a critical inflection point, presenting a generational investment opportunity. We teamed with the electric utilities industry at our core, as they were increasingly ready to transform their business and at the same time provide us and our partners with strong advantages to invest in this complex industry: they manage some of the most challenging technologies, control the network, understand the regulators, and are ready to deploy significant capital on innovation. They can be the key enabler in helping us source, screen, and scale brilliant entrepreneurs. By working together, we help them build the utility of the future. They help us make better investments. Together, we help the global economy get to net-zero faster.[87]

EIP was among the first venture capital and investment firms to create an at-scale business with its first fund launch. It recognized early that the utilities sector was at the nexus of four industries affected by disruptive and climate change policy direction—oil and gas, transport, technology, and the built environment—and these sectors would have to respond to challenges and requirements, as well as provide "a bird's nest on the ground" of opportunities for EIP to capture, and the investment party had already started.

In this 2013–2015 window, Southern Company was wrestling with how to gain market knowledge regarding disruptive technologies and market implications to help it position itself for the future. During 2015, connections eventually were made between the CEO of Southern Company and EIP to discuss their mutual views of the future and ways to mutually survive and thrive. These discussions ultimately led to Southern Company becoming the founding corporate partner with EIP.

In short order, other utilities were eager to learn that an investment firm that had experienced venture capital resources—plus executive-level, hands-on utilities industry expertise—was already in place for utilities to leverage and provide a source of value to address the issues and objectives described above.

As Mark Lantrip, the recently retired CEO of Southern Company Services and Chairman of the Southern Energy Resources Group, remarked:

> Southern Company's strategy in the 2014–2015 time frame recognized the emergence of disruptive technologies, expansion of infrastructure technology adoption, and proliferation of energy services providers. While we knew these events could be both a challenge to our market and customer position and an opportunity to participate in this market in some form, we were not as knowledgeable about what these markets were all about. An early discussion with EIP made it clear that going down the path of market discovery alone would not be sound strategically, economically, or from an enterprise risk perspective. EIP brought venture capital experience and insights into the nature, composition, and direction of the start-ups that were already active in the utility space, that we would have had to develop on our own. In addition, they offered a value proposition that fit our objectives of a quick ramp-up, financial attractiveness, technical competence, and risk sharing among similarly minded companies.[88]

After launching Energy Impact Fund LP (the Flagship Fund) in 2015, EIP set out to establish the largest coalition of forward-looking energy companies investing in the energy transition. By 2017, when EIP's Flagship Fund held its final closing, more than a dozen North American utilities, international companies, and non-utilities companies had become corporate members.

EIP's corporate strategic partners provide a cross section of some of the largest U.S. utilities, along with several smaller companies, and even international representation. This group of companies includes integrated electrics, combination electric and gas, and electric and/or infrastructure entities, each of which can have both common and unique priorities, given their market positioning and the specific market shifts affecting these segments.

EIP viewed three converging themes that created the need for an entity like itself: increasing growing demand, an imperative to create a sustainable energy economy, and increasing digitalization of the power value chain. It believed that technologies, innovative services, and new business models would sit at the center of a $20 trillion energy transformation market that would require significant infrastructure growth in ensuing years, to almost $50 trillion by 2030.[89]

When the Flagship Fund was launched, EIP's technology investment focus was broad, reflecting current views of technology solutions and their maturity, as well as a longer-term view of the areas that might become more critical in the future (e.g., low-carbon generation).

Initially, multiple energy impact markets were identified for pursuit, with multiple technologies encompassing these areas: energy storage, big data, smart grids, smart buildings, solid state lighting, connected sensors, low-carbon generation, microgrids, cybersecurity, virtual power plants, and new business, servicing, and financing models (see Figure 17).[90]

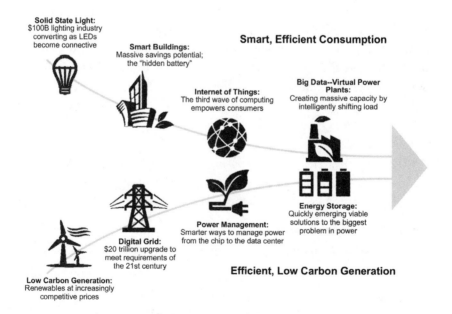

Figure 17. Investment focus.

(Source: Energy Impact Partners.)

This initial depiction of EIP's investment focus would soon further expand, however, as its thinking about the marketplace evolved, new technologies emerged, and the challenge of decarbonization increased.

That investment thesis proved to be correct, and EIP currently has more than 50 corporate partners—utilities comprising almost 30 of these—across North America, Europe, Japan, and Australia. EIP maintains several strategies targeting venture, growth, diversity, and credit investment directly in companies involved in the cleantech transition.[91]

Collectively, these utility corporate partners operate across four continents and 12 countries; spend more than $65 billion in annual capital expenditures, leveraging a market capitalization above $500 billion; serve more than 100 million customers; and represent the software, AI, infrastructure, data analytics, cybersecurity, transport, oil and gas, communications, home services, industrial, and hydrogen sectors.[92]

EIP's business strategy is straightforward—target important cleantech transition sectors; identify high-quality, high-impact, market-differentiated technologies; conduct structured partner-backed strategic diligence; select targets that offer distinctive market positioning and growth potential; exercise discipline in investment; provide meaningful governance and business support; collaborate continuously with corporate sponsors; build a world-class market analysis infrastructure; establish defined metrics and triggers for investment optimization; and most importantly, relentlessly connect the portfolio with its corporate partners to drive innovation and growth in their businesses.

EIP's Flagship Fund investment strategy identified guidelines for *how* the firm deploys capital:[93]

- *Focus on attractive growth segments.* With numerous options available, EIP seeks to invest in segments with the potential for disproportionate growth that can yield superior returns.

- *Leverage strategic partners.* EIP believes that the attainment of superior financial returns is advantaged by working closely with its strategic partners (i.e., its members).

- *Shun technology risk.* Focusing on proven technologies leads to avoiding risk and to superior returns, and EIP believes that its strategic partners bring valuable insights to investment.

- *Mitigate business risk.* EIP looks to avoid business and market risk by focusing on investments with demonstrable products and services, validated by customers and its members.

- *Focus on deals with manageable capital requirements.* EIP seeks to minimize financial risk by investing in companies with modest capital needs that can be met by available fund resources.

- *Practice valuation discipline.* The ability to earn superior returns is enhanced by investing at appropriate levels to secure meaningful ownership positions.

- *Structure carefully.* Prior experience in deal structuring provides protection from downside events and is supported by previous activity in complex private equity and venture capital investing.

Almost 40 cleantech sectors have been evaluated to identify market relevance, assess innovation potential, evaluate technology range, determine market readiness, and prioritize participation. This sector review resulted in the prioritization of supply decarbonization, tech-enabled infrastructure, reliability and resilience, and intelligent demand and electrification, and reflected a belief in underlying disruption potential, profitable growth, and high market interest (see Figure 18).

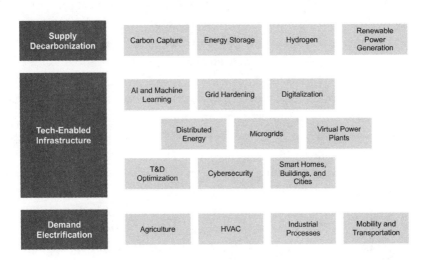

Figure 18. Technology building blocks.

(Source: Data from Energy Impact Partners.)

The evaluation of sectors—an expanded range of viable technologies—is reflected in its areas of current focus in early 2022. Many of the original technology areas remain, although they may have been integrated, separated, or added to reflect how EIP thinks about market needs, technology families, and investment priorities. The current view of the critical technology building blocks of the cleantech transition amounts to 17 based on EIP's outside-in perspective of market definition and technology application to societal challenges and utility operating priorities. This technology placement model should be considered dynamic and subject to continuous maturity and alignment as market priorities and opportunities evolve.[94]

Kevin Fitzgerald explained how EIP's results have confirmed the initial decisions for investing in the fund:

> Our thesis that the clean electron would be at the center of the fourth industrial revolution has proven to be correct. Our investments are centered on finding and nurturing the right technologies and start-ups that position the electric industry to be a key player in the cleantech transition that is underway in decarbonization, alternative supply and storage, grid modernization, communication, security, and electrification. Fund investment has been gratifying because it confirms we are focused on what our investors are interested in to prepare for the cleantech transition. We expect the range of our investments to continue to broaden as technologies continue to emerge, and, consequently, the EIP ecosystem will continue to grow to capture other areas of clean energy demand in the economy.[95]

Just as the technology thinking of EIP has shifted, the strategies that have emerged to guide investment priorities, market activities, and corporate partner positioning have similarly shifted. The key elements of its investment strategies reflect both investment discipline and market differentiation in its positioning as a substantial, global venture capital fund with many traditional utilities as corporate partners:[96]

- *Focus on attractive sectors.* EIP looks to invest in areas where buyer interest exists and EIP can add value, including intelligent operations, customer engagement, mobility, smart buildings and cities, distributed energy resources, and cybersecurity.

- *Find and win the right deals.* The ability to generate deal flow is a critical success element, and EIP looks to leverage its corporate partners for potential opportunities and position itself as a value-added investor and a partner of choice.

- *Be rigorous and disciplined in due diligence.* EIP leverages its deep market and investing experience to conduct purposeful diligence with its corporate partners and maintain a conservative posture on investment selection.

- *Structure investments for risk mitigation.* EIP offers extensive experience with managing the trade-offs between capturing upside and managing downside risks, which is accomplished through protective positions and value-adding capabilities.

- *Focus on value creation.* EIP works with its corporate partners on how to adapt operations, product strategy, and selling to the unique requirements of the energy industry to accelerate the growth trajectory of portfolio companies.

- *Keep a keen eye on monetization.* Close attention is given to working closely with portfolio companies to build a path toward multiple exit opportunities and actively nurture relationships with potential buyers.

CORPORATE MEMBER SUPPORT

As one of its desired outcomes, EIP's networking focus was driven toward creating opportunities for the start-up companies to demonstrate the applicability, viability, and value of their technologies or platforms for the utilities sector—particularly the most natural companies, the corporate partners. Since inception of the Flagship Fund, EIP has a proven track record in driving revenues from its corporate LPs to portfolio companies, enabling more than 350 contracts and delivering more than $1 billion in backing and business to a portfolio of 100-plus companies.[97]

Differentiation in philosophy, focus, and capabilities can influence how a potential investor views participation with a venture capital firm. EIP achieves that differentiation with its targeted corporate partners through how it has structured its business, collected necessary internal talent and perspective, developed its screening model, aligned investment purpose with corporate partner strategic intent, and collaborated with these corporate partners on a continuous basis. From inception, EIP has provided a "North Star" to its corporate partners related to cleantech direction, destination, and implications, as well as a conduit for market trends, information dissemination, target assessment, investment opportunity, deal structuring, and monetization strategy and execution.

EIP starts its collaboration with direct engagement with its corporate partners related to identification of sectors of business and operating interest and identification of potential market candidates from this group. It then continues this collaboration through a rigorous screening process involving analyses, interviews, and challenges. Through these processes, a population of more than 12,000 cleantech start-ups that EIP tracks can be screened down to several hundred potential candidates, and then screened down further to a short list of companies for deep due diligence, from which it will ultimately invest.[98]

The level of collaboration with corporate partners has evolved since the first Flagship Fund, and collaborations now extend between EIP and corporate partner, EIP and technology working group, and EIP and customer working group, with regular EIP visits, video sessions, and calls to companies. The purpose is to either inform about trends, discuss targeted opportunities, assess emerging technology attractiveness, or review current analyses and research. EIP is now an active, dynamic ecosystem that serves as the innovation hub for these cleantech companies to go to market and decarbonize the economy.[99]

Beyond this front-end structured investment screening, EIP is a hands-on general partner and provides or enables board of director expertise, market strategy advice, corporate partner networking, external strategic partnering skills to be applied, and market actions to be executed. As a result of these roles, the products or services of several of its portfolio companies have been selected for adoption by various corporate members to meet their market or operational needs.

To help drive strategy, technology scanning and assessment, partner support, and strategy optimization, EIP has more than 70 professionals that provide experience- and knowledge-based services for and to its portfolio companies, its investors, and its corporate partners. EIP gains deeper insights by working closely with its partners' experts in sector "deep dives."

It also provides partner corporate venture capital training and serves as a technology deployment liaison. These professionals are grouped into several organizational roles, such as firm leadership, business strategy, research and analysis, innovation, external advisors, and various back-office support. Throughout the year, this team provides its members with hands-on support and particular market-oriented capabilities related to investment rationale, structuring, and impact analysis.

EIP is not the only cleantech-oriented venture capital firm in the market, as firms like Sequoia Capital, Khosla Ventures, Breakthrough Energy Ventures, Riverstone Holdings, and Clean Energy Venture Group in North America, and Octopus Investments, Emerald Technology Ventures, and ETF Partners in Europe, among other locations, also actively participate in this space. However, it remains among the top venture capital firms in terms of scale, scope, and stature among its peers.

In addition, oil and gas companies, like Chevron, Shell, Total, and Eni, and utilities, like Engie, E.ON, EDF, NextEra Energy, and Exelon, have created internal corporate venture capital funds to participate in this ubiquitous transition that extends beyond all borders.

From a reputation perspective as an "investor of choice," the EIP market approach, scale and composition, and value-added contribution have proven to be leverageable with potential start-ups to create an enhanced value proposition for all engaged parties. From within its list of more than 100 companies where it has invested, EIP has exited and monetized 18 of these investments.[100]

EIP has already monetized a set of its portfolio companies in North America and Europe, including Greenlots, Ring, AutoGrid, Opus One Solutions, FirstFuel, Proterra, BHI, and AMS, among others. These start-ups had been evolving over a time frame beginning well before the founding of EIP and had matured their market readiness to the point where monetization was not only possible but optimal.[101]

Hans Kobler reflected on EIP's success to date and positioning itself for continued investment in new technologies and market participants that can lead to value creation for its members:

We are constantly scanning for new technologies that fit our net-zero investing strategies, as well as position our members to identify start-ups that support our member needs for the grid, network, and customer parts of their businesses. Our portfolio has been well constructed, blending a range of technologies with different potential market maturity cycles and risk and value profiles. The breadth of technology market categories, depth of unique technology developers and solutions providers, and stage investment opportunities have caused us to open our original aperture and tailor our strategies to fit these attributes. The opportunities may not always be this robust, but given the magnitude of the net-zero and modernization challenges, I think we are early in the cycle of technology maturity and market impacts.[102]

This track record has reinforced EIP's leading market position as the go-to cleantech venture capital and investment platform among the venture capital community and led to the determination that there was space for additional market participation, substantial incremental investment, and broadening of investment destinations and location focus.

During 2021, EIP continued to evolve and innovate by introducing additional unique offerings, such as Frontier (a deep decarbonization technology fund), Elevate Future (a fund to advance diversity in the energy transition), Flagship Europe Fund, and Credit Fund, which provided different best-fit options for its corporate partners. These funds have closed or will close in 2022, and they follow the existing investment philosophy and core technology categories, with several new technologies, like hydrogen, establishing a broadening core for market participation.

Each of these strategies serves a specific purpose, but collectively they offer comprehensive technology coverage and access, as well as financial support to companies enabling the cleantech transition, supply chain participants, and new diversity-based market entities:[103]

- *Frontier Fund:* This fund concentrates on bringing revolutionary technologies to market to solve the problems of climate change mitigation and decarbonize the global economy. It focuses on technologies for net-zero generation, breakthrough in storage duration and performance, carbon capture and sequestration, clean hydrogen and fuels, transport electrification, supply chain decarbonization, and industrial decarbonization.

- *Elevate Future Fund:* EIP supports expanded diversity in energy-related venture capital and for traditionally underrepresented groups and established this global fund to drive expanded sector diversity participation. Funding can be provided to partner supply chains and for start-ups through partnerships utilized with incubators, accelerators, and other private investors in their corporate partner footprints.

- *Europe Fund:* This fund extends the original Flagship Fund into the European market and technology community, where 1,800 investable companies exist at attractive lower valuations, with strong technology underpinning, and with lower costs for technology development, but are hampered by a lack of access to larger, more scalable markets. The fund will also leverage access to EIP's North America scale and resources.

- *Credit Fund:* This fund focuses on low-risk credit investments through use of available low-interest government loan programs (Small Business Association). The fund seeks opportunities to support start-up, middle-market, and growth companies that need access to capital for working capital, investment deployment, refinancing, and/or liquidity purposes, and match EIP's rigorous qualification requirements.

The strategies constructed and managed by EIP have had several monetization events, growing corporate partners, expanding start-up company participation, and growing internal EIP and corporate resources collaborating on market analysis, sector assessment, target deep dives, opportunity diligence, and portfolio enablement. EIP is also presently considering an infrastructure-focused strategy not only to meet the needs of its corporate partners but also to recognize the global market potential in this space that is measured in multiple trillions of dollars.

Hans Kobler commented on how he sees EIP's future growth:

> With the launch of our latest strategies, we are expanding our offering to invest in further critical building blocks of the energy transition and provide an expanded strategic partner group with more insights and opportunities to innovate. We believe our model is uniquely suited for these additional growth areas and expect to produce results for the benefit of our investors, portfolio, and partners.[104]

EIP has been successful in enabling the industry to accelerate its knowledge of the emerging technology sector and the applicability, functionality, and value related to these market offerings. This accumulated knowledge is invaluable to EIP's corporate partners and has enabled these companies to gain a breadth and depth of awareness likely not replicable without significant cost, time, and effort, if even possible under any alternative model.

The corporate partners of EIP have benefited beyond the value of initial and subsequent technology and market information through the ability to access a deep expert and analytical resource pool and enable start-up engagement and contractual mechanisms that provide even deeper insight into technology applicability, performance, and deployment benefits. As a utility-focused venture capital fund, EIP has continually exhibited the ability to provide not only insight to its corporate partners but, more importantly, foresight regarding what lies over the horizon and how to prepare for its arrival and impacts.

Joules Accelerator

Founded in 2013 as CLT Joules, its mission is to identify, advise, connect, and deploy cleantech start-ups across the Carolinas, an area rich with almost 300 energy- and cleantech-related companies, both established and in various stages of development and start-up. Renamed Joules Accelerator, it is located in Charlotte, North Carolina, operating as a 501(c)(3) non-profit chartered to collaborate with regional industrial, municipal, and university partners, and is the only climate tech accelerator concentrated on serving the Carolinas region.[105]

Joules Accelerator fills an identified regional gap for organizations focused on nurturing, enabling, and supporting start-ups that champion high-impact climate-related solutions, software development, equipment performance, asset safety, power delivery, and supply chain. Joules has worked to position Charlotte as the go-to location for human, intellectual, and financial capital to support qualified entrepreneurs in the energy space. As a derivative outcome, new high-quality, energy-related jobs would be created in Charlotte.

It is supported by a variety of highly recognized corporate and public sponsors—Duke Energy, Microsoft, Ernst & Young, S&C Electric, DOE, and the U.S. Economic Development Administration—which provide critical resources, intellectual capital, and funding support, among other types of direct and indirect assistance.[106]

Bob Irvin has been Executive Director of Joules since 2016. He is a 35-year utility industry veteran at New York State Electric & Gas, Duke Energy, and Tennessee Valley Authority. Most of this experience was in the strategy area, where he was responsible for market analysis, corporate growth, mergers and acquisitions, performance analysis, and strategy development.

INCUBATOR TO ACCELERATOR

Joules started as an incubator, focused on shepherding start-up companies through the early stages of the developmental life cycle. Start-ups in this stage of development may have little more than an idea they wish to pursue, with little to no revenues and little progress. At this stage of development, seed money sources are few, levels of investment are low, and the nature of assistance is often focused on internal processes and methods, rather than external markets and revenues.

Its role as an incubator reflected the nature of its own early purpose to drive local company development in Charlotte, with the intent to create new businesses. As is common to start-ups, many of the start-ups it worked with were relatively infant in their ideas, which resulted in a number of business casualties and ultimate failures.

During early 2016, the Joules board held a strategy review to assess the group's performance, define its challenges, and map a new path to a higher-quality, better-funded, and more successful future portfolio of start-ups. The enhancements to Joules addressed its vision, role, board, value chain emphasis, value proposition, funding, success metrics, branding, Southeast region position, national position, utility position, and alternative paths.

As a result of this self-introspection, Joules thought its best future positioning was as an accelerator, focused on fast-tracking and scaling-up start-ups to match the pace at which the market was moving. It also believed it needed to reshape its relevant market position and heighten the focus on corporate, utility, and funding partners; high-grade the quality of the start-ups it engaged with; and formalize the scope, structure, and delivery of the program it offered to these entities.[107]

Bob Irvin discussed his early days at Joules:

> After I came to Joules, I felt it was necessary to reassess the business model and challenge its viability moving forward. I believed the prior experience of Joules showed us that to be successful in the market, we needed to create a different persona than how we were presently viewed. It was hard to be a small incubator among many larger ones nationally, particularly when many of the start-ups we were mentoring were so early stage, at only a one to three level of technology readiness, which was too early for our corporate sponsors to effectively support.[108]

The results of this reassessment also changed the board composition, added an advisory group, expanded university outreach, clarified local and state engagement, expanded funding sources, and reconfigured the way Joules engaged with start-ups.[109]

The Joules program now brings together a broad community of

partners, advisors, collaborators, and sponsors, which is viewed as the foundation for innovation and collaboration. Joules focuses on connecting start-ups to a mix of utilities, corporates, universities, nonprofits, and municipalities from the Carolinas and elsewhere in the southeastern portion of the country.

The Joules agenda addresses the water, agriculture, transportation, shipping, industry, and energy sectors, with a focus on new technologies, climate change, product offerings, customer applications, and energy efficiency. Joules aims to help start-ups get access to a range of stakeholders that can provide or arrange technical validation, commercial support, and strategic partnerships. Start-up services include mentoring and demonstration projects to encourage venture capital investment, deployment, and corporate engagement.

It also maintains ongoing relationships with key partners, like E4 Carolinas, the Savannah River National Laboratory, the Research Triangle Cleantech Cluster, Ernst & Young, Honeywell, Trane Technologies, and Lowe's Corp. Further, it engages with a broader company network within the region and nationally, like ABB, Dominion Energy, Itron, Westinghouse, Hitachi, Siemens Energy, and Southern Company, among other well-known entities.[110]

Joules also interfaces with several state, public, and private organizations, like the North Carolina Department of Commerce, the South Carolina Department of Commerce, the City of Charlotte, the City of Raleigh, and the City of Durham, as well as North Carolina State University, Duke University, Clemson University, and South Carolina universities, among other entities.[111]

EVOLUTION OF JOULES

Joules's goal was to identify companies that were ready to go to market but still in front of a next-step Series A funding. The focus was directed at linking entrepreneurs to opportunities for piloting their devices, equipment, technologies, or offerings with a potential corporate entity or other type of stakeholder.

Like many energy incubators or accelerators, particularly those obtaining their footing when the cleantech transition was just beginning, Joules had its formative challenges. When Joules launched, the supply of regional-energy-focused entrepreneurs was small, utilities sector appreciation for cleantech was nascent, capital flows for cleantech were just initiating, and internal Joules resources were few.

Joules did, however, have several advantages to capitalize on. The Carolinas were a recognized education center with several highly visible utilities, and Charlotte was becoming known as "Nuclear City," with a strong presence of significant energy players. Charlotte was also a robust financial center for the Southeast, the regional universities provided a strong flow of engineering talent, and the CEO of Duke Energy in Charlotte was nationally renowned for his support of cleantech.

Joules operates with a cohort concept, where it brings a set of prequalified start-ups into the program to work with its internal team and other local mentors of various backgrounds for approximately 90 days. While Joules was initially focused on connecting these start-ups to both funding sources and potential companies, the ability to gain market traction was heavily dependent on the number, scope, and quality of the start-ups themselves.

In its first year after reconstituting in 2016, Joules had a cohort size of six entrepreneurs focused on several interesting clean technologies—thermal energy, power distribution products, and biofuels. By its second cohort in 2017, the cohort size had grown to seven companies, and the range of offerings expanded to IoT, wearables, solar cleaning solutions, EV charging, augmented reality, drones, and AI.

Its recent Cohort 9 in 2021 included six companies that further advanced technology coverage to DERMS, second-life batteries, EV fast-charging, lithium-ion battery safety, and CO_2 sensing. The newest Cohort 10 has expanded its focus on AI, direct current, long-duration energy storage, grid resilience, EV charging workforce enablement, and more (see Figure 19).[112]

The types of technologies addressed by the start-ups in the post-2015 era of Joules have focused on the downstream end of the value chain (i.e., beyond-the-meter and energy services), which is paralleling how the focus of the market has evolved, particularly as it relates to battery storage, EVs, AI, and DERMS over the last several years.

After a few years of operation, Joules underwent some timely introspection to assess its position and impacts and define the hurdles it needed to address. While its presence in Charlotte was beneficial and it had secured several partners and stood up a quality advisory board, Joules had much to do to move to the level of its own aspirations.

Cohort	Companies	Onboarding	Areas of Start-Up Concentration				
0	7	2014	Energy Management	Advanced Analytics	Wearables		
1	6	2016	DERs	Advanced Analytics	Energy Efficiency		
2	7	2017	Robotics	AR/VR	IoT/Sensors		
3	7	2018	Artificial Intelligence	Indoor Ag	Smart Grids	EV Infrastructure	
4	8	2019	EV Transportation	Water	Food Security	Grid Tech	Smart Cities
5	7	2019	Grid Tech	Workforce	Building Efficiency	Transportation	
6	8	2020	Geothermal	Cooling and HVAC	Electrification	Climate Tech	
7	8	2020	Climate Tech	Grid Tech	Cooling and HVAC		
8	6	2021	HVAC	Renewables Development	Virtual Power Plants	Hydrogen	
9	6	2021	Electrification	Batteries	Carbon Sensing		
10	7	2022	EV Charging	Batteries	AI/Predictive Analytics	DC Systems/Microgrid	DERMs Interconnection

Figure 19. Joules cohorts.

(Source: Data from Joules Accelerator, "Cohort Start-Ups," April 5, 2022; Joules Accelerator, "Cohort 10 Welcome and Introduction.")

Sustainable funding was a challenge and corporate support was limited. Deal flow was weaker than desired, and Joules's brand had not yet captured the visibility and prestige hoped for. Additionally, the effort expended to stand up Joules and quickly obtain market traction exposed some alignment shortcomings that needed to be addressed before its next market surge.

But by early 2016, the cleantech marketplace was gaining momentum, and the value chain destinations for new technologies were rapidly expanding into a host of new areas, like mobility, home automation, smart buildings demand response, advanced analytics, digitalization, indoor agriculture, micro-generation, rooftop solar, robotics, IoT, and AI, among other areas. To capitalize on this growth, Joules worked to refresh its strategy and elevate its governance, presence, and resource access, as well as scale up its go-to-market efforts. It tweaked its business model and expanded the sources of available funding and approach to securing more venture capital interest and commitment. Bob Irvin noted:

After refreshing our original market approach, we successfully elevated the type of start-up that became involved with us. The entrepreneurs behind these companies were still bright and energetic, but they now brought technologies to us that had received seed round or Series A funding and better developed products to discuss with corporate sponsors. These entities were now in a better position to demonstrate their technology and to potentially land demonstrations with utilities and corporate sponsors, which often led to customer contracts.[113]

With a new board of directors, an expanded advisory board (more than 250 in the network), expanded sponsors, and a broader innovation network, Joules has solidified its position and moved well past its own start-up challenges to a position where it is punching well above its weight.

Through early 2022, Joules had facilitated the raise of approximately $800 million in early-stage funding across its nine cohorts (see Figure 20). The total number of companies in the Joules portfolio today exceeds 70, with several headquartered in North Carolina. Almost 90 percent of prior cohort members are still in business and thriving, employing more than 1,250 people, many locally sourced in the Carolinas.[114]

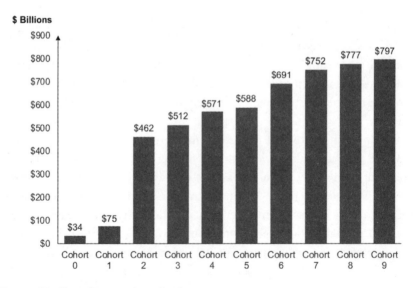

Figure 20. Cumulative cohort funding.

(Source: Joules Accelerator, "Cohort Overview and Funding," February 2022.)

Four cohort members—Atom Power (Cohort 0), SparkCognition (Cohort 2), Amply (Cohort 4), and WeaveGrid (Cohort 4)—are on track to achieve unicorn status with a market valuation above \$1 billion, and five other start-ups have successfully been acquired with a value in excess of \$300 million.[115]

ENTREPRENEUR OPPORTUNITIES

A primary role for Joules has been helping its cohort start-ups get known within the energy community—with utilities, commercial, and industrial entities—to obtain opportunities for these companies to pitch their technology products and services, demonstrate their technologies, and earn commercial contracts with these entities.

Joules uses several methods to accomplish this outcome: its core team engagement, periodic corporate sponsor interaction, the recent first Joules Camp, and the annual Joules Conference.

In 2021 Joules initiated an innovation sponsorship program called Joules Camp, which is designed to energize state communities about the cleantech transition. It also promotes public and private sector engagement and collaboration in the pursuit of sustainability goals, specifically within North Carolina.

The program involves 21 demonstration projects with 21 corporate partners working in 21 communities, and \$21,000 is provided in seed money per solution. It brings together start-ups, corporate partners, local communities, and local students to accelerate cleantech solutions over the course of a 12-month period.[116]

The program selected five technologies for the camp to demonstrate applicability to real challenges in North Carolina in the areas of water quality management (Varuna Tech), flood monitoring and intelligence (FloodMapp), solar-plus-storage (Yotta Energy), cross-enterprise collaboration (Centrly), and carbon accountability and sustainability analytics (Carbon Insights).[117]

In July 2022, Joules was awarded a \$96,000 grant from the Duke Energy Foundation to continue its Joules Camp efforts as a project-based community outreach program designed to energize North Carolina about climate tech innovation while promoting public-private partnerships in pursuit of sustainability goals. The program will pilot three to six projects per year (\$10,000 to \$20,000 per project), supported by the Joules team and three to six interns. Joules Camp exists at the intersection of start-up innovation, visionary entrepreneurs, corporate engagement, student education, and community adoption. Start-ups from the next cohort, along with previous cohorts, will be eligible to apply for the program. Joules sees this project as furthering its key priorities of business development, economic development, community engagement, and diversity, equity, and inclusion.

For six years, Joules has also held annual conferences in Charlotte with representatives from local government, corporate partners, EPRI, venture capital funds, and start-ups, as well as its board of directors. While COVID-19 interrupted these events over 2020–2021, in March 2022 Joules reengaged these stakeholders in an in-person conference featuring start-ups in its current cohort group, start-ups in National Grid Partners' venture capital fund, and start-ups in EPRI's Incubatenergy group.

Thirteen start-ups presented during the event, covering technologies like EV charging; transmission inspection, health, and performance; conductor technology; AI for monitoring; water heater efficiency; battery design, safety, and recycling; climate sensing and tracking; and load control. The companies presenting included the following start-ups:

- *ElectricFish:* Deploys direct current (DC) fast chargers in difficult-to-reach geographic locations for customers and fleets.

- *HeyCharge:* Provides charging solutions for EVs located in cellular- and Wi-Fi-denied environments.

- *Moment Energy:* Creates innovative battery management system solutions for second-life EV batteries.

- *Ribbit Network:* Develops and installs the world's largest grass-roots, open-source CO_2 sensing network.

- *Shifted Energy:* Balances the grid through monitoring, optimization, and customer-friendly load control.

- *Soteria Battery Group:* Works on improving lithium-ion battery safety through the use of durable, thin-film materials.

- *TS Conductor:* Designs improved conductors using advanced materials to reduce grid constraints and enhance conductor performance.

- *Xero Energy:* Provides customer application to evaluate water heater performance and assess alternative replacement economics.

- *Viridi Parente:* Builds battery-powered construction equipment ("green machines") designed to replace diesel engines and improve operating cost and performance and storage for grid use.

- *AiDash:* Utilizes AI and space-based monitoring of geographically distributed assets to transform operations, maintenance, and sustainability.

- *LineVision:* Provides a single platform to provide situational awareness and line health, while improving line ratings.

- *Linebird:* Utilizes drones to conduct inspection on hard-to-access transmission lines across all terrain while avoiding wildlife disruption, reducing inspection costs, and reducing cycle time.

- *Optiwatt:* Provides decision-quality data related to EV energy consumption and charging scheduling and tracking.

These start-ups represented their technologies and product offerings and conducted separate meetings with corporate sponsors about potential application demonstrations or adaptation. They were also able to network among themselves where their product offerings could offer opportunities for bundling or collaborative go-to-market opportunities.

Joules Accelerator's focus on early-stage cleantech start-ups and revenue-generating pilots is a critical differentiating feature for the program. Joules's success is measured by economic development (jobs), community engagement (events), and business development (pilots). Joules tries to focus on what is important to a start-up—for example, purposeful actions, fast execution, market focus, and commitments delivered. Bob Irvin summed up the approach that has made for a successful cohort experience with Joules:

We concluded we needed a unique formula to deliver success to our entrepreneurs, our sponsors, and Joules. Our formula starts with emphasizing connections between our advisors and start-ups, which lead to quick "yes or no" business development opportunities between the two parties. We know that a start-up's time is its most valuable resource. We want the total experience to be differentiating for the entrepreneur where it matters—in mentoring, market connections, speed-to-market, and funding access. If we can hit our marks in these areas, then we know we are making the experience with Joules personal, simpler, and rewarding.[118]

With this track record of delivery success, combined with a unique accelerator identity among the entrepreneur community, Joules has been successful in not only continuously attracting new cohort members but also delivering an experience that enables Joules to stand out among its larger, less attentive peer accelerators and create a distinctive persona among the start-up community.

As a result, Joules will continue with its 11th cohort in October 2022, with an intent to graduate this class in February 2023. It anticipates applying the same criteria for selection as it presently does—that is, mid-stage maturity with demonstrable technology application, prior investor funding at least at Series A levels, relevant technology application that can solve a clear market problem, and technology that can command ubiquity in market acceptance.

With a history of four cohort companies in line for unicorn valuation status and five having successfully monetized their companies, Joules is positioned to further demonstrate the value it brings to start-ups, corporate sponsors, and utilities in the Carolinas region and beyond.

CHAPTER 6

Profiles in Innovation:
The Innovators

THE range of external entities available to drive or support R&D and innovation activities of U.S. utilities serves as a catalyst and accelerator for the industry. This does not suggest utilities are insufficiently capable of successfully undertaking critical R&D and innovation initiatives. Rather, it identifies how utilities can utilize external force multipliers to complement their internal activities and leverage capabilities that do not make sense to maintain on a full-time basis within the company.

It just makes sense to capitalize on the leverage of third parties in areas where utilities are ill suited to conduct certain activities (e.g., basic research), do not have a constant need for capabilities, or can obtain needed capabilities at a lower total cost. As regulated companies, utilities do not have unlimited license to pursue R&D and innovation activities like an unregulated business does. U.S. utilities need to work within a tight regulatory framework that does not emphasize R&D and innovation activities as fundamental to a company's primary mission and does not reward these activities once conducted and deployed (i.e., full recovery of costs).

As noted earlier, certain utilities have been active in R&D and innovation since the mid-20th century, either on a stand-alone basis or as part of an industry-wide collaboration (EPRI or GTI). But while these prior activities have been individually impressive, they have been more targeted (e.g., coal-fired generation). In today's utility environment in the United States, the need for broad topical coverage, as well as specific areas for deeper inquiry, requires a more enterprise-wide focus and a concerted effort to optimize scarce resources against a possible R&D and innovation agenda that is expanding every year.

The constraints that overlay how the U.S. utilities industry functions within a regulated environment are not insurmountable; nor do they totally preclude the conduct of active R&D and innovation efforts at several companies. Several companies within the industry have been able to successfully navigate through these structural and regulatory challenges and demonstrate an innovation acumen that has served them well by embedding a curiosity about exploration, collectivizing the commitment to embrace innovation as a strategic enabler, and forging ahead on paths intended to build innovation into the corporate DNA.

Six utilities are profiled in this chapter that have been successful in standing up and/or executing effective enterprise R&D and/or innovation efforts: Ameren, Avista, Duke Energy, National Grid, Southern Company, and WEC Energy. While some similarities exist among these entities, they have each pioneered their own unique approaches to the pursuit of R&D and/or innovation.

These interviews reinforce the expectation that innovation is a bespoke undertaking—it reflects a well-established company persona, as well as preferences on *what* the right scope of the innovation could be, *where* to place its focus, and *how* to engage employees at the specific company. But the differences among these companies also point out that different innovation priorities, performance models, engagement approaches, and outcome emphases can still propel a utility toward its original objectives of expanding collaboration, enhancing operational performance and customer relationships, and moving the organization closer toward readiness for future market changes.

Disruptive technology evaluation, testing, and adoption is a common underpinning of these entities, with some companies focused on targeted in-house R&D, some on operating asset performance, some on grid and network modernization, and some on behind-the-meter offerings to customers. Where each company is concentrated depends on its historical legacy of exploration, its priorities for business positioning, its expectations from R&D and/or innovation, its needs for operating enhancement, its capacity for change, and its ability to translate ideation into real-world deployment.

- *Ameren:* This St. Louis, Missouri, utility provides electric and natural gas services to customers in the states of Missouri and Illinois. The company was one of the earliest utilities to formalize an emphasis and approach to pursuing R&D and innovation, and has been an active collaborator with universities, as well as an active investor through EIP.

- *Avista:* This multistate utility provides electric and gas services to customers in the Pacific Northwest. Based in Spokane, Washington, Avista has been a distinctive example of how a comparatively smaller utility has been able to define a sustainable innovation model with an emphasis on nurturing local start-ups while engaging the local community in its efforts.

- *Duke Energy:* This multistate utility is headquartered in Charlotte, North Carolina, providing electric and natural gas services to customers in the Southeast and Midwest. The company was active early in identifying, evaluating, and operationalizing new technologies for potential adoption, as well as creating an environment to encourage innovation across the company.

- *National Grid:* This multistate utility is headquartered in Waltham, Massachusetts, and serves electric and gas customers in the Northeast. It is owned by National Grid in the United Kingdom, which provides the benefit of a European perspective on the role innovation needs to play in leveraging technologies to transform the business and create the digital utility.

- *Southern Company:* This multistate, Atlanta, Georgia, utility provides electric and gas services to customers primarily in the Southeast, with additional customers in Illinois and other states. Southern Company has been an active participant in R&D since the 1960s and was one of the earliest advocates for elevated attention to innovation to achieve the clean energy transition.

- *WEC Energy:* This multistate utility is headquartered in Milwaukee, Wisconsin, and serves electric and gas customers in the Upper Midwest. The company has previously focused its historical attention largely on its coal fleet as its most significant portfolio element, although it is now pursuing performance enhancement and technology adoption across the company.

The utilities represented above provide a cross section of companies with different legacy histories, business portfolios, relative scale, and geographic dispersion. They are a microcosm of the U.S. utilities industry and provide a unique glimpse into how the sector is grappling with utilizing R&D and innovation to prepare for the clean energy transition.

As in the preceding discussion on innovation enablers, each entity is profiled over the remainder of this chapter. Key executives involved in leading and driving the R&D and innovation efforts at these utilities were interviewed to capture insights and perspectives on *what* they have been trying to accomplish, *how* they decided to pursue an enhanced R&D and innovation model, and *how far* along the journey they have progressed. More important, the interviews provide a view into the range of FOAK accomplishments—some illustrative of a long history of innovation and others a direct result of recent year ramp-up in innovation focus. Their experiences are rich in lessons for other utilities and instructive of how companies—large and small, experienced and inexperienced—have pursued an R&D and/or innovation agenda as an integral element of their future strategies and market positioning.

Ameren

Ameren is a combination regulated electric and gas utility headquartered in St. Louis, Missouri, and serves 2.4 million electric customers and 900,000 gas customers in the states of Missouri and Illinois. It also operates a FERC-regulated transmission company that invests in and operates local and regional transmission projects.

Like so many other U.S. utilities, Ameren focused its innovation efforts on developing and delivering energy solutions that would deliver safe, reliable, affordable service and cleaner energy to its customers through improved processes; the implementation of new technologies, products, and services; and innovative regulatory frameworks. The company believed that this focus would ultimately deliver sustainable, long-term value to its customers, communities, and shareholders.

This innovation focus reflected the external market and policy momentum around certain technologies, as well as Ameren's internal belief that the demise of the utilities industry propagated by external pundits was off base and did not adequately consider how utilities could leverage their experience and positioning to enhance the role of a utility. Rather than the industry entering a death spiral, Ameren believed it could be an enabler of innovation for the benefit of the network customers and shareholders.

The company particularly believed that innovation could directly create value to the customer in multiple ways: first, through producing lower emissions and carbon footprint; second, from enhancing system reliability by deploying enhanced technologies for greater visibility into network performance and risk areas; third, through lowering operating costs to reduce customer bills and improve affordability; fourth, from technology adoption to increase control, predictability, and value of the grid for customers; and finally, from digital technology implementation to achieve operational efficiencies and to improve its customers' experience with the company.[1]

As technology disruption became more evident, Ameren was able to lean on its presence and strong engagement with innovative companies in the St. Louis business community. St. Louis has long been home to innovative companies like Boeing, Monsanto (now Bayer), and Anheuser-Busch, as well as Centene, Express Scripts, and World Wide Technology. In addition, St. Louis has long been home to a robust entrepreneurial and innovation district, including the Cortex Innovation Community. Thus, while the utilities industry faced a different competitive environment, Ameren observed other companies competing in their markets and leveraging innovation to meet the challenges of their specific sectors.

As disruptive technology emerged as a challenge to the utilities sector, a more formal focus by Ameren on this evolution brought increased executive attention to innovation's importance. It also resulted in more concentrated messaging to employees about innovation's value and role in advancing the business operationally, meeting expanding and demanding customer needs, and creating value to customers and other stakeholders.

KICK-STARTING INNOVATION

Like most utilities, Ameren did not just flip the innovation switch at a single moment. Even prior to the emergence of the cleantech transition, the company continuously sought to advance its business through technology adoption and performance enhancements. However, as disruptive technologies became more functional and economic, and customer needs heightened, it became more committed to playing a direct role in industry evolution and transition occurring around the company.

As a precursor to standing up its innovation efforts, the company took its executive leadership team (ELT) to visit the Cortex Innovation Community (Cortex), a 501(c)(3) nonprofit that oversees the development of entrepreneurs in the region. Cortex is ranked as one of the top five innovation districts in the world and was founded in 2002, with local relationships that span the university and health sciences sectors, as well as entrepreneurs and start-ups across broad areas of interest.[2]

The Ameren ELT visited Cortex for an all-day immersion to learn how innovation is nurtured and how other companies do it successfully. The officer group spent time speaking with Cortex sponsors, mentors, and companies to obtain a firsthand view into the challenges and requirements for success. As a result of the time spent with Cortex, the company developed a perspective on what a more comprehensive and intentional innovation effort could look like, as well as how Ameren should position itself internally as a sponsor and externally as a community participant.

In 2013 a research facility was stood up in Champaign, Illinois—the Technology Applications Center (TAC)—to create a smart grid test bed to focus on network technologies and solutions. It was configured to enable testing of government-, customer-, and company-sponsored projects. TAC included an on-site substation, distribution circuits, a control building, monitoring, control devices, and beyond-the-meter testing capabilities to facilitate technology evaluation.[3]

Several entities sponsored various technology tests across a range of applications or technologies, like data flow controllers, cybersecurity, EV charging, interactional microgrid operation, solar panels, wireless communication, streetlighting, synchro-phased meters, transactive energy, real-time energy visualization, storage, and distributed energy resource (DER) integration, among others.

The Illinois TAC works with the technology or application sponsors like Schweitzer Engineering Laboratories, ABB, ARPA-E, EPRI, Opus One Solutions, and the University of Illinois Urbana-Champaign. Several start-ups also tested their offerings at TAC to assess operability and performance. A subsequent TAC has been established in Missouri, and while smaller in scale and activity, works with the University of Missouri–St. Louis (UMSL), Washington University, and Missouri University of Science and Technology.[4]

Unlike many other utilities that simply use their headquarters buildings as a host for innovation, in early 2015 Ameren set up a stand-alone innovation center—The Hub—at an adjacent facility that had previously housed a fleet garage. This facility included 8,800 square feet of usable space that was ultimately arranged to provide common collaboration space, test bench capability, and team meeting rooms.[5]

When asked about the philosophy relied on to formalize and stand-up Ameren's innovation effort, Warner Baxter, current Executive Chairman and previous CEO, explained:

As I stepped into my role as CEO in early 2014, it became clear the utilities industry was being disrupted by changing customer needs and expectations, new innovative technologies, and market participants. Our leadership team knew that while we had a solid innovation foundation focused primarily on R&D for our customers, we also knew we could not stand still. We had to think differently about how we operated our business and delivered value to our customers and stakeholders. That recognition prompted us to take several steps, including taking all our officers to our local innovation district to pick the brains of innovators, meeting with companies in our region outside of our industry that had established innovation programs, as well as meeting with some of the disrupters in our industry. At the end of the day, it was clear we had to be more intentional in our purpose and investments around our efforts, more agile in our execution, and more innovative in our thinking and actions. We created a case for change that described our future world so coworkers could understand our focus, making a point of linking our innovation efforts directly to our strategy and to focusing on customer benefits.[6]

The company made it a point to communicate that innovation efforts were not a "corporate" program. Rather, Ameren made a conscious effort to communicate that the power of innovation would be effectively tapped when all employees viewed the effort as centered on those directly involved in everyday innovation (the collective "we"), and not about the headquarters or leadership ("corporate").

After the company had addressed the *why* of innovation, it then formalized the *how* and *where* of its focus. It created a set of innovation categories that framed key technology, operating, and enabling areas to guide the structure of the internal teams and allow for a more programmatic approach to planning, execution, and management of overall project collaboration, performance, and impacts. Within each innovation category, a few full-time Ameren employees were involved, but most came from within the operating businesses on a part-time basis.

In 2015 the company also intentionally incorporated innovation directly into its corporate strategy. Three strategy categories—forward-thinking, growth-oriented, and foundational/enabling—provided guidance for more specific elements, which included electrification, innovative technologies, generation, transmission, energy delivery, customer products and services, and digital. The inclusion of innovation as a strategy element signaled the significance of this capability to the company and how Ameren was being intentional in embedding and leveraging these capabilities to benefit customers.[7]

Later in 2015, Ameren opened the 2,000-square-foot Ameren Innovation Center at Research Park at the University of Illinois at Urbana-Champaign, becoming the first major energy company to open facilities at this university. Ameren had a long-standing relationship with the university and recognized the value of locating this innovation center close to students and faculty, as well as other companies in this space.[8]

Ameren's initial innovation focus included EVs, storage, and distributed generation, which were all topical in the utilities and regulated sectors at the time, receiving high interest from the venture capital community. These areas were timely from a market readiness perspective, as they were beginning to experience rapid technology cost curve decline, as well as heightened interest from the various classes of customers most directly affected.

The initial focus of the Ameren Innovation Center was not limited to these areas. The full innovation agenda included other application-specific technologies in areas like robotic process automation, smart thermostats, and home energy monitoring and management. However, and perhaps most important to the company, was the fact that the innovation center enabled Ameren to provide internships to bright, innovative students from the University of Illinois. Not only did this effort enable the company to recruit many of these students, but they also energized the company's innovation efforts by bringing in fresh ideas and perspectives.

MATURING THE FOCUS

By 2017, Ameren adopted a more formal pilot vetting process that utilized stage gates to track and manage a project. Within this process assessment model, the internal innovation teams are able to more rapidly determine whether a technology or application could achieve a minimum viable product (MVP) before proceeding to the next stage gate. This model enabled Ameren to fail fast when it was clear that future viability was not going to be an outcome based on work performed to date, as well as allocate capital and people resources to those that looked more promising.

Ameren had matured to create more structure to its innovation effort and to align its areas of interest into five families of innovation—customer, grid/growth, competitive rates, IT/digital, and regulatory/policy—that the company would leverage to advance its market positioning and provision of benefits to customers:[9]

- *Customer:* This family enables new products, services, and solutions to be developed to drive increased customer satisfaction.

- *Grid/growth:* This family assesses the value of the grid, opportunities for investment in the traditional grid, and investment in nontraditional grid and non-grid products and services.

- *Competitive rates:* This family draws medium- and long-term plans to decrease the total cost base across the service territories.

- *IT/digital:* This family leads the development of an IT-enabled operating model and road map for Ameren, including infrastructure application, partnerships, and talent.

- *Regulatory/policy:* This family creates new customer and shareholder value through enhanced regulatory and policy frameworks.

Since stand-up of its innovation in 2015, the company has sought to ensure that its innovation agenda is directly linked to the corporate strategy. This is an intentional action as the company looks to create alignment throughout the business and line of sight into how innovation supports the overarching strategy direction and delivers on planned outcomes. Today, Ameren's corporate strategy focuses on several critical pillars to guide the enterprise and which serve to provide a "North Star" for its innovation efforts. The North Star for Ameren is provided by how the company articulated its vision, "leading the way to a sustainable energy future," and its mission, "to power the quality of life."[10]

Most of the innovation undertaken or supported by Ameren has been directed at the network, since much of the recent software, hardware, and solutions introduced in the market have been developed with this value chain element in mind. The company focuses on operationalization of technologies for the benefit of the system and the customer, as opposed to seeking commercial applications and revenue creation.

This posture reflects how the company's regulatory commissions in Missouri and Illinois see the purpose of innovation, and how value from its accomplishment should be directed (i.e., for system reliability, cleaner energy, and customer benefit). Thus, given these regulatory philosophies, Ameren uses operationalization and commercialization interchangeability since the results of innovation (i.e., developed products, services, or solutions) are directed at network deployment either as features, devices, assets, or systems.

The company defined a staged approach to innovation that would move at a pace to allow it to digest and assess its efforts and accomplishments to date, as well as reflect its maturity with embedding innovation. Rev 1 focused on the stand-up of the innovation centers and the setting of an agenda to drive early efforts. Rev 2 addressed execution against the initial innovation agenda and the conduct of ideation exercises, topical team discussion and collaboration, technology identification and evaluation, and project analysis and deliberation. This led to the determination of technologies that would continue through evaluation. Presently, in Rev 3, the company leverages the expertise of leading research organizations and company personnel to accelerate further its innovation efforts, including EPRI, GTI, and EIP, as well as efforts undertaken by EEI and AGA. The efforts of these parties enable the company to be more impactful with its innovation efforts.

The early innovation efforts of Ameren resulted in an innovation portfolio eventually centering around eight specific technology and support groupings. Some of the examples of work completed and outcomes over the period 2010–2022 include the following: electrification (electric bus introduction and fleet transport fast charging); energy storage (several battery installations); clean energy (renewables installations, augmented reality, data analytics, and neural networks); customer (customer segmentation, flexible payment, pick your due date, and outage notification); grid architecture (microgrids, drones, intelligent controllers, smart cities, and image processing); regulatory and legislative (energy efficiency, formula rates, modernization, and smart energy); grid growth (broadband and fiber); and culture (Ameren Accelerator, Cortex Innovation District, Incubatenergy Labs, and UMSL Diversity, Equity, and Inclusion Accelerator).[11]

These areas and outcomes illustrate the breadth of innovation that has been undertaken by Ameren over the last dozen years. While these technology and application areas are not unique to Ameren, they parallel the paths of other U.S. utilities and illustrate steady progress and accomplishment. They also recognize that the less tangible elements of innovation—regulatory, policy, and culture—are also important determinants of innovation outcomes, and are individually innovative.

Over its history, Ameren can point to a variety of FOAK accomplishments, ranging across different technologies or actions. These FOAK events are summarized below:[12]

- *1904 World's Fair:* At this event, a predecessor company demonstrated the world's first broad-scale electrification at a multipurpose site for this international event.

- *Private long-term evolution (LTE):* In 2019 Ameren completed the first utility-owned LTE field trial, which validated 14 use cases for distributed field automation and workforce mobility.

- *X-realities:* Ameren has implemented X-technologies (i.e., augmented, virtual, and mixed reality) to enhance work performance at its Callaway Nuclear Plant and in field operations.

- *Microgrid:* In 2016 Ameren designed and stood up a state-of-the-art microgrid for its Illinois operations that incorporated renewables, dispatchable load, storage, and transactive energy.

- *Nuclear storage:* Ameren became the first U.S. utility to store spent nuclear fuel in underground storage containers.

- *EV alliance:* In 2020 Ameren initiated a 10-member Midwest EV Charging Corridor Coalition to collaborate and coordinate the development of a seamless system to support EVs.

Through its focus on technology evaluation, ideation challenges, and sustained capital investment, Ameren has successfully undertaken, completed, and/or installed emerging technologies that can prove to be difference makers in operations, as well as contributors to enhanced customer benefit.

TAPPING INTO CROWDSOURCING

The company has held multiple collaboration or crowdsourcing events over time of various focus and duration. The initial collaboration event called the Summer Challenge was launched in 2017 and reflected a case for change that emphasized readiness for a more uncertain future from emerging technologies, new, unconventional market entrants, and policy shifts from federal and state agencies (see Figure 21).

This first enterprise-wide collaboration event was based on a request from employees for innovative ideas, and it extended over 48 hours, was open to the entire base of more than 9,000 employees, involved 100 four- to five-member teams, and received over 100 ideas based on a simple SharePoint site submission. These ideas split relatively evenly between information technology and business execution, and demonstrated employee interest in collaboration and innovation, as well as a willingness to engage in a manner that would benefit Ameren and its customers.

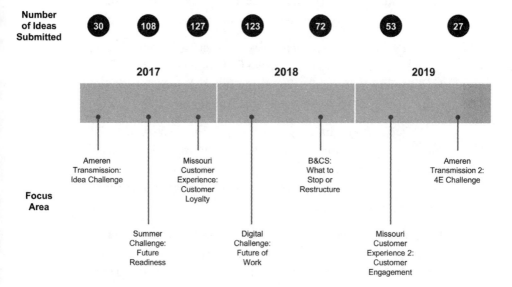

Figure 21. Crowdsourcing history and outcomes.

(Source: Data from Ameren, "Summary of Crowdsourcing Events," April 2022, internal document.)

The process Ameren followed was designed to achieve rapid idea processing (i.e., time-based screening) to assess which ideas had viability among those received, with the intent to quickly determine a go or no-go decision on potential impact and value.

In 2018 an Idea Hub was stood up, which initiated more formal crowdsourcing events and utilized a formal idea collection, information sharing, open comment, and employee voting platform. Since the employee base was already familiar with crowdsourcing, Ameren adopted frequent rapid crowdsourcing events, again lasting 24 to 48 hours, often several times each year, as well as targeted business unit challenges to obtain employee ideas. These events used a simplified summary format to provide meaningful information to event judges to understand, gauge, and select winning ideas and teams.

Over time, and until COVID-19, Ameren held multiple formal idea challenges that were targeted in business units and state organizations or were enterprise-wide:[13]

- *Ameren Transmission:* Two separate challenges were held in 2017 and 2019, with the first focusing on how to ensure Ameren

Transmission thrives over the next 50 years and the second addressing how to increase employee engagement and culture.

- *Missouri customer experience:* Two distinct challenges were also held in 2017 and 2019, with the first addressing how to increase customer loyalty, while the second focused on making it easier for customers to do business with Ameren.

- *Digital challenge:* In 2018 this enterprise-wide challenge addressed the future of work and how future business execution could be enhanced from technology enablement, process improvement, coworker experience, and/or safety/security/facility optimization.

- *Business and customer services:* Also in 2018, the corporate services organization conducted a challenge to employees to identify which processes or work activities could be stopped or restructured to focus on tasks delivering greater customer value.

Among its peers, Ameren is a prolific user of the idea challenge concept and has been successful in leveraging this model to continually engage employees on the topic of innovation.

As a reflection of the success of formal focus on innovation, several employees developed a risk-based analysis tool for gas assets—originating in one of the crowdsourcing events—which won Ameren recognition for the Smartest Digitalization Project in 2020 from *Public Utilities Fortnightly* in its annual assessment of the most innovative utilities in the United States. In addition, *Public Utilities Fortnightly* recognized an Ameren employee as a Top 40 Innovator in the nation for leadership in conceiving, architecting, and building the Illinois microgrid.[14]

VENTURE INVESTING

Like several of the companies profiled in this discussion, Ameren was an early investor in EIP's Flagship Fund, an $800 million fund initially composed of 10 U.S. utilities, as well as several industrial partners. This was one of the earliest sector-focused venture capital funds available to the utilities industry when announced in 2015. EIP has subsequently launched its second fund, increasing total assets under management to $2.5 billion.

This fund has multiple sub-funds, including a targeted European element, with Ameren focused on the Frontier Fund (electrification, renewables, and grid edge) and the Elevate Future Fund (diversity).[15]

Ameren Development Company, an in-house venture capital capacity, also invests in a local fund—Spirit of St. Louis—that focuses on early-stage companies with a local presence. This initial fund—with Cultivation Capital as its principal founder—invested in 24 companies, though it still focuses on seed and Series A funding to companies working toward larger and more permanent funding. With respect to this fund, it has invested in local, cross-sector start-ups in areas like financial technology, health care, and agriculture technology, as well as geospatial technology and direct-to-consumer offerings. Fund II will continue this investing model with another $12.8 million in funding to complete a similar amount in Fund I.[16]

The company is an investor and grant funder with the UMSL Diversity, Equity, and Inclusion Accelerator, which emphasizes empowering diverse start-up founders from underrepresented entrepreneurs. It also engages with various innovation team networks, like T-REX, ITEN, and Arch Grants, and participates with the National Center for Location Science and the Advanced Manufacturing Innovation Center.[17]

In Illinois in as early as 2012, Ameren, in combination with ComEd, invested $7.5 million through the Energy Foundry in fast-growing, top-tier-earning start-ups within the cleantech space, with an emphasis on creating more disruptive innovation in the energy sector.[18]

An additional element of its engagement with start-ups and incubators or accelerators is the Ameren Accelerator, which focuses on early-stage companies trying to develop a proof of concept. Ameren involves approximately 400 companies annually in a pre-seed stage competition, which has generally provided funding for six start-ups where the company believes the technical application concept has market merit, with each entity provided $100,000 in funding.

The first Ameren Accelerator Day was held in 2017, featuring seven start-up companies addressing digital data exchange, fiber sensors, grid resilience, industrial analytics, open-source smart plugs, distributed generation risk management, and online rebate incentives. Start-ups in the program were provided guidance and mentoring by Ameren subject matter experts, as well as faculty and staff from the University of Missouri System.[19]

In 2018 six additional companies covering wearable monitoring devices, logistical infrastructure for ridesharing and autonomous vehicles, ransomware remediation, electricity-generating floor tiles, data exchange integration, and visualization software formed another cohort for potential funding and development. In 2019 another six companies were selected for competition involving a mobile premise, building, and site energy management app; high-capacity lithium-ion batteries; energy efficiency; nano-materials for battery storage; smart radiator valves; and reservoir stimulation technology.[20]

In 2020 Ameren continued its collaboration with EPRI's Incubatenergy Labs effort. The 2020 effort marked the third year Ameren served as a participant and the second as a host for demonstration projects. Approximately 400 applicants from around the world, covering a range of technologies and start-up maturity, applied to the 2020 session, with 10 start-ups invited to partner with utilities and/or EPRI to demonstrate their solutions (four efforts of which Ameren hosted). These companies included the following:

- *ev.energy:* A wireless platform that optimizes EV charging to save customers money and fully use renewable energy, and delivers flexibility services to the grid (Ameren hosted)

- *IND Technology Inc.:* Technology that remotely detects and locates electrical faults before they occur, which could prevent power losses, wildfires, and other consequences (Ameren hosted)

- *PingThings:* An AI platform that processes, stores, and uses high-definition sensor data in real time at grid scale (Ameren hosted)

- *Recurve:* A software-as-a-service tool that analyzes how to use energy more efficiently and effectively in response to cost, carbon reduction, and other customer goals (Ameren hosted)

- *Grid Fruit:* Grid-responsive scheduling of machine cycles to provide demand management and flexibility from commercial food service refrigeration systems

- *Kognitiv Spark:* Augmented reality–enabled tool to help utility workers and supervisors solve problems and learn new skills on the job

- *LineVision:* Noncontact, overhead line sensor technology that provides situational awareness and asset health monitoring and increases capacity

- *RWI Synthetics:* AI-driven intelligent systems modeling tool to help grid planners with scenario planning and DER integration

- *SHARC Energy Systems:* A multifamily, campus, and commercial building wastewater heat recovery system to reduce carbon emissions, costs, and water consumption

Ameren has continued to pursue innovation through the many external innovators that have emerged and become involved in EPRI's Incubatenergy Labs, a multi-utility, multi-start-up accelerated technology demonstration that seeks to help these companies mature their technologies, source additional capital, accelerate their readiness to go to market, and expand the level of awareness and consideration of the net-zero challenge to the country and the company. For example, the company has utilized the capabilities of Dynamhex to begin a community-wide decarbonization dialogue.

Ameren has been an active participant in Incubatenergy Labs since its founding in 2019, participating as the host utility for more projects than any other peer utility. Further, Ameren has routinely engaged the selected companies as project participants and in some instances completed projects with past participants, fulfilling the promise and vision of Incubatenergy Labs of narrowing the timeline start-ups must endure as they seek to create customer and shareholder value through their products and services.

Ameren's strong commitment to participation in Incubatenergy Labs mirrors the commitment and resources the utility has made with EIP, where Ameren routinely ranks among the most engaged utility with both EIP working groups and portfolio company outreach and project development. This level of engagement and participation relative to its peers stands out, as many of the other companies involved with Incubatenergy Labs and EIP not only are substantially larger utilities but also allocate more dollars and human resources to these engagement efforts.

A fundamental underpinning of the company's innovation model is the emphasis it has placed over the past five years on digitalization to enable broad transformation goals of the enterprise. The digitalization effort provides a framework for innovation that encapsulates hard investment as well as soft enablers that can create discernable value to customers beyond direct capital deployment. As a practical matter, regulatory policies, mandates, and models all contribute to the nature, intent, and positioning of innovation on behalf of customers, and can provide the means by which value is captured from execution and delivered to customers. At present on the national stage, Ameren actively participates in EPRI's LCRI and facilitates a regional dialogue with the large industrial customers, universities, economic development organizations, energy carriers, sequestration companies, community leaders, and regional utilities. Ameren looks to understand the needs of all parties in the energy transition to a low-carbon economy, leveraging the LCRI initiative. This activity is crucial to establishing the planning timeline to support low-carbon technologies including hydrogen, carbon capture, utilization and sequestration, and long-term energy storage.

The innovation team is also currently working through the details of integrating a hydrolyzer at either its microgrid installation in Illinois or at its O'Fallon solar energy center to explore the use of hydrogen and fuel cell technologies to serve long-term energy storage needs.

Ameren has also joined EPRI's Climate Resilience and Adaptation Initiative (Climate READi), which is an innovative global program that leverages EPRI's collaborative model and convenes global thought leaders and scientific researchers necessary to build an informed and consistent approach to deal with the impacts to grid assets due to the changing climate.

The Climate READi framework will facilitate analysis and application of appropriate climate data among all stakeholders to enhance the planning, design, and operation of a resilient power system, providing a broadly accepted common framework, a collaborative approach to driving stakeholder alignment and a consistent approach for power system stakeholders to apply climate-related information, including extreme weather and localized climate data trends and projections at the asset level, with guidance for specific asset/system vulnerability analyses.

Mark Fronmuller, Ameren's Senior Vice President for Strategy, Innovation, Sustainability, and Risk, provided his thoughts on how Ameren's focus on critical technologies brings benefits to customers and to society:

Our innovation is guided by the Ameren vision—leading the way to a sustainable energy future—which rests on four pillars: environmental stewardship, social impact, governance, and sustainable growth. We are driving environmental stewardship forward with efforts like the DC fast-charging projects, coupled with large stationary batteries. This allows us to reduce the impact of DC fast chargers on our distribution circuits. We are also making a social impact through our St. Louis Vehicle Electrification Rides for Seniors program and Diversity, Equity, and Inclusion Accelerator, which provide direct support to disadvantaged communities in our service territory. We are enhancing our governance process by working with our peers in EEI and AGA to develop even more robust and consistent ESG disclosures. And we are driving sustainable growth through projects like the fiber infrastructure project, which potentially provides infrastructure for growth in all communities.[21]

Ameren's commitment to the pursuit of innovation as a means to deliver meaningful benefits to customers focuses on projects that provide immediate results, as well as emerging technologies that have the opportunity to reshape the energy delivery landscape in the future. Its orientation to bringing innovative technology to bear for strategic, operational, and customer advancement provides a foundation for meeting the challenges of industry evolution.

GOVERNANCE AND STRATEGY

In the early years of its innovation effort, Ameren adopted a structured model for leadership and oversight. This model leveraged a senior executive sponsor, targeted teams, and defined processes with oversight from the executive leadership team.

The early emphasis on innovation was initially led from the top—the chief executive officer and the chief financial officer (who were the sponsoring officers). From a governance perspective, the overall effort was initially overseen by an Innovation Steering Committee (ISC) that reported to the executive leadership team of the company. The ISC was composed of officers and directors from across the business. Each officer took a personal interest in leading enterprise messaging, targeted initiatives surrounding innovation within the company, and was visible in the stand-up of the effort.

Over time, the decision-making for specific projects was moved to the segments, yet still with leadership from the senior executive sponsor and oversight by the executive leader of the segment and the executive leadership team, as appropriate.

At present, the senior vice president responsible for strategy, innovation, sustainability, and risk leads the centralized innovation effort, with cross-segment advisors at multiple levels from within the Ameren organization and a formal team of two to three full-time resources (with four additional full-time resources dedicated to capital projects related to field technology deployment). However, the Ameren executive leadership team retains overall innovation oversight.

The company has continually evolved its strategy for innovation and its cornerstones for conceptualization, execution, and attainment. Like many utilities, it links innovation to customer benefits and growth, emphasizes collaboration among employees, and embeds innovation into its cultural fabric (see Figure 22).

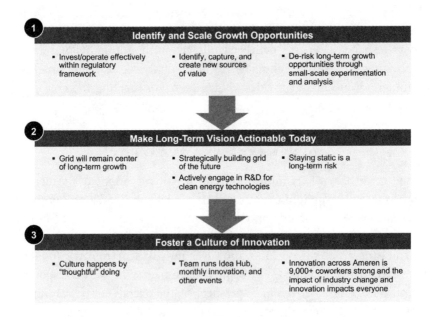

Figure 22. Innovation strategy core elements.

(Source: Data from Ameren, "2021 Annual Report: Fostering a Culture of Innovation," internal document.)

Ameren's innovation success is grounded in a strong corporate culture that can rapidly adapt to change. Another element of this culture is the willingness to constantly learn from its actions and results.

Warner Baxter shared several lessons learned that would benefit other companies that are still at more formative stages of their innovation thinking:

> Successful innovation must reflect strong senior leadership alignment—about purpose, priorities, and outcomes—which are fundamental to effective ideation and execution. Successful innovation also requires a solid governance structure and rigor behind R&D and innovation efforts. However, perhaps the most important thing that must be done is for senior leaders to engage with and consistently communicate to their coworkers that it is safe to innovate, and thereby create a culture of continuous improvement to create value for our customers and other stakeholders. At the end of the day, successful innovation is not a "corporate activity" done by a select few. Instead, successful innovation is a "we thing" that is driven by all coworkers.[22]

Unlike many peer companies that have been pursuing formal innovation efforts, in 2015 Ameren purposefully adopted a philosophy of recognizing innovation within its formal short- and long-term incentive plans. While not a specific and separate measure, the company adopts individual modifiers to the incentive framework to recognize that innovation projects are recognized for their accomplishment. This linking of management and employee incentives to innovation outcomes demonstrates the commitment of the company to actual accomplishments and reinforces its past messaging about the importance and value of innovation to business evolution and customer benefit.

As the company now moves into its eighth year of innovation pursuit, it continues to pursue a broadening agenda and build an increasingly visible persona with its customers, communities, start-up investments, and industry R&D organizations. The focus on low-carbon technologies and digitalization is a good example of where the company is actively engaging in evaluating a frontier technology with the potential to create a vibrant new energy carrier system and adopting more creative ways to think about utility performance delivery and value outcomes to customers.

Ameren continually seeks to advance the contribution from continuous ideation and idea conversion into a viable product for adoption within the business or with customers. Its focus continues to expand and evolve, combining a strong commitment to local start-up development and community purpose, as well as maintaining a larger-scale contribution to the broader national agenda for addressing decarbonization.

Avista

Avista is a combination electric and gas utility headquartered in Spokane, Washington, serving more than 700,000 customers in Washington, Oregon, Idaho, and Alaska. Since it was founded in 1889, the company has a rich history of innovation that spans more than 130 years and crosses all segments of the utility value chain.

Beginning in the 1970s, it became an active investor in technology-based start-ups, including what came to be known as Itron in the metering space, as well as ReliOn (previously Avista Labs), which was an early developer of fuel cell technology. It also launched competitive businesses in energy trading and marketing (Avista Energy), energy services and management (Ecova), fiber and telecommunications (Avista Fiber and Avista Communications), broadband communications (Avista Edge), and digital-enabled efficient buildings (Edo), as well as other financing and real-estate-oriented ventures.[23]

The Avista Energy, Ecova, Avista Labs, Avista Fiber, and Avista Communications businesses have been divested or dissolved, while Avista Edge is piloting broadband technology services to regional customers, Edo has started serving customer facilities outside the Avista service territory, and the financing entity and some of the real estate holdings remain. While Avista has monetized or disposed of most of its early investments, it remains active with start-ups and new technologies through its continued participation in two established venture capital funds, as well as its Mind to Market venture fund, its Start-Up Avista incubation hub, and its support of the Ignite Northwest community incubator.[24]

INNOVATION PLATFORMS

Compared to its peers, these prior innovative investment experiences are unique for a company the size of Avista, and it punches well above its weight with respect to innovation. The company likes to say that "innovation is in our DNA," as reflected by its long-standing history of activity and accomplishment.

But even more impressive is how early Avista committed to and invested in real innovation in disruptive technologies, far exceeding the imagination, scope, and commitment of its contemporary peers. Avista has been intentionally investing in innovation by committing internal employee resources and management focus for decades.

Avista has a long history of establishing new businesses across a wide range of operating areas, with some starting as investments in competitive entities, some as acquisitions, and others as unique stand-up subsidiaries. And some of these prior competitive businesses came to lead providers of products and services in their category after the company nurtured and developed them.

Many U.S. utilities, including Avista, opened energy trading and marketing businesses, but Avista also took a broader approach to developing consumer-oriented services, particularly in adjacent sectors—energy services and telecommunications—where its current or addressable customers could also benefit from technology deployment.

The early and most recent start-up businesses include the following (see Figure 23):[25]

- *Itron:* An early investment in 1977, this entity became the largest utility metering company in the United States and was eventually taken public in 1993.

- *Avista Development:* This non-utility subsidiary was formed in 1989 to invest in local real estate, businesses, and other assets that enhance the economic vitality of Avista's utility service areas.

- *Avista Labs (ReliOn):* This technology development center was created in 1996 to develop hydrogen fuel cells and subsequently sold to Plug Power in 2014.

- *Avista Advantage (Ecova):* Founded in 1996, it became the largest utility energy demand, billing services, and sustainability entity in the United States, before being sold to GdF Suez (now Engie) in 2014.

- *Avista Energy:* This business formed in 1997 to perform energy trading and marketing activities and subsequently sold to Shell North America in 2007.

- *Avista Fiber:* Incorporated in 1996, this subsidiary operated for approximately 10 years to provide metropolitan-area fiber optic network services to business customers in the Inland Northwest.

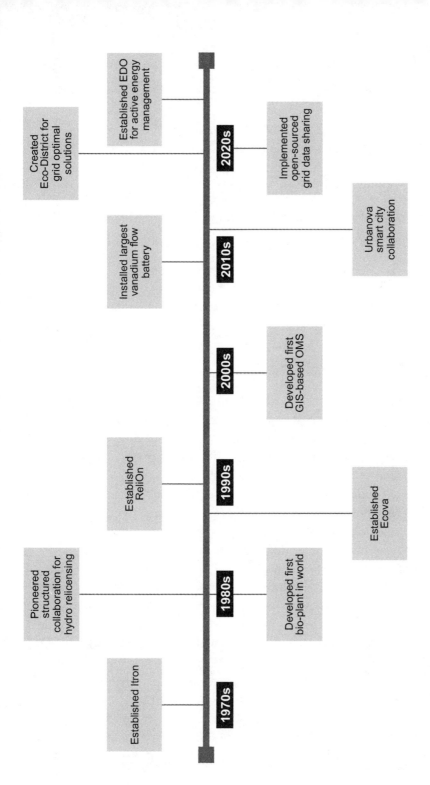

Figure 23. Modern–era first-of-a-kind innovation.

(Source: Avista, "Avista's History of Innovation," March 2022.)

- *Avista Communications:* This competitive local exchange carrier provided high-speed fiber-based services in small Pacific Northwest communities from 1995 until its dissolution in 2005.

- *Avista Edge:* Based on employee ideas, it provides internet and broadband services to municipalities, cooperatives, public utility districts, and internet service provider customers in rural areas.

- *Edo:* This expert active energy management business leverages its grid-integrated technology stack with building controls and renewable generation.

The Eco-District that powers Catalyst and the Scott Morris Center for Energy Innovation (Morris Center for Innovation) is unique in how the utility partners with building owners and managers. It collaborates with these managers to operate buildings in a grid-friendly manner, making the best use of the existing grid and avoiding costly capital construction, and ultimately making energy more affordable. Edo takes this Eco-District concept and replicates the model with others.

Since the majority of generated energy is used to operate commercial buildings, this sector holds significant opportunities to gain a deeper understanding of how the underlying building energy system is designed, operated, and consumes energy. By unlocking and analyzing a building's performance, operation, and consumption, Edo can implement energy efficiency measures to operate buildings more efficiently and, at the same time, understand how commercial buildings interact with the grid to leverage existing resources.

Avista's early investment in emerging technology companies (Itron), internal technology entities (Avista Labs), energy service and management entities (Ecova), high-speed broadband and internet service providers (Avista Fiber, Avista Communications, and Avista Edge), and facilities data analytics for active energy management (Edo) provides insight into adjacent technology and customer markets, as well as into specific technologies (meters, fuel cells, telecommunications, and shared energy) that could be deployed as part of a portfolio of utility and related competitive services.

Beyond these investment-oriented activities performed throughout the company, Avista has a rich experience in industry-leading R&D and innovation. Even in the early days of the company, it was recognized for its innovative nature and accomplishment, dating back to early in the 20th century, when the company constructed the longest transmission line in the world, the largest dam and generator in the world, temperature control for an electric range, and the electric water heater. Some of its more contemporary FOAK accomplishments in the industry include the following:[26]

- *Biomass plant:* In 1983 Avista opened this utility-owned electric generating station, which was constructed for the sole purpose of producing electricity from wood waste or biomass for use within its generating system and was an early user of renewables technologies.

- *Energy efficiency tariff:* In 1995 the company pioneered the first public benefit system surcharge (tariff) for energy efficiency, which went on to become the predominant model for energy efficiency programs across the nation.

- *Client server customer information system:* The company created the first modern customer information system at a utility in 1991, utilizing a user interface on a personal computer that enabled users to easily access and interact with information more quickly through drop-down menus.

- *Geographical information systems (GIS)–based operations management system (OMS):* Avista built and deployed the first GIS-based OMS in the industry between 1999 and 2001 to extensively model the company's electric and natural gas network, facilitating editing, design, and outage management system capabilities.

- *Urbanova:* This smart city collaborative is a unique public-private partnership experience, where the company was a prime mover behind its development and provided an early showcase in 2014 for driving innovation within the city of Spokane.

- *Vanadium-flow battery:* The company installed the largest battery storage capability of its type in North America (and Europe) in 2015, which became a test bed for this technology and an illustration of how scalability could be advanced.

- *Hydro plant relicensing:* Avista pioneered a novel approach for its time, engaging multiple stakeholders and interested parties in a collaborative-based model to secure a relicensing agreement from FERC in 1999.

- *Eco-District:* Avista was a prime mover behind the concept, design, and funding of this collaborative model, where the utilities and building owners and operators communicate across the meter and partner to create grid-optimal solutions.

- *Digital data exchange:* Leveraging smart city work at Urbanova and the Eco-District integrated simulator, an open-source data sharing structure was created in 2021 for utilities, vendors, academia, researchers, and labs to allow grid data sharing among collaborative partners.

- *EV charging:* The company was the first utility to conduct commission-authorized field testing of the full anticipated range of charging infrastructure in a pilot (i.e., level 1 residential, level 2 public, workforce, level 2 employer, and level 3 public).

Avista adopts a very straightforward definition of what innovation means to it—that is, turning observed market, customer, and operating opportunities into thoughtful ideas that can evolve into real solutions that provide compelling value to customers. This definition, similar to those of other peers in the industry, is underpinned by a simple philosophy that guides the company's approach to innovation—it should be directly linked to solving customer problems and enhancing the value of the customer relationship.

When Avista sold Ecova, it also lost the financial contribution from this business. It was then faced with the need to replace that contribution in the near term while maintaining a governor on the level of competitive business earnings in the range of 10 percent. This event was a catalyst for additional emphasis on innovation and leaning on the inherent capacity to develop new ideas to overcome this gap.

When asked about what drives Avista to be so engaged in innovation, Scott Morris, Chairman and retired CEO of the company, explained:

When you're a small company, you need to think about unique ways to grow, add value to customers, and potentially even create a new business. That means we need to think about ourselves differently and build a constant flow of ideas to provide a foundation for innovation and perhaps find the next Ecova. But having plenty of ideas to choose from also requires the courage to strategically invest and to have patient capital to allow an idea to mature. To succeed, we continuously need to inspire our employees and exercise our innovation muscles. Good ideas are a hallmark of our employees and part of our DNA, but it takes a little evangelizing and commitment to continuously improve how we work.[27]

During this same time frame, Avista was also recognizing that its external environment was changing and that the company would have to quickly adapt, improve its agility, increase its sense of urgency, and adopt a heightened level of customer focus to be successful in the future. It also meant that it would need to *think* differently to be able to *serve* customers differently. To help instill this concept, in 2014 Avista implemented a theme of "how might we," which is shorthand for stimulating how the company could reshape its fundamental thinking about solving the strategic, operational, customer, and financial challenges to serve customers differently and capture available opportunities during an era of rapid disruption.[28]

Avista adopted the concept of design thinking, which was intended to change how problem-solving occurred by starting with unmet customer needs, designing an initial prototype response, and then finalizing a tailored solution. To help engage employees and instill design thinking and a how-might-we approach to their work, the company introduced a mobile "innovation box." This box provided a creative way to encourage employees to bring ideas forward that "put the customer at the center" and focused on the customer impact as they worked to solve a problem. The box provided a visual metaphor to reinforce the concept of clear and directed thinking, simplicity, and compelling justification.[29]

To further instill this how-might-we mindset, Avista established an Innovation Workgroup (IWG) in 2014 to more formally focus on developing good ideas through employee collaboration. Instead of being led from the top levels of the organization, this was an organic group focused on all technologies and the differences they could make on the operating system and to the customers the company served.

The IWG conducted recurring employee meetings to increase awareness, solicit ideas, and communicate about the market changes it was monitoring. It also developed strategies, models, technology road maps, and action plans to guide ongoing and future efforts. In parallel, an Innovation Council was established, composed of cross-discipline and functional resources to provide additional input, expertise, and perspective to the IWG effort.

With smart city initiatives underway in large cities across the country, Avista wanted to test smart city technologies in a midsize city setting. In 2014 the company was a key driver and founding partner in Spokane's smart city initiative that later became known as Urbanova. This initiative was a collaborative arrangement with five partners—Avista, Itron, the City of Spokane, Washington State University, and the University District—to create a smart city technology proving ground.[30]

These entities worked to develop a "living laboratory" for future smart city design and adoption. Three projects were chartered for initial adoption: a smart city research grant (air quality), a smart and connected streetlighting pilot (LED fixtures and sensor packages), and a shared energy economy model (customer-shared assets and resources). This latter project—and the concepts it embraced—became a forerunner for what eventually became a foundational element of the Morris Center for Innovation, the Eco-District, and Edo.

While Avista is proud that innovation is part of its core DNA, it knows that relying on what made it successful in the past is not likely to be sufficient to secure its future success. It would need to make a step change to elevate its innovation game and build on its embedded DNA by "spreading the genes" beyond its existing internal core to like-minded entities and resources within its stakeholders—new employees, customers, vendors, and regulators—as each is a vital participant in the innovation process.

To further instill the innovation mindset across the organization, the IWG evolved into the Innovation Station. This group is staffed with about 20 Avista employees who volunteer to nurture ideas at early stages of their development cycle. The group generates ideas; teaches skills in design thinking, lean business canvas, and advocacy for inventors; and has facilitated several "pitch jams" for start-ups to prototype potential investment by Avista or other venture capital funds. All these activities help integrate the innovation mindset that permeates Avista.[31]

The Innovation Station is intended to reinforce a culture of innovation within Avista, encourage creative customer-centric solutions, provide a forum for fostering innovation, provide guidance and resource coordination internally and to start-ups, and contribute to the continued performance of the business. The Innovation Station also may subsequently provide very early-stage funding for Start-Up Avista events for ideas that emerge from the efforts of employees who work with and through this innovation group.[32]

To affirm its enterprise intent, in 2018 Avista developed four areas of corporate focus—people, customers, perform, and invent—to drive its purpose and emphasis as an enterprise. The invent focus area reflects a consistent objective to emphasize continuous innovation—and the generation of new business ideas that will enable readiness for tomorrow—through internal mechanisms and interactions, as well as through external engagement with stakeholders, partners, and customers. Like the other three focus areas, execution in the invent area incorporates four additional, critical actionable items to further drive achieving performance and expected results.

The invent focus prioritizes and reinforces Avista's commitment to sustained innovation within the business to improve competitive position in its various markets; enhance the capability, resiliency, and value of the network to the business; and anticipate and satisfy the emerging needs of customers, whether price affordability, service quality, grid and network performance, and/or regulatory policy. Taken together, these outcomes produce the return on innovation investment and set the stage for further value realization.

A CATALYST FOR SPOKANE

One of the most innovative undertakings Avista can point to in its rich history of innovation is the South Landing Project, which currently incorporates two distinct elements: the Catalyst building and the Morris Center for Innovation, which houses the Central Plant for the Eco-District that provides energy to these current facilities as well as future development.

This integrated development was the vision and brainchild of then CEO and Chairman of Avista Scott Morris and was partly a labor of love to enhance community and economic vitality—a desire to create a higher education immersive experience, help entrepreneurs develop their businesses, create an opportunity for energy companies to test their technologies on a simulated Avista grid, and showcase the future of shared energy in the region via this next living laboratory of innovative ideas, concepts, technologies, and integrated buildings.

Back around 2000, Avista and Morris played an instrumental role in creating and intentionally developing an area adjacent to downtown Spokane called the University District. Today, the University District has evolved into the city's innovation sector and is home to Spokane's smart city initiative Urbanova, six universities, and two medical schools. Yet growth in the University District had reached a plateau. So, when Avista learned that the company owned the property where a new pedestrian bridge would land, it was a natural incentive for the next phase of development, and it provided a unique opportunity to create something extraordinary.

Morris had a bold vision to create what he called the "five smartest blocks in the world." He wanted to create a space that was more than where smart city meets smart grid meets smart building innovations. The project would demonstrate the possibilities to integrate economic vitality, regional sustainability, and energy efficiency for multipurpose use in a single setting.[33]

As the company advanced its thinking on the potential benefits and outcomes of the Eco-District, it expanded its vision about the project and developed a more vibrant articulation of what could be created—the "five smartest blocks in the world." Within the footprint of Catalyst and the Eco-District, the integration of multiple technologies meant that current and future buildings, businesses, and customers would benefit from technology that could be deployed in a tailored manner that optimizes energy management, energy production, grid performance, asset productivity, and customer consciousness.

The vision extends beyond a simple redevelopment or revitalization effort, and Catalyst became the first-ever large-scale commercial building constructed from cross-laminated timber. Catalyst reduces the carbon footprint of traditional concrete and steel through integration with sustainable, efficient systems and architecture.

Avista would also develop and enable—in collaboration with several other partners with different expertise—a unique market offering called the shared energy economy. The finished product demonstrates how a utility can partner with building owners and operators to design, build, and actively manage a grid-integrated efficient building to help make energy more affordable for customers and the entire community.

The project would develop an innovation lab and collaboration center and create a connected Eco-District of buildings for energy sharing generation, utilization, and storage through installation of rooftop solar panels, storage, and other equipment, as well as leverage carbon-free technologies, digital grid, distributed resources, and adaptable digital devices. Integrating these features enables bilateral transactive energy activities to occur among the tenants, reduces adverse impacts on the grid, and enhances grid optimization. Plus, it would be funded through public financing and a nonregulated Avista entity, rather than by customers.[34]

The financing of the concept matured over time and resulted in a mix of public and private sources, including monies made available from passage of a state of Washington transportation bill in 2015, as well as other funds made available through the University District Public Development Authority, with direct funding from Avista. The combination of these funding sources laid the foundation for Avista's objectives, as well as demonstrated that Catalyst, the Morris Center for Innovation, and the Eco-District would serve to advance broad economic development objectives shared by Avista, the City of Spokane, and various colleges and universities proximate to the University District, thus creating a vibrant and successful public-private partnership.[35]

Using the earlier mentioned how-might-we theme, combined with a perpetually inquisitive mindset in place to start with, the company asked itself several key questions centered on what it could do to invent a different type of energy model for customers that was driven by environmental leadership, as well as the concept of energy sharing among customers. It thus asked itself:[36]

- Could we create a non-wired substation for less cost and higher benefit?

- Could we use an asset-based strategy and our University District investment to assist in redeveloping a red-light district in the heart of our city?

- Could we leverage the grid to meet needs for reliability while testing innovative solutions?

- Could we balance delivering reliable, clean energy at the most affordable cost to customers?

- Could we partner with building owners and operators in a manner that leverages the existing grid, maximizes the building's efficiency, and keeps the building's occupants comfortable?

These questions illustrate the nature and range of innovative precepts that were adopted and integrated from the start as Catalyst and the Morris Center for Innovation were designed and built from the ground up to interact with each other and the grid. This innovative mindset resulted in an entirely new transformative model for sustainable developments that demonstrated how environmental, energy, sustainability, and technology objectives could be integrated for the benefit of both the community and customers.

The company built on lessons learned while implementing the three American Recovery and Reinvestment Act (ARRA) grants it received in 2012 and other grid modernization projects that had also been completed. This collective experience provided insight into integrating customer benefits into designing and planning the Eco-District. For example, to scale and optimize technology, key elements of the Eco-District could be bundled—the Central Plant, installed technologies, grid integration and optimization, shared energy, partnering advantages, and data sharing.

The Central Plant includes centralized heating and cooling, electrical systems, rooftop solar, and storage that can be scaled to handle the requirements of the full Eco-District as the area is built out. Catalyst and the Morris Center for Innovation were completed amid the COVID-19 pandemic, and the Eco-District systems operated as expected, despite lower occupancy levels in both buildings.

While the Eco-District and the shared energy economy delivered on the initial promise of the Catalyst concept, it was recognized that even broader economies of scope could be realized when the full features of the Eco-District could be integrated, and layers of value could be captured by stacking use cases on one another to build a larger integrated value than the pure sum of the parts. In essence, the grid-integrated simulator allowed the Eco-District to operationalize the underlying technologies in a unique manner. The result was the creation of a new nonregulated, non-utility business called Edo so that other utilities can benefit from what Avista is learning.[37]

Scott Morris provided additional insight into how Catalyst, the Morris Center for Innovation, and the Eco-District came together:

I believed that simply relying on renewables for decarbonization was not enough to meet the country's needs and our industry's commitments. We had tremendous early success with smart cities and learned a lot about how to think about integrating technologies, buildings, and communications to achieve broader goals. We strategically recruited the right partners to help us and fortunately found [architect/design company] McKinstry, which was willing to think beyond the simple design concept of a "green" building and think about when energy is used and how that impacts peak demand and energy loads. We pushed them to design a building from the ground up, with innovative systems that would allow the utility to partner with building owners and operators to actively manage energy in a manner that maximized the building's energy efficiency, made the best use of the existing grid, and enabled load control, energy sharing, transactive energy, and energy affordability for our customers, all within a net-zero carbon footprint. No one had done this before.[38]

What started with a bold vision to create the "five smartest blocks in the world" resulted in unique and transformative outcomes (see Figure 24). It began with physical property (the South Landing), enabled a concept and a building (Catalyst), evolved to an innovation and collaboration center and a physical Central Plant (the Morris Center for Innovation), leveraged a new energy model (the shared energy economy), established an inclusive and integrated market area (the Eco-District), and created a new go-to-market business (Edo). The birth of an idea quickly evolved to a different way of thinking about addressing decarbonization goals—that is, leveraging non-wire solutions to achieve net-zero carbon emissions.

At present, the vision to create the "five smartest blocks in the world" has become a reality—the foundation is in place now that Catalyst, the Morris Center for Innovation, and the Eco-District have been completed. Avista is just beginning to pursue the next chapter of the "five smartest blocks in the world" and assessing exactly what next steps it will take to build out and complete the original concept.

The intent is to take the next step in increasing the value of the development by expanding the parties that take advantage of its presence (i.e., capitalizing on the natural industry clusters that exist in Spokane in health, higher education, and energy). This close presence provides an opportunity to bring them into a more active presence and relationship, as well as leverage the capabilities that Edo can provide at the nexus of energy delivery and the utilization of energy for health care and learning facilities.

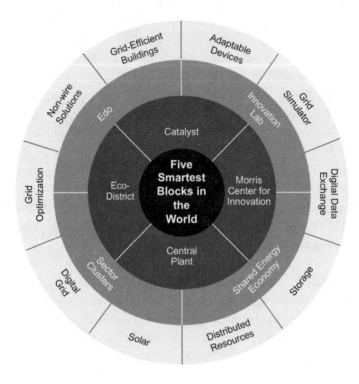

Figure 24. The innovation ecosystem.

An energy cluster is already taking shape within Avista's Energy Innovation Lab—it leverages the region's leadership in energy. The lab is located within 100 miles of leading research institutions like Pacific Northwest National Laboratory, Washington State University, and the University of Idaho, along with higher education institutions Gonzaga University and Eastern Washington State University. The region is also home to several energy industry leaders, including Schweitzer Engineering Laboratories, Itron, Engie, and McKinstry.

Avista's Energy Innovation Lab is in a unique position to bring together some of the brightest minds in the energy industry to address clean energy transformation challenges and evolve concepts into FOAK grid deployments. Avista sees this as an opportunity to scale this regional competency and develop energy thought leadership that will benefit the entire industry.

Today, it is obvious that Catalyst, the Morris Center for Innovation, and the Eco-District created a larger impact than originally conceived. There is a compounding effect when you recognize the total impact on the community and economic vitality from its development and stand-up. First, it resulted in two foundational buildings (a showcase) to drive further development. Second, it proved out the viability of the building materials, which supports further development. Third, it created new manufacturing facilities in the Spokane area, which enabled a ripple effect in new job creation. And fourth, it proved out the value from the simulator in providing a powerful tool for grid analysis, problem identification, and solution development.

Three elements that influence how the Eco-District participates are the experience obtained from the ARRA grant smart grid efforts, the current Clean Energy Fund work, and the DOE's Connected Communities grant. These current initiatives create learnings that further enable how the Eco-District formulates its market positioning and approach to energy sharing.

The specific capabilities of the grid-integrated simulator in the Morris Center for Innovation provides a valuable business tool for Avista's Energy Innovation Lab to conduct segment cluster analysis and load profiling to understand grid performance and provide solutions to observed conditions. These analyses can then be turned into distributed solutions that provide value to customers related to loads, patterns, and impacts. These outcomes help Avista fast-track innovation and accelerate its ability to test new ideas and then deploy them with confidence at utility scale to create game-changing outcomes.

Avista seeks to encourage, identify, and accomplish innovation at different levels. It is content with small innovation, like developing more energy efficiency programs and providing pool EVs to employees to drive for a week to become familiar with vehicle quality and performance. It also pursues large-scale innovation, like the Eco-District, and creating sector clusters, like the Spokane University District, with two new medical schools that have unique energy requirements. As a result of establishing these medical schools, Spokane now has more medical students than Seattle—leading to vibrant higher education and health-care sectors with large, complex, and demanding energy requirements that necessitate innovative ways to serve.

Avista invests in start-ups through three primary conduits: independent energy venture capital funds such as EIP and Energy Capital Ventures (ECV); direct investment in early-stage companies; and investment in internal ideas, generally incubated through Start-Up Avista events. The company was one of the earliest members of EIP, joining its original Flagship Fund in 2015, as well as its second Flagship Fund and its deep decarbonization-focused Frontier Fund. These funds have invested in more than 100 start-ups, with several already monetized.

EIP is the largest globally focused utility venture capital fund, with more than $3 billion in assets under management. The firm focuses on start-ups that are driving the cleantech transition, particularly as it relates to electrification, decarbonization, digitalization, and customer-centric technologies. While Avista was one of the initial 16 companies in the first fund as it sought to reduce exploration risk, there are now more than 50 partners in the EIP family of funds.

Avista initiated its second venture capital fund relationship in 2021, with ECV's utility focus exclusively on LDCs and attention directed toward companies emphasizing ESG imperatives and digital transformation of the industry in support of the clean energy transition. ECV seeks to identify, nurture, and grow businesses that center their R&D, innovation, and software and hardware on providing solutions to gas operations, renewable gas, hydrogen, and methane emissions, among other areas. Avista is part of an ECV member group that includes Black Hills Energy, NiSource, Eversource, National Fuel Gas, Southwest Gas, and Spire.[39]

The company has also created a pre-seed fund and incubator—Mind to Market—to provide pre-seed funding to very early-stage start-ups to create a minimally viable product that can prepare the start-up for traditional seed financing. Avista provides guidance and funding to start-ups in the region through support of Ignite Northwest that enable these companies to advance their development and lead toward commerciality.

These venture capital relationships provide a "force extender" for Avista in the start-up market and with technology evolution in general. These entities offer Avista expanded insight into technology trends, market adoption of technologies, and performance experience of specific technologies. Through EIP and ECV, opportunities emerge for the company to test and pilot potential technologies and serve to support broader transformation in the industry.

Through its Avista Development direct venture investments, the company advises and invests in early-stage businesses. While there have been numerous prior investments and monetization by Avista Development, several are currently active in the investment portfolio:[40]

- *Safeguard Equipment:* This entity focuses on personnel safety for utility field workers by providing them with personal detectors that can assess and warn of electrical dangers.

- *LevelTen Energy:* A focus on the clean energy marketplace is found through this entity, which provides a platform for commercial and industrial customers to procure renewable energy.

- *Rohinni:* This company transforms mini- and micro-LEDs through the use of new precision placement solutions for applications such as lighting and displays.

- *Open Energy Solutions:* This entity is building an open-source platform for utility operations that enhances interoperability of grid devices.

- *Edo:* This joint venture entity with McKinstry designs and develops buildings that can provide on-site clean energy, integrate with a local smart grid, and create grid interactive efficiency.

Edo represents a unique business opportunity for Avista as it seeks to replicate its Eco-District approach in other communities interested in blending net-zero carbon technologies with multipurpose buildings, along with grid integration and optimization, to provide a seamless model for accomplishing environmental, operational, economic development, and affordable pricing goals for communities and customers.

INNOVATION CULTURE

Avista's long history of thoughtful, purposeful, collaborative, and valuable actions has enabled it to continually sharpen its overall vision and mission about the role it seeks to project with respect to the environment and its customers. This continuous refinement of its purpose has led to a restatement of its core underlying enterprise values, with three principal values underpinning the business and the way it engages with its stakeholders—it is trustworthy, collaborative, and innovative. The notion of including innovation as a corporate value is generally left unsaid by U.S. utilities, even though most companies describe themselves as embracing innovation as a table stake to meet the challenges of the cleantech transition.

Avista CEO Dennis Vermillion commented on how he viewed the way in which the culture of innovation has developed at the company:

> We have had a long, rich history of innovation. It's amazing what we've been able to achieve through the years by intentionally taking actions and driving initiatives that have allowed us to strategically evolve our business. We encourage and recognize everyday innovation as a permanent part of our mindset—it is a capability that we practice and build every day. By constantly focusing on the value of innovation and asking how might we find better ways to accomplish our work, we keep innovation front and center for our employees. This creates a community of innovation both inside and outside of Avista so that we're better equipped to successfully meet the challenges our industry faces today and in the future.[41]

To reinforce its interest and focus on innovation, the Avista board of directors challenged the company in 2019 to consider and structure how to design innovation into its formal short-term incentive plan. Since the board viewed that Avista had become quite adept and continuously active in innovation, and "invent" was a formal corporate focus area and strategic objective for the business, why not find a way to incorporate a measure of performance in this area, just as traditionally done in other operating and financial dimensions of the business?[42]

And to help fulfill its commitment to sustained innovation, Avista recently developed and incorporated innovation into executive team incentives. This action signals the level of corporate and executive responsibility for the advancement of innovation throughout the enterprise and indicates the level of importance Avista places on its intent to continuously innovate.

Avista focuses more on impact to customers than receiving accolades or developing intellectual property, particularly since it focuses so intently on partnering, collaboration, and information and data sharing. However, while not an intentional objective of the company (a result of the various initiatives it has undertaken and the emphasis on innovation throughout the business since 2014), Avista has experienced a sharp increase in issued patents for technologies and applications it has developed.

The company is intentional about continuing and enhancing its innovation prowess with a willingness to challenge historical practices, eliminate friction in customer engagement, create solutions that provide meaningful impacts to customers, and further embed its culture of innovation within the business.

The Catalyst building, adjacent to the Morris Center for Innovation, and the Eco-District's shared energy model are major foundational elements of Avista's future—not just as a complex of grid-enabled efficient buildings but as a centerpiece that can be leveraged to establish an entirely different model for utility community engagement (i.e., the shared energy economy), to enable the development of new grid-related services, to enhance the value of the grid, and to increase community and economic vitality.

The transformational development is a testament that more than 130 years after Avista was founded, innovation continues to be an enduring value that still thrives with intention, helps the business navigate the constantly changing utility landscape, and positions Avista to evolve to successfully meet the challenges the future brings.

Duke Energy

Duke Energy is a combination electric and gas utility headquartered in Charlotte, North Carolina, serving more than nine million customers across the states of North Carolina, South Carolina, Florida, Ohio, Kentucky, and Indiana. It is the second largest U.S. utility by market capitalization, with more than $80 billion in equity valuation.[43]

Beyond its regulated operating companies, it also is involved with several nonregulated asset-, solutions-, or services-based businesses that target renewables, mobility, sustainability, consulting services, and energy product processing opportunities, inside and outside the Duke Energy service territory.

The company also participates in a corporate venture capital effort and partners with EIP and The Westly Group (Westly) to invest in, learn from, and nurture communications with energy-related start-ups.[44]

Duke Energy is a highly visible corporate entity and has a long-standing reputation for leadership across a vast range of industry issues. It has focused on preparedness for market evolution since the 1990s and has been at the forefront of utilities sector technology adoption across its integrated value chain for decades. By 1996, the company was the first utility to have won the Edison Award three times for its contributions to the industry, particularly around technology innovation.[45]

Over its almost 120-year existence, the company has observed shifts in generation sources, environmental attitudes, technology advances, regulatory policies, and customer behaviors. But today, it is experiencing simultaneous changes in all these areas, and these shifts are leading the company toward a different composition of future assets, as well as an elevated purpose and role for the utility and its relationship with customers.

TECHNOLOGY ASSESSMENT

As one of the largest U.S. utilities, the company maintained an early R&D organization within the enterprise. This organization can be traced back to approximately 1960, focusing on generation, transmission, and distribution. This organization stayed in place until the mid-1990s, when industry events changed corporate priorities and resulted in these capabilities being distributed within the business.[46]

But even before this R&D organization appears to have formally existed, the company was innovating in unique ways. In 1949 the company installed its first microwave system for communications and control, beating Southern Bell by a year. In 1950 the company created a truck-mounted mobile generation source for use in remote areas. And in 1958 it created the first multicompany nuclear consortium to build a demonstration plant in South Carolina.[47]

In 2007 an Emerging Technology Office (ETO) was established within Duke Energy to help the organization achieve its overarching goals to maintain an industry-leading strategic and operating position. The genesis of the stand-up of the ETO was the recognition by the then CEO (Jim Rogers) that the future would require an advanced view of how technology would serve to enable the grid of the future, particularly how the network architecture would be configured and enable enhanced control over this collection of assets and devices to increase the value of the network.

The then CEO had chartered the ETO to look over the horizon to identify future technology challenges that could disrupt the business and develop a strategic response to these factors. The ETO was intended to support the company's strategy for effectively preserving and enhancing its competitive market position. The stand-up of the ETO was believed important to Duke Energy's future, as technology availability and performance were dramatically changing the generation supply and delivery landscape and customer requirements and preferences.

The intent was to stand up an internal organization that would anticipate and prepare for emergent threats and opportunities that could alter the company's business model, approach to operations, interfaces with customers and stakeholders, and priorities for action. The organization would focus on understanding external drivers and assessing how new technologies could fit into Duke Energy's future and how soon.

With this framework in mind, the company could assess multiple technologies simultaneously, knowing that some would be eliminated from consideration, while others would receive close attention because of their accelerating maturity, and others could be regularly monitored since their evolution and economic parity could take several years to unfold.

The ETO is a multidisciplined organization dedicated to coordinate technology evaluations across Duke Energy and was not intended to function as a stand-alone gatekeeper within the business. Rather, it was intended to act as a center of expertise that would anticipate new technology availability and lead technology evaluations and deployment readiness, leveraging business subject matter experts (SMEs) for technical assistance, since the range of technologies was broad to track, evaluate, and demonstrate. The ETO collaborated with DOE ARPA-E and other institutions to stretch its access to technical expertise that could be applied to technology assessment.

Duke Energy also created the Envision Center in northern Kentucky, a 10,000-square-foot facility that opened in 2008, providing a demonstration center for the smart grid, complete with a smart home, solar panels, and EV charging—which was well ahead of its time for an integrated display of smart-grid-related technologies by a utility.

At the time of its initial stand-up, the ETO was focused on potential technologies on the radar in 2007, including clean combustion, capacitor banks, energy efficiency, smart grids, demand response, EVs, broadband over power lines, and advanced nuclear (including SMRs).[48]

By 2014, the ETO's scope of assessment continued to include the above technologies, as well as expanding to energy storage, renewables, microgrids, water efficiency, and distributed generation, and was actively working with OEMs, vendors, and solutions providers. For the technologies it tracked and evaluated, the ETO developed technology road maps and potential timelines for introduction, with three defined value and developmental periods: commercial readiness (1 to 3 years), extended testing (3 to 5 years), and technology investigation (5 to 10 years or more).[49]

By 2022, the ETO had progressed to the point where it was tracking dozens of emerging technologies and applications and actively involved with dozens of start-up companies in either identifying emerging technologies, tracking technology readiness, evaluating application performance, investing in commercial readiness, and/or partnering for adoption.

As expected, today's broad industry technology agenda and distribution of effort reflect accelerating retirements to the generation fleet and emerging technologies where near-term deployment is possible and value can be added to the grid and customers. Thus, technology evaluation and deployment within the ETO has been grid-centric, given the breadth of solution availability and the emergence of the grid as a source of value. The

ETO focuses on leveraging technologies that can enhance this distribution intelligence and optimize system performance.

While the ETO has been highly visible in the market since early in its life cycle, it has become particularly active over the last eight years as availability of disruptive technologies and opportunities for utilities have exploded. The ETO fills a role within the company as the eyes and ears on the technology market, whether applicable to its core businesses (smart grid), beneficial to the entire enterprise (digitalization), or at the leading edge of solutions directed at enhancing the value of energy to customers (home hubs).

The ETO consistently interacts with numerous start-ups, OEMs, and solutions providers, entertaining requests to test their products at the Mount Holly Emerging Technology Innovation Center, as well as inviting selected start-ups to demonstrate their applications and their fitness (i.e., reliability and performance) for Duke Energy's grid requirements. This interaction between start-ups and the ETO is intended to increase visibility into technology application, but also to help these entities advance their products to commercial readiness, which can benefit Duke Energy.

This innovation center functions as a lab for testing new software and hardware that can support grid monitoring and/or be directly connected to the grid to fulfill more direct system purposes. It frequently engages with other utilities, universities, DOE labs, EPRI, or start-ups to evaluate or test technologies that could hold promise for the company's adoption and deployment.

Duke Energy CEO Lynn Good believes that mastering the application of emerging technology through digital platforms is critical to the company's ability to move the business forward in a more competitive and demanding operating and customer environment. She believes that innovation should happen throughout the enterprise, regardless of location. She noted her thinking on investing resources now to advance the role of technology within the company, as well as enhance the customer experience:

> We are focusing on technologies being developed during the 2020s that will lead to broad adoption in the 2030s, when they are more mature and ready to enhance business value. We want to adopt technology that solves the problem—not just deploys a generic solution—and pursues real outcomes through the design thinking model we have adopted. The technology we adopt should help us improve productivity throughout the business and enhance the

value of our assets and our relationships with customers. When we think about evaluating technology innovation, we consciously blend business experience with digital capability, so the needs of the business are fully embedded in the technology solution we deploy.[50]

Two of its most visible and significant technology deployment successes are the microgrid and storage installations established at the McAlpine Creek and Mount Holly facilities.

The first key facility for R&D and innovation testing is the McAlpine Creek substation that initially focused on testing lithium-ion batteries from a variety of OEMs, utilizing a range of different technologies. The McAlpine Creek substation became a test bed for battery storage in 2012, early in the industry's technology testing era. Its work emphasized the use of specific use cases to capture the operating experience of lithium-ion batteries for extended periods. In 2013 the effort then began to develop the McAlpine microgrid, the utility industry's first distribution-based microgrid.

The microgrid consisted of a lithium-ion battery and solar to support an adjacent City of Charlotte Fire Station with near seamless islanding and reconnection. In 2019 an Eos zinc aqueous battery was added to the site to test non-lithium ion–based battery chemistry performance. The Eos battery and the microgrid were operated until 2021. In 2022 a nickel hydrogen-based battery was to be installed and tested.

In 2016 the first utility-based technology test and development center—the Mount Holly Emerging Technology Innovation Center—was opened to engage with entrepreneurs and OEMs on new products for technical efficacy. Mount Holly provides a test bed for new grid and network technologies and internally developed innovations to understand their application and test their performance and value. Today, it is an islanded, self-contained innovation center that houses micro-generation, batteries, solar, bundled solar and storage, EV charging, advanced meter testing (AMI) and other demonstration facilities.[51]

The Mount Holly facility not only is designed to support the evaluation of Duke Energy–created and vendor provider devices but also allows OEMs and vendors to utilize the innovation center in tandem with the company. A key aspect of the Mount Holly facility is that the ecosystem matters as much or more as the stand-alone technology—that is, integration is more powerful than simple application. New deployment is fine, but not if it is disruptive to existing assets and systems. While many U.S. utilities have been conducting pilots on the deployment of smart grid, microgrid, storage, and/or fuel cell facilities, the Mount Holly microgrid and McAlpine Creek storage installations are unique, FOAK stand-ups, preceding other industry installations and incorporating multiple technologies and integrated elements.

Beyond the McAlpine Creek and Mount Holly illustrations, Duke Energy and its ETO have a history of R&D and innovation since 2007, with multiple FOAK applications of technology or business expertise. Some of the more recent instances include the following:[52]

- *Carbon calculator:* The company became the first utility in the United States to calculate emissions at the customer level based on the customer's specific generation sources and create a plan to bridge the gap between sustainability goals and actual emissions through supply portfolio adjustment.

- *Customer prototype lab:* This capability was created in 2009 to test, research, incubate, and operationalize ideas for how to enhance the customer experience in areas like rate models, EV charging, and outdoor lighting, with more than 175 product prototypes developed.

- *Smart cord:* This technology enables Duke Energy to integrate power monitoring, data collection, and data transmission electronics into all plug cords. This patented technology is expected to potentially create a significant annual revenue stream in the future.

- *Fixed-fee EV charging:* To meet the expanding needs of a growing customer segment, the company designed and is offering a fixed-fee subscription arrangement where Duke Energy will actively manage EV charging requirements through a mix of pricing models and signals.

- *eTransEnergy:* The company established this unique line of business to create a commercial EV business designed to alleviate fleet owner concerns over conversion, financing, maintenance, and fleet optimization with tailored services to owners.

- *Direct current:* The company has been active in evaluating direct current application with three specific areas of development and/or installation for direct current microgrid and solar-plus-storage at Mount Holly and the first certified revenue billing meter.

- *Renewables battery integration:* The company conceived and installed an at-scale (36-megawatt) installation in 2013 at the Notrees wind farm in Texas to test and demonstrate the viability of integrated storage with stand-alone facilities.

- *Residential storage:* In-home batteries with demand response capabilities were installed in a residential community, along with selective solar panel installation, to provide multiyear insight into premise and network impacts.

- *Battery and storage microgrid:* The company installed and integrated the first commercial deployment of these technologies in a public use setting to provide for optimized charging of EVs.

- *3D printing:* The company worked with Northern Kentucky University to design and print multiple battery training simulators to demonstrate the complexity of lithium-ion batteries in operation.

- *Methane leaks:* Infrared satellite imaging through spectrometer use identifies dramatically more gas leaks in real time than manual technician inspections. This enables repair of methane leaks in record time and materially reduces CO_2-equivalent emissions of the gas system.

The ETO maintains a view of near- and long-term technology readiness that extends across more than 25 technologies, from the typical current areas of industry-wide focus to over-the-horizon technologies that may take 15 to 25 years to develop and be implemented on a mainstream basis (recall the earlier discussion about utility technologies' period of 15 to 25 years before general acceptance of the technology itself) (see Figure 25).

Figure 25 suggests that the ETO—and any utility R&D and innovation entity—has a robust challenge to maintain active scanning and evaluation over various families of technologies, with so many assets, devices, and applications that can be deployed across the business. The challenge of not

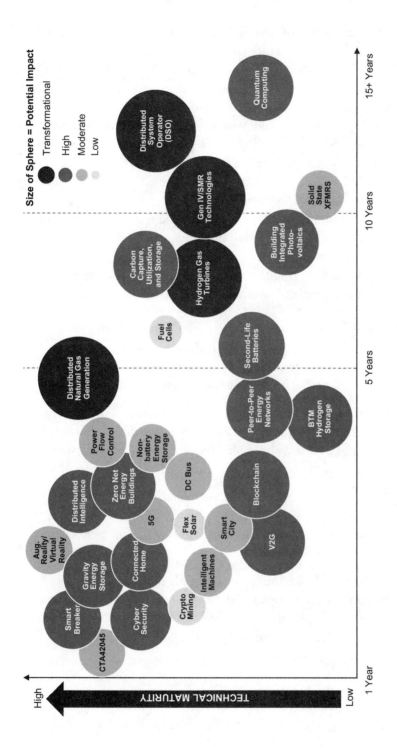

Figure 25. Future technology availability.

(Source: Duke Energy, "Emerging Technology Office: Quarterly Flipbook," February 2022, internal document.)

just scanning and evaluating emerging technologies but also determining how best to deploy the inherent capabilities of these technologies requires utilities to dedicate sufficient resources and funding to stay ahead of the technology curve and ensure readiness for adoption as a primary strategy for the business.

While other established companies provide regular updates to executives on innovation progress, the ETO provides a continuous view of emerging technologies, software developers, applications and end use cases, and OEMs and vendors. Every quarter the ETO addresses not only its activities but details about specific start-ups and technologies, active project updates, future technology readiness, and technology hype curves. This information seeks to go beyond informing about progress by providing insights into market events and directional trends.

Currently, Duke Energy is involved in four initiatives with five highly visible partners, as well as several investment vehicles with which it is involved:[53]

- *Hydrogen:* The company is leveraging a DOE-supported study on the integration and utilization of hydrogen at a combined heat and power plant, along with Siemens and Clemson University, to evaluate hydrogen production, storage, and co-firing with natural gas.

- *Advanced nuclear:* Duke Energy is partnering with TerraPower to provide consulting and advisory services to the design and development of a FOAK sodium-cooled fast reactor and to understand the challenges and opportunities of plant installation and operations.

- *Energy storage:* The company has partnered with Honeywell to test its extended-duration flow battery technology, which can triple the length of storage capability compared to current technologies available in the market.

- *Venture capital:* Duke Energy was an early investor with EIP in its Flagship Fund focusing on grid edge and electrification opportunities, while The Westly Group offers more targeted investment in other areas of company interest, such as buildings, electrification, and secure supply chain.

The technologies above—along with carbon capture and sequestration, renewable natural gas, advanced renewables, pumped storage hydro, energy efficiency, and demand response—constitute the types of avenues that Duke Energy is following to achieve zero-emitting, load-following resources that can enable the company to achieve its net-zero emissions goals.

To support achieving its technical and market objectives, the company partners with entities like the above and, importantly, with numerous universities, like Purdue University, the University of Kentucky, the University of North Carolina–Charlotte, Northern Kentucky University, and others.

The ETO provides a distinctive technical awareness, evaluation, and demonstration capability to Duke Energy for understanding and pursuing potential grid advancement and value. As an early pioneer in these areas within the utilities industry, the company built an emerging technology canvas that has enabled it to monitor multiple technologies as they progress from the nascent to commercial stages of development. More importantly, it is providing contemporaneous insight into technology applicability and readiness, and to how the company can optimize adoption to enhance the value of the grid and improve system performance for customers.

DIGITAL PLATFORM

Like other companies, Duke Energy recognized the need to do more than explore technologies and invest in start-ups to prepare for the kind of future it anticipated to evolve. It knew it needed to prepare the entire organization to think more deliberately about targeting capital deployment toward new and more grid and customer solutions, and act more aggressively to high-grade its execution capabilities and significantly shrink its cost profile.

In 2016 the company initiated an enterprise-wide transformation program to pursue these objectives and produce meaningful impacts for the enterprise. Company-changing targets were set across all business units and corporate functions, focused on the cost structure first, but also directed at capital deployment, customer experience, and new revenue stream creation.

Brian Savoy, Executive Vice President and Chief Financial Officer (and formerly the executive officer responsible for transformation), remarked about framing this effort:

Before we started, we wanted to build the *why* for the transformation for our employees. It was clear we wanted to define and own our destiny. It was also clear that to effectively serve our customers in the future, we had to understand and anticipate their future needs, as well as leverage innovation to improve the customer experience at all levels of our business. We concluded that transformation for us needed to be defined both inside-out and outside-in and focus on the *why* and *how* of our business purpose, particularly as it could be advantaged through smart application of technology, like artificial intelligence and machine learning.[54]

An early focus of the company related to its current digital presence, emerging operating requirements and opportunities for the future, and capabilities of a digital platform that could enable the nature of innovation that Duke Energy was seeking. In particular, the transformation program was intended to extend beyond operating performance into new customer products and services. To illustrate its importance to Duke Energy, the digital program grew from less than 10 resources at inception to approximately 450 today.

Three core themes formed the focus of the company's digital platform: connected customer, intelligent operations, and digital technology (see Figure 26). Connected customer focuses on creating a different customer experience through frictionless digital transactions and valued outcomes. Intelligent operations radically change the approach to work and the application of AI for decision-making and performing tasks. Digital technology is deployed in the form of mobile applications and analytic services that empower worker safety and productivity.

The focus on the digital platform includes several key capability areas, including product innovation (design thinking), analytics (data science), data (platform and visualization), modern architecture (API factory), user experience (web interface), and automation (robotics).

Several of these capability areas provide a foundational element or a delivery system component for one of Duke Energy's principal innovation desired outcomes—developing customer-tailored, innovative products and services that provide demonstrated value to customers and raise the perception of the Duke Energy brand as a smart and committed solutions developer for customers. To illustrate this prowess in transformation and innovation, the company has tracked and reported to its board of directors a five-year level of value produced of more than $1 billion between 2017 and 2021, with the annual benefits largely extending into perpetuity.

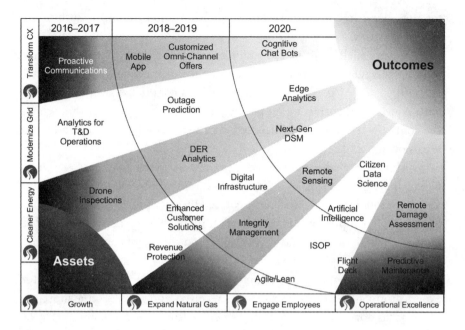

Figure 26. Digital road map.
(Source: Duke Energy, "Digital: Board of Directors," June 27–28, 2018, internal document.)

EMPLOYEE COLLABORATION

In 2016 Duke Energy initiated an internal effort to conceive and stand up an innovation crowdsourcing event (i.e., inviting the employee base to submit innovative ideas for enterprise benefit) that would enable the company to both identify well-thought-out ideas to enhance the business or the enterprise and provide a platform for employees to engage in creative thinking about how to advance the market position of the company.

The intent of the crowdsourcing event—the Energy Evolution Crowdsourcing Challenge—was structured to look over the horizon to question *how* externalities could shape the future regarding the emergence of disruptive technologies, nature of impacts to the enterprise, timing of these impacts, shifts in customer needs, changes in customer positioning, potential product and service application, and opportunities provided by market disruption. Employees were asked the specific question, "Given the significant changes taking place in the energy industry, what are your ideas for how our company can meet the evolving needs of our customers at work and home?"

The event kicked off in 2017 and was conducted across the enterprise to identify valuable ideas that could enhance operational, financial, market, and customer positioning. The event was conducted over two weeks, with continuous voting by employees using the Spigot platform, which the company had previously licensed, on the ideas submitted by employee teams or individuals.

During the challenge, almost 13,000 employees from across Duke Energy participated in the event, with just under 400 discrete ideas generated, subsequently evaluated, and scored. Ultimately, almost 60,000 views of the challenge platform occurred, with more than 8,700 votes provided on the portfolio of ideas and more than 3,000 comments on the ideas provided from the employee base.[55]

From this broader population of ideas, a 38-person subject matter expert group sifted through the ideas received and agreed on a short list of 75 ideas for more detailed assessment, ultimately producing a list of 20 ideas that were selected for additional scrutiny by this review group and pairwise voting by employees. These 20 ideas were aggregated into six categories previously defined by the company: customer service and communications (13 ideas), products and services (4 ideas), distribution and grid (2 ideas), and new business models (1 idea), with none of the final 20 ideas included in the categories for new technology or regulatory and economic development.[56]

From this point, the idea owners were invited to present to an executive committee, with ideas evaluated on three criteria: innovativeness, ease of implementation, and impact. Four winning ideas were selected by the executive team for further development:[57]

- *Track My Service:* This service provides real-time order status and notifications for residential, builder-developer, and small-medium business customers through a web portal, mobile app, email, text, and GPS tracking to enhance the customer experience.

- *Improving outage restoration and damage assessment through technology:* This app-based technology allows response teams to accurately assess, record, log, and locate physical storm damage to reduce repair time, routing time, and resource utilization.

- *Automatic installment on an increase in deposits—residential:* Risks from nonpay disconnect, returned payments, or recurrent nonpay disconnect status are assessed an increased deposit and make monthly installment payments to satisfy deposit requirements.

- *Mobile charging stations:* These stations supply mobile device charging capability—potentially through a partnership—to disaster areas and large events so customers and attendees can charge their devices and keep in contact with friends and family.

The crowdsourcing event served to elevate the collective understanding of the employee base about the evolution of technology and the risks and opportunities this presented. Indeed, the idea platform was subsequently used on more than 30 occasions.

But conducting this event was just one step on the path the company adopted to drive more focus to the need to continuously innovate and reinforce to employees how important continued ideation would be to operating and market success.

Other employee engagement opportunities intended to elicit additional ideas to advance Duke Energy were conducted, such as for the Midwest commercial generation business, although these events were more targeted in focus (topics) and more directed in participation (groups) and rapidly conducted over several days. Outreach to vendors also existed where ideas were submitted, with those passing a review screen invited to Charlotte to present their ideas.

After these events, a cross-discipline approach was stood up in 2018 to address "innovation for the future." This multidisciplinary group brought together resources from customer solutions, distribution, digital, and information technology to define an approach on how to deliver continued innovation consistent with the priorities of the business. A formal model of discovery, incubation, and acceleration was established in 2018 to provide a continuous, structured basis for ideation. This model was informed by lessons learned from the crowdsourcing event.

INNOVATION FOCUS

The company decided in 2018 to formally stand up an innovation center that could provide a separate space where employees could gather to dialogue about ideas, discuss technology use cases, evaluate technology value, advance market-ready applications, and create business cases to justify investment for deployment or marketing. The facility, Optimist Hall, contains 80,000 square feet and is now staffed with more than 400 resources composed of both Duke Energy employees and external contractors, organized and led by business units, with test bench and demonstration capabilities. The scale of the innovation center and focus on products and services signal that the grid-centric nature of earlier innovation is quickly shifting to more customer centricity.

The emphasis on products and services has resulted in more than 80 identified offerings, with at least 50 of them having the potential for meaningful contribution. The offerings developed and taken to the market to date include customer mobile applications, building concierge services, streetlighting efficiency, Perfect Power, energy management programs, and home asset protection services, among other offerings in the solutions stack. To support the pursuit of productization, the company partnered with IBM, given that company's experience in product development, product selection, product marketing, and go-to-market expertise.

When Duke Energy approaches customer solutions development, it keeps several considerations in mind. First, the offering needs to solve a real problem and produce a compelling outcome; if it doesn't, find a better bet. Second, while the company tries to look at potential products and services early in their maturity, it adopts a rigorous scalability lens—that is, if it isn't ultimately scalable in the market, let it go. Finally, the product or service needs to produce real value to customers; if it is hard to tangibly illustrate, then move on.

A particularly important element to have in place to make utility innovation successful and outcomes valuable is effective governance. This process for transformation and innovation at Duke Energy is the responsibility of the enterprise-wide Senior Management Council (SMC), which oversees and coordinates innovation activities throughout the company and establishes priorities for investment. In addition, the enterprise board of directors has been regularly engaged to communicate market trends, transformation and innovation accomplishment, and future direction and priorities to close the governance loop.

One of the key pillars of innovation involves the regulatory area, which has an influence on the competitive environment and utility positioning. The company actively pursues opportunities in this realm and utilizes annual regulatory dialogues to discuss market, technology, and customer trends, providing commissioners and staff a deeper understanding of the market challenges the company is facing and the nature of its responses. This focus enables Duke Energy to ensure that its regulators have sufficient information available for developing effective regulatory policy to address the needs of its regulated utility and customer stakeholders.

Not only does the company actively work to achieve transformation and innovation value outcomes, but it also spends considerable time working with state regulatory commissions to address industry trends, technology maturity, disintermediation implications, product and service potential, and adoption value to the customer. This focus is intended to position Duke Energy to secure the regulatory "permissions" to continue to pursue its path toward attractive brand positioning and high customer satisfaction.

The company regularly reviews the affiliated interest rules in place that govern the relationships between regulated and nonregulated business elements to assess the boundaries of potential market participation. It also continuously brings ideas to its commissions about regulatory reform that can advantage customers, while reducing risks to Duke Energy. These ongoing analyses and proposals help position the company to optimize the value of its innovation activities.

Regulatory innovation is a valuable outcome, as it can include new pricing models, expanded rate structures, performance-based ratemaking, multiyear rate periods, technology introduction, customer value, incentives, and issue treatment, all of which can create certainty for utilities and customers and incent desired behaviors. The company actively pursues innovation across these and other areas and believes they are fundamental to increasing long-term value with reduced risk.

Another innovation pillar, adopting new business models, is a popular discussion topic within the utilities industry—even though no single business model is the right outcome and utilities need to be adept at simultaneously operating within multiple business models that reflect the range of their businesses.

But Duke Energy is taking a different approach to business model innovation; rather than seek to craft a different business model, it focuses on stretching its business model—that is, starting with what is already in place within the current business and regulatory construct, but aggressively leveraging these foundations to enhance the art of the possible in grid capability and customer value and expand the boundaries of the regulatory paradigm. In essence, the company sees a pragmatic path to the cleantech transition and customer revolution by moving deliberately through a series of linked actions that produce desired outcomes.

Duke Energy's innovation activities have continued to mature to reflect growing internal capabilities and play a vital role in positioning the company to meet evolving customer expectations and advancing the business into the digital age. Over 2021–2022, the company's innovation efforts increasingly focused on responding to market changes from ratcheting inflation and increasing borrowing costs. These responses included leveraging and enhancing its customer digital presence for new products and services that would produce new revenues, as well as deploying new technologies like light detection and ranging imaging linked with machine learning growth algorithms to enable smarter and more efficient vegetation management planning and execution.

In 2021, Duke Energy implemented a unique cross-business (generation, transmission, and distribution) capital planning tool—Integrated System, Operations, and Planning—to capture, build, and analyze a range of available data elements to support detailed mid- to long-term prioritization and allocation of future investment (i.e., the optimal use of the next investment dollar for customer and system benefit). This machine-learning-based tool addresses *where* future capital investment would be optimally directed (e.g., resiliency, EVs, or renewables) and provide regulators with more detailed data to understand Duke Energy's needs and support their own decision-making.

DIRECTED SOLUTIONS

Beginning in 2020, the company reinvigorated its focus on additional ways it could capitalize on its accumulated technology experience and go-to-market expertise by evaluating available market gaps and opportunities it could build businesses around. Duke Energy was reconstituting a previous renewables services business it had owned and commercializing its prior R&D and innovation into market-ready offerings that would help its customers with a range of energy-related challenges or problems, leverage its prior ETO and other source knowledge, and create new revenue streams for the company.

Duke Energy Sustainable Solutions did business under a previous name before being restructured in 2021, with a focus on helping large power users lower energy costs and emissions and increase resiliency. This entity serves customers throughout the United States and focuses on distributed generation, off-site renewables, energy resilience, fleet electrification, cloud management, and electric and mechanical systems. The company offers a range of services, such as energy infrastructure as a service, renewables financing, operations and maintenance services, and full life-cycle management to customers.[58]

Duke Energy One provides advisory services and programs to a range of customers related to existing on-site equipment (HVAC), planned site installation (charging stations), entire facilities (security protection), and building services (information modeling). This line of business was originally established by Cinergy, prior to its 2006 acquisition by Duke Energy, and operates nationwide across multiple industries.[59]

The company stood up its eTransEnergy business in 2020, which provides end-to-end services and helps logistics and last-mile delivery businesses, municipalities, transit agencies, school districts, public authorities, and other institutions with electrification of their fleets. This subsidiary offers multiple services, like analysis and planning, financing, charging infrastructure, on-site renewables and storage, and operations, optimization, and maintenance, and operates inside and outside the Duke Energy service territory.[60]

In standing up eTransEnergy, Duke Energy is leading the U.S. utilities industry by establishing a FOAK commercial business that utilizes a go-to-market model consisting of initial and ongoing advisory and financing services, on-site facilities-based energy services, and critical analytic-based fleet optimization support. The creation of eTransEnergy signaled the company's view that the interest of commercial fleet owners justified directly addressing this segment and building a national business that would contribute earnings to Duke Energy and support broader goals of decarbonization.

Duke Energy also has created a commercial transmission business that consists of two partnerships with other asset owners to participate in critical projects outside the company's service territory—American Electric Power (AEP) and American Transmission Company (ATC). The ATC partnership involves the 500 kilovolt Path 15 line in California and connects the transmission grids in northern and southern California. The AEP partnership relates to the 765 kilovolt Pioneer Line that was built to provide a link between two regional transmission organizations—PJM Interconnection and Midcontinent Independent System Operator.[61]

In the future, Duke Energy will further emphasize continually perfecting its digital platforms, mining transformation for sustained business improvement, and leveraging innovation for commercial growth and customer loyalty. It expects its operational priorities will continue to be refined and that its commercial capabilities will be substantially perfected. It is anticipated that AI will be ubiquitously embedded in the business and naturally augment decision-making. The company also expects that it will be able to execute with increased speed and agility, the aperture of market and innovation interests will widen, and the appetite for risk will expand, although within a well-defined set of parameters.

Lynn Good expects that Duke Energy's transformation and innovation journey will need to sustain itself, as the marketplace is dynamic. She believes that future success will depend on how employees, regulators, and customers understand and view the results of these efforts:

> It's critical for us to prepare our employees for the future, and I believe they are gaining a deeper understanding of our future purpose and mission. We are also working hard to help our regulators understand how the utility marketplace is evolving, the new demands it creates, and the paradigm changes it requires. It's clear that our future success depends on how we change the customer value equation from being historical price takers to viewing us as valuable energy partners focused on providing solutions to their problems or needs. Our purpose and role with customers are continuously evolving, and we will look different to them in the future.[62]

The company believes that it is already capturing the benefits of the previous R&D and innovation work it has conducted. These benefits include financial value from transformation pursuits, operational value from ETO research and testing, brand value from customer innovation platforms it has created, and indirect value from greater employee engagement. The company believes it has created a greater sense of urgency within employees, that employees recognize that change will be constant, and that flexibility in decision-making, adaptability to unforeseen circumstances, and overcoming discomfort with the lack of certainty will be key attributes of its ongoing competitive model.

Duke Energy sees that its role has moved beyond dramatically transforming its own legacy model in just a few years to that of an active transformation agent for regulators, investors, employees, and customers.

National Grid

The National Grid Group is based in the United Kingdom, where it serves eight million electric customers, but it also serves more than five million electric and gas customers in the states of Massachusetts and New York.

Aside from its U.S.-regulated business, National Grid has several subsidiaries, such as the Electricity System Operator (overseeing the U.K. electric grid), Gas Transmission (operating the U.K. natural gas system), National Grid Electricity Distribution (operating multiple U.K. regional electric companies), and National Grid Ventures (investing in transmission, interconnectors, renewables, and LNG assets). It also owns the Silicon Valley–based National Grid Partners (NGP), which invests in a wide range of start-ups critical to the clean energy transition. NGP also leads company-wide disruptive innovation efforts across National Grid, including new business creation.[63]

Because of a much earlier paradigm shift in the regulatory model reflecting new governmental policy initiatives, National Grid's U.K. business advanced faster and further in market design and competitive readiness than in the United States, particularly relative to advancing the frontiers of performance. This U.K. experience is extremely valuable to U.S. operations and is openly shared to enable transfer of learnings and adoption of proven approaches to transforming the business for the cleantech transition and elevating the focus on customer benefits provision.

The approaches to innovation across the U.S.-regulated utility regions vary depending on the philosophies of each executive team, the local regulatory environment, and the needs of the business. The company adopted a mix of models at various times, including investment in external venture capital funds, the launch of its own direct corporate venture capital arm (NGP), regulatory policy advancement, disruptive technology deployment, and an emphasis on fundamentally transforming the overall business from top to bottom. This utility-wide transformation utilizes a digital adoption philosophy and model to define *where*, *how*, and *how far* to drive the business toward new platforms, products, and positioning.

The focus on digitalization often leverages new technologies as a basis to define and deliver new and innovative ways to execute the business, simplify and streamline resource deployment, leverage capital for operations and maintenance, and develop viable, attractive products and services to satisfy customer needs.

In a general sense, transformation programs in today's utility operating environment are table stakes and often not that transformative as many companies are pursuing simple cost takeout to prepare for the future. However, when fundamentally changing the way a company works and leveraging digitalization through emerging technology adoption—distributed generation, storage, augmented reality, machine learning, EV charging, digital enablement, and advanced metering—form the backbone for this transformation, the nature of innovation evolves, the breadth of innovation expands, and the value of innovation elevates.

GLOBAL INNOVATION

As the perspective on regulated utilities industry evolution began to shift after initial serious focus on carbon emissions took hold in 2010–2012, National Grid established an enterprise-wide Global Technology and Innovation Group (GTIG) to oversee the planning, execution, and measurement of innovation across the commercial and regional operating components of National Grid—both in the United Kingdom and the United States—and to act as an internal team focused on disrupting the company itself.

The company recognized that an active innovation agenda was both a market prerequisite and a competitive differentiator to prepare for and meet the challenges and opportunities of the cleantech transition. As a result, National Grid stood up a range of initiatives to drive innovation throughout the business and prepare it for the drive toward decarbonization, decentralization, and digitalization, which would collectively birth the cleantech transition.

Somewhat coincident with the stand-up of an innovation platform was the introduction of a revolutionary model in the state of New York called Reforming the Energy Vision (REV). Through regulatory overhaul, REV is remaking New York's utilities to encourage the cleanest, most advanced, and most efficient power system operation. The scope of REV includes an emphasis on renewables, building efficiency, clean energy financing, sustainable and resilient communities, energy infrastructure modernization, innovation and R&D, and transportation—all considerations that also affect the Massachusetts utility, although no formal program exists there.

The public reception to this program certainly provided insight to National Grid on the future direction of policy and a call to action for response.

To start with, the company defined its view of innovation with tangible outcomes in mind and clear benefits operationally or commercially: "Activities must have a clearly defined benefit; be a first implementation of a product, technology, or way of working; or fall under a regulatory innovation mechanism."[64]

This definition provides a framework for *where* to look for innovation and *how* to assess its value. National Grid first asked itself three questions: *Where* do we innovate? *How much* do we invest in innovation? And *what* value do we get from innovation? Asking these questions enabled the company to frame the reporting dashboards that were subsequently developed and adopted.[65]

These three simple questions were further supplemented by additional introspection to provide insights into National Grid's innovation model, addressing topics like cost and benefit relationships, partnering arrangements, portfolio alignment, project selection and approval, strategy alignment, business alignment, measuring success, regulatory impacts, and alignment to other commitments. These elements provided the framework for assessing and measuring value outcomes, as well as context for aligning these outcomes with other business influences and activities.

The acknowledgment of the value of regulatory innovation is an underpinning of the company's pursuit of internal and market-facing activities. It is a critical dimension for achieving intentional outcomes from innovation and ensuring that realized value recognition is an integral component of capital investment, performance execution, and product commercialization.

John Pettigrew, Chief Executive of National Grid, commented on how the company prepared to pursue a more aggressive innovation model:

> We knew the future market environment was going to be different, much different from the past—technology applications would be more powerful and customers far more demanding. And we knew our company would need to think very differently about our purpose and the capabilities we would need to succeed in this future. We started more directly preparing for this future in 2014, when we conducted an extensive outside-in market assessment to understand direction and the challenges and opportunities that could create for us. We created specific internal organizations to help enhance our

knowledge base and our understanding of implications that could arise from technology adoption and customer need expansion. And we put more emphasis into designing an innovation model that was disciplined and linked directly to our strategy.[66]

The company established an internal Group Technology Team to ensure and accelerate understanding of significant emerging technology trends for the sector and National Grid. This team would leverage its relationships in the broader energy innovation ecosystem, as well as with other technology centers, such as at universities, the venture capital community, and the supplier population.

At one point during its early innovation efforts, the company had more than 500 innovation projects in flight. These projects were linked with the most significant problems or issues that the operating companies faced, as well as adopting a more structured model for innovation project evaluation. This upgraded approach would include a stronger governance model and enhanced discipline in project value creation and monitoring.[67]

Consequently, it initiated tracking and reporting the results of its innovation at the enterprise level, as well at its major country operations in the United Kingdom and United States. In 2019 NGP began an ongoing initiative to capture and assess the activities, progress, and value of the R&D and innovation agenda being conducted across National Grid. This effort was stood up to bring coherence and insight into these activities and outcomes and provide a measurable barometer of achievement.

The accomplishments of FOAK projects or initiatives are a part of National Grid's history and have played a role in advancing its business and providing value to customers:[68]

- *EV100:* National Grid became the first U.S. utility to join the EV100, an initiative of the Climate Group that has committed to conversion of their fleet vehicles from gasoline to electric and/ or charging by 2030, with an emphasis on fast-tracking electrification across its service territories.

- *Silicon Valley presence:* The company was the first utility to locate its corporate venture capital fund, NGP, in Silicon Valley, where a deep reservoir of entrepreneurs and potential investment partners was also present to advance technology scouting and continuous innovation community access and collaboration.

- *Robotics:* Boston Dynamics has worked extensively on deployment of robotics for use by the company, including early deployment of "Spot," the mobile robot dog, to conduct equipment condition inspections, monitoring, and analyses at facilities like hydroelectric stations and substations, with IBM now joining this partnership to provide additional focus to AI-based applications.

- *Electric bus supply:* The company initiated a novel approach to utilize dormant battery-supplied school buses in its service territories during the summer months as an integrated source of power supply to the grid, providing an available vehicle-to-grid element that could be quickly added to support voltage levels and availability to meet peak requirements.

- *Curbside EV charging:* In partnership with Connected Kerb, the company is enabling roadside charging in south London in the United Kingdom, utilizing technology deployed through public charging bays that offer simple, efficient, and cost-effective drive-up roadside charging for motorists within a neighborhood setting.

- *Zero-carbon region:* The company is leveraging CCUS and the hydrogen economy to enable the largest region-directed industrial cluster in the Humber area of the United Kingdom to move to zero carbon through adoption of emerging technologies and development of a new onshore and offshore infrastructure footprint and delivery system.

- *T-pylon:* A new structural design for transmission line supports was developed using a T-pylon model and installed in Somerset in the United Kingdom to mitigate the impact of the company's electricity infrastructure on the environment and reduce the costs of new line construction, representing the first fundamental redesign in almost 100 years.

- *North Sea link:* The company designed and installed the longest subsea interconnector link in the world between the United Kingdom and Norway in a partnership with Norwegian system operator Statnett, which will enable renewables energy to flow in both directions and provide access to a broader set of resources to reduce carbon emissions.

- *SF6 replacement:* National Grid partnered with Hitachi to develop and deploy a solution to refill greenhouse gases present in gas-insulated busbars and switchgear with a more environmentally friendly solution—a fluoronitrile-based gas mixture—which is equivalent to taking more than 100,000 cars off the road by 2050.

Ultimately, the GTIG in 2018 evolved into NGP to accelerate innovation across the energy industry. NGP established the NextGrid Alliance (NGA) as a collaborative forum for utilities across the globe. NGA was convened to coalesce more than 100 utilities ("a coalition of the willing"), multiply the available points of view from an expanded collaborator set, share energy transition and innovation-related information, engage relevant start-ups, and build a deeper set of learnings about technologies, applications, and outcomes (see Figure 27).[69]

NGA positions itself as a change leader in the industry and as a catalyst and convener for this initiative—that is, bringing companies together to broaden the collective value of engagement across a wider swath of the global utilities industry. In essence, NGA acts as a force multiplier that extends beyond relationships with venture funds that many utilities already maintained, and opens more doors to enable broader, deeper, and faster industry and individual utility awareness and to expand the nature and degree of benefits that can be developed and shared.

This alliance values the power of the coalition and seeks to utilize a range of mechanisms to create opportunities for NGA members to come together frequently through a combination of an annual summit, technology showcases, introductions to start-ups, and executive roundtables. To date, it has convened five targeted working groups—electric transmission, cybersecurity, corporate venture capital, net-zero, and innovation—that meet quarterly and will continue to add new initiatives as guided by its member utilities.

NGA is considering expanding this utility-focused global group to potentially include other sectors adjacent or related to the electric industry, like other utility types, energy providers, and industrial companies, with some closely involved as energy carriers.

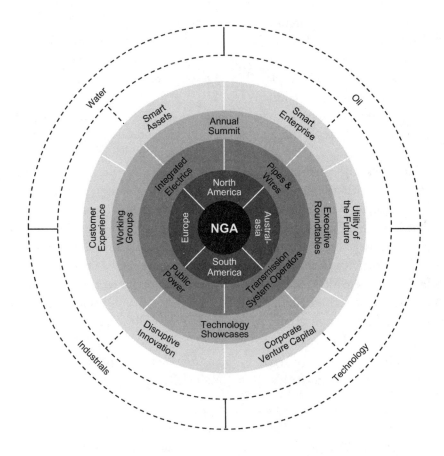

Figure 27. NextGrid Alliance model.

DIGITAL REVOLUTION

National Grid became acutely focused on how its future could unfold in 2014, when it stood up Shaping Our Future, a program directed at reviewing current strategies and operating models in light of the changing external landscape. This intensive dive into current U.K. and U.S. electric utilities—and to some extent natural gas—addresses the changing landscapes, the opportunities for National Grid this could create, and the potential implications of opportunity-pursuit-captured input from a broad executive team within the company.[70]

Multiple scenarios were developed to frame the future and define *how* it could unfold, with circumstances constructed to address key conditions like smart distributed networks, technology displacement, gas asset continuity, and carbon emission outcomes. These scenarios shaped possible futures that were "at the plausible edge of extremes, so collectively they would capture likely outcomes."[71]

The external market analysis and internal introspection focus on market conditions, industry direction, response drivers, and value pools and levels available to National Grid in its current and potentially future markets. The value pools it focused on included renewables generation, electric transmission, distribution infrastructure, and distributed energy resources.[72]

As a result of the Shaping Our Future exercise, the company concluded that it was well positioned across many businesses, although the growth potential was more limited in several markets, as these were already mature and experiencing declining growth. Alternatively, several emerging growth businesses were identified that were closer to the customer end of the value chain and that exhibited high potential for elevated and sustained growth. Ultimately, three core strategies emerged to drive the future:

- *Drive a step change in core business performance.* Emphasize as the near-term focus with a strong rationale for change.

- *Look for opportunities to grow the core business through disciplined business development and mergers and acquisitions.* Leverage strong operational performance to pursue core and attractive business options.

- *Future proof the business against technology and value shifts.* Build positioning and capability to pursue small investments at the customer end of the value chain.

In 2016 the company had secured board approval to undertake an expansive transformation program focused on dramatically repositioning itself for a different future that would create meaningful benefits to customers, stakeholders, and shareholders.[73]

As a result of this strategic program, National Grid determined that an enterprise-wide strategic transformation program was needed to align governance, strategies, capital, technologies, processes, costs, performance, products, regulation, customers, and change management to meet the emerging needs of the market and prepare for a more challenging future than the current norm.

Transformation was intended to fundamentally aid the business in executing in the future in a manner far different from its recent history. At that time, the company was focused on upgrading its core operating power and gas systems that had been incompatible because of multiple mergers or acquisitions and/or aging out. For example, none of the underlying gas operating systems were similar and required massive investment to achieve both replacement and integration, as well as align with the company's desire to use technology as an enabler to enhance operating simplicity and productivity.

National Grid's focus on transformation reflected a model tailored to fit its circumstances and needs. This model was process-based to enable clarity and visibility, pushed strategy execution into the teams, and emphasized performance management and continuous results reporting. The scope of the transformation addressed five critical areas—asset management, grid operations and management, field force, customer experience, and internal operations—to which the company intended to reimagine the approach with the intent to leverage a digital way of thinking and executing across the business.

A formal focus on transformation is not unique within U.S. utilities, as almost all companies have been emphasizing fundamental change over time to prepare for competitive markets, ensure earnings goals are delivered, and/or substantially retool their technology infrastructure. However, National Grid (the enterprise) adopted an illustrative formula to explain its effort—Imagination + Innovation + Technology = Digital—a concept not distinctively articulated universally across the U.S. utilities industry.[74]

Ben Wilson, National Grid's Chief Strategy and External Affairs Officer, described how the company crafted its digital transformation model to support its future view of market success:

The emergence of new technologies opened doors that had not been available to us in the past, particularly with respect to digitalization. But we knew we needed to find the right balance between leveraging technology, applying it to our business, and utilizing it to create value to our system and customers. Digitalization was both an enabler to achieve our overall strategic positioning objectives and an element of fundamentally changing the way we work and our perceptions of the art of the possible with respect to capturing value. To transform our company, we needed to take advantage of the natural evolution in technology maturity but bend it to our specific needs for grid operations excellence and customer value expansion.[75]

National Grid's approach is distinguished from many other U.S. utilities, particularly in the electric sector, by the concerted emphasis on a rapid and pervasive digital transformation and the parameters of its approach (i.e., emphasis on root causes, aggressiveness in outcome pursuit, and ownership "pushdown" for results). For example, the focus of many of the projects it undertakes is on identifying the frictions within the business (i.e., the inherent issues in role definition, work purpose and value, work design and interfaces, and work execution complexity). Successful digital transformation projects are not exclusively driven by technologists; rather, they reflect far broader disciplines and more applicable perspectives from operational staff who composed the bulk of individual teams to provide a fit-for-purpose view.

The breadth of this approach signaled that the company intended the digital journey to be all-encompassing—top-to-bottom redesign and end-to-end business engagement and alignment—which would enable and embed innovation within the business.

To frame its strategic intent, National Grid crafted a North Star to drive its digitalization efforts: "Digital should now propel us toward National Grid's transformation goals across all strategic initiatives—both stand-alone products and broader technology and data platforms."[76]

This ambition led to designing a three-step process to guide and drive the digitalization journey:[77]

- *Spark:* Use internal crowdsourcing to engage employees to develop a digital adoption methodology, create initial digital road maps, and validate the first wave of digital products to support succeeding stages of the journey.

- *Scale:* Utilize employee teams to identify and capture the network effects and impacts available from demonstration of digital adoption and prepare products and services to scale at an enterprise level.

- *Evolve:* Leverage the digital journey; product, service, and solution development; and associated strategic and execution learnings to permeate the entire enterprise and accelerate adoption and innovation velocity.

In October 2019, National Grid convened "Hack-a-Future," a weeklong, immersive ideation session to generate a large number of technology-enabled products, services, and solutions and digital concepts and ideas. This initial brainstorming session included almost two dozen employees—with more involved in subsequent sessions—and was intended to surface one to two digital concepts for subsequent validation with team members and facilitators.[78]

The company believed it knew its processes well, along with the systems underlying operations, where frictions existed, and a view of the likely future. It decided to frame an event that would enable the company to have active employee engagement in fundamentally transforming the *what*, *why*, and *how* of work execution. The company decided that if it truly desired significant transformation, it should "imagine what the future could be, and how it would be more valuable to its customers."[79]

After some early instruction, facilitation, and brainstorming, 50 ideas were developed for detailed evaluation using a rapid-fire *Shark Tank* format where short pitches were made to justify these concepts. From a total of 50, the ideas were progressively reduced to 10, then 3, and finally 1. The ideas were built around fundamental rethinking of the needs of the business, aggressive challenge to the status quo, design thinking of the outcomes desired, and definition of how to rapidly bridge the gap from concept to adoption, with an emphasis on creating tangible value.[80]

The selection of the winning ideas was based on three specific attributes—desirability, feasibility, and viability. The company's goal was to push the boundaries of existing thinking, and therefore the business, and reflected an overall mandate for operating efficiency and readiness, positioning, and advantage from electrification.

In 2019 a digital road map was created to capture the intended efforts of the company, establish the objectives of the program, determine the priorities for execution, define the expected outcomes, and align resources against planned timelines. This road map was used to capture all the product concepts (product canvases) and how they linked together to transform the underlying end-to-end processes. Digital products provided the ability to break the overall transformation into smaller, discrete pieces and think about life-cycle change, as opposed to a delayed "big bang" outcome.

While the digital road map laid out the path toward achieving significant value outcomes across multiple projects, it also reflected the distinctive levels of change (and value) that would inure from pursuing a range of technology-based projects. A "horizon" concept was used to differentiate among innovation technologies. The first horizon reflected technology already in place at National Grid; the second horizon referred to where technology was available that could be pursued at National Grid; and the third horizon related to where these technologies would provide breakthroughs in performance and value.

From these events, a number of "lighthouse" projects were initiated that were intended to produce meaningful outcomes from adoption and execution. An initial focus of the first electric business digital project—dubbed "On My Way"—related to building a simple, technology-enabled platform for outage work planning, field execution, and work order closeout. This enabled individuals and crews to self-direct their work and plan, schedule, and deliver planned work, with control over decision-making within the contours of overall work priorities and risks.

This process substantially shortened the application conception-to-adoption schedule, reducing the closeout period from 77 days to instantaneous after an initial MVP was developed following initial and second-stage investment for new capabilities. Changing work planning, execution, and closeout practices is certainly transformative, but the innovative aspects emerge when technology design and application are centered on problem-solving and customer benefit, rather than just operational excellence.[81]

The "On My Way" application fit the critical needs of the sponsoring executive and team members (i.e., digital foundation, scalable application, distinguishable product, enhanced capabilities, business simplification, enhanced productivity, risk mitigation, data analytics, radical outcomes, and high-value benefits).

It also satisfied the objective of leveraging the MVP approach to the product life cycle, which allowed the company to focus on what can be accomplished quickly and add near-term value, rather than attempting to constrain accomplishment until the perfect solution became available. These MVPs were based on specific use cases for targeted sets of stakeholders and were designed to eliminate process and technology frictions and displace factor inputs (e.g., labor, technology) that were at the root of low productivity, high cost, and poor performance. The MVP concept still allowed for future enhancements to be made to the initial product, enabling early value to be provided to address core issues, yet work could continue post-release to further extend product development and increase total value.

To enable the foundational technology replacement and integration, National Grid adopted a traditional, linear waterfall approach—sequential development assessing requirements, design, implementation, testing, and adoption—to drive this program and deliver on the planned benefits of lower operating costs, faster and cleaner flow-through of transactions, and greater business insights.

Meanwhile, the next layer of electric operating systems was also approaching end-of-life and would need replacement. However, rather than use the waterfall approach, the electric organization used a digital agile model that emphasized rapid and tailored application development. This approach turns the traditional ground-up model around to one where the focus is on solving the frictions mentioned above, and doing it quickly and visibly.

The agile model was viewed as a more progressive and productive model to adopt because it involved constant builder-user engagement that emphasized problem-solving and the use of sprints and scrums to engage the team and stakeholders in rapid iterative and incremental processes directed at moving quickly and focusing on the value of the outcome.

A purpose of this transformative project was to paint the picture of the future and coach executives and managers on *how to think* in response to market, technology, and execution challenges. Thus far, the focus of National Grid has been on operationalization of its transformative technology projects, but it is moving toward a commercialization mindset. The company has additional projects in the pipeline after "On My Way," such as "FutureNow," which is focused on optimizing electric asset investments through more sophisticated prioritization of customer dollars. The company's initial digital road map established a portfolio of 13 products over six years, anticipated to deliver ongoing benefits for customers. But this road map is a dynamic one that continues to evolve, and the company adds new product concepts, merges old ones, and unlocks additional sources of value as it learns. For example, both the road map and overall expected value for "On My Way" look very different from the way they did in late 2019.[82]

The underlying strategy for the products that National Grid offers is based on addressing a few targeted areas, affecting operations, corporate support, customers, and employees (see Figure 28). The previously mentioned digital road map enables the company to take a targeted view of its activities and apply discipline about resource and deployment priorities. This focus on stakeholders and outcomes is a cornerstone of the digital transformation.

By the end of 2019, National Grid was ready to pivot from its initial short-term focus of creating products to demonstrate the value of digital adoption and establishing the foundation for a digital future, to the next step of its digital transformation—the long game—by reorienting and reinforcing these digital capabilities to deliver achievement of the full scope of strategic objectives and business ambitions of National Grid. With this move, digital is placed at the core of all programs intended to deliver on the strategic goals of each business unit.[83]

National Grid subsequently created a digital acceleration organization designed to deliver all digital products, enabling technologies and data platforms in a coordinated and synergistic manner across the business that delivers network effects for the entire organization.

Figure 28. Digital focus areas.

(Source: Data from National Grid, "Strategy Briefing: Digital Strategy," January 29, 2019, internal document.)

The digital acceleration organization would manage a hub-and-spoke operating model, incubating new products and platforms before supporting them within the spokes, in collaboration with the business units and functions. The digital acceleration team also incubates the five foundational digital enablers required to scale this new way of working throughout the organization (i.e., digital methodologies and ways of working, a standardized hub-and-spoke product operating model, digital talent and culture, modern IT systems and data platforms, and a comprehensive governance and funding system).[84]

The digital road map is constantly adapting to reflect the experiences gained during the first few years of the transformation—more ideas are emerging, products are expanding and moving toward integration, and direct linkage to customers is increasing. While the breadth of the program and direct outcomes are increasing, challenges remain regarding the pace of how quickly change is occurring, benefits are being realized, and total value to customers is accumulating.

National Grid recognizes that it is still early in its digital journey, and that where it goes in moving from its present stage of progress to its future end state needs to be revisited and refined. Consequently, it is rethinking how to deploy its resources and against which priorities, but the commitment to being outcome-focused and value-oriented will only become more elevated.

John Pettigrew further commented on how he sees the digital transformation enhancing National Grid:

We have been very successful in utilizing our digital transformation to rapidly and dramatically move the company to an elevated plane of performance. At one point, we had 500 innovation projects underway throughout the company, focused on operations, service delivery, customer engagement, and product development and introductions. Some of these projects provided incremental benefits, but others were very meaningful to the business, yielded individually significant outcomes, and demonstrated our ability to conceive, execute, and deliver on our objectives. This early project success told us we needed to be very disciplined in project prioritization and execution and that measurement of our progress and delivered grid and customer value outcomes would be an important dimension to emphasize.[85]

To reinforce its commitment to meaningful, achieved outcomes, National Grid continually focuses on ongoing scorekeeping on innovation projects and impacts, both qualitative and quantitative. In early 2022 the company had 230 innovation projects (both in flight and planned), with 74 percent having specific success measures and 54 percent having both financial and nonfinancial targets. The 230 innovation projects align across eight categories, with primary impact from customers and stakeholders (60 projects), followed by low-carbon future (52 projects), design optimization (40 projects), and system operability (36 projects).[86]

VENTURING OUT

National Grid began to invest in venture capital in late 2015, when it was an early participant in the initial Flagship Fund of EIP. The company still maintains its initial investment in this fund, but it subsequently launched NGP to establish an on-the-ground presence in Silicon Valley and exert more direct control over its start-up investments. NGP was formed in 2018 with a challenge by National Grid to "disrupt ourselves" internally and advance the energy systems of tomorrow. It seeks new technologies that are grouped in four families—modern assets and operations, smart enterprise, customer-focused solutions, and utility of the future. These categories include technologies such as AI and analytics, the cloud, IoT, and cybersecurity, but its field of vision is not limited to just these areas.[87]

It has more than $400 million of investment funding, with a $350 million portfolio of investments across more than 40 start-ups, such as AiDash, Dragos, and Urbint, among others, and is the lead investor in more than 50 percent of its positions. To date, it has also exited six investments in these start-ups to recognize their maturity and monetize these results to demonstrate the level of available returns.[88]

A fundamental element of NGP is its business development organization, which is charged with identifying priority technology areas for potential start-up company investments meeting current, emerging, and over-the-horizon needs of the operating companies, as well as enabling the demonstration and deployment of related technologies into these entities. While the investment teams source a wide range of potential start-ups to consider for investment, 75 percent of these companies need to satisfy certain thresholds for strategic impact. Presently, the focus of NGP and the National Grid executive team is expanding to address

Horizon 3 objectives, which relate to technologies not yet deployed (perhaps anywhere) and can provide measurable future impact to the business, including creation of new revenue streams and potential new business stand-up.

A group of 20 National Grid senior leadership individuals serves as a sounding board for identified opportunities and can sponsor investments, allowing them to be designated as strategic and thus count toward the 75 percent goal. As part of the process of potential investments in compelling future technologies, an advisory board of 12 internal leaders is also empaneled to imagine over-the-horizon needs of the business and provide ideas and idea validation within NGP around high-impact technology areas, particularly FOAK. On occasion, OEMs, software developers, and solutions providers direct perspective to the advisory board about market offerings and potential adoption value. While the business development group has a natural focus on the NGP portfolio companies, this team acts as an "honest broker" in ensuring nonportfolio companies are fully considered and evaluated for investment.

The evolving NGP organization is focused on extending its reach beyond Horizon 1 and 2 technologies, which generally support and sustain the business, toward Horizon 3 technology opportunities. These technologies could provide significant revenue growth and value potential to National Grid and its operating companies and open the spending aperture to significant future investments NGP may make and the level of business contribution that could arise.

The operating companies within National Grid are beneficiaries of new technologies developed by the portfolio companies of NGP, such as for work and asset management from Copperleaf (which is being leveraged for the aforementioned FutureNow product), vegetation management with AiDash, asset management through Cogniac, renewables enablement from LineVision, building efficiency with Carbon Lighthouse, AI and machine learning for customer interface from AptEdge, incident prediction through Urbint, cybersecurity with Dragos, and real-time energy management from Copper. This collaboration provides multiple proof points to the value of technology adoption and deployment against meaningful needs for utility operations decision-making, closing capabilities gaps, and building knowledge and analytical capacity.[89]

NGP actively engages with the start-up community, acting as both an incubator and an accelerator. NGP maintains a Disruptive Innovation

Center of Excellence (DCOE) that offers a series of experienced-based support from National Grid employees or other companies in the broad energy ecosystem to help start-ups convert great ideas into projects and products that can become vibrant, independent businesses.

The DCOE offers access to internal NGP resources to engage, learn, and apply experience to their business. This group also provides access to internal subject matter experts, as well as experienced investors and operators that can aid these start-ups with sweat equity to enhance the prospects of business success. Finally, the DCOE is a vehicle for obtaining capital to further advance start-up progress.

NGP also operates a Ventures Acceleration Team that creates an immersive experience for National Grid employees to help them hone their entrepreneurial and innovation capabilities. This includes initiatives such as a Venture Fellows program, placement of National Grid executives on start-up advisory boards, a company-wide "Future Forum" monthly speaker series, and Silicon Valley immersions for National Grid leadership teams. Finally, the Ventures Acceleration Team provides the opportunity for National Grid employees to participate in intense design sprints around key topical areas for one month.

National Grid Ventures is another market-focused business within National Grid and looks for competitive business opportunities in asset-based businesses like electric transmission, interconnectors, LNG, battery storage, metering, and wind and solar. It provides direct investment into these identified project, technology, and partnership opportunities, all of which are outside of the natural, core-regulated business. Some of these partnerships include TenneT, RWE, Drax, Equinor, and WindEurope, with the company (National Grid Electricity Transmission) also partnering with six universities in the United Kingdom to work on decarbonizing the electricity system. The company also seeks opportunities in clean energy innovation, competitive transmission, offshore wind, and CCUS.[90]

This competitive business provides National Grid with insights into adjacent competitive markets, preserves the ability to participate in new projects, and secures an additional earnings stream in high growth areas. While still relatively small within the overall enterprise, National Grid Ventures is positioned to pursue growth opportunities across multiple markets in Europe and the United States, as well as position for additional opportunities that could emerge because of National Grid's scale, reach, and reputation.

The company is in the midst of creating the strategic, operating, and value platforms needed to sustain and advance its future market positioning. It has successfully launched its approach to innovation and employee engagement, created multiple paths to technology investment, stood up and executed an enterprise rethinking of *how* it does work, invested in major market participation capital projects, and is aggressively pursuing the identification and capture of new sources of value.

National Grid's digital transformation is at the heart of the company's journey to create the utility of the future by dramatically reshaping the way it works, adopts technologies, redefines the value equation for both itself and customers, and embeds innovative thinking throughout the organization. While the digital road map still has several years to run to achieve its initial objectives, the journey does not conclude at the end of the indicative timeline. Rather, the pursuit of value will continue as the scope of value broadens, the sources of value expand, and the levels of value realized point to additional opportunities to continue to enhance benefits created for the business and its customers.

Southern Company

Southern Company is a very large combination electric and gas utility headquartered in Atlanta, Georgia, serving nine million customers in Georgia, Alabama, Mississippi, Illinois, Tennessee, and Virginia, with the third-largest market capitalization among U.S. utilities of more than $80 billion. It also owns an independent power producer (gas and renewables) and a leading energy services company (distributed energy infrastructure), both of which operate in multiple additional states in the United States. It also owns a fiber-based regional communications carrier and private network that operate across internal and rural purposes.

The company was formed in 1924 when its operating companies in Alabama, Georgia, Florida, and Mississippi created an interconnected system in the southeastern portion of the United States. In 2016 Southern Company acquired AGL Resources, a holding company for several local natural gas distribution companies that also maintained a presence in Georgia, as well as in Illinois, New Jersey, Maryland, Tennessee, and Florida through acquisitions it had made over time.

A distinctive portion of Southern Company's business is Southern Linc, created to provide mission-critical voice service, particularly during emergencies, across its electric utilities. It was recognized that organizations outside of Southern Company had similar communication needs, and Southern Linc marketed an unregulated wireless offering for commercial customers within its territory. The network began to be utilized for wireless connectivity to fill the operating companies' data needs, such as SCADA (supervisory control and data acquisition), going live in 1995 and officially launching in 1996.

This network was a purpose-built, push-to-talk (PTT) Motorola iDEN (integrated digital enhanced network) 2G system, providing wireless connectivity across the company's 120,000-square-mile service territory. This system, while effective for PTT communications, was not capable of meeting emerging needs of a future digital and interconnected electric grid. In 2012 Southern Company decided to replace the aging iDEN technology with a 4G LTE system, providing an enhanced communications platform with the capability to incorporate advanced technology, strengthen network security, and optimize available spectrum.

The company's electric utilities have identified more uses for the upgraded network than anticipated, leading to a 150 percent increase in the number of data devices operating on the network since launch, with more use cases in development. The LTE network positions Southern Linc to expand its services frontier, providing an opportunity to become a "utility of utilities," managing wireless services for other utilities and leveraging its expertise in owning and operating a utility-grade, mission-critical network.

In addition, a separate entity was founded in 1997—Southern Telecom (STI)—which owns, invests, deploys, and operates dark fiber and colocation capacity across its footprint (which is leased from Southern Company's local operating companies), as well as an STI-owned system running from metro Atlanta across Georgia to Jacksonville, Florida. STI also operates a leased fiber and colocation system from Jacksonville to Miami, Tampa, Orlando, and Daytona, largely ringing the state. This 1,500-route-mile fiber system provides long-haul and "middle/last-mile" capability connecting Atlanta to other cities and rural areas in the Southeast with high-speed broadband. It serves wireless, wireline, and satellite carriers and private networks of commercial entities.

Southern Power, another separate, unregulated subsidiary, focuses on generation projects—initially in natural gas and now renewables—and has sought to develop projects with precontracted output agreements to reduce development and market risk to Southern Company. This model is an extension of an earlier wholesale market model where Southern Company would create unit power sale contracts to regional utilities in the south.

R&D CAPABILITY

Over its rich history, Southern Company has been widely recognized for its R&D and innovation efforts. These endeavors go as far back as 1916, leading to a steady history of equipment design, technology adaptation, demonstration projects, government grants, research center stand-up, federal government-sponsored studies, and industry-leading environmental advancement. Southern Company utilized many of its generating plants, transmission and distribution assets, and myriad other resources across its portfolio to host this technology testing and introduction.[91]

A formal research and development department was first formed as part of Southern Company Services in 1969 in Birmingham, Alabama, and flourishes today as the R&D organization for the Southern Company system. Since Southern Company—like most utilities in this time frame—was heavily dependent on coal-fired generation, much of the early work was similarly focused and led to a broad portfolio of plant design, technology testing, and environmental remediation projects. As the staff of the R&D team were reminded, the group was there "to serve as a lookout for signs that will characterize tomorrow, so that we can be prepared for it, or perhaps even influence what it will look like."[92]

Beyond these early supply-related efforts of the R&D group, and in parallel with EPRI's activities, the company was an early activist in promoting broader efficient electrification across its electric operating companies during the 1980s. The company was at the forefront of aggressively pushing electric heat pumps as a substitute for natural gas for space heating, as well as pursuing other industrial electric end uses (e.g., electric infrared heating for process applications) to create additional opportunities for developing new sources of electric load or sales.

These activities carried over into other industrial or transportation settings, such as shipping ports and airports, where displacement of diesel oil with electricity was advantageous in reducing dependence on imported oil while reducing emissions. As a result of this focus, in the 1990s, the operating companies established several technology application centers, which provided an opportunity for industrial customers to test application of electric technologies, such as infrared, induction, ultraviolet, and others, for their own industrial heating, drying, and curing processes prior to installing them at their facilities.[93]

But even with its early efforts, including significant air quality research, the company has not been entirely predisposed toward coal-related assessments and pilots—its strategy has always been to utilize a portfolio approach in looking for options to provide solutions. Many Southern Company R&D initiatives were conducted well before the topical issues became mainstream, with testing of solar energy, fuel cells, and EVs all occurring before 2000. In addition, a range of FOAK technologies were tested within Southern Company, such as smart grids, power dispatch computers, liquid solvent-refined coal, stack-gas flow monitoring, coal gasification, integrated distribution management, molten-carbonate fuel cells, and fiberglass scrubbers, among other areas.[94]

A distinguishing element of R&D focus in the early 2000s was the company's work on carbon capture and sequestration (CCS). In 2007 the company conducted a carbon sequestration pilot project at Plant Daniel in Mississippi to demonstrate the feasibility to safely store CO_2 in saline geologic reservoirs. The project successfully injected 3,000 tons of CO_2 into a deep saline rock formation 8,500 feet underground, becoming one of the world's first pilot injections of CO_2 at a coal-fired power plant.[95]

Over the next decade, Southern Company developed what was at the time the world's largest start-to-finish demonstration of CCS on a pulverized-coal power plant at Plant Barry in Alabama, in a global partnership that included Mitsubishi Heavy Industries (MHI), DOE, EPRI, and others. The project captured more than 250,000 metric tons of CO_2, transported and injected more than 125,000 metric tons of CO_2, and led to the commercialization of MHI's technology.[96]

Within the same period, Southern Company began managing and operating DOE's primary CO_2 capture research facility, the National Carbon Capture Center, which has so far completed more than 127,000 hours of testing of 70 technologies for developers from seven countries, reducing the cost of CO_2 capture by approximately 40 percent. Today, the facility's research encompasses CO_2 capture for natural gas power generation, CO_2 utilization, and direct air capture.[97]

Through work with DOE's Carbon Storage Assurance Facility Enterprise Initiative and the Southeast Regional Carbon Sequestration Partnership, Southern Company's geologic sequestration R&D continues to evaluate CO_2 source and sink synergies in the Southeast and demonstrate the ability to safely store large volumes of CO_2 in EPA-permitted wells. The company is also engaging in numerous DOE-funded front-end engineering design studies to advance transformational CCS technologies for natural gas power generation toward commercialization.[98]

Several other specific research centers have been established over time within the Southern Company footprint or plant portfolio (some with EPRI, DOE, or other institutions), such as the Electric Vehicle Research Center, Mercury Research Center, National Electric Energy Testing Research and Applications Center, Power Systems Development Facility, Water Research and Conservation Center, Energy Storage Research Center, Ash Beneficial Use Center, and the Schatz Grid Visualization and Analytics Center, which illustrate Southern Company's commitment and prowess in R&D.[99]

As the shift away from coal-fired generation occurred because of increased climate change attention, so too did the R&D effort expended on this generation source within the fleet. In addition to CCS for natural gas power plants, such as through the National Carbon Capture Center, Southern Company would primarily become focused on advanced nuclear, hydrogen, and renewable energy technologies. This R&D provides a foundation for Southern Company's goal of achieving net-zero greenhouse gas emissions by 2050.

And over the last 10 years, the level of interest in grid edge and beyond-the-meter technologies has also ratcheted up with focus given to different end uses, electrification, and locational assets for homes, buildings, sites, and transportation. For all these areas, the R&D group—in conjunction with Southern Company's operating subsidiaries—asks itself several fundamental questions:[100]

- *What is good for the customer?* What technology will reduce energy bills and increase productivity, product quality, customer comfort, or safety?

- *What is good for society?* What can reduce emissions or water consumption, or support economic development for everyone?

- *What is good for Southern Company?* What new business models, markets, and opportunities are available?

The R&D group has established four primary strategies that apply across the enterprise value chain businesses. These four elements include developing a sustainable energy future through customer-focused, cost-effective solutions; providing delivery and storage solutions that meet reliability, resiliency, and flexibility needs; developing technologies that support expanding customer needs; and leveraging and advancing existing infrastructure through minimizing cost and improving efficiency (see Figure 29).

Hundreds of specific technologies fall within the overall scope and include traditional areas like CCS, reliability and resiliency, and environmental controls, among other areas, as well as unique emerging technologies, like zero-carbon energy carriers, low-carbon transportation, negative-emission solutions, energy storage, dispatchable renewables, integrated energy delivery, data analytics, and sustainability solutions.

To support its R&D agenda and take advantage of external expertise,

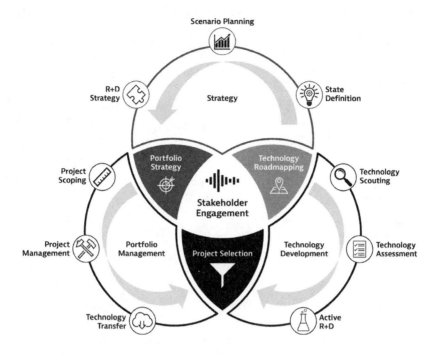

Figure 29. R&D innovation framework.

(Source: "Southern Company Background: Research and Development," 2002, internal document. Graphic by Patrick W. Crossley. Used by permission of Southern Company.)

facilities, and funding, the R&D group has maintained collaborative relationships with federal agencies, universities, and commercial entities, including DOE and its National Laboratories, NEI, TerraPower, General Motors, General Electric, GTI Energy, MIT, the Global CCS Institute, International Energy Agency, Georgia Institute of Technology, Battelle, and the Nuclear Regulatory Commission, among others.[101]

Southern Company has continually expanded the scope of its R&D and innovation efforts across its family of electric and natural gas utility companies. For example, the R&D group worked with the NREL to develop an original idea that would later evolve into the HyBlend Initiative, in which more than 30 industry partners are collaborating with five national labs toward solving key challenges that could enable natural gas utilities to blend hydrogen into existing infrastructure or convert infrastructure to dedicated hydrogen service.[102]

In June 2022, Georgia Power Company, Mitsubishi Power, and EPRI demonstrated the successful validation of blending hydrogen and natural gas at Georgia Power's Plant McDonough–Atkinson facility. This FOAK project was conducted on one of six gas turbines at the plant and was the largest test of its kind globally.

Southern Company has also recently initiated new sponsored research efforts around economy-wide decarbonization (EPRI and GTI Energy), Generation IV nuclear (DOE), energy storage (DOE), carbon capture for natural gas power generation (DOE), direct air capture (DOE), and smart neighborhoods (DOE). Each of these efforts involves collaboration with unique other parties that represent OEMs, universities, and vendors, among others.[103]

This involvement with third parties has also led to leadership or participation in a range of other cross-industry or utility-specific initiatives:[104]

- *Hydrogen Council:* The company joined this global CEO-led coalition with a long-term ambition to foster hydrogen as a pathway to the cleantech transition. This is one of several arrangements where diverse avenues for decarbonization are being pursued.

- *Electric Highway Coalition:* This group is composed of 14 utilities committed to enabling the highway system from Texas to Florida to Maine to provide a network of direct current fast-charging stations that will offer reduced driver charging time.

- *Low-Carbon Resources Initiative:* The company has joined with EPRI, GTI Energy, and more than 50 other utilities and industrial companies to pursue a range of decarbonization initiatives using low-carbon generation and low-carbon energy carriers like hydrogen, synthetic fuels, and biofuels.

- *Alliance for Transportation Electrification:* This group is composed of almost the entire U.S. utilities industry, as well as OEMs, charging station providers, and other affiliates to share policy and technical information about regulatory outcomes and open standards and interoperability.

- *Molten Chloride Reactor Experiment:* This was an agreement with DOE to design, construct, and operate the world's first critical fast-spectrum molten salt reactor, along with a collaboration of TerraPower, Idaho National Laboratory, Orano Federal Services, CORE POWER, EPRI, and 3M.

- *Novel Microbial Electrolysis System Collaboration:* Southern Company Gas is leading a project with Electro-Active Technologies and T2M Global to pursue the production of hydrogen from food waste as a means of decarbonizing waste products.

These and other initiatives compose a continuous chain of critical future technology evaluations and developments that can have substantial impacts on Southern Company as an enterprise, as well as on its customers and society.

CROWDSOURCING AND COLLABORATION

In early 2014, Tom Fanning, the company's CEO, recognized both a need and an opportunity related to the nature and pace of industry change that was beginning to occur and the direction of travel it was following. The need was ensuring that the full employee base was aware of the significance of the technology and competitive challenges to the traditional core business and that business as usual would no longer be sufficient to ensure that Southern Company maintained its premier position within the sector.

The opportunity was to utilize the presence and potential impact of these externalities as a way to galvanize the employee base to prepare for these challenges and utilize the collective resources of the company to "invent its future," rather than wait for it to overtake Southern Company. The CEO believed that harnessing the almost 25,000 employees across the Southern Company system would offer a wealth of enthusiasm, experience, and brainpower to forge a new and compelling view of the company's innovation persona.

Tom Fanning reflected on what he wanted to accomplish through the crowdsourcing event:

Our surrounding environment was rapidly changing from new policies, technologies, and competitors. I wanted our employee base to test the boundaries of the future and ask the disruptive question

"Why not?" The event provided a means for a cultural intervention to destroy historical hubris and provide cover to shift our focus to adapting behaviors to a new environment where risk-taking was encouraged. In a sense, we were seeking to celebrate the revolutionaries among us that had bold ideas yet didn't think they had freedom to explore them. I wanted to capitalize on our diversity of thought and use collegiality to turn our thinking to the expectations for tomorrow.[105]

A case for change was developed that communicated the surrounding externalities that were emerging and framed the challenges they provided to Southern Company—that is, it painted a picture of a possible future. This case for change was meant to inform the entire employee base of *how* the energy and utility worlds could look different in just a few short years, as well as *what* these impacts could mean to Southern Company.

After a crowdsourcing event model was selected for use, its parameters needed to be refined and the model architected. The CEO wanted to emphasize active participation from all employees and continuous collaboration among them. The modification of an event into a contest (SO Prize) was determined the best option to meet these expectations and create the internal buzz that would excite employees about engagement. To demonstrate the company's commitment to full participation, a collaboration platform was implemented to allow the employee base to like an idea, comment on an idea, or vote on an idea depending on their prerogative and the stage of the contest.

The SO Prize was framed around six reinforcing leadership themes that would form the basis for the contest and communicate the expectations from its conduct: necessity, culture, collaboration, challenge, breakthrough, and commitment.[106]

Necessity framed the purpose for innovation within the company as a requirement, not an option. Culture signaled the intent to build innovation into the company's DNA and embed a culture of innovation within the business. Collaboration recognized teaming as an optimal way to enhance the quality of ideation and take advantage of different experiences and views. Challenge emphasized the desire to obtain high-quality ideas from the teams and encouraged them to "think big." Breakthrough emphasized the need to accelerate Southern Company's readiness for the future and create high impacts to the company's growth potential. Commitment reinforced that the executive team would be actively supporting the effort and ensure any obstacles to execution were removed.

The kickoff started with the CEO asking employees to "look around the corners of the future" and addressing areas like customer expectations, demand for electricity, public policy, generation portfolio, and workforce. Employee communications used traditional internal channels like the home page and Southern Today (the company's intranet), which were then complemented by the CEO delivering the message directly to all employees through an email and a "Tom Talks" medium (i.e., an intranet and streaming channel used to communicate with the entire employee base).[107]

Initial ideation and submission began in early May and established a four-week schedule for initial idea descriptions, with first-stage idea review and qualification for continued assessment to be completed by mid-July.

Almost 1,000 ideas were received across the enterprise from 565 teams and individuals, with more than 4,000 comments received from employees as they reviewed the ideas submitted to the collaboration platform (see Figure 30). All ideas received were screened and rated against four criteria related to the degree of change to the business model, technology, Southern Company itself, and the anticipated impact from adoption. Some of these ideas related to common areas, such as EVs, and the idea owners and teams were encouraged to extend from collaboration with teams to integration across teams to enhance the power of the idea.[108]

Figure 30. SO Prize highlights.

(Source: Data from Southern Company, "SO Prize: Inventing Southern Company's Future—Commemorative Edition," 2014, https://www.southerncompany.com/content/dam/southern-company/pdf/public/SO_Prize_2014_commemorative_book.pdf.)

From the almost 1,000 ideas submitted, several hundred were short-listed for more detailed screening and rating based on the screening conducted. To down-select from several hundred ideas, the internal SO Prize office undertook a deep dive on these submissions and evaluated and selected 50 ideas that were viewed as interesting, well developed, innovative, and impactful to the business.

This list of 50 ideas was further short-listed to 20, which is where initial monetary awards kicked in. To move from 50 to 20 prioritized ideas, an executive review panel of internal officers and several external entity representatives were constituted to undertake a deeper, structured review of idea quality, change level, and impact. The employee base was also engaged for the first time in voting in parallel with the executive review panel, and the ideas receiving the most votes across each group were selected for further development by the teams and idea owners, with more attention provided to economic impacts, predicates for adoption, and costs and timing of implementation. More than 14,000 employees company-wide participated in the voting stage to arrive at 20 ideas, and six honorable mention ideas were added to the awards group.[109]

After additional team idea expansion and refinement, team coaching, and business case support from the SO Prize office, the 20 ideas were further down-selected by the executive review team, as well as through "pair wise" voting (i.e., multiple head-to-head rankings) to six winners. These six ideas were then presented in person to a leadership team in an event that was live streamed to all employees. Each of these teams received a separate monetary award, and several also received another financial award to further develop a proof of concept or charter a pilot within the business. By the end of the SO Prize contest, more than 40 percent of the employee base had participated in the event at least once.[110]

The six winning ideas—all finalists were selected—addressed a wide range of ideas that stood out from the broad list of ideas initially submitted:[111]

- *A path to move away from carbon in the transportation sector:*
  The use of hydrogen as a carbon-free fuel source has long held interest, and this idea capitalizes on Southern Company's generating fleet as a source for hydrogen for transport, industrial, and residential use.

- *rEVolution—a Southern Company plug-in EV concierge and infra-structure initiative:* This idea seeks to transform the EV buying experience via a one-stop shop where the company provides customer education, enables EV acquisition, offers customer service, and provides charging.

- *Empowering people, expanding opportunities:* Customers are at the center of Southern Company, and this idea focuses on creating a menu of services for customers that can enable payment options, product access, and new services, including in a bundled model.

- *Unmanned aerial vehicles (UAVs) for inspection and control:* This idea is built around the acceleration of UAV testing, development, and deployment with an intent to capture and process data more effectively and efficiently for enhanced performance and cost control.

- *Water, water everywhere:* With Southern Company's territory including the Gulf Coast, a focus on how to capitalize on that presence led to an idea for development of multiple desalination plants to both increase water quality and lower long-term supply costs.

- *SoConnected:* This idea is directly driven at the customer and understanding latent needs, using data analytics to match them with available Southern Company solutions and create individualized solutions.

These ideas all included definition, scale, and timing of the creation of new revenue sources for the business. The development of these winning ideas was consistent with the original intent to identify ways to enhance Southern Company's future market position—including with customers—and to develop new avenues for growth and strengthen its "right to win." The differentiating element is that these ideas were developed in 2014, well before they became mainstream and topical across the industry—an example of the power of harnessing collaboration within the business.

Several key takeaways resulted from the SO Prize that were of additional interest to Southern Company executives. First, the messaging about the future company external environment and strategy was not as well communicated as believed and was not being heard by the employee base, despite the various communication mechanisms used and instances accomplished. Second, an artificial ceiling existed for new ideas rising through the organization and the various layers of management. Finally, the SO Prize revealed that there was pent-up enthusiasm among millennials for energy innovation at Southern Company, which was reflected in the demographics of the teams and individuals involved. These were all important messages for the Southern Company leadership team to realize, particularly since the company was now formally committing to building a culture of innovation throughout the enterprise.

The event was thus a catalyst for developing the next stage of Southern Company's innovation model and the stand-up of a more permanent capability within the company. It also became a model for a subsequent SO Safe contest, which focused on improving overall operating safety and collected more than 900 ideas; numerous One-Day Challenges that simplified the SO Prize model; and SO Prize–like contests sponsored by Georgia Power Company and Alabama Power Company that focused on improving the business. These events, executed through virtual collaboration, resulted in over 40 percent of employees participating and more than 4,000 additional ideas.

ENERGY INNOVATION CENTER

As a result of the SO Prize contest, a stand-alone Energy Innovation Center (EIC) was stood up in 2015 in the middle of the start-up community at Technology Square in midtown Atlanta, adjacent to the Georgia Institute of Technology (Georgia Tech). The EIC is recognized as the first formal innovation center within the U.S. utilities industry and created an open environment for ideation, exploration, collaboration, development, and commercialization for Southern Company.

The EIC was chartered to reinforce Southern Company's commitment to innovation and act as a catalyst and facilitation hub for ideas within the company with three primary areas for its mission: developing new products and services, evolving business models, and empowering a culture of innovation. The emphasis of the EIC was to help convert ideas into solutions for the business, where they could be operationalized, and for customers, where they could be commercialized, as well as making Southern Company the world's leader in customer-focused innovation. Southern Company intended the EIC to fulfill its strategic intent—innovating for the benefit of customers and increasing value for customers through products and services.[112]

Several roles were established for the EIC to address—innovation culture, market recognition, partnership expansion, and product development—which became the initial focus areas for pursuit. Of these functions, innovation support and strategy development were enablers to the mission, while product development was to be growth-oriented and consistent with the notion of commercialization of ideas.

The EIC did not view its purpose to create a centralized innovation organization that acted as a gatekeeper, but rather to be a go-to resource center that identifies new technologies or unmet customer needs, creates collaboration forums with other innovation idea owners and teams to bring projects to fruition, and enables the flow of ideas, technologies, and information across the enterprise. Thus, it was intended to be a front door to innovation ecosystems both internal (employees, operating companies, and R&D) and external (universities, national labs, other innovation centers, and technology, consumer, and industrial companies).

In this sense, the EIC could be thought of as a center of expertise available to support the full enterprise, as well as drive specific activities on behalf of the entire business, such as being a clearinghouse for information dissemination on trends, technology economics, end use cases, pricing models, and partnering potential. It also provided a focus on the protection of intellectual capital that had been and would continue to be developed within the company. As the EIC functioned through the years, it expanded its technology evaluation into areas like blockchain, AI, virtual reality, logistics electrification, photovoltaics, batteries, wireless power, and digital twins, as well as continuing to think about how to enable innovation across the enterprise, creating and commercializing new products and services, and building a culture of innovation.

Over its formal existence, the EIC created partnerships with AT&T, Lyft, Cox Automotive, DowDuPont, Honeywell, Connex, Panasonic, Electrify America, Accenture, Samsung, and Vivint, among other companies, to explore technologies, evaluate end use cases, and develop market-ready offerings. These relationships complemented those maintained at the Southern Company level, such as EPRI, DOE, Bloom Energy, and esVolta, which addressed broad initiatives and enterprise impact.[113]

Between 2016 and 2018, EIC received numerous awards and acclaim for innovation from national organizations like Business Culture Awards,

Innovation Collaboration Awards, Georgia Tech, EEI, Innovation Leader, IDEO, Spigot, Smart Cities Expo, EPRI, and *Public Utilities Fortnightly*.[114]

In 2019 the company determined that after five years of innovation hosting at EIC, enterprise, operating company, and external market activities had evolved to the point of rethinking the role of EIC and reassessing its original purpose and momentum given these shifts. Since the EIC was established in 2015, Southern Company had acquired distributed energy subsidiary PowerSecure, which became a sandbox for testing emerging solutions like fuel cells.

The company had also made the founding investment in the climate tech venture fund, EIP. To help integrate and leverage insight from these strategic investments, a new internal organization, New Ventures, was established. New Ventures brought an integrated focus to the competitive businesses, partnering, venture capital, and inorganic growth—and was fast becoming a significant scouting and origination vehicle for strategic growth for the company and the leading influence on innovation purpose, priorities, and investments.

In parallel, the engagement of Southern Company resources directly with EIP was expanding to a level not originally anticipated, leading to the portfolio companies of EIP working more broadly with the operating companies in providing technologies for testing, adoption, or further incubation. This engagement was a long-time goal of Southern Company to not be a passive investor, and it enabled the company and members to bring technologies more rapidly to market settings to assess impacts on local operating systems.

After this self-assessment, the company determined that the EIC's original purpose and role had been well served, but the broadening role New Ventures was playing on the national level (e.g., interface with EIP, OEMs, and key innovators) and the building recognition that the operating companies were well positioned to interface with local innovators combined to suggest a new model would be more advantageous. It was decided that a transition and devolution (i.e., realigning roles into the New Ventures R&D and/or operating companies) would be the appropriate next step to continue the advancement of innovation and increase the ownership of unique operating company product and service go-to-market models. EIC would then be repurposed as a virtual entity, with the existing physical presence continuing as a showcase for new technologies and a collaboration center for the enterprise.

As Mark Lantrip, the recently retired CEO of Southern Company Services and Chairman of the Southern Energy Resources Group at the company, remarked:

> The EIC successfully expanded our position in the innovation community, identifying technology applications for the business and sustaining our focus on collaboration. But we knew we needed to further evolve, using applied innovation to achieve the leading market positioning we were pursuing. The alignment of several commercial businesses like PowerSecure, Southern Power, and Sequent, along with other market-facing activities like EIC's platform, EIP, and operating company activities allowed us to create a coordinated, customer-focused approach to meeting market needs from "big iron to beyond." At the core of this go-to-market approach, we believed customer-centered innovation coordinated throughout the enterprise but emphasized at the local level would strengthen our success.[115]

This step was taken to reflect external market evolution and create more local engagement and accountability within the operating companies, as well as align technology assessment and testing for products that were bridging the responsibilities of both R&D and EIC (e.g., storage, micro-generation, mobility, and smart cities).

VENTURE CAPITAL POSITIONING

Shortly after the EIC was stood up, Southern Company continued its efforts to identify and pursue opportunities for additional R&D and innovation engagement and exploration. The timing of these efforts was propitious, as EIP was just beginning to formulate the idea for a venture capital fund focusing on energy start-up investments. The general partners at EIP worked closely with Southern Company to craft the concept of bringing together selected utilities interested in learning more about emerging cleantech technologies, creating a shared funding model, and minimizing the risk of these activities. It was a fund created "by utilities and for utilities," leveraging the strengths and expertise of its limited utility partners to seek out young ideas and companies needing not only the investment dollars but the strategic support and commitment of the utilities themselves to be successful—the *Shark Tank* of the energy space.

In 2015 Southern Company became the founding member of what turned out to be an initial major membership commitment of $50 million from four U.S. utilities that serve as an advisory board to stand up the strategic direction and collaboration process for this fund. These utilities, along with several other industrial companies and financial institutions, ultimately helped EIP surpass its modest $250 million fund goal by almost $500 million. All members were focused on the cleantech transition and an opportunity to leverage a multi-entity organization like EIP for the collective benefits of the members, as well as to advance their individual strategic market position and future value creation.

This initial EIP fund totaled just under $700 million in original funding and focused on U.S.-centric investments in areas like EV charging, DERMS, virtual power plants, smart thermostats, software-as-a-service, microgrids, cybersecurity, transaction platforms, AI, analytics software, and digital, among other areas. It also successfully leveraged this investment by creating an SBIC-backed credit fund. Ultimately, EIP invested in dozens of companies, and it has monetized several of these investments, such as Ring, Opus One Solutions, FirstFuel, AutoGrid Systems, and others.[116]

In 2021 EIP closed its second fund, which approximated $1 billion, and expanded its focus in Europe, as well as in a focused decarbonization fund and a diversity investment fund. The close of Fund II created assets under management of approximately $2.5 billion, with Southern Company again a prime strategic member.[117]

While the EIP member companies can make investments in these companies alongside EIP, Southern Company generally does not participate in that manner of direct investment. However, when an idea comes from within Southern Company, it is eager to support those ideas. In 2018 one such idea was incubated and born at Alabama Power Company, which developed an idea to create and sell fractional shares of its carbon credits generated by its own renewable facilities. In this way average retail customers could, for example, "green their online purchases" for as little as 25 cents to cover the carbon footprint created by the in-home delivery of their goods. This resulting company, called Cloverly, was supported by Southern Company for two years before it was finally spun out in 2021.

In parallel with the timing of the EIP venture fund participation, the company made the first large-scale acquisition in the industry of a commercial enterprise focused on network and grid edge technology development and deployment when it acquired PowerSecure for $430 million.

PowerSecure was a nationally known distributed infrastructure company specializing in distributed generation (smart grids), utility infrastructure solutions (advanced metering and lighting), and energy efficiency (building envelope). Southern Company viewed PowerSecure as a natural fit with its customer-centric focus and compatible with other products and services offered by its operating companies.

Since 2014, Southern Company had also been active in dealing with a variety of potential and active partners leading up to 2019, when it reconsidered realignment of its internal facing (EIP) and external directed (corporate) growth and investment activities (i.e., PowerSecure, EIP, Bloom Energy, and Amazon). The decision was made to consolidate oversight of the competitive businesses, like PowerSecure and Southern Power, while also bringing together other innovation and growth capabilities, like Customer Solutions, partnerships, and capabilities and solutions acquisitions (as PowerSecure was), as well as coordinating with the operating companies on their specific innovation activities.

The New Ventures organization was stood up in 2016 to build the cleantech capabilities of Southern Company as an enterprise, while nurturing local innovation among the operating companies. This organization essentially evolved out of part of the mission that was performed by the EIC, but elevated and reinforced its role in enabling strategic business development by the operating companies, its competitive businesses, and Southern Company as an enterprise. In a sense, it acts as a bridge between available technologies from EIP portfolio companies, PowerSecure, or elsewhere to the needs of the Southern Company operating companies.

But the focus of New Ventures is not exclusively internal, as it maintains a close working relationship with EIP in helping commercially align its portfolio companies seeking demonstrations, pilots, and adoption contracts with the Southern Company operating companies. New Ventures also maintains a range of partnering arrangements with OEMs and other entities that bring platforms, technologies, or products and services that can be aligned and integrated as customer solutions consistent with operating company priorities.

In 2022 the company went through an exercise of reassessing its future path to determine whether any calibration to its objectives and strategic path were necessary. It considered alternative paths—one titled Fortress Southern, where more attention was directed at the operating elements of the business, and a second called Brave New World, where increasing disruption, potential disintermediation, and sustained growth would be required. The executive team concluded that Brave New World was the likely future condition, and the company would have to be strategically aligned with these requirements. It also considered the importance of innovation to either scenario, as well as how to embed it into ongoing measurement. As CEO Tom Fanning summarized:

> To achieve sustainability of any significant corporate endeavor, you need to be intentional about its importance to the business. We have been discussing with our board the value of measuring what is important to the company, and they have been supportive of adopting innovation as part of our short-term and long-term incentive plans. We anticipate that we will shortly incorporate both qualitative and quantitative metrics into our compensation management and measurement processes to reinforce the significance of innovation as a fundamental objective of Southern Company.[118]

Southern Company has evolved its innovation capabilities and expanded its innovation reach since it formalized its enterprise activities in 2014 with SO Prize. It has also continued to grow its core R&D capabilities and research breadth as the emergence of disruptive technologies increases. To further this innovation mission, these capabilities have expanded within the Southern Company Gas business through its focused reduction of methane emissions through production of renewable natural gas to increase its clean, sustainable energy sources.

As its experience and successes have grown, it continues to lean in to its employees throughout the business for new and impactful ideas that produce products and services that offer the solutions that customers are seeking.

With well-developed capabilities over a five-decade involvement with applied R&D, combined with an almost 10-year purposeful focus on innovation and collaboration, Southern Company is positioned to continue to move toward successfully positioning the business to navigate an era of decarbonization of resources and digitalization of business execution. Its ability to consistently leverage collaboration throughout the enterprise has created numerous opportunities to bring innovative ideas to fruition and bring value to customers through offerings designed to meet emerging needs and preferences.

WEC Energy

WEC Energy is a large integrated electric and gas utility holding company with operations in the states of Wisconsin, Michigan, Illinois, and Minnesota. Headquartered in Milwaukee, Wisconsin, it serves almost five million customers and is one of the dozen largest utility holding companies in market capitalization at more than $30 billion.

The company has expanded through three external mergers and acquisitions involving Wisconsin Southern Gas, WICOR, and Integrys Energy Group. It operates primarily through its regulated subsidiaries of We Energies, Wisconsin Public Service, Peoples Gas, North Shore Gas, Minnesota Energy Resources, Michigan Gas Utilities, Upper Michigan Energy Resources, and its unregulated entity, WEC Infrastructure.

WEC Energy has experienced several periods of sustained high growth that has required substantial expansion of its generation fleet within very short windows, such as a four-fold increase of the portfolio between 1945 and 1965. Since most of its fleet was coal-fired, this also led the company to consider new construction techniques and environmental management or remediation actions in concert with these supply additions.[119]

The company is highly regarded in the U.S. utilities industry and the Public Service Commission of Wisconsin (PSCW), is widely recognized for its insightful and evolved regulatory policy initiatives, and encourages its regulated companies to think in a similar manner to act innovatively for the benefit of customers.

Utilities can pursue innovation in several different ways depending on their philosophies and circumstances—for example, they can aggressively focus on formal enterprise-wide innovation approaches, utilize specific messaging to drive innovation outcomes across the enterprise, or leverage operational excellence to produce superior results that can further enable the business in different investment or action dimensions.

WEC Energy adopts an approach that reflects its strengths—that is, actively managing cost levels and delivering high-quality service and affordability to enable it to secure its business position to subsequently leverage these outcomes for the benefit of the operating system and its customers. Said differently, WEC Energy seeks to "do the right things right" within the business to enable it to pursue a broader agenda of change and innovation of its choosing, such as pursuing environmental leadership in generation or developing innovative regulatory mechanisms in areas like EV tariffing.

The company does not pursue the bleeding edge of innovation; rather, without fanfare it looks to identify innovative ways to steadily operate its business and quietly pursue the fundamentals of operations with a view of the future in mind. WEC Energy has been referred to as the "execution king," meaning it is known for predictable performance, low costs, and successful regulatory relationships (i.e., "classic WEC") (see Figure 31).

These outcomes position it to deploy cash from the business for capital investment that enhances fleet or system performance and creates customer-facing enhancements that improve the customer experience. It is this virtuous cycle that positions the company for readiness for an environmentally and customer-responsive future, continued operational execution success, and pursuit of innovations within its business.[120]

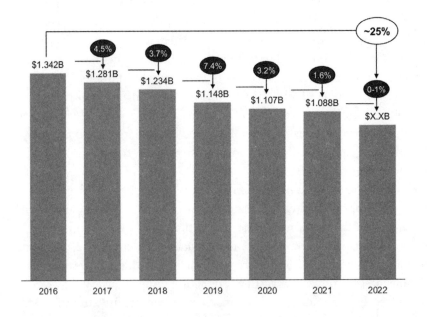

Figure 31. Focus on operations and maintenance efficiency.

(Source: Adapted from WEC Energy, "Our 'ESG' Progress Plan: Investing in Efficiency, Sustainability, and Growth," May 22, 2022, https://s22.q4cdn.com/994559668/files/doc_presentations/2022/05/05-2022-May.pdf.)

WEC Energy has demonstrated continuous leadership as an environmental steward, energy efficiency promoter, and air quality advocate. It has accumulated decades of design, construction, and operating experience across these areas, with public, regulatory, and Wall Street accolades for its aggressive and responsive actions. This historical track record of policy accomplishment has set a standard for other utilities and developed into a fundamental underpinning of the company's persona.

During the 1960s, a focus on energy conservation began to develop among public interest groups and at regulatory commissions nationwide, resulting in the creation of the EPA in 1970. This was occurring because rates to customers were increasing at a rapid pace from asset growth, commodity prices, and inflation, as well as general concern about the preservation of resources and the environment. At one point in the 1960s, WEC Energy adopted a moniker for itself as the "beautility" as it focused on the aesthetics to reduce "visual pollution" and complement its other targeted efforts on air and water quality.[121]

While California was generally at the forefront of this movement in the 1970s, it was not alone, and Wisconsin became a fast follower for energy conservation in the Midwest. The PSCW has a reputation for forward-thinking and responsible regulation and was well aware of the challenges WEC Energy's operating companies and customers were facing. One of the early innovative actions undertaken by WEC Energy in the mid-1970s was to create a formal focus on energy conservation, well before most states outside California.

WEC Energy started with the simple notion of customer education in the mid-1970s and used these communications to increase perception of the need and establish the platform for various programs created to encourage, incent, and shift energy consumption patterns across all classes of customers. The company moved from the awareness stage to specific programs, such as incenting customers to shut off or allow remote control of their water heaters during peak electricity demand hours.

Gale Klappa, Executive Chairman of WEC Energy, provided his perspective on how the company thinks about its priorities and objectives:

> Our focus is on the fundamentals—on being the best in the business at executing—and we work to measure and improve our performance every day. That mindset drives thoughtful and prudent innovation.

I believe the company's endurance, expansion, and success have validated our approach. By any objective measure, we have been able to create lasting value for our customers and our shareholders. Now we're positioning ourselves to pursue even more meaningful benefits for them in the future.[122]

From this program, WEC Energy moved to add programs in several other areas, like time-of-use rates, seasonal pricing, energy audits, interruptible rates, and others to create a portfolio of almost 30 specific programs. This number does not seem to be high compared to what other utilities were required to offer in subsequent years, but it should be remembered that for the late 1970s and early 1980s, this portfolio illustrated an industry-leading role for which WEC Energy received broad recognition and awards.[123]

Within the next several years, these early and innovative conservation programs were expanded under a "Smart Money" program with compact fluorescent light bulbs; interest-free loans for efficient heating, cooling, and ventilation systems; and rebates for home appliances (including air conditioners and water heaters), which again was ahead of many utilities in scope and again won WEC Energy regulatory recognition.[124]

While the company had relied on OEMs for R&D related to coal-fleet improvements, by the mid-1980s it was expanding its R&D focus to new technologies, like nuclear fusion and superconductivity, and establishing its own demonstration projects for wind, solar, and stored cooling.[125]

POWER THE FUTURE

One of WEC Energy's broadest and most aggressive transformational pursuits related to its mix of current generation resources and the reconfiguration of its fleet portfolio. In September 2000, WEC Energy announced its $7 billion Power the Future program, which was focused on ensuring reliable and reasonably priced power from the company. It was viewed as more than a simple financial investment—it was intended to be an investment in communities, the economy, and the environment.[126]

The scope of this program included retiring older, less-efficient coal resources, upgrading and maintaining existing plants, increasing the presence of renewables in its supply portfolio, and adding air quality control systems at various plants (see Figure 32). In addition, Power the Future extended to upgrading the existing distribution network. The program was

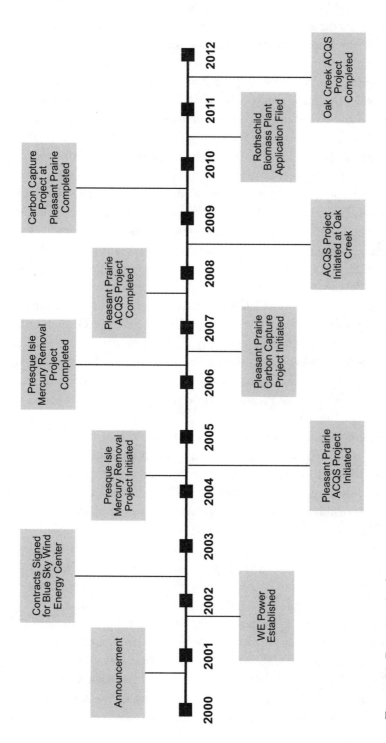

Figure 32. Powering the future.

(Source: Data from We Energies, "Powering the Future," 2012, internal document.)

purposeful in its design and signaled a powerful reinvestment message to stakeholders interested in environmental remediation and future emissions avoidance and reduction.

It resulted in the creation of the We Power subsidiary to design, permit, build, and own the plants, although Power the Future could not directly operate them and would utilize long-term leases with We Energies for its production output. This construct was adopted to comply with the requirements of the Wisconsin Legislature's Leased Generation Law of 2001.

The Power the Future program resulted in new plants being built and sold. For example, the sale of the Point Beach Nuclear Plant was announced in late 2006 and ultimately finalized in 2007. Proceeds of the sale were used to offset customer rate increases from the new build. This was a significant event and one of the earlier nuclear plant sales across the industry, resulting in a long-term purchase power agreement to support the company's load levels.

Between 2000 and 2013, WEC Energy added renewables wind farms—the Blue Sky Green Field Wind Energy Center and the Glacier Hills Wind Park—as its first renewables supply sources, two 545-megawatt natural gas units at Port Washington, two 615-megawatt coal plants at Oak Creek, and the Rothschild Biomass Cogeneration Plant, in addition to air quality systems work at the Pleasant Prairie and Presque Isle coal plants.[127]

To enhance wind asset performance, the company implemented breaker reconfiguration, which generally results in reduced curtailments by a regional transmission organization. And when WEC Energy turned its attention to solar, it focused on utility-scale installations rather than smaller commercial sector opportunities. This move allowed WEC Energy's assets to best match customer peak needs and leverage the more than five-times-higher capacity rating of solar over wind.

This construction and remediation cycle involved more than $7 billion in capital investment over the roughly 13-year period of its execution. At the end of this time frame, WEC Energy had dramatically revamped its generation supply portfolio and substantially reduced its carbon, mercury, and sulfur emissions across the larger plants in its fleet. This major program reshaped the company's future and set it on a course for enhanced fleet performance, particularly with respect to plant efficiency and heat rates.

As is typical of "classic WEC," not only was the Oak Creek Plant able to blend coal and natural gas, while operating in the top 5 percent of all U.S. coal units in plant efficiency, but it was also one of only two

1,000-megawatt coal plants in the Midwest that achieved top decile operating heat rates. These operating achievements were preceded by favorable construction cost and schedule results, a discipline that has typified WEC Energy's performance on its large capital projects in generation for decades. The approach to design and construction at Oak Creek has also enabled conversion from coal to gas to occur, which will provide a stable firm capacity bridge on the road to net-zero emissions.

Throughout the Power the Future program, WEC Energy looked for ways to incorporate innovative design and construction features, such as installing extended conveyors and utilizing a more efficient intake and pumping system at Oak Creek, leveraging a FOAK mercury removal process at Presque Isle, and conducting first-time testing of a chilled ammonia technology at Pleasant Prairie. All these innovative technology applications were instituted to drive cost, performance, and environmental improvements to key plants in the fleet portfolio and deliver on WEC Energy's commitment to its stakeholders.[128]

The entire Power the Future program extended between 2000 and 2013 and covered power plant retirements, upgrades, replacements, additions, and modifications. Part of Power the Future also included a FOAK demonstration project to separate CO_2 from a coal-fired power plant. This effort was consistent with the company's mantra for carbon of "reduce, reuse, recycle," which had particular applicability to coal combustion products like coal ash.[129]

The Power the Future program illustrates how WEC Energy's inherent performance model and discipline manifest in exemplary construction, operating, and performance results. It also demonstrates the linkage between the company's performance execution capabilities, creation of business and customer value, and ability to turn discrete activities into innovative outcomes.

INNOVATION AND INVESTMENT

WEC Energy believes that innovation is demonstrated, not just claimed. Its persona is not to bring attention to itself or create high visibility over its activities; rather, it seeks to achieve innovative results through being smart about investment, dependable about operations, and valuable to customers.

The company has relied on its operational prowess to drive innovative outcomes through high performance, rather than adopt broad initiatives like crowdsourcing or stand up formal innovation organizations. While an innovation focus can materialize in several forms (e.g., formal or informal, continuous or episodic, pervasive or targeted, breakthrough or incremental), it is the results achieved, rather than the methods taken, that distinguish the effectiveness of these efforts.

Despite a more operational approach to innovation, WEC Energy has produced several FOAK examples of innovation over its long history. These examples span a range of areas, although the dominance of innovation in the generation business is apparent:[130]

- *Mercury removal:* The company adopted a novel technology—Toxecon, a carbon injection and filter system—for installation at its Presque Isle coal plant that has resulted in industry-leading mercury capture at an industry-leading rate of more than 90 percent.

- *Chilled-ammonia carbon capture:* A globally funded pilot project utilized a new technology for carbon capture—a chilled-ammonia process developed by Alstom—to develop a proof of concept through a continuous-mode, fully integrated process.

- *Coal combustion sales:* Other companies pursue coal ash sales, but WEC Energy is recognized for achieving record levels of combustion product disposition, achieving industry-leading alternative use levels (e.g., paving and concrete) greater than 98 percent.

- *Wet scrubber:* This technology was installed at the 1,200-megawatt Pleasant Prairie Power Plant, the first time a wet scrubber was used at a 100 percent Powder River Basin coal-fueled plant, which produced a beneficial, reusable by-product of gypsum, rather than materials simply landfilled.

- *Selective catalytic reduction (SCR):* At the 1,100-megawatt South Oak Creek Plant, the SCR was installed using a "tail end" model (i.e., after air heater installation) and included a steam coil used to reheat the exhaust.

- *Intake system and conveyor:* The Oak Creek Power Plant underwent novel redesign and installation changes (i.e., the intake system, lift pump, and conveyor system) to supplant traditional industry design and construction techniques.

- *Green tariff:* A certified green tariff program was introduced to enable customers to procure renewable energy from WEC Energy's Energy for Tomorrow program to meet their interests in environmentally friendly supply sources.

- *Reciprocating internal combustion engine (RICE):* The company has been an early adopter of RICE units for use in its system for continuous, peaking, or stand-by purposes, but more importantly, leading in deploying this technology at scale.

- *Hydrogen blending:* The company is using a 25 percent/75 percent hydrogen and natural gas blend to test hydrogen within an existing RICE unit and to explore the viability and versatility of hydrogen as a component of a sustainable future generation strategy.

Over time WEC Energy has continued to increase its activities in a range of technology areas, with the above hydrogen blending project at a generating plant in the Upper Peninsula of Michigan enabling the company to inform its thinking about how hydrogen fits into future business readiness and positioning. Scheduled for completion in Q4 2022, this blending testing will serve as a unique demonstration project for the company. The company is partnering with EPRI, which will act as the lead for technical implementation and dissemination of results to the industry.[131]

WEC Energy has extended its innovation capability to the development of LNG for new plants, but with a slight twist—focusing on direct vaporization and injection into the natural gas distribution system. This allows the company to maintain high reliability during "needle peaks" and avoid additional capital for expensive interstate pipeline expansions.

Gale Klappa described how he views the company's positioning for the cleantech transition:

There's no doubt the industry is moving rapidly toward one of the most significant transitions in its history. We want to play a role in helping to shape the future of a clean energy economy. And the lens through which we focus our investment plans can be summarized in three words—affordable, reliable, and clean. When we succeed in driving toward greater efficiency and decarbonization, we will have made a lasting impact on our customers, our public stakeholders, our shareholders, and our environment.[132]

Beyond its continuing investment in environmental remediation, new generation, and new technology application, WEC Energy has also invested in a venture capital fund led by Invenergy—Energize Ventures—that closed its first $150 million fund in late 2018. This fund focuses on cleantech transition areas such as advanced energy storage, distributed energy, data analytics, mobility, cybersecurity, and AI. It has invested in start-ups like Volta Charging (mobility), SparkCognition (AI), DroneDeploy (aerial inspection), Nozomi Networks (operational technology security and IoT), and Aurora Solar (solar software), among others. WEC Energy is among several partners in its investor group, including GE Power, GE Renewables, and Schneider Electric, as well as other institutional, individual, and family entities.[133]

Two portfolio companies were named to the 2022 Forbes AI 50: Aurora Solar and Matroid. The list honors standouts in privately held North American companies making the most interesting and effective use of AI technology. These two firms represent two of the (only) three sustainability-focused firms on the list and is evidence of an ability to identify leaders when investing at the intersection of digitalization and sustainability.[134]

WEC Energy is positioned as a highly regarded utility with exceptional financial capability, operational performance, and enduring regulatory relationships. It commands a superior valuation because of its consistently delivered results, which are built from strong execution, carbon management, and attractive regulatory outcomes.

Dan Krueger, Executive Vice President for WEC Infrastructure and Generation Planning, discussed the value the company produced from Power the Future:

WEC executes with extremely high levels of financial and operational discipline. This level of execution creates space to further innovate by finding leading ideas and then fitting them to what our customers need and when they need it. We take this approach because we place our customer focus at the center of everything we do—from strategic planning to design and construction, operational planning and delivery, and storm response, through to everyday engagement with our customers.[135]

The company is not flashy; rather, it is steady and demonstrates its innovative capabilities through disciplined execution, operating productivity improvement, operations and maintenance expense management, and balanced regulatory outcomes. It is quietly innovative, yet recognition of these outcomes remains understated. The pursuit of new or evolved technology adoption across its system—particularly in generation—is a critical element of its operating strategy and is borne out by the breadth of its recent investment destinations, like LNG, biomass, RICE, and batteries. Innovation in the U.S. utilities industry can look very different across companies, and WEC Energy's version is not revolutionary but extremely effective in producing results for the business and customers.

CHAPTER 7

Platform Stand-Up

WITH accelerating movement toward the cleantech transition, U.S. utilities are being prodded to move from being patient subscribers to targeted, industry-sponsored R&D, to active participants in a broad R&D and innovation community. Where traditional R&D was a simple process of dedicating funding to an internal effort, supporting OEMs and vendors or relying on federal government-led efforts, the broader scope of innovation now offers a wider set of participation options that are not driven by concentrated investment or dependent on the results of a few third parties.

And while utilities historically focused on targeted R&D intended to address key assets where the investment was well worth the value received (e.g., coal-plant design and operations), large-scale bets like this have given way to smaller-scale investment in broader technology applications within the business. Utilities now have redirected their attention to the multiple microelements connected and operating within their grid and network systems that provide the level of visibility necessary to enable performance enhancement, like hardware, software, sensors, and controllers.

Even when utilities maintained some type of an ongoing formal role for their R&D activities, this role was typically compartmentalized within the business and not a natural platform for the expanded needs of emerging innovation. The truth, however, may be even more stark—what experience may have existed in a company's history had likely atrophied because of funding constraints, technology cycle lengths, and regulatory challenges, among other factors. As a result, interest waned, funding receded, and no one noticed over time. A high degree of dependency on third parties had evolved for new ideas, new technologies, and new methods, with the attendant limitations to utility influence and control.

As executives assessed *what*, *where*, and *how* to take initial steps toward adopting a more highly visible and valuable innovation model, they were faced with several key questions. First, *what* should drive how they think about innovation's purpose within the business? Second, *where* in the organization should innovation be led to enable innovation to thrive and succeed within the company? And third, *how* should innovation be positioned and executed to optimize its pursuit?

This chapter addresses these questions and the other considerations utilities face in standing up an innovation platform within the enterprise and its audiences—board of directors, leadership team, middle management, and employee base—as well as establishing the fundamental internal support elements related to supporting this effort on a sustained basis.

While the challenges faced by utilities are common across the sector, the approaches taken by the previously profiled companies differ to reflect their corporate philosophies, priorities, starting points, constraints, and capabilities. This is not surprising since the utilities industry consists of a wide range of players, representing a broad diversity in geography, scale, composition, regulation, and positioning.

In truth, while the U.S. utilities industry is dedicated to a common purpose—safety, reliability, quality, and affordability of services to its customers—it has always been unique in how differently some companies operate their businesses with respect to standards, requirements, processes, and metrics.

It has never been so standardized that only a single way of conducting the business became the model for all utilities. Each company has always exercised its judgment over its own operating choices, and obviously the choice selected reflects prevailing conditions and preferences. Just as common asset operating networks can be designed differently, utilize different components, apply different tolerances, and reflect different risk judgment, so too can an innovation platform. Particularly when blueprints or road maps are not naturally portable across companies, starting points are not consistent, and prevailing circumstances are, by definition, different and unique.

The discussion that follows provides insight into just how different innovation approaches can be among utilities. The adage that "no one size fits all" seems to be apropos for the utilities sector, and some may aver there should never be any expectation to the contrary, given how differently utilities operate similar businesses.

To the casual reader or an interested observer, the insights that emerge from this discussion are instructive but not dispositive of any single model. Each utility executive considered what provided the best fit for their company at the time. Rather than be guided by what others had done, these executives demonstrated one of the core elements of being innovative—tailoring a model that was fit-for-purpose to apply in their distinct environment and the objectives of the company.

Purpose and Aspiration

While the U.S. utilities industry has been aware since the mid-1990s that an era of energy supply competitiveness was sweeping across the globe and would disrupt their traditional businesses, the early pace of related change still took some years to gain firm footing and become more revealing in impact.

Even with the great fanfare afforded to the liberalization of energy markets in Europe, Asia-Pacific, and Latin America, the United States did not move as fast or as uniformly as other countries in adoption. This timing off-ramp from immediate adoption provided companies sufficient time to conduct informed decision analysis of options, select an appropriate strategic path, restructure the current business model, transition to the steady state, and take stock of the impacts and implications of related changes.

But this first transition—market unbundling—reflected the adoption of new policies, which were initiated at the governmental level. With policy as the catalyst, utilities had ample time to react and act without worrying about other causative externalities. That is not the case with preparing for the cleantech transition—which involves the next stage of net-zero market evolution.

The market has evolved to a different place than what was enabled by simple unbundling and restructuring an existing integrated business. At present, the market is characterized by a confluence of *technology push* and *customer pull*. This is a very different dynamic than one driven by policy. Granted the policy shift to market unbundling partially birthed today's environment of technology- and customer-driven change, but it has been the proliferation of new technologies—assets, hardware, or software—that has accelerated its pace.

As utilities determined that the observed market information signaled a surge in technological advancement, coupled with a shift in customer sentiment, this caused a change in internal perspective as well. The alignment of these two perspectives combined to redefine industry attitudes about possible futures and accelerate expectations of the sector—the future is here now, and our preparation window has shrunk.

Utilities are juggling two distinct dynamics in facing up to the cleantech transition. First, the impacts and implications are more subtle than in policy-based restructuring, which was about *where to play* along the value chain. The current challenges are about *how to play* in a selected market and succeed. Second, the drivers behind the current cleantech transition—technology and customers—are not in utility control at all, and decisions need to be made in "market time."

Where policy-based restructuring had years of advance planning time to work through the definition and design, the cleantech transition is happening in full view in real time. Utilities can leverage their history since the restructuring of the 1990s and early 2000s to assess their current position, whether still integrated or unbundled. The fundamental item to determine is the purpose of the business—that is, whether the legacy role as an incumbent energy provider or distributor is accurately defined, or whether it should be expanded or enhanced to meet market demands.

Thus, utilities are faced with a formative question regarding how to think about innovation in the future. At one end of the spectrum is leveraging external changes to maintain and improve overall business outcomes. This positioning reflects a more risk-averse view of innovation—support it and adopt its outcomes when proven. At the other end of the spectrum is actively embracing innovation and utilizing it to significantly enhance the positioning and performance of the business. This selection reflects a more aggressive view of the value of innovation—drive it and instill it as a core characteristic of the culture.

Innovation is not about just keeping abreast of industry developments, piloting new equipment or solutions when possible, and then applying them broadly once proven out. Innovation should be about continuous exploration and discovery of new technologies and approaches; actively shaping OEM and vendor response to industry operating issues; encouraging and incenting employees to think differently about the business; and intentionally bringing new technologies, products, services, or solutions to the customer.

With the industry in a continuing transition, the mindset of utility leadership should acknowledge that accelerating change is inevitable and an opportunity to capitalize on. This suggests utility executives recognize that innovation is a substantial lever to be utilized to respond to the externalities affecting the industry, and that it should be considered as an aspirational platform undertaking, rather than as an adjunct to the status quo. Innovation is about advancement and a bridge between current and future states. If utilities aspire to be meaningful players in the energy space in the future, innovation is the catalyst to enable that to occur.

In a *technology push–customer pull* environment, an incumbent can easily be disintermediated (directly, operationally, or commercially) if an OEM or vendor convinces a customer they can deal directly with them in an expanded form of asset or capability provisioning (e.g., microgrids, DERMS, demand response, rooftop solar, EV charging, and so on). It is critical for utilities to get it right on defining the *what* and *how* of their future role. Will they be a passive system operator or an active OEM, vendor, and customer partner?

Utilities do not relish the potential adverse outcomes of being disintermediated from their core assets or customers to any degree. Once allowed, it is a slippery slope toward irrelevance in the market. Thoughtfully defining how innovation plays a role in addressing the cleantech transition is key to positioning innovation as part of the fundamental business strategy.

If utilities desire to meet their customers where they have needs, they will opt to be aggressive with new technology deployment because it bridges both need dynamics. While OEMs and vendors want to interconnect with the incumbent network host, customers want to take advantage of emergent technologies that can offer the perception or reality of more personalization, such as influence, control, information, insights, and choices. In essence, is the incumbent in place to simply ensure energy supply and delivery, or is its purpose to also satisfy customer needs in a way that optimizes the value of the network?

The question of purpose—and therefore the role—of utilities in the future with respect to innovation is not much of a choice at all. The U.S. utilities industry needs to be at the forefront of innovation within the industry and is best suited to enable the evolution to, and through, the next energy transition. The real question relates to how visible and active the industry will be in shaping and executing the nature of its role: Will it be facilitator, enabler, interconnector, integrator, or optimizer?

Given the choice, most utilities would opt for a role that extends well beyond facilitating, enabling, and interconnecting. They would prefer to remain fully engaged with and valued by both their customers and the potential new market entrants who will deliver new technologies for utility or customer use. If companies believe their role is to shade toward being an integrator and optimizer, then they need to be highly visible and active in innovation with these OEMs and vendors and their customers.

Utility managements do not need to *decide* whether to emphasize and pursue innovation, but they do have to *define* their purpose and objectives of being an active innovator. Will they pursue breakthrough innovation or simple business improvement? Will they focus on future technology evolution or near-term application? Will they emphasize customer-value-centered offerings or operational deployment? Will they demonstrate industry leadership or risk-averse adoption?

Passive, disinterested observation or intentional obstruction will not enable them to maintain the coveted role they possess or convert that role into an even more valuable solutions platform for the future. This suggests that utilities need to be in front of the new technology wedge, not behind or under it, and that adequate recognition of the value of innovation exists throughout the company. When a utility can clearly articulate the linkage between its purpose, role, strategy, and innovation, then it will be in position to put in place an innovation platform that enhances the value of the company to its customers, vendors, and OEMs.

The "North Star"

U.S. and international utilities recognize that becoming an active part of the innovation community is not a choice; it is a table stake to be successful in the environment of the future. Technologies are already evolving beyond proof of concept, customers are already making decisions about what they want, vendors are already installing new types of equipment on the network, and markets are already expecting utilities to respond in ways that preserve and enhance the future.

Thus, innovation by the utilities industry, like for any other sector, is a natural expectation of investors, competitors, and customers for any business that they invest in, compete with, or rely on—it is at the core of successful competition and customer "ownership."

Once a utility moves past addressing the rationale for embracing innovation as part of its competitive mindset, the next step usually is defining its expectations from this emphasis. Innovation is an aspirational undertaking, whether targeted on a solution to a problem or focused on competitive market positioning. Consequently, how utilities think about innovation typically reflects how they think about their future market positioning aspirations—their "North Star."

For many utilities, their North Star has always been the continuation of the successful alignment of the four corners of their business purpose: providing high quality and affordable service to customers, operating safe and reliable assets within the system, maintaining good relationships with relevant regulatory stakeholders, and ensuring shareholders earn appropriate returns on their investment in the business. That is the tried-and-true formula for success of regulated, publicly owned utilities, and it has worked that way for well over 100 years.

But with the additional dimension of the cleantech transition looming, the North Star, as it relates to innovation, needs clarity to avoid overgeneralization or misappropriation. The North Star is generally recognized as a navigational beacon for travelers or a symbol of hope and inspiration. In essence, it establishes a visible guide to a company toward its future, even if the path is not always clearly marked.

It seems appropriate that in an era of escalating change and disruption, defining a company's North Star with respect to innovation is a foundational element of *how* it pursues innovation, *where* it directs its efforts, and *what* defines its objectives. The North Star for utilities in the current environment is consistently directed at reinventing the future of the company and establishing a durable and resilient enterprise to withstand the test of time.

Different companies have their unique view of their North Star or innovation vision. It depends on how they see themselves currently positioned in the market and whether they are vulnerable to the many externalities that surround U.S. utilities. It also reflects how they think about new technologies and change in general—whether they are requirements or enablers, threats or opportunities. For some companies, significant change may always be a threat, while for some it is always an opportunity.

The key in developing a company's North Star for innovation is particularizing it to the entity itself and aligning it with the overall guiding strategy in place. The North Star for innovation across U.S. utilities does not center around amount of spend, scope of interest, speed-to-market, or level of value, although these are not unimportant considerations. Rather, it is about *how* a company perceives its purpose in undertaking more concerted innovation efforts. Successful companies will use innovation to accomplish multiple purposes: create a strategic theme, illustrate a case for change, galvanize the employee base, secure the business, respond to customers, preserve future opportunities, and shift the culture.

Utilities have generally been able to articulate a rationale and purpose for undertaking and emphasizing innovation but are often more challenged in aligning defined priorities with existing business strategies. At its core, innovation seeks to understand possible futures and convert that foresight into addressable operational or market opportunities. But with multiple opportunities comes the need for optionality to provide flexibility and avoid placing the wrong bets on policies, strategies, technologies, or regulation. This flexibility is needed because the future is not certain and is not simply a set of binary options to choose among.

Utilities need to be adept at identifying likely direction and available options in the pursuit of innovation and positioning themselves to select the most informed choices based on what is known and can be reasonably expected to occur. Since markets change and technologies can become outdated, utilities need to guard against placing outsized bets on "winners" and preserve the ability to pivot as market drivers evolve.

All these expectations are reasonable to pursue from standing up or accentuating an innovation platform. The purpose of innovation in the utilities industry is to position a company to convert new technology into practical and beneficial application for the business and into value for its customers. Whether innovation is to be operationalized early or commercialized later is less important; what is important is that innovation that is pursued directly links with the priorities and strategies of the utility.

Effective Messaging

Once the executive team has established its North Star, its next agenda item in standing up its innovation platform is to communicate the underlying rationale for this intent. It is one thing for the leadership team to set a course, but an entirely different challenge to communicate *why* and *why now* to the broad employee base about this intent.

In 2013–2014, when utilities began to think more consistently and curiously about innovation, it was no longer a hot topic in American industry; it had achieved that status 15 years prior. No longer was innovation novel; it was accepted practice and mainstream across American industry—except in the utility vernacular.

Again, utilities had not been bereft of R&D activity in the past, but the current drivers and future focus that began to emerge on their radar screens around this time created a different dynamic to be addressed. Policy evolution, particularly around reduction in carbon emissions and the burgeoning interest in renewables as a viable non-carbon supply source, had begun prior to 2010, but it was now gaining momentum.

The acceleration of this policy shift at the federal and state governmental levels occurred just as a boom in entrepreneurs was occurring related to the advancement of network-focused hardware and software. Numerous start-up software and solutions companies were sprouting up, each with a different take on how utilities networks could be configured and operated, particularly regarding interconnection of micro-assets. Suddenly, the historical policy and regulatory compacts underlying the utilities sector began to look a little shaky, and the future became even hazier.

While the utilities industry was not caught unaware of these externalities, the pace of change is usually underappreciated by industries undergoing such events. The time horizon expected to future events looks a long time away—until it isn't.

At one company where I consulted, savvy executives saw that the traditional utility environment was changing around them in ways that had not been experienced before and were less predictable. Future outcomes and timing weren't always clear, but executives instinctively knew that the level of preparedness for these outcomes was not where it should be.

Significant effort was expended in painting a picture of a possible future and defining the potential timing horizon for employees. These actions reinforced the fundamental shift away from historically predictable and measured change—from managed evolution to inspired revolution. Frequent communications were used to further explain the nature, breadth, and pace of change, and to educate this group on how their future roles and responsibilities could be affected.

But the picture was not intended to simply focus on the downside of what could happen, but also to illustrate how the future could look in a positive sense (i.e., opportunities for the company and its employees). Continual engagement with employees was recognized as critical to driving the message home and ensuring the necessary level of understanding in the employee base.

Messaging focused on encouraging an environment of collaboration across the enterprise. Employees were encouraged to engage with one another in dialogue and work together to visualize the future and find solutions to emergent challenges and opportunities. At this company, increased collaboration was viewed as a paramount objective of innovation, not just around any short-term event but as a permanent part of how to work across boundaries for the benefit of the enterprise.

Thus, the principal task centers on *how* to inform, educate, and excite the broad employee base about what changes lie over the horizon and *what* the company needs to do to prepare for these future shifts and, most importantly, take advantage of them. The communication also needs to paint the picture for how to be ready to meet these challenges and to emerge intact and prospering.

Focusing on the successful launch of the effort is crucial to how the message is heard and how it is digested within the employee base. This launch messaging—whether through traditional or nontraditional channels—establishes the tone for the enterprise about innovation, not just at the outset but through succeeding periods, which could be years. Whatever channels the launch utilizes, it needs to be bold and not come across as just another initiative. It needs to immediately excite the employee base and create its own buzz about the direction of the company. After all, employees do not often get the chance to invent (or reinvent) their company during a time of turmoil.

Since the communication needs to reach all corners of the enterprise—generating plant operators, pipeline operators, storage operators, transmission system operators, distribution system operators (DSOs), customer service representatives, and headquarters staff—the message needs to be clear, strong, uplifting, persuasive, and with a bias toward action. Companies use a variety of mechanisms to get their messaging across, such as town halls, CEO streaming, brown bag meetings, website discussions, all-hands web meetings, internal publications, blogs, and small team meetings, among other mechanisms.

But if a company needs to communicate with a broad, dispersed, and diverse group, it needs to do it extremely well because it is the first impression that matters. If the employees can't grasp the rationale, or the messaging is vague and incomplete, or expectations on action are confusing, it is hard to recover from that outcome.

Any initial messaging needs to be framed from the perspective of both the company and the employee. If it is going to fully capture an employee's attention and achieve the desired response, it needs to establish the predicate (*what* is occurring), frame the impacts (*what* could result), define the ask (*what* to do), create an urgency (*when* to act), and embed the purpose (*how* to proceed).

Some companies use a vehicle called the "case for change" to deliver the initial message. This storyline lays out the changes in policies affecting the industry, the implications of these policy changes, the trends surrounding the industry, the disintermediation opportunities presented to competitors, the potential impacts to the company, the opportunities available to the company through observed trends, the readiness requirements to meet identified challenges, and the role that employees could fill in positioning the company for future success.

Using this kind of public response to executive concerns over externalities effectively creates a call to action to the entire enterprise. It lays out the drivers and the challenges, the ramifications and the opportunities, the actions and the benefits, and the expectations and the outcomes. The case for change is the foundation for an enterprise-wide effort and establishes the road map for execution.

For any effort that is intended to be enterprise-wide, the employee base is looking to the top of the organization for a signal of just how important the effort is and how serious executives are about its purpose and expectations. Like so many other enterprise-wide efforts in utilities, the CEOs often find themselves as the focal point for visibility and voice.

Savvy CEOs use a variety of mechanisms to help communicate their messaging and its importance. For large utilities with more than 10,000 employees, it is hard to reach the entire employee base in a timely and seamless manner that provides adequate insight into messaging purpose and intent and still further provides the "power of the position" to reinforce executive commitment without requiring omnipresent physical presence. And it is even harder to make it work in much larger companies.

Fortunately, current technology enables CEOs to overcome some of these challenges and reach large and remote groups (if not all) employees through mechanisms like a variation of TED.com, videoconferencing, and in-house streaming. The mechanism is far less important than the message, but many an initiative has gotten off to a rocky start because initial communications were not adequately planned and addressed.

Once the case for change has been laid out, a company can immediately initiate its efforts to build a vibrant innovation platform, or it may utilize additional methods to engage the employee base as a precursor to deeper actions. This is further discussed in a subsequent chapter.

Leadership and Placement

Another formative question that emerges when a company announces it will elevate its innovation game relates to what level to align overall responsibility and accountability for the effort within the enterprise. In practice, CEOs are often the natural selection focus because anything that reaches across the entire organization (e.g., business restructuring, cost streamlining, and so on) is the logical domain of the office, with the business unit leads owning their vertical unit issues.

The CEO is a logical starting point for driving innovation across a company because the intent is to motivate the total employee base to expanded collaboration and cooperation. No other position has an equivalent level of stature to move an entire organization in a new or different direction. But being a visible champion for innovation does not mean that a CEO needs to own the day-to-day leadership of innovation simply because they are at the top of the organization.

Often, transformational change within a business may be the brain-child of a CEO because of their overall experience, market awareness, or general prescience, or because they themselves are a force of nature and possess a capacity and style of exhorting employees into action. In some cases, CEOs have built their reputations as being successful change agents and leading companies into transformative activities, creating a personal leadership brand that employees gravitate toward.

In the early days of utility focus, it was typical for the CEO to be the face of innovation because employees were generally unfamiliar with the term and thought they were not licensed to be innovators. This position was recognized as having the broadest perspective about future direction and would either be a catalyst for change or an impediment. And if the case for change had already been established, chances are pretty good that the CEO was a principal architect. So, if the organization needed to shift its focus or priorities, it was going to count on the CEO to make it happen anyway.

It is difficult to argue with having the CEO as the face or champion of innovation; after all, the role is the focal point of company strategy and direction. And no other position commands the respect of an employee base as does the CEO role. If a company is serious about innovation—or any other transformative change—the CEO is critical to its success. No other position has the same gravitas to draw employees together, ensure commitments are followed through and obstacles are removed, and aspirations are turned into realities.

But CEOs are busy individuals and can be absent from their offices for extended periods because of inside or outside business responsibilities. Maintaining the CEO as the face or champion of innovation and creating opportunities for consistent, ongoing messaging are the best ways to ensure the employee base sustains its belief in the effort and its importance to the company. Determining how to position innovation within the business—formal or informal, integrated or diffused—is next to figure out.

After the innovation launch is conducted—whether through a high-profile event or plain-spoken communication—a company needs to consider how to reflect this new emphasis organizationally. As stated earlier, innovation is not an initiative or a program as those things connote a term and an end. Innovation is also not a typical process with roles and boundaries, as it reflects multiple interactions, multiple disciplines, and unconstrained time frames. Endorsing innovation as an important strategic platform and capabilities lever communicates a commitment to change, as well as an intent to redefine the company in the market and reshape the boundaries of creative ideation within the company.

There has been no uniformity in model among utilities standing up an innovation capability. Some companies use formal approaches where a specific organizational unit is established to frame, oversee, support, integrate, and optimize all innovation work, often reporting directly to the CEO. Others elect not to establish a unique, executive-led reporting unit to the CEO, but to create a unit within another logical part of the business, like strategy, corporate development, marketing, or operations. This approach provides a home for innovation but maintains it within core groups. Still, other companies choose not to establish any formal organization under the notion that it is not a specific individual or organization that has responsibility for innovation; rather, innovation is the responsibility of all individual employees.

Three alternatives exist for defining how to position innovation within a company. There is no right or wrong option because each one reflects a philosophy within that business about how it chooses to position responsibilities, align relationships, collaborate across groups, and drive to attaining objectives. Some corporate cultures are command-and-control-oriented, where more structure is viewed as preferred, while others are more resilient and flexible and believe engagement and openness are beneficial (see Figure 33).

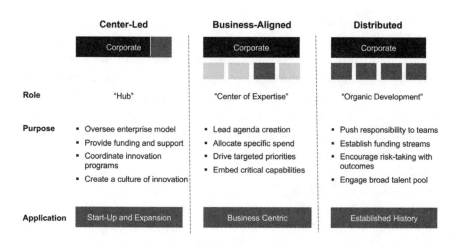

Figure 33. Innovation placement models.

- *Center-led:* This model creates a formal organization (at least at inception) intended to signify importance and commitment, as well as provide a hub for pursuit of various ideas, technologies, and offerings. This hub also serves as a face to the broad innovation community of universities, laboratories, incubators, and start-ups. The innovation organization could be a separate report to the CEO or part of a service company, if one exists.

- *Business-aligned:* This model places innovation closer to groups focused on business growth, strategy definition, and/or operations execution. It maintains a certain level of visibility of innovation while it focuses on activities conducted a little closer to the business core. Hub responsibilities would also follow placement in this model. The innovation organization could reside in a logical business unit where its value would be highest.

- *Distributed:* This model does not establish any formal organization and purposely pushes innovation down to the group, team, and individual. It treats innovation as a viral phenomenon that changes its shape repeatedly. Under this model, no market hub responsibilities are assumed to be executed. This devolved model could serve to avoid centralizing innovation under any specific owner and emphasize its ubiquity.

Any of the above approaches could be adopted without necessarily increasing the risk of attaining actual outcomes, as the formal versus informal structure decision comes down to the philosophy of the senior executives. However, for utilities that have less experience and insight into disruptive technologies, go-to-market models, and product, service, and solution development, there are benefits from taking an enterprise view over a local one, particularly in a stand-up situation.

Even for large utilities, the launch of an enterprise-wide effort is complicated as resource selection and assignment can be vexing, such as defining needed capabilities, identifying skilled candidates, and transferring people between organizations. For small to midsize companies, the challenges are even worse as the available resource complement is already busy and the talent pool is simply smaller. And since a dedicated innovation team is what it takes to typically succeed, the constraints of existing resources are governors on just how broadly scoped the innovation effort can be.

The most straightforward approach to standing up the innovation effort is to initially house it at the enterprise level, both to reinforce its visibility to the full organization and to give it close access to members of the full leadership team (which after announcement all become innovation ambassadors). This placement offers initial simplicity and avoids other complications, such as priority attention, cross-business coordination, and idea ownership, and if placed elsewhere, alignment may add another layer of complexity. This does not mean that innovation leadership will interminably remain at the corporate level but that the interests of the enterprise are best served by securing a clear and simple stand-up as rapidly as possible.

For a new effort with the visibility and importance of innovation, it is important to secure firm footing before launching a host of random and unconnected activities. As a highly visible and celebrated enterprise effort, innovation stand-up is often expected to demonstrate almost immediate, visible results, even though it is embryonic. This focus on "more, better, faster" is normal but unfortunate, as it reflects an internal view in the employee body that just announcing corporate intent and pulling a few resources together will change the near-term trajectory of the business.

The desire for near-term results needs to be tempered by the reality that innovation is played as a long game, and success is measured in years versus weeks and months. Consequently, after the initial announcement of an enhanced focus on innovation throughout the business, attention needs to be given to the details of the stand-up itself.

The company needs to affirm the day-to-day aspects of the stand-up and leadership of the effort or group. The CEO can still function as the innovation champion for the enterprise, but there is much to do regarding the fundamentals of location, leadership, strategy, agenda, staffing, infrastructure, presence building, and communications:

- *Location:* The choice exists to house innovation within or outside the headquarters facility. Ensuring the ability to easily collaborate and openly dialogue with colleagues is generally the foremost consideration.

- *Leadership:* The day-to-day innovation effort needs senior executive direction to provide broad business experience and represent the needs of the effort with the collective senior team.

Leadership at this level also increases the clout necessary to secure adequate funding.

- *Strategy:* The strategy for the innovation effort needs to fully integrate with the enterprise strategy. Establishing both near-term and long-term priorities for focus is grounded in how the enterprise views its overall expectations and priorities.

- *Agenda:* The scope for potential innovation is as wide as the range of ideas that can be generated. Setting a clear agenda is the critical linchpin to confirm where the business sees potential value and avoid chasing disconnected ideas that dilute the resources available.

- *Staffing:* Scaling the dedicated innovation team is a challenge as it needs to balance scope, capabilities, and number, with expectations. Once the actual resource requirements are determined, they need to be released from their host organizations quickly to staff up.

- *Infrastructure:* Once the location to house the innovation team is known, the related infrastructure to support facilities, workstations, conference rooms, communications, videoconferencing, and demonstration capabilities needs to be sourced and installed.

- *Presence building:* An immediate need exists to publicize the existence of the innovation effort within the nearby innovation community. Attention also needs to be given to creating more national recognition and building relationships with OEMs, vendors, and partners.

- *Communications:* An ongoing capability needs to be housed or assigned to enable the innovation team to continue to create visibility into the agenda, activities, and accomplishments of the innovation effort.

If a utility is serious about pursuing innovation as a strategic differentiator, then it will need to be connected to the innovation ecosystem of players, wherever they may reside. A utility would also want to be aligned with force multipliers like venture capital funds, research labs, and so on that can extend their market reach in a coordinated manner. Additionally, a utility would seek to garner internal executive support for innovation on a multiyear and sustained basis. All these outcomes are more difficult the further innovation efforts are diffused within the organization.

Some companies have attempted to further enhance their approach to innovation by establishing critical mass to their actions. For example, Ameren, Duke Energy, Exelon, and Southern Company created formal innovation centers outside existing company headquarters after standing up their initial efforts. The centers were staffed by dedicated employees from across the business who were focused on standing up the effort, accelerating the innovation learning curve, and leading internal efforts on technology assessments or adoption use cases.

For Ameren, an unused facility adjacent to the headquarters building was repurposed to provide for open collaboration within the employee base and to serve as an ideation space and "war room" for the various teams that had been created. At Duke Energy, an older building in Charlotte was refurbished to provide a stand-alone space for significant numbers of employees to gather, ideate, collaborate, and develop solutions.

Exelon created a space removed from its headquarters, which allowed it to be part of a start-up and incubation community in downtown Chicago. And Southern Company also created its Energy Innovation Center in a separate facility in the center of the technology community in midtown Atlanta.

All these companies recognized that if innovation activities were intended to be successfully conducted and expected results realized, several elements needed to be addressed: the innovation ecosystem community needed to be close at hand to enable walk-in discussion and natural collaboration; the facilities needed to provide for both small- and large-scale collaboration, as well as test bench capabilities; and employees needed space for ideation away from the day-to-day requirements of the business.

Innovation stand-up and adoption are far more challenging than innovation introduction and announcement. Visible, formal leadership and structure are critical to reinforce the message that the future organization intends to move further and faster on innovation than the legacy company imagined possible. But standing up an innovation effort does not make a company an effective innovator. It takes continuous attention to what is occurring in the marketplace and the innovation community to stay abreast of new trends, technologies, use cases, competitor inroads, investor sentiments, and customer attitudes to build a robust set of current and prospective information and data to drive future strategies and priorities.

More importantly, it takes a vision of what the CEO and executives seek to achieve from their innovation efforts to set the stage for how to make innovation sustainable. Like so many other success elements in a business, that vision usually centers on people expectations—what executives truly want, what employees can deliver, what barriers to outcomes exist, and what the current culture can accommodate.

Organization and Resources

Defining the *what* of the innovation organization itself is a necessary predicate for then determining the *where* or location of the organization. This task is pivotal to positioning the organization so it can bring necessary resources and emphasis to the execution of the innovation strategy. This initial organization is a foundational structure that can be expected to evolve over time as market and innovation experience is gained and the growing pains of stand-up are ameliorated.

The organization initially established needs to be well structured but also reflect sound organizational principles. These principles include being clear in design and accountability, fit-for-purpose to match the utility's objectives, strategy- and market-focused, simplified and efficient, effective in enabling interfaces and decision-making, scalable and portable, and flexible for the future.

The sponsoring executive needs to frame the organization to be structured in a manner that is outside-in (i.e., intentionally designed to match market challenges), instead of reflecting functional or conventional approaches to organization. The stand-up of the innovation organization is an opportunity to demonstrate to the employee base that leadership understands the nature of the challenge and is prepared to think more dynamically than has historically occurred.

A traditional organization model for innovation could follow a functional, market-based, or topical approach. The functional approach could define responsibilities along a typical planning-execution-support model where resources are aligned by primary activities. The market-based approach could establish responsibilities to match go-to-market areas like storage, mobility, renewables, DERMS, or behind-the-meter. A topical approach could be adopted to reflect responsibilities in areas like strategy, policy, product development, and communications, among other areas.

A different model for innovation is required to step outside how executives typically think in the normal course of business. For innovation, the structure needs to be unconstrained by organizational design norms (like spans) and reflective of the kinds of challenges that the enterprise faces (like growth and disruption).

The organizational model for innovation needs to reflect the philosophy of leadership and be designed with a strong market orientation in mind. An outside-in "straw dog" model for potential capabilities of an innovation organization could be designed along the lines of Figure 34. This model illustrates a hybrid structure of capabilities, where certain natural functions, like strategy and product development, are in place, as well as support functions like business support (in addition to more market-oriented areas like product management, venture capital, and ideation and development).

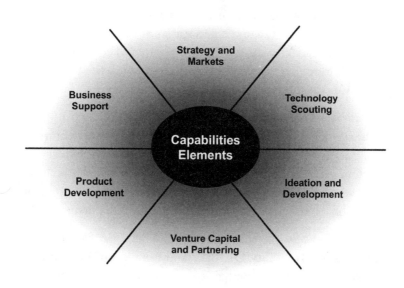

Figure 34. Resources for innovation.

This "straw dog" model as an illustration of an innovation model that is designed with an outside-in perspective might not fit everywhere, depending on leadership prerogatives, but it could fit anywhere as an initial innovation organization structure. The principal functions shown would reflect the following logic and composition:

- *Strategy and markets:* This organization would conduct external market scanning and development of the innovation strategy and game plan. It would focus on identifying external trends, such as policy proposals and direction, peer strategies, disruptor actions, customer requirements, potential opportunities, and creating a multiyear blueprint for innovation.

- *Technology scouting:* This organization would conduct technology scanning and oversee the early identification and evaluation of new technologies and their applicability to the business. It would function as a screening partner to identify potential new R&D or application for further assessment by the businesses.

- *Ideation and development:* This organization would coordinate the conduct of ongoing ideation sessions with vertical product teams and establish or arrange the necessary test benches or developmental lab facilities for exploration or proof of concept. This is a specialist group that would support on- and off-site test activities with OEMs and vendors, as well as with customers.

- *Venture capital and partnering:* This group would identify and manage relationships with third-party investors and venture capital funds, as well as identify potential private or public ecosystem partners that could align to support knowledge sharing and accelerate market entry. The organization would also identify additional market channels and collaboration to pursue.

- *Product development:* This group would take a vertical view of markets (e.g., mobility, DERMS, and storage) and also address challenges like origination, pricing, and go-to-market strategies. This organization would charter and oversee various projects in flight within the innovation team and closely align with other internal business units in analysis and assessment.

- *Business support:* This group would perform certain administrative services for the group, like planning and budgeting, infrastructure management, and communications. This organization would also arrange the provision of certain other corporate-level services, like recruiting and compensation, project management, and internal technology support.

The initial product development vertical areas would reflect the priorities of the enterprise and the key areas of interest for market assessment. The number of product areas will need to be managed so that they reflect critical market areas versus a broad cast across the universe of potential product areas. The entire organization needs to be established with an eye toward building it out as experience is gained and a sense of priority and opportunity are affirmed. While the initial innovation organization needs to have sufficient scale and mass to be effective, it is also embryonic and does not need to create a quick cash drain on the enterprise.

More importantly, the innovation organization—both initial and evolved—will seek part-time resources from the business to supplement those from within the group. It is essential to recognize that there are few "renaissance" resources (i.e., broadly erudite) available within most companies, and it is important to directly involve resources from the business to leverage their expertise and enable effective handoff to the businesses at the appropriate future juncture.

As the innovation model matures, it will naturally evolve with project execution experience, as well as with shifts in market focus and expansion of verticals or modification of other market-facing units like venture capital, partnering, and ideation and development. As this model matures, the nature, number, and capabilities of the team will also likely expand, although the permanent members may rotate in and out. And potentially, certain innovation activities could be pushed down into the overall company organization to reflect evolved emphases on linking innovation directly to the business.

This chapter focused on the stand-up of an integration effort and some of the considerations that need to be addressed at formation. Sometimes, the largest hurdle to get over is understanding what innovation is and what it isn't. It is not an initiative or a process because it is intended to be perpetual. It is not an organizational unit because it is not a gatekeeper for the enterprise, and the spirit is intended to permeate the company thinking. It is a permanent mindset that focuses on creating a regenerative model for creative thinking and novel action, and it is a ubiquitous platform that can be accessed and tapped into on demand and drives collaboration across an enterprise.

The next chapter picks up the innovation cycle at a later moment, when companies sometimes hit the wall on progress and find the need to revisit *where* they are and *how* they got there. Consideration of these execution and growth hurdles is just as important as formation activities. In fact, the need for an innovation refresh is often the best means to reinvigorate the overall effort and reenergize the employee base.

CHAPTER 8

Achieving Success

O NCE the launch of the innovation effort is announced, and purpose, priorities, and leadership are in hand, the real stand-up work
begins. Observed experience suggests that with even the best of
intent, it will still take several weeks to months to completely address and
resolve the issues of scope and infrastructure (*what*), location (*where*),
and staffing (*who* and *how many*) that are core to bringing the effort to life.

The stand-up of the innovation effort parallels starting any new
organization—little to nothing exists. No road map is in place to provide
a guide through the process, everyone is generally new to the topic and
team, and neither the remainder of the enterprise nor the new team knows
exactly what to expect or do next. Although typical, given these inherent
challenges, what could stand in the way of success?

As the innovation team is built and assembled, companies have to navigate a period where almost everything appears to be in flux: people are
transitioning out of existing jobs; the team is meeting together for the
first time; the agenda is still to be developed; priorities need to be established; timelines need to be fixed; projects need to be defined with roles
and resources identified; budgets need to be determined; and clear linkages
to the rest of the enterprise need to be put in place, among a host of other
stand-up areas requiring attention. This is the core "blocking and tackling"
that precedes and underlies getting to the point where the team can focus

on ideation, evaluation, and market introduction, and then aggressively pursue the intended innovation agenda.

The first order of business is to architect the plan (the punch list) to attack stand-up execution requirements, and then design the blueprint (the road map) to propel the effort from its starting point through steady state. The punch list is the same as usually what exists for any project (i.e., areas, tasks, responsibilities, timelines, and outcomes), and the faster it can be developed, the better. The road map is critical to understand because multiple dependencies permeate the stand-up process—the agenda is driven by defined priorities, task timing depends on available resources, and infrastructure is tied directly to team scale, among other circumstances.

Creating the punch list and road map will be among the least innovative activities the team will ever undertake; however, doing both well enables the team to initiate and complete fundamental activities faster and vigorously turn attention externally to the marketplace.

Successfully completing the kinds of activities enumerated above provides the innovation effort the foundation to directly move from stand-up to execution, with the focus now directed externally versus putting an organization and capabilities set into place.

After announcement of the innovation effort enables utilities to effectively function from an organizational perspective, the focus and shape of the innovation model will evolve in an unpredictable manner. Prior hypotheses will not always prove out, and market conditions will generally not be quite as expected. The pace of change will likely be accelerated, with the market altering course. Utilities need to go into their innovation efforts expecting to be continually surprised and to be agile enough to pivot on short notice. Consequently, utilities will not rely on innovation stand-up version 1.0 for an extended period. Like opportunities in the market, the initial model will be perishable and evolve to what each utility learns in its specific market.

Building Momentum

Standing up an initial innovation model is consequential to a utility as it establishes the framework for leading subsequent efforts. Even though decisions still need to be made to flesh out the innovation team, these are relatively straightforward and do not capture a large part of innovation leadership's time.

What should occupy the leadership is to ensure that after announcement or launch, the innovation effort gets off to a purposeful, smart, and rapid start. This certainly means that formation activities do not extend beyond a reasonable execution time and that there is no lapse in decision time for critical items. The innovation team needs to operate in market time, which is fundamental to its purpose and mandate. Competitors think this way and do not allow internal impediments to slow down work that is linked directly to market success.

There is a wide range of emerging technologies around which an innovation agenda can be crafted. A key challenge to utilities as they stand up their innovation efforts is to get the agenda right—not overly broad, but not too limited; not excessively ambitious, but not unchallenging; and most importantly, built around what will matter to their customers and the overall business.

A fundamental issue that many companies face when standing up an effort is defining the *what* and *how* for the focus of innovation. A company might ask whether it should assess from an internal or customer perspective, prioritize performance or positioning, evaluate through an enterprise or business unit lens, address near- or longer-term issues and opportunities, focus on quantitative or qualitative outcomes, drive to operationalization or commercialization, and emphasize revenues or costs.

The answer to many of those questions is a qualified yes; it depends on the utility's philosophy and circumstances. To be effective, any innovation scoping assessment needs to consider the opportunity, the impacts, and the outcomes to the current provider's business, as well as the related benefits to customers. But the capacity of an innovation effort to address a broad innovation agenda is constrained by the size of the team, the experience of the individuals, the priorities of the strategy, the nature and capabilities of external partners, and the time to market of opportunities.

As discussed in Chapter 2, there are numerous primary technology areas that are receiving attention from utilities because of their timeliness, applicability, and functionality. These include those related to mobility, batteries and storage, DERMS, hydrogen, AI, and behind-the-meter developments like domotics, among many other over-the-horizon technologies. All these technologies are between nascent and early stages, and utilities are actively engaged in assessment and adoption at various levels of commitment. The innovation team needs to be able to not just focus on the identifiable technologies but also have the curiosity and bandwidth to look over the horizon for what may be upon the industry in the next 5 to 10 years.

Regarding the innovation *what* and *how* focuses above, an innovation team needs to consider the scope of ideation and evaluation to be broader than technology as a single category. Earlier, I addressed the three critical types of innovation: *incremental, advanced,* and *breakthrough.* Generally, utilities tend to look internally for improvement whenever an undertaking like innovation is chartered. It is natural to look at *what we do,* and then determine *how to do it better.* That is the lowest threshold and provides the greatest population of "slow, fat rabbits" to capture within a short time frame to improve operations.

But that only gets a company to the point of *incremental* innovation—improving what we do rather than dramatically evolving the approach and methods to significantly advance the business. That takes longer to accomplish and requires more open-mindedness to radically different thinking about *how* to perform (e.g., with respect to technology application). Of course, that brings more potential risk to the company into consideration, since both utilities and regulators are generally risk averse, and there is no certainty that expectations will materialize.

The final innovation type, *breakthrough,* is a major shift in the role of a utility and how it performs its work. This form of innovation is even more stressful to companies because, as the level of related risk ratchets upward, the more changes lean to the side of being game changers and being difficult to explain to regulators and customers (e.g., new services or markets).

Utilities need to be agile enough to think beyond incremental and performance enhancement types of innovation. They need to think of themselves as disruptors to their own business and approach the challenge from competitor and customer points of view. They need to ask themselves, "*How* does my competitor think about disintermediating me?" and "*How* do my customers think I should be adding value to them?" These questions suggest that companies should expand the scope of *where to look* for innovation and think of both hard and soft sources for innovation application (see Figure 35):

- *Processes:* Improving *how* activities are conceived and executed offers almost ubiquitous applicability to identify *incremental* to *advanced* opportunity.

- *Technology:* The assessment, evaluation, and adoption of emergent technologies—particularly digital—offers high-value opportunity to achieve *advanced* to *breakthrough* impacts.

- *Regulatory:* Evolving traditional regulatory paradigms and standard models is an important but often overlooked source for meaningful impact to the business.

- *Products and services:* The identification and development of new products, services, and solutions offerings is a traditional way to create the bases for all types of innovation.

- *Business models:* Redefining *how* to make money in role, delivery, bundling, channel expansion, or pricing creates opportunities for enabling *advanced* and *breakthrough* outcomes.

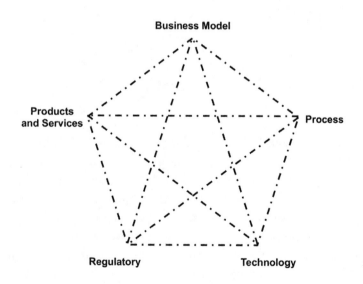

Figure 35. Focus areas for innovation.

Most utilities have found it easier to focus on *incremental* innovation in some areas because it is the most natural (i.e., more tangible, more common, least difficult, or least risky). That is why innovation advancements made by utilities tend to relate to the operations side of the business, where thinking is traditional, labor intensity is high, productivity is mixed, processes are antiquated, and technologies are outdated. In a different sense, most utilities do not think about products, services, and business model innovation, as these have not been a natural place to look. Utilities do not offer many discrete, unbundled products and services, and the formula for profitability is a function of ratemaking.

But this is changing as technologies open up opportunities for broader customer engagement about the role a utility can perform for a customer, services it can provide, and how it can create value for that customer. Similarly, new technologies open the aperture on redefining the fundamental business model and how utilities can expand their sources of value to be captured, particularly in pricing.

If utilities adopt a broad view of innovation—one that is not only operations centered—they can unlock the potential to reshape the incumbent-customer relationship. If they can think more commercially about the innovation they pursue, they could then have an opportunity to change the nature of the value equation as well.

Fit-for-Purpose

Where and *how* utilities determine to pursue innovation should directly align with *what* they are interested in accomplishing within their future business. Their innovation agenda should directly reflect their strategies and priorities, both of which are informed by their current market and infrastructure positioning, their perspective on the future direction of key market drivers, and their expectations for future internal or external outcomes.

Innovation is art, not science—there are no sacrosanct rules; nor are there prescribed paths to success. Each utility is driven by its own set of influences and expectations. Consequently, the innovation model—and therefore the longer-term platform—needs to be designed to be fit-for-purpose (in a nonlegal connotation); that is, the quality of the outputs and outcomes meets the standard of expectation of the entity. Stated differently, the innovation model is established to meet the goals each utility sets forth when it decides to stand up its innovation activities.

Why is this important? Since there is no paint-by-number approach to innovation, the degree of flexibility in approach is extremely high for individual utilities. Further, utilities do not start from the same market or operational position, thus the purpose, priorities, and expectations of each company are uniquely different. Consequently, an innovation model that works for one company may not work for another, regardless of how similar in scale, composition, or strategy they appear to be.

Utilities need to recognize that while they share many of the same challenges, risks, and objectives of their peers, how one company sees pursuing innovation as a source for advancement in customer engagement will be different from its peers because underlying regulatory conditions, pricing positions, and go-to-market approaches differ. Similarly, one company's perceived need for distribution operations innovation will differ because current technologies in place, system performance, and local operating conditions are not the same as for another peer. And a company interested in creating new sources of revenue from expanded products, services, and solutions will look at the environment differently than another utility that has already been seeking ways to enhance customer engagement and increase the value of the customer relationship.

Utilities can and do continually scan the strategies and actions of their peers to understand their focus and direction, as well as share experiences about operational complexities, regulatory frameworks, and customer attitudes. These observations are interesting and useful and provide welcome peer insights, but they are less valuable to designing an innovation model that will be fit-for-purpose to any specific utility.

Companies need to design the innovation model they choose to stand up to be unique and differentiating, because it not only addresses their direct strategic challenges but also reflects the inherent persona of the enterprise—the philosophies, priorities, norms, and values specific to their entity. Fit-for-purpose innovation model design will be tailored to the needs of the specific company and framed by consideration of several baseline elements:

- *Current challenges to business positioning:* A foundation to the innovation model is understanding *what* the key challenges

to the business are. Declining performance, customer dissatisfaction, capabilities gaps, customer relationships, technology
shortcomings, market disintermediation, market perception,
peer positioning, and value shortfalls can all hint at areas where
pursuit of innovation could be advantageous.

- *Root causes for perceived challenges:* The above challenges can be
influenced by *how* the utility views its fundamental performance.
Sluggish demand, increasing costs, insufficient resources, inefficient processes, asset failures, regulatory problems, customer
dissatisfaction, employee malaise, and competitor growth can
all point to opportunities to leverage innovation in technology
adoption, offering expansion or capital dedication.

- *Perspectives on market evolution:* A more important consideration will be *how* the future may look versus a preoccupation
with current position. Policy evolution, technology proliferation,
customer optionality, interoperability standards, competitor
encroachment, and AI are all even more impactful considerations to drive the future innovation model.

- *Aspirations for future positioning:* Framing the future innovation model will also need to consider just *where* the utility sees
itself in this disrupted future. Trade-offs exist over whether a
utility seeks to be a market leader, a competitive peer, or just an
operationally excellent provider. This decision has a considerable impact on establishing its priorities and aggressiveness in
resource allocation and dedication.

- *Value contribution from innovation:* The expected outcomes from
innovation are also important to further define and shape the
parameters of the model. Utilities have choices of *what* to expect
from their innovation model and can choose whether to focus
operationally on technology deployment for performance or
shift the emphasis toward commerciality and seek revenues from
new products, services, and solutions.

These considerations allow the utility to frame its fit-for-purpose innovation model with an informed perspective on *why* to undertake a focus
on innovation. Since there are choices to be made regarding the focus and

intensity of the innovation model, getting the rationale (*why*) and intent (*what*) correct is critical to being able to then design the innovation model to match what executives are attempting to achieve.

To make an innovation model fit-for-purpose, it should be designed with the intent to define and illustrate the key elements that the utility wants to establish as core to the manner in which the model exists in the current company operating environment. These elements will define the position within the business, alignment with other operating organizations, movement from ideas to realization, and the specific outcomes it intends to achieve.

- *Role:* The model should be clear about the specific role to be fulfilled by the dedicated team. The intent should be to acknowledge its positioning as an adjunct to the current business and to enable advancement of the business outside of traditional channels.

- *Priorities:* Specific projects and objectives of the model should be clear to the overall enterprise, complementary to the existing strategy guiding the business, and concentrated on improving enterprise readiness for the future.

- *Capabilities:* The model should enable the necessary skills within the resources dedicated to ongoing execution to be obtained, whether from the permanent team, within the business, or externally, if required.

- *Interfaces:* The model should also illustrate and explain that the dedicated team will maintain several key ongoing relationships with its executive sponsor, the leadership team, the business units, key functions, and project teams to ensure transparency and awareness.

- *Decision rights:* It should be clear that the intended model does not centralize any decision rights in the core team; rather, it intends that group to function as an extension of the business, and key business decisions will be made at the appropriate levels of the business.

- *Collaboration:* The model should clearly establish that its intent is to be a fully cooperative and collaborative innovation effort, blending expert team resources with non-team experts through project staffing from within the organization.

- *Risks:* Recognition of the existence of various business risks should be an inherent element of the model, and a clear process to identify, assess, and mitigate risks between the dedicated team and the appropriate affected parts of the business will be in place.

- *Community:* The model should recognize and embrace the need to participate in the broad innovation ecosystem and incorporate resources, processes, and funding to accomplish and expand the visibility of the business.

- *Partnering:* The model needs to recognize that external market knowledge and positioning exist outside the dedicated team, and that these capabilities will be leveraged to enable all expertise and channels to the market to be fully exploited.

- *Impacts:* The desired outcomes from model execution (e.g., revenues, earnings, strategic position, market value, and future flexibility) should be clear from the priorities already established and the specific projects that are undertaken through the model.

- *Value:* Building and capturing value through innovation are critical elements of success, and the nature of value to the business that is being pursued should be identifiable to the enterprise through the intent and focus of the model and the project.

- *Communication:* Using the dedicated team to keep the enterprise fully informed of its activities and progress, as well as to build visibility and momentum to the agenda, should be an embedded element of the model.

The initial fit-for-purpose innovation model should take a 360-degree view of the manner in which the model will align, execute, and contribute to the business. By its design and content, it should illustrate differentiation from the present business and communicate that the innovation model in place is uniquely positioned to drive the nature of change the enterprise is seeking.

This model will not be the only innovation model that will be adopted over the course of the enterprise's pursuit of innovation. The model will likely further evolve to fit emerging business needs as more experience is gained and as externalities affect how the business sees that it needs to be positioned. This may involve only some slight updating, it may involve a repositioning or partial devolvement to the business, or it may be radically repurposed to match new or modified needs of the business.

Governance and Alignment

The model, organization, staffing, and infrastructure for standing up innovation are all critical dimensions of positioning the overall innovation effort effectively within the utility. But two important dimensions often under-considered are the overall enterprise governance model regarding innovation and the alignment of the innovation model with the existing enterprise strategy.

The top-down governance model for utilities is well established and operates seamlessly across the vertical business segments, service entities, and subsidiaries. It generally works so well because it has been almost perpetual in its design and execution, carried over with modest change from CEO to CEO. The decision-making processes are straightforward, and the decision rights are well defined by role, group, and position.

But most governance processes are designed from a top-down perspective—a cascading level of mechanisms that link the enterprise to the segment, the segment to the business unit, the business unit to the function—with the discrete management mechanisms (e.g., committees) including representatives from across leadership and management. These governance mechanisms are designed to function top-down under the working assumption that the collection of multiple existing mechanisms cover the business holistically.

A newly stood-up innovation model would effectively exist outside the normal governance process and would need to be "designed in" to the process or covered through an existing mechanism. If the innovation model is intended to be viewed as an enterprise undertaking, then it needs to be specifically designed in as well, or it may become subordinated to being only a topical discussion point, rather than a stand-alone focal point.

There are several ways in which to accomplish this emphasis and visibility: incorporate innovation as a distinct topical session for leadership team review (not just buried in general updates) with executive sponsor presentation responsibility; establish a separate innovation council within the executive team to meet separately with sponsors and teams to directly focus on progress, issues, and accomplishments; and/or require regular update and decision guidance presentations, if not otherwise incorporated into regular governance sessions.

While typical governance processes focus on the reports of the CEO on emergent enterprise issues and executives providing regular issue and performance updates in their vertical domain, less time is spent as a group on the strategic issues of the enterprise or talking directly about strategy itself. By comparison, innovation is a recurring topical point, where strategy is occasional and operating performance is constant. Innovation is a uniquely different strategic subject area as it permeates the enterprise at multiple levels and across multiple organizations. Further, innovation addresses intellectual rather than physical inputs, and outputs address market offerings, core business transformation, and outcomes achieved, rather than operating assets and customer and regulatory issues.

The objectives of recognizing the uniqueness of innovation are twofold: embed innovation into formal governance processes to continue to reinforce its importance to the enterprise, and then engage the executive team in an innovation exploration and discovery experience on a contemporaneous basis. In this sense, innovation governance is not just an extension of the general management model and focused on information sharing but a natural vehicle to enable the leadership team to learn in real time about innovation as a strategic enabler and a fundamental element of the enterprise mindset going forward.

The other focus of governance is attaining concurrence that the direction of the innovation model remains consistent with the objectives of the enterprise, and that alignment exists across and within the business on priorities, performance, and positioning.

Since innovation execution cuts across the enterprise, and at any time all the various business segments or units may be engaged or affected, it is essential to ensure the respective vertical businesses and organizations are aligned on focus, implications, and outcomes. Innovation projects can easily cross businesses and corporate support functions and create intentional and unintentional impacts to those entities or individuals not directly involved in the specific projects in flight. Accordingly, mechanisms need to exist to ensure there are no surprises or regrets when projects reach readiness to transfer ownership from innovation to the business.

In addition to governance at the enterprise level, alignment within the lower levels of the business needs to occur on a simultaneous basis. On the one hand, direct engagement of business resources via integration within the project teams provides a means to enable the businesses to have direct eyes on project parameters, activities, progress, direction, and indicated outcomes. This is the most direct means by which project insights can be obtained on a contemporaneous basis and management can stay informed. But limited status reporting is a poor mechanism for simple progress information sharing when another mechanism can be adopted to provide greater benefit to involved or affected business units.

The utilization of regular innovation forums at the business unit level offers a deeper and more natural mechanism for information sharing, but also for business unit education on critical matters related to projects and market-based insights. This mechanism offers broader and deeper insights that can be missed if the focus is overly directed at an individual project.

Here, the recurring engagement of innovation leadership with business and functional counterparts provides broader communication of ongoing market and project insights to the "customers" of innovation, thus allowing the business unit and functional leadership to obtain deeper insight into emergent challenges to their domains, as well as greater appreciation for the work being performed on their behalf.

These forums do not add onerous complications to the existing governance process; rather, they provide a specific opportunity for operating executives and managers to focus on innovation as an enabler to their business, understand the progress and challenges with specific projects, and communicate additional business innovation interests to innovation leadership. The investment of a couple of hours bimonthly is modest for the value that can be obtained by the businesses.

A more critical outcome for focus is ensuring that the innovation agenda is fully aligned with the direction and priorities reflected in the enterprise strategy. The innovation agenda is not the province only of the innovation team; it is the product of full consideration of the market readiness, technology evolution, and business improvement needs of the company, where the strategy team is acutely involved in architecting business direction and priorities.

This should be relatively easy to ensure, but the challenge is that strategies are not usually reconstructed each year, only refreshed. In contrast, the innovation agenda is reset each year based on direct insights obtained from the projects underway, as well as market experience obtained from engagement with the broad innovation ecosystem and continuous scanning of market, technology, and customer trends.

Certainly, projects can have longer than a single-year license to be pursued, but each project has stage gates, milestones, and recheck points to ensure that the initial purpose, scope, and execution remain in line with the original intent and market direction. Ensuring that the innovation agenda, priorities, and expected outcomes are consistent with the strategy is simple to accomplish and reflects dual development between the strategy group and innovation leadership.

Since an existing strategic plan is usually in place when a company stands up its innovation model, the agenda is naturally informed by the direction and priorities reflected in this preexisting plan. Thus, the innovation agenda is guided by the strategy that has been developed and adopted. This does not mean the innovation agenda is limited to the four corners of the strategy, since a multiyear strategy cannot anticipate year-to-year externalities and market shifts, and an agenda is usually constructed post-strategy release.

Rather, the innovation agenda starts with the overall guidance from the strategy and incorporates a more dynamic view of the market and the needs of the business into its annual agenda. It can adopt the strategy as its North Star, but it has the advantage of being fully contemporaneous and reflective of a current view of the market and competitors. The innovation agenda should always be as current and intentional as possible to meeting the needs of the business, and more importantly, with the real-time influences underlying market direction.

The innovation agenda can be directly aligned with the enterprise strategy by linking individual projects to related focus areas within the strategy— whether during a common planning cycle or when the agenda is developed outside a normal strategy development process. This crossmatch of strategy and innovation focus directly aligns two separate logic paths and identifies if any gaps exist in intent or focus. It is doubtful that there would be substantial incongruence between the two formal planning outcomes, but ensuring alignment is simple to accomplish to confirm there are no mixed signals between enterprise and innovation priorities.

Culture of Innovation

Much attention is given to the stand-up and launch of an innovation platform, but far less thought is directed at nurturing, augmenting, enriching, and sustaining the platform itself. The innovation platform is intended to be perpetual; that is, it never diminishes and only flourishes. With stand-up and launch near term, tangible activity can be directly observed. But with creation of a platform, it only attains this end state when its accomplishments are visible over an extended time frame and at an enduring level of contribution to the enterprise.

The utilities industry is still very much at the embryonic level of development, and it has its own set of hurdles and growing pains to surmount before it can ever move to the growth and maturing stages to reach a position of embedding innovation into enterprise DNA. But it is important to recognize what a desired end state from standing up the innovation model looks like, and the actions that can be undertaken early, while continuously building a foundation for this outcome. While utility-to-utility perspectives can vary on what an innovation end state can look like, it will at least enable seamless collaboration, cooperation, and continuous value contribution to the business, all of which can create dividends in perpetuity.

A few companies have used structured approaches to innovation, which have given the appearance of adopting developed and tailored models. And as explained earlier, some have used formal events or contests to solve problems or engage the employee base in a prescribed activity. But these tend to have a discrete challenge to solve, are different in intent than building a durable culture, and do not stand the test of time. Utilities have not cracked the code to embedding innovation within the four corners of the business on a sustainable basis. And the utilities industry has yet to elevate innovation to a true competence level that can be viewed as expert or repeatable.

Building a sustainable culture of innovation can be thought about across multiple recurring dimensions: engagement, communications, measurement, incentives, and funding (see Figure 36). These dimensions are important elements of the process of moving from shaping an innovation culture (i.e., using enthusiasm and outcomes to build commitment to innovation) to embedding a culture of innovation (i.e., creating the durable organizational DNA and zeal that buttresses and extends an innovation platform).

Earlier, the use of sponsored, enterprise-wide activities, like formal ideation events or contests, was introduced to galvanize the employee base and introduce innovation to the organization at the launch. But the use of such a formal event does not need to be limited to a one-time event or a series of 24-hour scrums. A utility wants to have its employee base continuously and deeply engaged in thinking about innovation and providing multiple mechanisms to encourage engagement as a foundational element of building a culture of innovation.

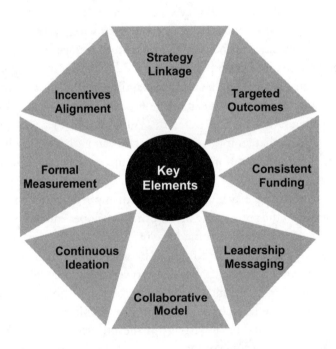

Figure 36. Embedding a culture of innovation.

The same concept holds true after a launch, and there are no limitations to encouraging employee engagement in innovative thinking. Similar crowdsourcing events could be held periodically, and for longer periods, to secure ideas across the business. They could also be held with vendors and customers to obtain broader and different perspectives around business challenges and innovative solutions. The intent is to provide opportunities for the employee base to engage as a body, rather than just as individuals when a project may need their assistance.

A key dimension of building awareness, enthusiasm, and commitment to innovation is the utilization of highly visible, recurring communications across the enterprise. At a minimum, an innovation website needs to be created so employees can follow activities, projects, collaboration, and accomplishments on a regular basis. The methods of communication should also include recurring communications from the CEO through traditional and nontraditional channels; inclusion in normal business organization meeting agendas; vignettes of project day-in-the-life activities; technology trends, adoption, and parity updates; and illustration of how innovation created tangible value as a result of its pursuit and adoption.

These communications can be streamed to employees, posted on the home page, or made a recurring part of an innovation portal. The topics to be covered should reflect executive determination on what is important to them and valuable to the employee base. It certainly will measure the items mentioned above but can also bring focus to areas like new channels to market, partnering arrangements, products and services developed, market recognition, and industry activities. Communication is a valuable tool in breaking down silos that can exist within the business, but it needs to be continuous, not episodic. Providing open insight into innovation activity is a core building block of creating a culture of innovation.

The final dimension relates to funding innovation within the enterprise. The investment made in innovation is incremental budget, not repurposed spend. It has to be made under the proposition that innovation is as much an investment in the future of the company as capital is in the growth of the enterprise. Funding is not a flexible item; it needs to be multiyear and growing to meet the expanding needs of the business and the architecture of the end-state platform.

Like certain capital investment is nondiscretionary for asset replacement or growth, innovation investment also needs to be thought of as a core element of the investment stack and not a discretionary amount to be argued year to year. If innovation investment is viewed as flexible, it will signal a lack of commitment and cause the employee base to lose faith in the messaging of the champion. Taking a long-term view of the value of innovation is a fundamental element of building and illustrating a culture of innovation.

If a culture of innovation can become embedded in a utility, it will still need to be championed by the CEO. No other role has the cachet of the CEO, and no other position has the same soapbox level to champion from. Most utility CEOs have a term of less than five years, so innovation needs to be timeless and not aligned with an individual. It can be easy for a succeeding CEO to decide that an entirely new strategy is needed that does not consider innovation as critical. It can also be easy for a new CEO to assume that after a certain time frame, the innovation platform exists and does not need the same nurturing and commitment to sustain it.

A solution to avoid this occurrence is to ensure that the board of directors—which has an extended life well beyond single CEOs—has been actively engaged with the innovation model and is as much a champion of it as the original sponsoring CEO. This level of support ensures that a culture of innovation is protected, if already in place, or is further enabled if embedding the culture is still a work in progress.

Utilities need to move beyond treating innovation as a rallying cry in a time of industry disruption. They absolutely need to view innovation and strategy as conjoined, compatible, and complementary. They need to begin to think like traditional competitive firms in the market, where innovation is a distinctive characteristic of being a dynamic and effective competitor and a market maker.

Regardless of the innovation stage at which the utilities industry finds itself today, the role of innovation needs to become more elevated within the business and a core dimension of the utility market model. Utilities need to direct specific attention to a few core building blocks—visible commitment, executive alignment, strategy linkage, intentional value, sustained engagement, continuous reinforcement, and adequate funding. All these elements are critical to successfully sustaining a robust culture of innovation.

Committing to embedding a culture of innovation within the utility can produce real advances in market positioning, technology adoption, and strengthening of customer value and relationships. Utility executives need to be comfortable with knowing that building a culture of innovation is not a short-term effort; it will take at least five years for it to become visible and truly embedded, which stresses the patience of executives accustomed to chasing annual earnings goals. Those companies that embrace innovation as an ingrained mindset and commit to it as part of the enterprise persona position themselves for differentiated market, financial, and customer success.

CHAPTER 9

Operationalization to Commercialization

EVEN though several innovation headwinds exist regarding the adequacy of investment, sustainability of internal commitment, and continuity in messaging, U.S. utilities are making strides in moving their organizations toward more active open thinking within the enterprise. Many companies have made innovation a boardroom topic and an element of their definition of a high-performance organization.

But most utilities still wrestle with where their priorities about innovation should lie. Are they principally focused on the business, the environment, or the customer? Most companies would default to the notion that the obvious answer is all of the above, but even that answer requires a decision about *what* to emphasize across these choices and *how* to direct internal and external resources to achieve high-impact outcomes.

Fundamental to this determination is *how* utilities envision the intent of innovation. Recall the earlier discussion on the stages of innovation—*incremental, advanced*, and *breakthrough*. Each of these outcomes can be relevant to companies, depending on their objectives and appetite for risk. And each can apply to various aspects of a company's innovation platform or portfolio, depending on the aggressiveness of the underlying idea.

Given their history and mental makeup, utilities tend to direct much more innovation attention to operations than they do to customers, even though that is the opposite thinking of most industrial companies. Thus, internal application of innovation within the business tends to trump that related to external market pursuits.

Recall also that innovation typically consists of five areas of focus—processes, technology, regulatory, products and services, and business models. These innovation areas are introduced and briefly contrasted in an earlier chapter, but they are further explained here to illustrate the linkage to application and outcomes.

Clearly, process innovation relates to improving or simplifying performance and is generally more limited in achieving sea change outcomes (i.e., it yields *incremental* results). Technology is a more diverse innovation category and naturally applies to operations at the fleet, grid, and network elements of the value chain, but it can also lend itself to enhancing customer engagement and opening new revenue streams.

When technology innovation is asset-based (e.g., new design, functionality, and performance in supply or delivery), it is more likely to be about equipment or devices like boilers, turbines, inverters, synchrophasors, sensors, monitors, controllers, or software, among a host of other equipment types. These asset products are conceived and fabricated by OEMs, designed by software developers, deployed in operations by the utility, and likely to reflect *advanced*-stage impacts.

However, when technology innovation is customer-focused and directed beyond call centers, billing systems, and engagement mediums, it is less about operational execution and more about meeting customer needs and preferences and providing new offerings. And when technology extends to direct customer engagement and impact (e.g., demand response and transactive energy), it is decidedly more about market interface and impact, and less about operations. In these cases, innovation is likely to be moving within the *advanced* (and perhaps to the *breakthrough*) stage.

Obviously, products and services are centered on top-line opportunity or customer options and likely to yield *advanced* or *breakthrough* stage outcomes. This innovation capability has not been a historical strength of utilities, but they are neither precluded from more vigorous pursuit nor devoid of fundamental capabilities to be successful.

Innovation directed at business models (i.e., the linkage between strategy and economic outcomes) defines how an enterprise captures value and can create *breakthrough* outcomes. These results occur by fundamentally reshaping the enterprise strategy, changing the bases for go-to-market models, and redefining *where* and *how* value is created through reconsideration of roles, engagement, origination, offerings, value sources, pricing, channels, and partnering to revolutionize the utility-customer relationship.

To be more direct, processes and parts of technology innovation generally create *incremental* impacts and can be thought of as *innovation with a lowercase i*, which is not to diminish the value of this stage. More market- and customer-oriented elements of technology innovation can be characterized as *advanced* and *Innovation with a capital I* in the next stage. New products and services generally address a void that has remained unfilled with customers in any appreciable manner for quite some time. But when utilities do expand and focus attention on their offerings to customers, they are tacitly striving for the *advanced* stage level, with the potential for these offerings to enable the *breakthrough* innovation stage to be realized (i.e., *INNOVATION in all caps*). And when business model innovation is a focus, it is the most impactful area and almost by definition reflects this *breakthrough* stage as well.

The varied areas for innovation focus and stages of innovation levels create a challenge for utilities with respect to where they choose to prioritize and position themselves to capitalize on innovation (and R&D) to address their most pressing business needs—operationally or commercially. The challenge for companies is to choose the path that best fits their strategic focus—emphasize operational excellence, resilience, and reliability, or tailor their priorities more directly to growth, markets, and value.

A focus on operationalization is typical for this industry, but sooner or later it needs to evolve from a disproportionate emphasis within a company to a blended and balanced model, where customers are at the center of the innovation focus and commercialization is viewed as the higher strategic purpose. The key question for utilities to answer is: *How* do companies pivot their focus from an operations orientation to one that emphasizes commercial success?

Operationalization

The history of most utilities is heavily influenced by drivers such as demand growth, system expansion, and operating performance, all of which represent a view toward delivering safe, quality, reliable, affordable service consistent with regulatory expectations. The public nature of utilities has always made them susceptible to criticism about operational performance, so a heightened sensitivity toward operational efficacy was natural.

Utilities managements are always attuned to technology evolution that can enhance operating performance in line with the attributes above. After all, if technology adoption can positively affect service delivery and price outcomes, then it is not a hard sell to executives for budget commitment. And utilities managers do not often get in trouble or even receive serious pushback for advancing ideas that offer perpetual benefits in the core elements of operations.

So it is no wonder that an emphasis on operations is a safe priority and receives far more innovation attention at this stage than commercial aspects of the business. That means that related investment follows this prioritization and is an easier decision for executives to make regarding *where* to spend its limited resources.

The bulk of utilities employees have backgrounds in various engineering disciplines, as one would expect within a business that focuses on operating power plants, transmission grids, and network systems. These assets are the backbone of utility operations and represent most balance sheet assets and the bulk of annual capital investment. Consequently, these business units, and the assets they operate, typically receive an outsized level of executive attention to ensure operations and asset stability, durability, effectiveness, and efficiency.

The utilities industry has been an active adopter of new technologies for decades, even though it is generally not a rapid deployer of these advancements given its propensity to be risk averse. As noted earlier, the industry is an enthusiastic user of pilots and testing that can last years or decades before evolving into full, ubiquitous deployment. In a technology environment where new equipment materials, designs, functionality, intelligence, diagnostics, and performance are constantly advancing, the industry will have to become more adaptive to this rapid evolution and the arrival of the next big thing.

For example, a plethora of new technology innovations are appearing that focus on utility operating areas and offer improvements to traditional technologies, as well as introduce new approaches, models, hardware, software, and intelligence:

- *Supply:* Given the range of generation fuel sources, attention is directed at advanced technologies, like nuclear fusion, small modular reactors, renewables, fuel conversion, battery storage, coal combustion products, boiler improvement, turbine life cycle, heat recovery, heat-rate improvement, process automation, hydrogen, cooling systems, and several other areas.

- *Environmental:* A predominance of R&D and innovative thinking is focused on carbon reduction and/or capture, as well as for other emissions, like mercury nitrogen oxide, sulfur dioxide, and ammonia, along with other areas. But focus is also provided to methane emissions and renewable natural gas as areas for exploration and development in the LDC sector.

- *Grid:* R&D and innovation in this area are largely directed at transmission operations impacts from variable energy resources, dispatchable synchronous generation, electromagnetic fields, engineering software, sensing technologies, drone deployment, substation upgrades, line resiliency, and visualization and decision support, among other technologies.

- *Network:* The delivery system is the beneficiary of many sources of OEM innovative technology, like distributed generation, broadband communications, distributed energy resources, long-duration storage, virtual power plants, and failure analysis, among other options. Gas LDCs also are exploring advances in leak inspection, corrosion control, and pipeline maintenance.

- *Electrification:* An emphasis on electrification within utilities is receiving substantial interest with additional focus on gas infrastructure and end use replacement. Areas like power quality, advanced buildings, end use optimization, personal and fleet mobility, AI, and electric substitution for diesel, propane, and oil are also receiving considerable attention.

From the above discussion, it is clear that utilities have many emerging technologies to follow, evaluate, and consider adopting when they are commercially available to deploy in the supply, grid, and network businesses. Of course, there are additional customer-directed technologies that are also emerging, but these are described in the next section.

This creates a decision dilemma for utilities (i.e., *how* to determine *where* to focus and *how much* attention and investment should be applied). While utilities are large entities with strong balance sheets and cash flows, they still do not have infinite time and capabilities to stay engaged on all emerging technologies, at least not on an equivalent basis. Hard, but practical, choices need to be made.

So, *where* does a utility normally turn? Usually, it errs on the side of familiarity and chooses to focus on the most fundamental operating areas of the business because it never hurts to explore technologies that enhance asset security, operating reliability, or equipment analytics.

If the first choice for technology adoption is operational deployment, then the choice of where to focus—either through externally conducted R&D or internal innovation—will depend on the company's assessment of *where* the challenge may be most acute (e.g., environmental management in generation), or *what* level of improvement or impact can be realized most rapidly (e.g., system-wide distributed resource integration in networks).

Historically, generation has received the greatest share of discretionary capital because of its scale and the concentration of related investment. Hence, the most logical destination for attention and resources might be around accelerating the move to decarbonization and pursuing technologies related to carbon capture and new hydrogen sources. This would enable previous commitments to net-zero goals and offer a new use for assets like renewables and nuclear power.

Alternatively, utilities might focus on the new primary destination for new capital—the delivery network. This business unit has quietly displaced the power supply business as the largest destination for new capital expenditures and is facing fundamental operating improvement necessity and abundant technology opportunity.

New hardware and software technologies are continually being developed and installed that can help utilities enhance network efficiency, offer predictive insights into asset risk, enable integration of existing assets and devices, create new sources of power supply, protect assets against disruption, and facilitate the support of mobility, all of which strengthen operating asset condition, provide increased insight into network performance, and/or support new demands on the system.

When the results of new technology adoption and deployment in the delivery network can include more efficient equipment use, lower operating costs, avoided system risks, asset and device interconnection, energy grid optimization, and smarter overall configuration, it is easy to see that this part of the utility business can be a primary beneficiary of R&D and innovation efforts.

It is hard for utilities to not emphasize operations and rather focus on the operationalization of innovation (and R&D). After all, it is often seen as more directly deployable and less revolutionary than FOAK power supply technologies, or more easily implementable than entirely new software applications.

The operationalization of innovation will likely hold the high ground in the near term for U.S. utilities. The adoption advantages in day-to-day deployment are easier to grasp and generally entirely consistent with how regulators view the purpose of innovation in the utilities sector. But even if this is true today, the time is rapidly approaching when operations-oriented technology, R&D, and innovation will be complemented by elevated attention to addressing the existing and future needs and opportunities of customers.

Commercialization

Since utilities are regulated entities, they tend to believe that the current regulatory paradigm and the utility business model that focuses on the asset base and customer prices will continue unabated. Utilities often think that the era of the customer (i.e., when customer centricity is paramount and really matters to market positioning) is still some time in the future. This has been the conventional view and reflects utilities' belief that customers do not care about anything more than quality service at an affordable cost.

For more than 100 years, they haven't been wrong. When retail competition emerged in the mid-1990s in the United States, there was a rush of customer sign-ups to non-utility marketer options because the opportunity existed. But utilities also were required to serve default customers (i.e., those that chose to stay with their incumbent as a provider of last resort because of trust, complacency, or risk aversion), and that amount can often exceed 65 percent of the customer base in competitive markets.[1]

Utilities and other pundits tend to believe customers are inert—they are hard to get to switch, take an interest in nontraditional activities, or move outside their comfort zones, even when presented with choices. This stickiness is true, but could that be because the relationship with their utility has largely only been about account setup, commodity service, occasional outages, and account close? What have utilities offered to customers other than alternative billing payment plans, energy efficiency audits, renewables supply rates, service warranties, online marketplaces, and more timely outage communications? And most of these offerings are relatively new and far from ubiquitous.

Consequently, many utilities have never truly focused on active engagement with their residential customers (or commercial and industrial ones, for that matter) for the purpose of meeting latent needs or pent-up demand. This often occurred because the utility was never truly aware of the customer's interests or motivations and never had a portfolio of offerings—interesting, exciting, or valuable—to bring to market. Some companies established "retailcos" in the mid-1990s to attempt to bring diverse products and services to customers, but when these were established, utilities often lacked market trust—offerings were narrow, their value was hard to discern, they were not well marketed or priced— or were themselves uninspired and uncommitted to the business; thus, none were successful.

Utilities have tried to engage customers about their current needs and future aspirations. Several have conducted surveys and held customer forums to explore their brand perception, market positioning, and value to the customer. But it is a heavy lift for utilities to convince customers to think about utilities as anything other than what they have always seen— the commodity provider sometimes disappointing to deal with, often slow and stodgy, and seldom swift, agile, or creative.

But this historical position of many utilities does not preclude them from becoming more effective competitors or more valuable to customers. As the profiles of the six companies in Chapter 6 indicate, they are already leveraging innovation to develop solutions to customer needs (though limited) that can unlock future market opportunities. Utilities will never be OEMs; nor will they be software developers, but they can partner with them to develop products, services, solutions, and platforms that fundamentally help transform the purpose and role of the utility, as well as the perceptions of customers regarding their value as providers. Thinking in this manner will help utilities move toward a more commercially oriented mindset (see Figure 37).

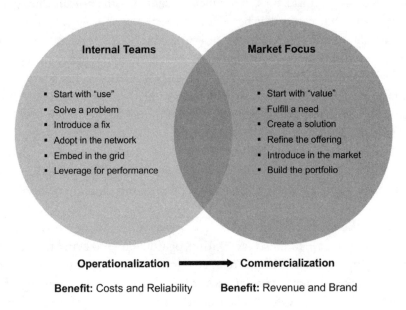

Internal Teams

- Start with "use"
- Solve a problem
- Introduce a fix
- Adopt in the network
- Embed in the grid
- Leverage for performance

Market Focus

- Start with "value"
- Fulfill a need
- Create a solution
- Refine the offering
- Introduce in the market
- Build the portfolio

Operationalization ➡ **Commercialization**

Benefit: Costs and Reliability   **Benefit:** Revenue and Brand

Figure 37. Operationalization to commercialization.

The emergence of new entrants into the end user marketplace (e.g., Nest with smart thermostats, Ring with smart home security, NRG Home with tailored energy plans and services, and so on) opened the eyes of utilities to a different breed of marketers and fulfillment companies. These entities addressed various residential customer need gaps with products and services that offer attractive features (e.g., set-and-forget, protective layers, personalized plans, and so on) and differentiate the customer experience.

Entrance of these vendors set a tone for utilities—if they do not think about meeting residential customer needs in areas where they should have natural rights to compete, then others will capitalize on that vacuum. And for large commercial and industrial customers, where natural rights are less solid, the challenge is more daunting as energy bills are far higher on absolute or relative bases, energy availability is far more complex and valuable, and these customers are already familiar with OEMs and vendors, which have provided hardware or software in the past—these customers already are experienced energy buyers and more demanding in their relationships.

Utilities now need to pivot from a concentration on innovation for operations to a heightened attention toward customer innovation and identification and fulfillment of their priorities, needs, and opportunities. This elevated innovation focus now needs to optimize energy use, expand high-value energy solutions, and create higher relationship value to a customer's premise, building, or factory. This is the perfect opportunity for converting abstract ideas into tangible value.

To be successful with commercialization, utilities need to address several challenges to position themselves to leverage their natural rights to sustain the customer relationship and change the value lens through which they have been viewed:

- *Rethink the value equation.* Utilities need to high-grade their value proposition with customers and move from impersonal billing and limited touchpoint engagement to a demonstrated value-added model, where tailored services and solution streams expand the conventional role.

- *Embed an ownership mindset.* The customer relationship model should be redefined to shift from a de facto license to serve to a conviction that all energy-related needs of the customer are the province of utilities to provide.

- *Create a product development engine.* With internal clarity of the right to serve, utilities need to stand up a product, service, and solution ideation and design capability to conceptualize, create, and bring a continuous stream of offerings to customers that meet and anticipate needs.

- *Expand the pricing model.* New products, services, or solutions will require different approaches to pricing than utilities have utilized in the past, leveraging a range of options, like subscription, marginal cost, value-for-service, and shared benefits, among other approaches.

- *Secure innovation partners.* Utilities can never house the full capabilities set needed to be commercially successful, requiring them to create multiple arrangements with OEMs, vendors, solutions providers, and venture capital firms to leverage specialized skills and positioning.

- *Build the go-to-market model.* How utilities approach market entry and participation will be substantially different from what is performed today and accelerate the design of new and broader approaches for branding, solutions bundling, market channels, and platform design.

- *Secure regulatory support.* The ability to capture the full value of commercialization necessitates that utilities obtain the permissions required to participate in new markets, as well as gain approval for *where* these activities can be housed and *how* they can be priced.

This last element deserves additional discussion, as it is a challenge for utilities to address and overcome. Regulators have not historically been traditional supporters of R&D and innovation because of wariness around the outcomes, specifically expensive failures for which customers receive no benefit. Accordingly, regulators have either not been supportive of utility-conducted R&D and innovation and refused to endorse it, limited the recovery of costs to industry-supported R&D (such as from EPRI and GTI), or allowed utilities to pursue these activities as a below-the-line expense that could not be recovered from customers.

While there are numerous OEMs focused on supporting or enhancing the hard assets of utilities, there are thousands of software developers, solutions providers, and platform integrators vying to serve the customer sector. Emerging technologies are developing in a constant stream, with expanded end uses evolving as technologies are adapted to be fit-for-purpose.

New market offerings are emerging in a host of areas related to customer energy consumption and management, electrification in mobility, source-to-grid marketing, and micro-generation. Non-technology innovation is also occurring in smart solutions, service pricing, energy sourcing, regulatory permissions, nontraditional financing, and risk mitigation. Some of these areas focusing on the customer side include the following:

- *"Smart" everything:* The adoption of behind-the-meter technologies is apparent from the presence of smart appliances, smart micro-generation, smart sensors, and smart charging, by which customers can leverage technology for energy control and management.

- *Pricing:* Conventions beyond average pricing, like marginal costing, expanded time-of-use rates, revised interruptible rates, flat rates, value-for-service, and other variations will offer customers more options and the ability to select plans that fit their needs and send the right price signals.

- *Home automation:* Technologies are emerging to simplify customer energy management, like home hubs, domotics, and control devices that allow homeowners to further accomplish energy management and control through various intelligent devices.

- *Financing:* Alternative approaches to funding customer energy initiatives, such as nontraditional sources like energy banks, state and local grants, and subscription services, either provide new sources or enable different approaches to obtaining energy source access, such as renewables.

- *Micro-generation:* Customers can access a range of alternative sources for energy, such as micro-turbines, reciprocating internal combustion engines (industrials), rooftop solar, vehicle-to-grid, and fuel cells to provide increased control over supply or hedge supply risks.

- *Mobility:* EV adoption is increasing among individual customers, as well as within corporate fleets, leading to technology or go-to-market advances in EV charging, fleet conversion, pricing options, vehicle-to-grid, financing, infrastructure services, and energy services.

- *Demand response:* Large commercial and industrial customers have been beneficiaries of this technology for over a decade, but many customers still do not participate in these programs, and residential customers are a largely untapped market.

- *Transactive energy:* Customers can participate in local markets through their ability to leverage technologies that facilitate premise-, building-, or facility-to-grid energy sharing that enables customers to sell or swap available energy back to the utility or DSO when imbalances exist.

The range of market offerings described above covers a wide collection of both emerging technologies and creative imagination. Many of the areas result in tangible products, services, or solutions, while others change the model used by utilities for charging customers for energy, services, or participation.

But what differentiates these offering areas is that most create new revenue streams and an expanded commercial relationship with customers. Thus, innovation effort in these areas can directly lead to commercialization of outcomes versus simple adoption and deployment within the asset base. While asset deployment drives the earnings base at a known return level, products, services, and solutions can create new top-line revenues, incremental margins, and customer penetration and stickiness.

Although these revenues and margins are admittedly small when first initiated, they provide a utility an opportunity to burnish its reputation as an innovative customer solutions company and create new demand sources in customers that did not previously exist. This outcome should be a primary goal for utilities concerned about redefining their purpose and role as a preferred energy solutions provider and high-value partner with customers, extending beyond the legacy position as a pure commodity provider.

Thus, utilities are going to be drawn to commercialization because it advances market positioning at a time when the competitive environment is heating up and the potential for customer disintermediation is growing. Elevating the value of commercialization to equivalence, or better, with an operations emphasis offers the opportunity to utilities to think and act more like their non-utilities sector peers, which are constantly focused on funneling new products, services, and solutions to their customers.

It is important to acknowledge that market opportunities do not last forever, particularly when there are so many well-funded OEMs and vendors that already have footholds in the utilities sector. Ideas are perishable unless quickly acted on, as customers can source the offerings that flow from these ideas from a variety of channels, depending on type (e.g., OEM account representatives, industry expositions, venture capital funds, industry periodicals, consulting firms, and a myriad of entrepreneurs).

The time to market is a critical dimension for utility awareness. The industry does not move with the sense of urgency of competitive sectors, and with its deliberative nature, it can naturally extend market-time-sensitive readiness beyond the window of opportunity. To optimize commercialization, utilities need to think at market speed—from ideation through evaluation, proof of concept, and testing to offering readiness.

This is one of the hallmarks of bringing a commercial mindset to market engagement—that is, being able to navigate traditional internal avenues of approval to achieve accelerated outcomes that illustrate the organization is a different enterprise than its legacy past.

Successful commercialization may not always be a controllable providence of utilities. They may be the originator of an idea to bring to customers, but for hardware, software, or asset solutions, they are neither the OEM nor the developer. Thus, they are dependent on third parties to fill the capabilities gaps, whether that is computer code, fabrication, delivery, or integration.

And it is highly likely that to be successful in the solutions and platform areas, they will work as partners with one or more entities. Partnerships are notoriously perilous when it comes to making decisions and meeting commitments. Thus, effective commercialization requires utilities to possess deft capabilities to navigate among multiple parties for contracts, governance, decision-making, and go-to-market activities.

However, it is one thing to decide a company is going to emphasize innovation commercialization and an entirely different matter to be successfully commercial from the innovative thinking and development activities conducted. Several predicates need to be addressed to enable commercialization to flourish (see Figure 38).

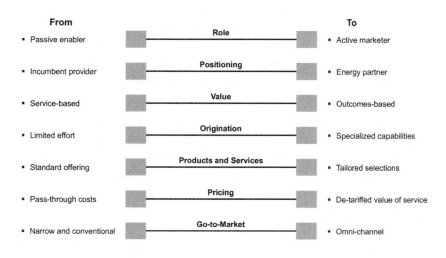

From

- Passive enabler
- Incumbent provider
- Service-based
- Limited effort
- Standard offering
- Pass-through costs
- Narrow and conventional

Role
Positioning
Value
Origination
Products and Services
Pricing
Go-to-Market

To

- Active marketer
- Energy partner
- Outcomes-based
- Specialized capabilities
- Tailored selections
- De-tariffed value of service
- Omni-channel

Figure 38. Creating the commercial mindset.

Recall that the definition of innovation adopted for this book centers on two premises: the sustained development and *deployment of new ideas* that measurably *enhance the value of the business*—for both shareholders and customers.

Ideation is the foundation for all innovation, but it falls short of its full promise if it cannot ultimately be converted into commercialization value (i.e., products, services, and solutions) that can be monetized in the market. This does not suggest that operations-oriented innovation does not produce value, but it recognizes that result is directed at a different outcome—that is, the system or asset versus the customer, and functionality, performance, costs, and risks versus revenues and margins.

Moreover, most businesses have a commercial orientation—including utilities—since they serve, seek to retain, look to attract, and continuously engage with customers. Frankly, innovation is expected by customers of any company if it wants to continue a perpetual relationship with them. This may be even truer for a utility that operates under a franchise agreement that depends on how it performs and is viewed by mobile politicians but inert customers. Utilities are competing every day for the right to serve these customers, even though they do not always think in that manner.

More recently, the explosion of disruptive technologies has caused regulators to become highly interested in R&D and innovation and the potential impacts to existing utilities' competitive position. These regulators now discuss technology on a regular basis and exhibit more awareness of and attention to the way it may affect the direction of the industry and its regulated companies. And some regulators are allowing recovery of R&D and innovation expenses.

Some of the products and services that utilities could offer to customers may be provided under a tariffed-rate structure, but many do not fit this model, particularly where they are services- or value-based. The concerns of regulators, however, do not constrain utilities from market participation through a nonregulated business that operates outside the utility. This already happens in some states in areas like renewables, energy services, battery storage, and warranty services, among others. To optimize commercialization, utilities will likely, although not exclusively, utilize a nonregulated entity to provide for more open market access and competitive freedoms.

This occurrence brings the topic of business models into discussion. A regulated business is separate and distinct from a nonregulated business, with each employing a unique business model (i.e., linking strategy and economic outcomes through *how* it makes money). While pundits like to discuss how utilities will need to design a new business model, the truth is that they will have to define multiple business models. A core model will exist for the regulated business, with one for each nonregulated business, since these lines of business are usually quite unique (e.g., EVs, energy services, transactive energy, behind-the-meter, and so on), and *how* they charge or create revenues can be vastly different.

Defining and standing up differentiated business models is an art, not a science. Consequently, executives need to take a highly strategic approach that is market backed, rather than the traditional approach that has served them in the past. These new business models are simultaneously more expansive in what they address, while being individually unique in *how* they are applied.

It is possible (if not likely) that any one line of business could have multiple business models, as the range of offerings, the relevant target customers, and the optimal pricing approach could be extremely unique. For example, there are nine ways for utilities to make money related to EVs: make ready (regulated), financing, charging station infrastructure, fleet conversion and operation services, vehicle-to-grid energy, energy services, after-market batteries, information management, and control and coordination (all nonregulated), each having different drivers and parameters to drive pricing. Thus, the broader the market segment value chain, the more complicated the overarching business model and pricing approaches.

It is inevitable that the utilities industry will migrate from an operationalization emphasis in innovation (and R&D through other entities) to a more elevated focus on commercialization. Innovation for utilities will still be a binary option for both operations and customers—neither need be excluded or underemphasized.

As utilities find the right blend of operations-directed and customer-centric innovation, they will create a sweet spot where operating deployment and commercial potential is fully realized. When this occurs, utilities will have optimized their innovation strategy, met the needs of multiple stakeholders, and moved closer to creating the integration platform described earlier.

CHAPTER 10

Innovation Strategies

THE utilities profiled in this book have been successful in pursuing innovative outcomes in their businesses, whether formally (organizations) or informally (activities). While some companies have adopted a mix of organic (internal-driven) and inorganic (external-supported) models, others have simply relied on the capabilities of all employees, with a light touch on formalization.

However, there are some utilities in the United States that have yet to truly engage in innovation activities, and even more that have been episodic and uncommitted to it as a strategic activity. Certainly, every utility is constantly reminded by the flood of articles, conferences, and news stories about innovation's contributions and merits to companies and customers. But they do not always act on this information or regularly engage with their regulators, boards, and employees on its importance and value.

The companies that have been successful with making innovation a critical component of their persona have been committed to highlighting its importance to the business in achieving readiness for the cleantech transition, as well as utilizing its benefits for business advancement and customer benefit. These utilities view innovation as a table stake to success and a means to differentiate themselves in their sector, business community, start-up ecosystem, regulatory environment, OEM and vendor population, and customer base.

Several specific strategies emerge that can enhance the quality of a company's innovation model and platform and at a minimum define a path forward to elevate the level of innovation quality and value:

- *Innovation to strategy: How* the importance of alignment enhances innovation value

- *Services to solutions: How* utilities can shift their focus from support to offerings

- *Projects to products: What* mindset shifts are necessary to enable commercialization

- *Constraints to approvals: How* internal thinking needs to become more aggressive

- *Measure to incent: What* actions can drive employees to embed innovative thinking

- *Communications to inspiration: Where* companies can elevate their messaging

Utilities already have an articulated corporate strategy, although it is often quite general and tends to reference decarbonization, electrification, grid modernization and resiliency, customer centricity, and regulatory outcomes, with an occasional one-word mention of innovation as a supporting element. The above strategy elements are not a substitute for a company's corporate level strategy that presently exists. Rather, they are intended to provide greater definition to innovation-specific strategies that can then be aligned with enterprise-level strategies.

Each of these strategy elements can, however, contribute to advancing the position and effectiveness of innovation within a utility. These strategy elements are not intended to be one-off additions to an existing innovation strategy, assuming such a specific strategy is in place (as opposed to a general set of objectives that are not truly strategic). The intent for utilities should be to ensure that in addition to a robust enterprise strategy, an innovation-focused strategy also exists, integrated directly with the key elements of the enterprise-level strategy.

All the strategy elements above are intended to broaden the appeal of innovation within a utility and add to the value of innovation to a company. They also provide a set of mindset shifts that would be advantageous for utilities to adopt to optimize their present innovation efforts, as well as pursue additional benefits on behalf of shareholders and customers that can be demonstrated to regulators.

Innovation to Strategy

The need for tight integration between overall corporate strategy and innovation activity is key to closely aligning the direction and priorities of the enterprise with the focus and intent of innovation. Too often innovation is only seen as tactical and supporting, as opposed to strategic and guiding, which affects how utilities think about and execute it.

In today's environment, utilities tend to focus on macro-themes (e.g., decarbonization and electrification) that describe an overall goal for outcome attainment or market opportunity. These two themes are usually addressed in terms of net-zero carbon emissions for decarbonization and new uses like mobility in electrification or asset replacement, which depend on innovation to enable these outcomes. Other strategy themes can sound like platitudes (e.g., regulatory positioning and customer centricity) and clearly do not have direct linkages to innovation. Innovation as a strategy theme itself is less common among utilities, even though it has much to do with company direction, emphasis, and outcomes.

But whatever the strategy themes or the elements are, innovation efforts should be directly linked to these directional guideposts in a manner that allows clear connectivity between underlying strategic objectives and related innovation execution, whether for technologies, products, services, solutions, business models, or capital investments.

Thus, a strategy focused on decarbonization may refer to coal retirement, which is not directly related to innovation but is clearly related to replacement with renewables, batteries, biomass, hydrogen, or other technologies that depend on innovation for operating performance, system support, new sources, or new energy systems in the future.

The same is true in electrification that seeking or creating new electricity uses is a market opportunity outcome, but attainment is partially dependent on developments in batteries for EVs and charging infrastructure for individual and fleet use.

In both cases, the ability to take advantage of the carbon reduction or load growth opportunity is linked to technology development, parity, and/or availability. The attainability of these identified outcomes means that utilities need to be on top of relevant technology maturity, functionality, economics, and evolution, as well as how adoption and deployment would be structured and cadenced in the grid or network.

As Figure 39 shows, most strategies in the utilities industry today build from a macro-theme of significant change in market focus and/or business model, which usually have a fundamental grounding and alignment with innovation. Decarbonization is not accomplished without capacity replacement, largely from renewables, storage, and energy efficiency. These are directly enabled by enhanced technology availability, viability, and scalability, which, in turn, are enabled by innovation in materials, design and fabrication characteristics, unit cost economics, and operating performance levels—all of which find their roots in innovation.

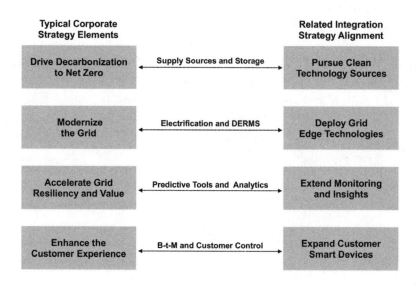

Figure 39. Strategy and innovation integration.

The same is also true for grid modernization and resilience—the priority is for asset hardening, digitalization, and smart equipment installation, all of which are linked directly to software solutions and hardware upgrades enabled through innovative application development, precision manufacturing, and network control technologies.

Integrating strategy and innovation is a natural occurrence, as there is a symbiotic relationship between them, one not usually occurring successfully without the other. Integrating strategy and innovation does not require redefining the strategy, changing its priorities, establishing new targets, or realigning roles and responsibilities. All it takes is to stand back and see the natural objectives and enablers between the macro-themes and the innovation focus.

To integrate innovation activities with strategy necessitates aligning the strategic objective with *how* it is achieved (i.e., *what* factors will contribute to the expected outcome). Innovation plays an integral role in enabling and accomplishing the strategy, even more so when the expected outcome is technology evolution in assets, equipment, controls, devices, and underlying software. Other critical elements of innovation (i.e., ideation, testing, piloting, and deployment) combine with other go-to-market elements, such as origination, offering development, pricing, channels, partnering, financing, branding, technology savvy, and innovation prowess to enable strategy objectives to be achieved.

Going forward, strategies and objectives need to link directly to the innovation elements supporting these outcomes. And innovation priorities and activities need to be conceived and conducted to specifically support the pursuit and attainment of each of the strategies, where relevant. Drawing this alignment will ensure that goals, outcomes, and means are clearly linked, and that integration occurs between overarching objectives and supporting activities.

Services to Solutions

The utilities industry also tends to think narrowly about products and services in terms of the way they are designed and purposed. Most utilities offer a range of different types of services (e.g., energy efficiency, demand response, EV charging, backup supply, microgrids, and so on) and have the capability to offer many more depending on their view of their purpose and role.

Utilities are using innovation to evaluate a host of technologies that provide new equipment, enhance operating performance, provide more operating information, or enable interconnection to, or within, the grid. These technologies can directly apply to customer sites or facilities, like assets, sensors, monitors, controllers, or data and intelligence.

Similar to products discussed above, utilities tend to focus on the unique purpose and aspects of a service (i.e., reliability, performance, control, or information) rather than the issue or problem it is intended to resolve. This is also a legacy mindset that needs to shift to not just the services offered but the solutions intended to result.

A solutions-based approach provides a utility the ability to view innovation from the perspective of the end user, whether residential, commercial, or industrial. This design thinking perspective allows the front end of the innovation cycle to work backward from an expected outcome to address the identified system or customer need or gap. Thinking about solutions in this manner enables the innovation effort to be accelerated because it starts with fully understanding the problem so the right solution can be conceived through an informed focus on design from the beginning. This ultimately allows an innovation team to shortcut a traditional scientific process that emphasizes iterative discovery and evaluation.

The vernacular of solutions is not common in utilities and more often refers to traditional information technology solutions. Use of solutions in the innovation context refers more to the pursuit and adoption of technologies, methods, and hard and soft assets that deliver a clear resolution to an indicated gap or problem. Solutions can include new offerings, new pricing options, new uses, and new outcomes. All these end results can enhance the value of a service or product to a customer and/or the value of the grid to a utility.

Moving to a solutions orientation does require a change to the fundamental focus on traditional products and services, as well as the attendant implication of moving to design thinking for innovation planning; the elevation of value into innovation execution; and the natural requirement of robust identification and measurement of value sources, level, and timing.

This move will also cause an evolution in thinking about *what* utilities are trying to accomplish through innovation and *how* they can best achieve it. Solutions are the critical destination of innovation outcomes and a perfect barometer of the nature and degree of success realized because they are the definition of the bridge between understanding a problem and disposing of that problem.

But solutions are just the next logical step toward creating and embedding a vibrant innovation platform, which is the natural extension toward a distinctive, end-to-end, and sustainable model for innovation. For a utility, an innovation platform is the culmination of a journey from formative stand-up to initial definition and prioritization, followed by attainment to broad employee engagement, testing and piloting, design offering, solution development, and finally to an integrated platform model.

The innovation platform is not a conceptual framework; nor is it a physical feature. Rather it is a construct focusing on positioning a utility for recurring ideation, idea development, conversion, market readiness, and offering delivery. The platform is built on real ideas, actual solutions, observable momentum, and tangible contribution, all grounded in value demonstration, rather than the bricks and mortar of a technology or a facility. It is the internal equivalent of a market-facing business model as it defines *how* innovation is executed, value is produced, and going-forward agendas and priorities are established—the way innovation is conducted in a utility.

An innovation platform is intended to signify common purpose and intentional outcomes, as well as institutional permanence. While utilities want innovation to be organic and dynamic, adding more shape, substance, and formality to its pursuit through a tailored platform does not constrain creativity, individuality, or freedom.

Embedding a platform does not necessitate abandoning prior principles and approaches, but it does require the willingness to think about innovation in a more incisive, end-to-end manner. Bringing an innovation platform to life means refining and scaling innovation's orientation toward purpose, priorities, visibility, leadership, structure, commitment, outcomes, and value. A distinctive innovation platform that is visibly embedded in the DNA of the utility organization, as well as clearly discernable to market participants, can enable the utility to bring greater focus to its ideation and conversion efforts, accelerate its outcomes and results, and elevate its strategic position as an advanced-thinking company—all of which contribute to more valuable solutions being delivered to the market and customers.

Projects to Products

The utilities industry tends to think of innovation in operational versus commercial terms and frequently reverts to traditional nomenclature in describing its execution process. Consequently, innovation activity is typically described as a project, since it involves dedicated and assigned resources, a defined analysis, and an expectation for an outcome.

And with an operational orientation, it is easy for projects to be referred to under a loose descriptive term, as the work conducted generally focuses on tangible areas like smart grid, EV charging, storage, and distributed resources, where network deployment is an expected outcome. Innovation in these areas usually leads to asset or equipment installation, expansion of operating capabilities, extension of operational insights, and improved functionality within the grid, and readiness for these end results requires some amount of lead time to complete.

Even on the residential customer side of the business, the term *project* is used to describe the focus and effort of innovation. While the utilities sector is far less active beyond-the-meter, it does spend time considering new products, services, and solutions for customers and uses traditional project performance and delivery processes to drive to an outcome. However, developing new pricing structures, payment options, equipment provisioning, and home services, among other areas, does not fit the traditional project nomenclature as in operations. These offerings are typically directed at revenue growth, offered through alternative channels, priced differently than electric or gas service, and can have additional service features beyond the single offering—the definition of a product.

An operations orientation will likely continue the need for a project orientation over some portion of the development-to-readiness life cycle because that is the way utilities have historically thought. Notwithstanding this traditional project mindset, the nature of thinking in utilities needs to shift from innovation for internal operations to the conversion of available knowledge, technologies, and capabilities into offerings beyond internal application. These offerings could extend to current customer relationships, adjacent customers, related sectors, and/or broader geographies. And when this focus exists, then innovation has moved to productization.

Utilities often do not realize the applicability of the outcomes of their innovation efforts beyond their immediate operating needs. They do not appreciate that a technology application, an analytical tool, a device, or a third-party relationship may have value to other entities. And a customer-directed offering, by definition, has value, regardless of how it is priced in the market.

The utilities sector is not deeply experienced with unique customer need assessment, customer segmentation, product development, pricing, partnering, origination, distribution, financing, or branding—all critical capabilities of a product-oriented, go-to-market model. But sooner or later, they will need to develop, deploy, and demonstrate these skills, particularly if they are going to change how they think about optimizing customer relationships and capturing business opportunities.

Utilities need to think of innovation more strategically, not just to explore the art of the possible to enhance the business but to consider it in a broader context—*where* and *how* value is created within and outside the business. And this definition of value extends beyond rate-basing an asset or equipment for an earned return on investment (ROI)—it extends to reshaping its fundamental purpose, changing market and customer expectations of the utility, strengthening customer relationships, redefining value to customers, and positioning the utility for expansion of its role with customers.

In the past, when utilities would undertake innovation projects, they would not adopt a market-based view of technology adoption—they would utilize their view of internal readiness for deployment, even if the broader market was moving past them. As mentioned earlier, it was not uncommon for utilities to take 15 to 25 years to move from evaluation through testing, on to piloting, and finally to ubiquitous deployment for technologies regardless of scale and complexity—a lifetime for competitive markets and companies.

That kind of decision-making and deployment time frame cannot exist in the technology-driven environment that surrounds utilities today. Utilities need to think like competitive companies, even though they are not at all like these kinds of entities. The utilities can, however, think with more of a market-back mindset and orientation to action.

In a previous project, I conducted primary research with industrial, consumer, and utilities companies to understand their time frames for commercializing product offerings. While utilities believed they generally had at least three to five years to bring an offering to market, competitive companies believed they had no more than two years and generally only one year before market advantage was lost. This time frame difference occurs because competitive companies start with a clear picture of unmet needs, supported by a vision of future needs customers may not even recognize yet.

Contrast that with utilities that are new to innovation, have no frame of productization and commercialization, and believe they are constrained by regulation, whether true or not. For utilities, time is an enemy, not a friend, to thinking about enhancing value to customers, like a competitive company naturally does.

Moving from projects to products is an important dimension of a utility's innovation strategy. It is not enough for innovation as a strategy to link directly to the corporate strategy in the obvious areas. The innovation strategy needs to reflect the underlying products, services, or solutions—whether operational or commercial—that underpin each of the relevant strategies.

Consequently, a corporate strategy (like electrification) may align with an innovation strategy (like mobility) that addresses financing, charging technology, charging fees, commercial fleet conversion, commercial fleet services, vehicle-to-grid, energy services, and battery repurposing, among other areas. The read through on the corporate strategy should reflect mobility as a fundamental element of electrification but also recognize these potential products as part of the execution of the overall innovation strategy in support of electrification.

When utilities start to think about shifting their mindset from projects to products, they will quickly come to realize that it requires front-end thinking about back-end technology, application, or equipment adoption versatility (i.e., the use cases that extend beyond original innovation priorities). For example, 12 to 13 use cases exist for storage within an integrated utility, with more existing once the focus shifts from the overall grid to discrete applications in other sectors, like water, mining, and oil and gas.

Productizing innovation project outputs also necessitates that utilities learn to think about *how* to define a product and *how* to take it to market. Products can be unique (e.g., EV charging installation and fee pricing) or bundled into a package (e.g., EV charging installation and fee pricing, smart home devices, renewables supply, warranty services, and transactive energy, among other areas). But a utility needs to think end-to-end at an early stage, not late in the individual product development cycle. And the same is true for commercial and industrial customers, except their needs can be more specific about supply reliability or broader about total equipment monitoring and control.

The move from a project to a product orientation will open up different and more market-oriented ways of thinking about creating and delivering value. It will also improve the efficiency of delivering multiple projects, since they can now be thought of as market opportunities, not just technical activities, and capitalize on the innovation productivity that comes from starting with outcome and use over evaluation and continuous testing.

Constraints to Approvals

Regulatory commissions have recently been slightly more conceptually supportive of utilities pursuing innovation than in earlier years, although this has not directly extended to much change in supportive regulatory outcomes related to innovation desirability, cost recognition, risk mitigation, and/or approval. In fact, most commissions prefer not to deal directly with the issue at all, or they establish principles that perpetuate, not resolve, the central question on risk assumption.

To begin with, the regulatory arguments against utility cost recovery seem to conflate R&D (long-term) with innovation (short- and intermediate-term). R&D does exhibit greater risk as it carries more uncertainty about technology discovery, future outcomes, and investment efficacy. On the other hand, innovation is directed at process, technology, regulatory, products and services, and business models that are usually pursued for tangible, near-term outcomes in the business, such as improved processes, system implementation, regulatory enhancements, new-but-simple customer offerings, and changes to *where* and *how* utilities do business.

However, the presence of risk in long-term R&D should not be the end of the discussion about innovation, particularly where process, technology, and regulatory innovation are easier to assess and identify outcomes.

Utilities do not undertake innovation to get little or no results—they are not in the business of basic research or open-ended discovery. Rather, utilities usually direct existing resources to finding ways to improve productivity or operating performance, reduce operations and maintenance costs and capital expenditures, and/or create win-win regulatory outcomes. Even bringing new products or services to customers is not pursued unless tangible benefits to customers can be identified (e.g., more options, easier engagement, cost avoidance, reduced uncertainty, and/or increased service value).

Often, regulatory arguments suggest the risk-reward ratio on R&D and innovation cost recognition is asymmetrical in favor of utilities—that is, if it works, the utility receives disproportionate benefits, while if it doesn't, it bears no risk from failure. A regulator's view of a "heads you win, tails I lose" approach is not the norm and need not be the basis for decision-making over the efficacy of utility R&D and innovation investment. And from an innovation perspective, very little risk exists in the areas identified above, with possible downstream exception of business model innovation.

If R&D investment worries regulators, then use below-the-line treatment of the investment, deferred recovery of costs, time-based matching of costs with benefits (although costs always precede benefits that emerge), a lower rate of return on higher-risk discretionary undertakings, or return penalties for failed investment, if necessary. When companies know the rules about R&D investment recovery, they can make informed decisions about *whether* and *how* to proceed. But stifling R&D because antiquated regulatory policies do not reflect the current and future technology environment will only prolong the time it takes for technology benefits to reach customers and exacerbate utility readiness for the cleantech transition.

Some companies already have made risk-reducing moves by participating with other peers in venture capital funds where syndicating fees paid for participation vastly outweigh the risks of self-performed R&D. As an example, spreading technology discovery and maturity costs across 40 entities in EIP substantially reduces an individual company's exposure from the level it would have had to invest to achieve remotely similar benefits.

So, if new technology adoption is one means to help achieve and accelerate decarbonization or electrification, and support achieving other public policy attainment, shouldn't the notion of cost recognition for innovation supporting these outcomes have merit and be a necessary element of regulation? If so, then isn't the question really considering *how* to provide support to innovation, rather than *if* cost recognition should occur?

It is time to shift from a regulatory environment characterized by innovation constraints to one where innovation is expected and incented. In this environment, innovation is an open dialogue between regulators and utilities, focusing on market-based mutual priorities and expected outcomes.

State commissions have several regulatory means available to provide incentive to utilities to be willing to invest in innovation. For example, perhaps an agreed annual amount of innovation funding could be directly allowed in rates, or specific basis points off the return on equity could be dedicated to innovation, or innovation outcomes could be reviewed for value, leading to an asymmetrical or symmetrical sharing.

There are numerous regulatory approaches to addressing innovation cost recognition and recovery, so getting to a reasonable answer should not be difficult. But getting a responsive policy in place is not as simple as selecting one of the examples above. To be successful in obtaining helpful innovation cost recognition and recovery requires dialogue and collaboration between the regulator and the utilities it regulates to reach concurrence on the purpose, scope, and outcomes from spending on innovation itself.

Regulators have a legitimate reason to know what a utility is considering spending on innovation when the utility wants to obtain specific approval for cost recognition and recovery. And it is not unreasonable for the commission to understand the purpose of the spending, the manner in which these funds would be expended, the expectation of outcomes, and the specific benefits to be derived by customers and the utility. These are fundamental justification questions where a utility should be happy to make the case for innovation spend and the relationship between their costs and customer benefits.

But this dialogue should not expand into a regulatory commission exercising its judgment over that of the utility on *where* the dollars should specifically flow—they are less informed than the utility about market and technology evolution, and even less aware of how individual technologies can be most effectively deployed.

Regulators should be focused on whether proposed expenditures are justified as legitimate responses to the needs for grid and network modernization, reliability, and/or optimization. They should also be focused on understanding the indicated needs and wants of customers for enhanced provider engagement, broader customer choice and control, increased access to available technologies, and expanded offerings that respond to customer lifestyle preferences. Commissions should view these interactions with their utilities as foundational, instructive, and beneficial, not as budget requests.

This regulator-utility dialogue should not happen during a rate case when friction naturally exists about rate increase requests. It would be more appropriate to conduct this dialogue outside a formal hearing process where open engagement, thoughtful deliberation, and policy design can be conducted with a single purpose in mind—that is, *what* is important to customers as users and for utilities as operators and providers.

The assessment of *whether* and *how* innovation should be considered, recognized, and recovered is about the art of policy, not about the mechanics of rate making. Regulators do not need to assume that utilities will be profligate spenders and unmindful of execution risk. Similarly, utilities should not assume that the automatic answer is no to innovation need and value. The whole purpose of the dialogue is to come to a collaborative view that purposeful innovation has a value to all involved parties—customers, regulators, and shareholders—and that constraining its pursuit affects customers the most.

If regulators and utilities can come to a fundamental agreement that innovation is necessary to conduct to reflect the changing environment around them, and that neither side is interested in taking or allowing excessive risk, or requesting or allowing unfettered spending, then common ground can be built. The next step is just about determining the parameters of the purpose, priorities, content, means, and outcomes of innovation spending.

Utilities can always spend shareholder money and treat it as a below-the-line item not recognized for rate making. But if the common goal is to ensure grid and network vitality and customer benefit, this is a self-defeating outcome and a detriment to innovation activity, not just a constraint on spending level.

Measure to Incent

The stand-up of the innovation model brings new excitement to a utility but also requires that strong management processes be in place to guide and drive performance as an organizational unit and a project manager and executer.

Utilities are new to incorporating innovation as a critical element of their business strategy, but every day they are focusing on mastering the fundamentals of executing their innovation models. Most companies are not far enough along in their innovation journey to point to many significant examples of operational or commercial success. But they do recognize that the ability to sustain innovation as a critical enterprise undertaking is dependent on their effectiveness in measuring organization and project progress.

Traditional approaches and metrics in place for an established business are less relevant to assessing the performance of an innovation organization and its work. Traditional, results-driven metrics are less useful to a stand-up organization, particularly where activity, participation, and accomplishment are the hallmarks of innovation. While hard metrics may be more useful at a later time, soft metrics are more relevant in the near term when utilities are trying to gain their footing and attract interest and participation within the larger enterprise.

Utilities with formative or existing innovation models can consider metrics in five key areas: engagement, ideation, productization, commercialization, and innovation ROI. These metrics provide a life-cycle view from adoption to accomplishment and have differing degrees of applicability across the innovation journey:

- *Engagement:* A primary measure of innovation success is the participation and collaboration among employees—knowing whether this participation rate is increasing or decreasing is important to gauge the value of prior and current messaging.

- *Ideation:* Innovation falls dramatically short of its intent if it is not constantly producing a steady flow of new ideas to the business that can be qualified for vetting and subsequently passed through the screening process for detailed assessment and potential adoption.

- *Productization:* Too many innovation activities start as the normal execution mechanism for utilities—projects—with little attention directed toward the outcomes to the business and the way in which they can be converted into implementable products inside or outside the business.

- *Commercialization:* The ultimate goal of innovation is to convert outcomes into tangible benefits for shareholders and customers that lead to measurable value, either as quantifiable impact from business adoption or as market solutions that can create additional value streams.

- *Innovation ROI:* Ultimately, the arbiter of innovation success is whether the tangible investment and sweat equity are delivering on the expectation established by management for demonstrable value—either captured or created.

With most utilities still in an early window of stand-up and activity, traditional performance, impact, and results metrics, like ROI and value contribution, are premature to apply. But an emphasis on engagement within the business is relevant from day one, and a focus on employee awareness and participation are two measures that do capture a view of internal acceptance and momentum. These outcomes typically measure the success of communications within the organization and how well the innovation message is being heard through the enterprise.

At early stages, engagement metrics, such as messaging and participation, are more relevant than outcome-based measures. Companies should measure how frequently they communicate, what mechanisms are used, how many interactions occur, and how employee innovation attitudes are changing, such as creating an annual culture index. They should also measure how many employees engage in innovation education—formal training, portal access, frequently asked questions, or online programs—and how many participate in innovation projects themselves.

Once innovation stand-up has occurred, emphasis turns to what is being accomplished, such as the process and results of employee ideation. Innovation success comes from a steady stream of high-quality ideas generated within the business. This measurement focus relates to the depth of the idea pipeline and ability to move ideas from concept to evaluation to realization. The pure number of new ideas generated—through specific formal events (crowdsourcing) or unique employee undertakings (sprints and scrums)—is the starting point for measurement. Total idea numbers are an important barometer of employee participation, as is the amount progressing from ideation to adoption (see Figure 40).

How well the innovation model nurtures, evaluates, and decides on idea quality and application is critical to achieving innovation expectations. These processes enable shifting utility cultures from endless study to rapid adoption.

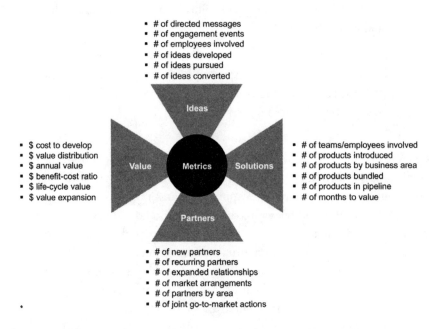

- # of directed messages
- # of engagement events
- # of employees involved
- # of ideas developed
- # of ideas pursued
- # of ideas converted

- $ cost to develop
- $ value distribution
- $ annual value
- $ benefit-cost ratio
- $ life-cycle value
- $ value expansion

- # of teams/employees involved
- # of products introduced
- # of products by business area
- # of products bundled
- # of products in pipeline
- # of months to value

- # of new partners
- # of recurring partners
- # of expanded relationships
- # of market arrangements
- # of partners by area
- # of joint go-to-market actions

Figure 40. Innovation measurement.

Many utilities focus first on enhancing business operating performance in terms of cycle time, quality, productivity, or unit cost because it is most easily measurable. They also focus on deploying new technologies to support execution and generating visible changes to related process execution.

Operationalization of innovation is measured from both adoption and value perspectives. While plenty of good ideas continually percolate within operations, what matters is how many are actually proven and adopted and can be applied to the business. How long it takes for ideas to move through innovation evaluation is an important metric since time equates to money. Realization of value is the ultimate barometer of success, whether increased performance, reduced problems, or avoided expenditures.

Once the innovation model becomes more embedded, management then turns to how to monetize its ideas. Converting ideas into commercial value is not constrained just because utilities are regulated. Innovation addresses new products, services, technologies, and solutions, as well as new ways to harvest value from existing assets and systems. Commercialization value (margins) is the outcome innovative companies pursue. Relevant metrics relate to how many ideas are monetized, the robustness of the pipeline for future commercialization, and how long it takes to move an idea from concept to value.

Fundamental to commercialization value is the return on innovation investment, both capital and labor, that underlies ideation and monetization. This is not a familiar metric to utilities but is common to established innovators. The relevance of this metric increases as the innovation model matures, sufficient project activity develops, and there are outcomes to measure this financial result. While new metrics will be adopted to enable innovation measurement, they should not operate outside the existing performance management framework.

An emphasis on measurement of innovation engagement, activities, progress, and outcomes was previously mentioned as a critical performance tool for use in managing innovation. Utilities need to become comfortable measuring activities they never had to consider in the past, like ideas and collaboration. How well the organization converts ideas into accomplishments and contributions is an important barometer of whether innovation is succeeding against its charter and against its end-state goal.

But also of importance is the ability to demonstrate changes that occur over time. Trends in volumes, instances, and topics are just as important as pure period-to-period activity comparisons. The measurement system should not just be considered a tracking process but also provide insights that underlie the metrics being reported. To increase interest among the users and readers of the metrics, stale number tables should be replaced by active graphical presentation to bring the story to life and enable trends to be more distinguishable over time. Building an awareness and appreciation for model and project activity and accomplishment helps nurture the culture of innovation.

A key dimension relates to aligning incentives within the business with the desired behavior a company seeks from its employees. Employees need to feel they have the freedom to ideate, as well as the freedom to fail without penalty, if that occurs. But utilities have been slow to consider innovation as an outcome just as important as business performance and contribution.

Utilities need to become comfortable with the notion that if they want to make innovation important to employees, then they need to reflect that desired behavior among formal incentives. Just as employees are incented to meet budgets, execute well, and avoid operating discontinuities, they should also be incented to take reasonable risks and pursue success. Company lore chronicles instances in which acting boldly was not celebrated but punished. Many employees remember a culture where, instead of risk-taking, avoiding failure at all costs was embraced. Encouraging employees to pursue risk-taking within bounds is part of building a culture of innovation.

But to cement that culture into employee DNA requires that tangible demonstration of value to management be provided. What works better in a utility than the annual incentive plan and the long-term incentive plan? For optimum benefit, specific metrics should be incorporated into executive, manager, and employee planning and accomplishment measurement.

For executives, the value weighting of this metric should reflect its importance among all key performance indicators that determine performance payouts, just as have traditionally been measured across financial, operational, and customer categories. But since managers and employees tend to be evaluated on macro-corporate goal attainment, this metric could be specifically called out and weighted such that those employees who participate, ideate, collaborate, and produce outcomes are assured of an outsized bonus (if not already provided through other innovation value methods).

Regardless of the design of the incentive model, the key desired outcomes are for the employee base to see that executives have skin in the game in a meaningful way, that employees derive a tangible and emotional connection to innovation, and that their sense of ownership of ideation and value to the business are further enhanced.

Communications to Inspiration

While most utilities do a great job of informing their employees about actions, events, and outcomes, they are often less adept at exciting and persuading employees about new directions and expectations—and that is exactly the intent of innovation. Certainly, describing a crowdsourcing event is relatively easy to do; however, developing a compelling case for change for innovation is more exacting. And engaging employees about the differences between the current state of operational execution emphasis and the future state of commercialization value capture is an even more daunting task.

Utilities have several internal communications mechanisms at their disposal—internal streaming, employee portals, dedicated innovation portal sites, regular and targeted employee emails, on-site brown bag forums with executives, and other digital pushouts. But many utilities do not make it easy to find out about innovation occurring within the company or to dig deeper on innovation projects, programs, progress, or outcomes. When companies do have active links to innovation, the range of quality content can be stark.

This lack of content sometimes has a lot to do with the lack of general home page upkeep, but also the lack of imagination about understanding what employees—and customers and other stakeholders—want to hear about and what companies should be talking about. Of course, it can also reflect a desire not to draw too much attention to the topic, knowing the industry trepidation to be signaling strategies to competitors and adding to the list of issues that intervenors like to raise in regulatory proceedings. But this is a matter of content precision, not one of content availability.

For the best utilities, an innovation tab sits right at the top of the home page, but these are few and far between. Other utility websites take between two and four clicks to get to something resembling an innovation topical page—if a multi-click deep dive can even surface a landing spot. And even if an innovation page can be found, the depth of content can be light and the reference examples not truly representative of innovation activities in action.

The industry thus has a tremendous opportunity to elevate its game about communicating with employees and beyond. It is not a difficult task; nor is it too demanding a task to take on. Refacing a home page to enable a direct link to an innovation page is relatively simple. It is more demanding to build out this page and subsequent click-throughs to more details, but this is also not an extensive rebuild.

What does require thought, however, is the nature, breadth, depth, quality, and value of the information provided. For starters, an innovation page should be a compelling read—revealing, interesting, and relevant. This does not mean that confidential information is given away, but that the focus of the information provides a view to employees about the scope of innovation, efforts in progress or completed, impacts to the business, and next stages for innovation focus. For a reader, a view into *what* work is transpiring, *where* it is being done, *what* is hoped to be achieved, *how* this will create business value, and *why* this is important to the business should be the purpose of the innovation home page.

With this scope of content as an appropriate starting point, attention can then turn to the nature of the content itself. Of course, the content needs to be current and not out-of-date—leave that for the compendium of stories that can be used to provide a history of prior situations. The presented content should cover fundamental elements like innovation purpose, priorities, and intent, along with current topics such as overall messaging (from an officer sponsor), selective current innovation project initiatives (projects of the month), recent events like new partnerships (universities), external appearances (conferences), demonstration pilots (vendors), technology deployments (system purposes), funding receipts (DOE), business benefits (values), and collaboration events (crowdsourcing), among other topics that a company would like to address.

Perhaps surprisingly, when utility innovation home pages exist, they show a broad range of approaches to design with varying degrees of breadth, and depth mostly limited. The intent of a company innovation home page should be to inform the employee base about purpose, activities, and outcomes, but also to seek additional employee participation in innovation teams and collaboration with ongoing initiatives. An innovation home page is a low-cost–high-return mechanism to recruit resources and knowledge to support ongoing efforts.

But creating an innovation home page is not an end game, it is only a start. The intent is not just to create interest about current and past innovation undertakings but to educate the employee base about what is happening in the industry regarding new technology development, future technology evolution, venture capital investments, and the external entities and activities the company is involved with in executing the overall innovation effort. All these dimensions paint a picture of the future, of which most employees do not have any awareness.

It is a broader intent of an innovation effort to communicate to the executive group about a different level of information targeted at extending their understanding of more critical themes, like technology trends, technology options and maturity, competitor technology adoption, technology providers, funding availability, technology economics, internal technology pilots and deployment, and individual project nature, purpose, and progress.

The innovation home page can be a logical site for some of this information, but this nature can be involved and technical and perhaps beyond the intent of the site. And the nature of the information is difficult to present and display without excessive description that partially defeats the intent of driving more employees to the home page.

Perhaps a more valuable mechanism is the preparation of a quarterly, comprehensive discussion on innovation that is directed at senior executives. It is not uncommon for innovation efforts to have limited upward access and exposure to senior executives as a group. In these cases, this contact may be through an executive sponsor or limited in discussion scope to what the management team *wants* to know. However, the more important issue relates more to what this team *should* know.

Since innovation is subject to annual funding process challenges, the full awareness of the executive team to the full innovation perspective—industry, technology, and projects—is a critical element of ensuring that outcomes and value, as opposed to only costs and projects, are available to this group.

Providing a regular, face-to-face update (and companion fact-based document) to the executive team, based on the comprehensive topical elements described above, ensures this team can stay informed at an appropriate level. But more importantly, it provides an opportunity to directly engage this team in meaningful discussion about what it should know beyond the current project agenda, specifically the direction and pace of technology travel, the risks and impacts of technology acceleration or direction to the business, the key decisions this team should be focused on, the value-in-play from technology adoption, and the manner in which the company can capitalize on technology evolution.

This level of innovation discussion can go a long way toward alleviating any misconceptions about technology challenges and opportunities, the value of innovation, or the nature of future opportunities available to the company.

The six strategies described in this chapter help align innovation strategy and emphases with the direction and intent of the corporate strategies that, in part, depend on innovation for attainment. But there are other available strategies to complement those described. For example, utilities need to expand their horizons regarding partnering with third parties. Even though they are EPRI and/or GTI members, or partners with venture capital firms, or contract directly with portfolio companies in various funds, or have long-standing relationships with OEMs, vendors, software providers, and solutions providers, they have far less direct experience in partnering as a critical adjunct to business execution.

Utilities need partnerships because they are neither chartered to nor experienced with conducting many of the critical technical activities directly involved with detailed discovery, proof of concept, development, and distribution of various products, services, or solutions. Partners are a force multiplier that can help utilities gain from investment, collaboration, design and development, and commercialization experience.

Utility and third-party partnerships with the types of entities identified above will not occur overnight, as there are many trepidations that exist on both sides of an agreement—congruence in views, governance models, value equations, and go-to-market models. However, it should be a goal of the industry to make these kinds of technical capabilities, supplemental capital, pricing savvy, and market-reach capabilities a fundamental part of their innovation strategies. It is very foreseeable that any individual utility will evolve into a *partner of partners*, with multiple relationships that enable broader, deeper, and faster engagement in the markets of the future.

CHAPTER 11

Refreshing the Agenda

THE U.S. utilities industry is amid a continuing strategy realignment as it proceeds through the cleantech transition and into perhaps a more directional, but far less clear, future evolution. Most U.S. utilities have announced their approaches, goals, and timing to get to net-zero emissions, yet the path to attainment is neither certain nor attainable under present industry, political, financial, and regulatory models.

The time frame between the earliest date to achieve net-zero of 2030 and the latest announced target date of 2050 is wrought with uncertainty. First, global estimates for necessary capital to fund the attainment of net-zero in 2050 are in the hundreds of trillions, spanning from $125 trillion to $275 trillion. It is unclear how funding at that level will be provided into a changed utilities industry model and, more importantly, how it will be absorbed by utility customers—whether related to new renewables and transmission build-out, electrification, or gas replacement, among other drivers.

In addition, most utilities—and other sectors as well—will have at least one new CEO (and perhaps two) by 2030, and with the average tenure of CEOs at around five years, maybe as many as six to seven by 2050. In addition, there are seven national elections by 2050. These are well-appreciated factors that can change, if not derail, the path to net-zero. But factors, such as global disruption, customer impacts, capital availability, policy shifts, and new science can further affect the ability to achieve planned outcomes, delay the timing of goal attainment, and/or shift the focus of the industry.

Even though a portion of the die has been cast for the future utilities industry path to net-zero given known assumptions, succeeding net-zero achievements remain back-loaded and subject to off-ramps or outright change because of gaps in the five factors mentioned above.

Significant impact on carbon emissions is not dependent on policy; it is dependent on technology—some of which that has yet to be tested, perfected, scaled, or even discovered. Achieving broad net-zero goals by 2050 does not seem that difficult for a society where technology has held a dominant position in its evolution. But 2050 is less than 30 years away, and breakthrough innovation at that level is complicated to realize in just about one-quarter of a century.

It is not the discovery and proof-of-concept stages that are the constraining factors; rather, it is the ability to first scale technology for adoption and then achieve ubiquity to produce full expectations of results in the necessary time frames. While massive technology introduction takes decades to accomplish, the task is much more difficult when immutable goals have been established, substantial gaps in technology performance exist, and the to-be-incurred costs are not just significant but—based on the little we know, understand, and can anticipate today—no more than 25 years in the future.

This situation leaves utilities with the challenge of aligning planning for the future in an uncertain environment, where announced goals and targets depend on technologies that do not yet exist or are not perfected (e.g., long-duration storage, CCUS, hydrogen as an energy carrier at scale, SMRs, and other technologies), and depend on policies that have been enunciated but are more cliches than realities. That level of technology evolution uncertainty is a bad place to be on a planning spectrum that relies on a high level of known inputs and outputs, even if outcomes are more unpredictable. Combine that with the unknowns of policy and regulatory predictability and potential financing instability (e.g., ESG), and the picture becomes even cloudier. And the questions of *who pays*, *how much*, and *when* are nowhere close to resolution, particularly when customer affordability is under siege from unstable energy and inflationary factor costs.

The journey toward net-zero is long and unlikely to be without some twists and turns from the current straight-line path. To achieve net-zero by 2050 is playing the long game, but the first steps have already been played out (i.e., numerous coal plant retirements, dramatic renewables installation, and economy-wide sentiment for thinking differently about climate cleanup). The focus on long-term climate objectives is clear, but the incessant ESG rhetoric about constraining access to financing for companies (and even industries) on a 30-year journey is a distraction, particularly when some of the largest emitters in the world refuse to adhere to what the financial community considers established norms.

To move from net-zero goal setting to attainment, cleantech is the transition bridge between where the industry is today and where it needs to be in the future. Utilities will not bridge the gap without technology breakthroughs on a larger scale than what has been achieved to date.

These circumstances make the need for, and more the value from, innovation increasingly critical to utilities. Innovation as an effective platform becomes an imperative rather than a complementary instrument of executives as they work to move their organizations forward. Creating and embedding a robust and effective innovation platform is a table stake component of a utility's competitive positioning strategy, just as innovation importantly is a critical element of any distinctive strategy.

The path through the cleantech transition and on to net-zero is enabled directly by technology evolution. Thus, the future agendas for both a utility and innovation need to adopt innovation as a centerpiece of activity and accomplishment. For the utilities industry to be successful in preparing for a net-zero environmental outcome, along with subsequent operational and customer engagement impacts and outcomes produced by this massive industry shift, all utilities need to continue to elevate their innovation game—sometimes dramatically—or risk falling behind and being unprepared for one of the largest supply reformation and revolutionary market opportunities to ever present itself to companies.

With these net-zero challenges facing the U.S. utilities industry, companies need to reimagine their future strategies, with innovation elevated to a centerpiece on the path to the future, albeit accompanied by a healthy dose of flexibility. Innovation needs to become even more visible in companies, as they will become increasingly more dependent on direct (corporate venture fund) and indirect (external venture fund) investment, as well as internal activity at the enterprise, line of business, and operating company levels.

The future agenda for innovation in utilities will need to become more aspirational, demanding, and far-reaching. While innovation in the industry has become more visible, it has yet to reach all corners of the industry and is far from becoming a table stake for how companies position themselves for the future. The future agenda to be set for innovation thus needs to be purposeful in design, aggressive in execution, and targeted on outcomes.

Innovation 3.0

The ability of utilities to move through the present industry state of play will be heavily affected by the nature and intent of company innovation models. To be sure, utilities will seek to elevate their games to match the intensity of the evolution of the market. Utilities will also continue to rely on a mix of internal ingenuity and external expertise to shape and execute their innovation efforts. Relying on only one or the other will not be sufficient to enable utilities to move to either the next level of innovation to ensure their desired market positioning and success, or the next level of enabling strategies, navigating markets, deploying technologies, and engaging customers.

Remember, only a few companies originally possessed and maintained real R&D (mostly applied) capabilities over an extended time frame, and most of those company capabilities have atrophied, leaving just a couple of utilities with in-house expertise. So, relying on external organizations and laboratories is a necessity, but not an end in itself—R&D has to be accompanied by internal capability, particularly when new technologies are exploding around the industry.

Companies will ask themselves whether more effort with innovation focus will really be necessary and ultimately worth it. They will rechallenge the notion that they have not always been innovative, at least where they think it matters. And they will rethink how value actually emerges from all the innovation efforts they undertake—all reasonable questions for companies in an industry relatively new to practicing imaginative and sustained innovation.

Innovation 1.0—the first era—started with just a few companies pursuing investments in or acquisitions of start-up companies with technology solutions viewed as beneficial to utilities in preparing for the future. This version of innovation also reflected the formative activities of these companies, rather than a broader participation rate across the industry. This early era included the stand-up of discrete innovation centers in these companies as well.

Innovation 2.0—the second era—saw a second wave of companies become engaged in innovation after they had further assessed the nature and pace of technology introduction and seen the progress that the era 1.0 companies were achieving. This tranche of utilities also followed the venture capital path with a mix of internal and external fund investments, which seemed to limit the industry's interest in start-up acquisition. These companies learned from the era 1.0 companies and adopted some of the approaches utilized by their peers in earlier years.

Innovation 3.0—the third and current era—is where the industry now resides with four to eight years of experience between the earlier era 1.0 and 2.0 companies. This era is just beginning, characterized by broader recognition of innovation need and value, along with an increasing awareness that the cleantech transition is accelerating and causing utilities to rethink their planned timelines for action. This era also reflects a deeper awareness among the employee base; increased interaction with customers, OEMs, software developers, and solutions providers; more concrete examples of the types of innovation being pursued and accomplished; and a broader determination of innovation value.

This era will be the one where almost all aspects of innovation will need to be addressed and enhanced. By the time this era evolves into innovation 4.0 at some future date, it may be known for illustrating the level of value outcomes that can be realized when innovation is fully integrated into enterprise strategies, whether for the cleantech transition, growth priorities, business enhancement, or customer advancement.

In setting the innovation agenda, companies will need to think about what they can do with all available resources, whether internal team, external partners, or key stakeholders (i.e., regulators and other third parties).

The future innovation 3.0 agenda will address a full range of actions to enhance the innovation platform and continue to elevate its importance inside the company, as well as with the full range of relevant stakeholders. This innovation 3.0 agenda could address enlarging the scope, focus, and accomplishment of the platform:

- *More visibility:* Innovation has succeeded in gaining some recognition and notoriety within companies—the next stage will be to increase the consistency of this visibility, the innovation agenda, and the alignment of priorities to market evolution.

- *More integration:* Strategy alignment is still somewhat nascent at the present—going forward, the corporate strategy and innovation agenda (as well as strategy) will be closely aligned with direct connectivity between purpose, priorities, and outcomes.

- *More collaboration:* Many employees have been involved with innovation teams and activities in their utilities—future employee engagement will need to make a concerted effort to encourage more employees to participate and extend the idea pool.

- *More communication:* Utilities tend to not talk very frequently or deeply about innovation activities and accomplishments—the communications agenda needs to view messaging as an innovation virtue, regularly describing trends, technologies, projects, products, and value.

- *More crowdsourcing:* Industry use of formal events is mixed, ranging from across a whole company, to a single business or function, to not used at all—crowdsourcing is a powerful tool, but even more valuable when conducted company-wide with purpose and to customers and OEMs.

- *More solutions:* Much innovation to date centers on enhancing operational performance versus advancing business capabilities—future focus needs to emphasize creating real solutions to system or customer problems.

- *More commercialization:* As asset operators, utilities tend to focus on operationalization of innovation areas in need of technological enhancement—recognition that commercialization is key to creating new revenue streams and delivering customer impact is a primary goal.

- *More partnering:* Utilities are limited in funding, market experience, technology evaluation, product development, and creative pricing—increasing the leverage of experienced third parties is a smart force extender and a critical means of increasing reach and position.

- *More measurement:* Most utilities have not evolved innovation measurement into a key process for assessing model traction and success—future utility efforts should emphasize more formal indicators of innovation engagement, productivity, and contribution.

- *More incentives:* Linkage of innovation to compensation through traditional incentive mechanisms is not a routine action by utilities—like most things, when measured and aligned to performance evaluation, efforts are more likely to produce desired results.

- *More outcomes:* Few utilities emphasize or even speak to the production and realization of value to customers—an orientation toward outcomes that produce tangible value as an innovation purpose needs to be adopted by the industry to reinforce its purpose.

- *More ROI:* Formal evaluation of return on innovation spend seldom occurs within the utilities sector—adopting a financial discipline that incorporates direct quantitative assessment of investment and value created is key to focusing teams on contribution over activity.

Following an agenda structured around an enhanced view of innovation engagement, positioning, and value will be key to achieving the intended purpose of the overall effort. It will also signal and reinforce the importance of continually elevating and reinforcing the promise it can deliver to the utility, system, and customers.

Partner of Partners

It will be difficult for utilities to approach the cleantech transition solely depending on their internal capabilities. In many respects, a utility's innovation muscles are just beginning to be exercised, and core strength, mass, growth, and flexibility need to be developed.

There are many actions utilities can take that can help them elevate their innovation game. Some rely on traditional activities undertaken by companies, such as evaluation of technologies for deployment, while others are not the historical domain of utilities, like developing solutions. These capability extensions are necessary elements of innovation but not areas where utilities have had to become experts in the past.

If utilities are going to succeed in positioning for the cleantech transition, they will first need to develop or access innovation capabilities that extend beyond their traditional experience and deploy them in ways they have seldom pursued. But utilities are not likely to be able to produce a complete portfolio of capabilities to meet customer needs or determine that market opportunities (and market position preservation) are enhanced through an extension of relationships.

I have previously referenced the logical need for utilities to leverage third parties (i.e., other competitive companies and market sources) where these capabilities exist. These sources are force extenders—partners—that both complement and supplement the experience and capabilities that a utility brings to innovation.

These partners complement the internal capabilities of utilities by enhancing those that already exist (such as market, customer, and technology awareness and financing capacity) and supplementing them with different and/or deeper capabilities in product development, go-to-market model, and market access, which are developed through experience acquired over decades of market participation and competition.

The utilities industry does not have a long or recognized history of successful partnering with third parties, and even joint venture and co-owner arrangements with other utilities are difficult to frame, paper, stand up, execute, and endure. Sure, there are individual examples of successful external partnering arrangements by specific utilities with venture capital firms and universities, but far fewer between utilities and OEMs, technology firms, and consumer companies. These are the types of entities that are real force extenders to utilities and difference makers to future market positioning and cleantech transition success, as they bring capacity, credibility, relationships, capabilities, and channels to leverage and extend.

The types and range of partners that can be beneficial to utilities create a wide aperture of source possibilities: OEMs in energy supply, telecommunications, technical equipment, and monitoring and control devices; vendors in the form of software and hardware developers, solutions providers, and data analytics; consumer-oriented companies in home products, services, and beyond-the-meter offerings; venture capital funds, whether broad or targeted; and universities, laboratories, and research institutions.

Each of these partner types offers something unique and different to a utility focused on expanding its internal capabilities and extending the reach and value of a relationship of this kind, and each is composed of numerous attractive entities that can provide value to a utility:

- *OEMs:* These partners provide deep technical expertise, from design concepts to distribution channels on assets, self-contained equipment, individual or system-wide information management, and smart devices for customer data collection and analysis, control, and insight.

- *Traditional vendors:* These partners develop directed operational and operating support tools that enable utility performance execution and/or management, as well as the development of data repositories for use in building long-term operating profiles.

- *Consumer-oriented companies:* These partners target this specific beyond-the-meter customer segment, with a focus on offerings that enable services to be provided to or for customers and enable greater customer insights through available information and the ability to control energy consumption.

- *Venture capital funds:* These partners bring financial capacity to complement utility investment levels and support company market information access, technology assessment, and technology application use cases through deeper technical resources than utilities can devote.

- *Universities, laboratories, and research organizations:* These partners conduct ongoing R&D—basic and/or applied—through a depth of broad and specialist scientific resources and skills that focus on a broad and deep research perimeter unable to be supported by a utility.

Each of these partner groups brings a level of differentiated capabilities and expertise in areas useful to utilities and comprises a useful collective of innovation sources. These technology and service providers can expand market knowledge and awareness, enable faster technology evaluation and deployment, accelerate commercial product introduction, increase the breadth of capabilities available to meet emerging customer needs, and reduce the costs and risks of innovation on a stand-alone basis.

But the goal is not just to be a single partner with a single entity. Rather, a broad knowledge ecosystem exists of potential partners available to a utility to address the technology environment and dynamics that are evolving. Utilities can benefit through simultaneously partnering with providers in areas like broadband, mobility, storage, distributed energy resources, grid edge offerings, beyond-the-meter, and cybersecurity, among other areas.

These available partners can be utilized under a range of combinations and arrangement types to function as knowledge enablers, investment multipliers, and commercial accelerators for savvy utilities—the definition of being a partner of partners.

Becoming a partner of partners and broadly engaging across the relevant third-party landscape recognizes that the energy ecosystem is broad but interconnected and complicated to navigate, and customer positioning can be advantaged through the ability to high-grade internal capabilities and integrate related market offerings.

Not all utilities are positioned to be an effective partner of partners—they may be too small to attract interest, believed to be too narrowly focused to add sufficient value to a large partner, or unable to successfully navigate internal risk management barriers and overcome inertia over agreement conditions and commitments to participate.

Regardless of the challenges that exist to identify, structure, and execute an effective partnering arrangement, the utilities sector can dramatically benefit from joining with industry participants that bring the experience and capabilities of longstanding market participation in technology development, solution creation, or go-to-market models that take years or longer to perfect.

There is no substitute for the nature and depth of innovation savvy, market knowledge, customer positioning, and time-to-value benefits that single or multiple partners can bring to a utility still early in its innovation journey and trying to evolve from an operationalization to a commercialization focus. They may be difficult to create, but the value of these benefits far exceeds the efforts necessary to stand up these partnering arrangements.

Value Differentiation

As discussed through the last several chapters, the purpose of innovation is to produce meaningful and valuable enhancements to the business, whether processes, technologies, regulatory outcomes, products and services, or business models. These are not mutually exclusive, and all can be the focus of innovation simultaneously.

Compared to the early and recent periods' focus on innovation formation, demonstration, and momentum, the focus of the utilities industry now needs to shift to a more intense emphasis on the outcomes it produces and the value it realizes. This outcome and value-realization focus will sharpen the ability of utilities to gauge and demonstrate expected outcome attainment and enable measurement of actual value provided to the business and customers.

The utilities industry has generally focused on measuring and managing activity and project performance it undertakes. But innovation activities do not always lend themselves to the exact same, time-tested approaches utilized in the past. While outcomes are at the core of project execution objectives, going forward, the measurement orientation for innovation needs to emphasize value realized far more than it has in the past. This means that while qualitative measures like progress, effectiveness, learnings, and changes are still important, the focus needs to shift to more quantitative metrics that address tangible areas like cycle times, reduced costs, productivity gains, products delivered, load impacts, new revenues, capital investment, and return on innovation investment, among other areas.

But refocusing on these types of innovation outcome and value measures is good for the utilities industry. It has developed similar processes over the years in the normal course of business and can easily and quickly adapt these methods to innovation. A benefit of adopting these types of quantitative measures for innovation is that it reinforces its purpose and focuses teams on *why* they are pursuing meaningful outcomes from their efforts. More purposeful measurement of innovation outcomes also enhances the ability of the company to demonstrate value from innovation execution for its board of directors, executive leadership, investment review boards, and regulators.

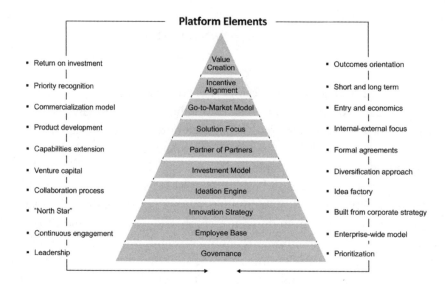

Platform Elements

Left	Center (Pyramid)	Right
• Return on investment	Value Creation	• Outcomes orientation
• Priority recognition	Incentive Alignment	• Short and long term
• Commercialization model	Go-to-Market Model	• Entry and economics
• Product development	Solution Focus	• Internal-external focus
• Capabilities extension	Partner of Partners	• Formal agreements
• Venture capital	Investment Model	• Diversification approach
• Collaboration process	Ideation Engine	• Idea factory
• "North Star"	Innovation Strategy	• Built from corporate strategy
• Continuous engagement	Employee Base	• Enterprise-wide model
• Leadership	Governance	• Prioritization

Figure 41. Framing the innovation platform.

This measurement and demonstration of value is fundamental to the ongoing success of the innovation effort and sits at the pinnacle of the innovation platform previously discussed. As illustrated in Figure 41, the innovation platform is not a physical construct but a way to think about the fundamental building blocks of innovation, from the inception of employee involvement through the development and commercialization of solutions and realization of value. The platform is integrated and reflects a linkage between purpose, prioritization, execution, markets, and value.

The platform itself is simply a way of organizing the building blocks of innovation that determines its objectives, direction, methods, alignment, and outcomes, ultimately leading to value realized. The ability of a utility to demonstrate its model for *how* innovation is managed, initiated, focused, funded, executed, and delivered is fundamental to understanding and demonstrating *how well* this effort fulfills its intent.

As important as value is to assessing benefit to the business, it is also important to be able to clearly identify *where* and *how* value is produced from the projects conducted within the business. The identification and measurement of value needs to start with something that is measurable (e.g., a project), which is discrete and has both inputs (costs) and outputs (productivity, capital, operations and maintenance, load, revenues, and so on). Using project data as the basis for measurement simplifies the task and aligns *what* happened as a result of the innovation effort. This type of approach to value identification and measurement also provides a simple and portable basis across all projects.

While general measures like inputs and outputs are straightforward, they form the collective basis for value measurement (i.e., ROI). Ultimately, this is the overall arbiter of project and platform success since it provides the cumulative view of all outcomes, whether successful or not.

Another dimension of the measurement of innovation value relates to the use of demonstrated outcomes and value in an external context—as a proof point of company prowess to the board of directors, investors, and regulators. Certain utilities are widely known for having differentiating capabilities in areas like financial management, regulatory relationships, plant operations, or distribution operations, and are highly valued by investors for these skills.

When utility innovation efforts begin to produce noticeable operating impacts and value contributions, perhaps certain companies will be recognized by investors and receive differentiating recognition for the quality of the innovation platform that has been built. This accomplishment will be achieved not only by pointing to innovation outcomes but by demonstrating enterprise-wide fusion of innovation into an embedded element of a utility's DNA.

Future Positioning

The U.S. utilities industry is well positioned financially and operationally to address the challenges of the cleantech transition. And many companies are creating the foundation for ongoing innovation through the activities they have already conducted and their intentional focus on thinking differently about planning, executing, and managing their businesses.

But like the cleantech transition, the innovation journey is still early in its formation, with no shortage of areas to address and no indication that the path to the future is clearly defined. This leaves the utilities industry with a need to refresh its innovation agenda and strategies to reflect these uncertainties and chart a path to elevate its innovation game to match the challenges that technology evolution is creating for executive management teams.

To begin with, utilities need to step back from their current innovation posture and rechallenge all the underlying precepts guiding them to this current point in time—that is, the drivers influencing original strategies and planning, the targeted outcomes initially determined, the early priorities established, the milestones adopted to guide progress, the adequacy of projects already completed and underway, and the sufficiency of the effort to date relative to external changes underway.

This is a logical step for utilities to be regularly taking as part of their innovation strategy development thinking to keep their planning relevant and on point. After all, the outlook for future technology evolution considered in the early years of innovation stand-up in 2013–2016 was outdated by 2019, which has itself become outdated by 2022, and will continue to be superseded every two to three years. This will occur because of accelerating policy development, diverging attitudes about priorities, evolving technology costs and performance, and shifting market perspectives.

Consequently, to ensure their future innovation success, utilities need to reassess several defining elements of their early innovation planning with an eye toward both fine-tuning and wholesale redesign:

- *Strategy focus:* The industry shaped its innovation strategy around readiness for an uncertain future, even before the cleantech transition became topical as a driving influence. This original emphasis is still relevant, but additional focus can be directed at positioning innovation as a fundamental element of enterprise strategy success. *Strategy focus extends beyond the cleantech transition to new influences on leveraging technology to advance business performance and redefine the utility role with customers.*

- *Priority setting:* The initial stand-up of utility innovation models focused on addressing observed business execution gaps and embryonic market opportunities, like EVs. These priorities are also still relevant but have broadened to reflect the proliferation of operating performance enhancement opportunities. *But attention needs to further shift to thinking about the customer domain and new opportunities to improve value delivered in the form of products, services, and solutions that improve insight and increase options.*

- *Organizational positioning:* Innovation efforts tended to be more centralized at formation because of their unique aspects and the initial low level of familiarity across the business. It has now become more devolved to reflect a sentiment that it cannot be solely owned at the corporate level and should be embedded in an organization's cultural DNA. *However, with increasing visibility and impacts, the value of innovation grows and suggests that regardless of where positioned, successful execution benefits from hands-on senior executive visibility and leadership.*

- *Employee participation:* Early crowdsourcing events were designed to galvanize the broad employee base and introduce new ways of thinking and execution to the business. These events had early success but have been used with less regularity than is their intended purpose. *To optimize innovation results, more success can be obtained by continuing to involve the employee base— by business segment, unit, function, topical area, external trend, or competitive challenge.*

- *Innovation messaging:* Effective communication is an art, and one where utilities often struggle beyond providing factual information. While early innovation communication was tightly linked to informing and exciting the employee base, it typically fell off fast after enterprise events had concluded and innovation became localized and episodic in many utilities. *Employees would benefit from revitalization and expansion of messaging purpose and continuity to incorporate information about technology trends, projects underway, and project accomplishments.*

- *External collaboration:* Utilities have been active partners with various entities in the venture capital community since early in its formation. But they do not attempt to collaborate with other third parties much beyond industry organizations like EPRI, GTI, and universities. The range of other entities like OEMs and solutions providers is broad, with the value of vendor engagement viewed with skepticism. *Regardless of this perspective, there is tremendous value in engaging more directly with customers about their perspectives, priorities, needs, and decision values.*

- *Innovation emphasis:* Utilities tend to center their innovation attention on the near term over the long term (the business of today), and the tactical over the strategic (the gap that exists). While valuable to the business, these targeted areas of attention do not address the critical future needs of an industry in evolution. *Innovation falls short of its promise if it does not focus on the emerging needs of the business to embrace new technologies, new customer roles, new market offerings, and new sources of value creation.*

- *Incentive alignment:* The alignment of innovation with incentives is still very new to the sector, with only a handful of companies adopting it to date, which is no surprise. Modifying the incentive model is difficult if it sends the wrong signals to boards of directors, employees, investors, and regulators. *But nothing signals the intent and commitment of executives to desired outcomes better than to link innovation execution and outcomes to the compensation system in a visible and meaningful manner to expand it beyond this single level.*

This chapter has largely been more about what comes next, than what has transpired to date. The next few years promise to provide significant challenges to the utilities sector in navigating the cleantech transition and readying for attainment of net-zero commitments. As utilities move into the innovation 3.0 era, they will assume a heightened leadership role for broader enterprise engagement; expanded technology evaluation, piloting, and deployment; accelerated project execution; and greater value contribution from innovation endeavors.

The success of the utilities industry with innovation through the next few years will depend on the vitality of the steps taken to further elevate its importance within the business and position it as a valued element of a company's operating philosophy and DNA. Utilities do not need to try and become Google, Apple, or Amazon, but they do need to think and act more like them where it matters—producing outcomes and value that are important to the business and customers in visible, useful, meaningful, and compelling ways.

Notes

CHAPTER I

1. Barry Jaruzelski, Robert Chwalik, and Brad Goehle, "The Global Innovation 1000: What the Top Innovators Get Right," *strategy+business*, October 30, 2018, https://www.strategy-business.com/feature/What-the-Top-Innovators-Get-Right.
2. Jaruzelski, Chwalik, and Goehle, "The Global Innovation 1000."
3. Jaruzelski, Chwalik, and Goehle, "The Global Innovation 1000."

CHAPTER 2

1. The Edison Foundation Institute for Electric Innovation, "Electric Company Smart Meter Deployments: Foundation for a Smart Grid 2021 Update," April 2021, https://www.edisonfoundation.net/-/media/Files/IEI/publications/IEI_Smart_Meter_Report_April_2021.ashx.
2. National Conference of State Legislatures, "U.S. State Greenhouse Gas Emissions Targets," September 2021.
3. "Energy Policy Act of 2005 Summary," *Wikipedia*, September 25, 2022, https://en.wikipedia.org/wiki/Energy_Policy_Act_of_2005; U.S. Department of Energy, "Tax Incentives for Energy-Efficiency Upgrades in Commercial Buildings," August 2005, https://www.energy.gov/eere/buildings/tax-incentives-energy-efficiency-upgrades-commercial-buildings.
4. S&P Global Market Intelligence, "Managers of $10 Trillion in Assets to Cut Portfolio Emissions Up to 65% by 2030," accessed October 24, 2022, https://www.spglobal.com/marketintelligence/en; see also UN Environment Program, "UN-Convened Net-Zero Asset Owner Alliance," accessed October 24, 2022, https://www.unepfi.org/net-zero-alliance.
5. Climate Action 100+, "2021 Year in Review: A Progress Update," January 2022, https://www.unpri.org/download?ac=15751.
6. BloombergNEF, "Corporate Clean Energy Buying Tops 30GW Mark in Record Year," January 31, 2022, https://about.bnef.com/blog/corporate-clean-energy-buying-tops-30gw-mark-in-record-year/.
7. Bureau of Economic Analysis, "Personal Income and Outlays, December 2021," January 28, 2022, https://www.bea.gov/news/blog/2022-01-28/personal-income-and-outlays-december-2021.

8. "October's CPI Report," PUF's Where's Energy, *Public Utilities Fortnightly*, accessed October 13, 2022, https://www.fortnightly.com/today-from-puf/octobers-cpi-report.

CHAPTER 3

1. Institute of Entrepreneurship Development, "The 4 Industrial Revolutions," June 30, 2019, https://ied.eu/project-updates/the-4-industrial-revolutions/.
2. Institute of Entrepreneurship Development, "The 4 Industrial Revolutions."
3. Institute of Entrepreneurship Development, "The 4 Industrial Revolutions."
4. Klaus Schwab, "The Four Industrial Revolutions: What It Means, How to Respond," World Economic Forum, January 14, 2016, https://www.weforum.org/agenda/2016/01/the-fourth-industrial-revolution-what-it-means-and-how-to-respond/.
5. "Bell Laboratories," *Encyclopedia Britannica*, September 14, 2022, https://www.britannica.com/topic/Bell-Laboratories.
6. Catherine Jewell, "Global Innovation Index 2021: Tracking Innovation through the COVID-19 Crisis," *WIPO Magazine*, September 2021, https://www.wipo.int/wipo_magazine/en/2021/03/article_0002.html.
7. Jewell, "Global Innovation Index 2021."
8. Jewell, "Global Innovation Index 2021."
9. Jewell, "Global Innovation Index 2021."
10. Jewell, "Global Innovation Index 2021."
11. Jewell, "Global Innovation Index 2021."
12. Jewell, "Global Innovation Index 2021."
13. Barry Jaruzelski, Robert Chwalik, and Brad Goehle, "The Global Innovation 1000: What the Top Innovators Get Right," *strategy+business*, October 30, 2018, https://www.strategy-business.com/feature/What-the-Top-Innovators-Get-Right.
14. Jaruzelski, Chwalik, and Goehle, "The Global Innovation 1000."
15. Jaruzelski, Chwalik, and Goehle, "The Global Innovation 1000."
16. Jaruzelski, Chwalik, and Goehle, "The Global Innovation 1000."
17. Jaruzelski, Chwalik, and Goehle, "The Global Innovation 1000."
18. Jaruzelski, Chwalik, and Goehle, "The Global Innovation 1000."
19. Jaruzelski, Chwalik, and Goehle, "The Global Innovation 1000."
20. Jaruzelski, Chwalik, and Goehle, "The Global Innovation 1000."

21. "List of Largest Corporations by Market Capitalization," *Wikipedia*, September 27, 2022, https://en.wikipedia.org/wiki/List_of_public_corporations_by_market_capitalization.
22. Jaruzelski, Chwalik, and Goehle, "The Global Innovation 1000."
23. Jaruzelski, Chwalik, and Goehle, "The Global Innovation 1000."
24. "List of Largest Corporations by Market Capitalization."

CHAPTER 4

1. Edison Electric Institute, "Industry Capital Expenditures," June 2021, https://www.eei.org/-/media/Project/EEI/Documents/Issues-and-Policy/Finance-And-Tax/bar_cap_ex.pdf.
2. Tom Flaherty, "Reimagining Purpose," *Public Utilities Fortnightly*, July 2020, https://www.fortnightly.com/fortnightly/2020/07/reimagining-purpose%C2%A0%C2%A0.
3. Flaherty, "Reimagining Purpose."
4. Flaherty, "Reimagining Purpose."
5. Flaherty, "Reimagining Purpose"; S&P Global Market Intelligence, "Utility R&D Spend," n.d., unpublished document in the author's possession.
6. Mercom, "2019 Q4 and Annual Funding and M&A Report for Battery Storage, Smart Grid, and Efficiency"; Mercom, "2019 Q4 and Annual Solar Funding and M&A Report." Reports are available at https://mercomcapital.com/clean-energy-reports.
7. Mercom, "2021 Q4 and Annual Funding and M&A Report for Battery Storage, Smart Grid, and Efficiency"; Mercom, "Annual and Q4 2021 Solar Funding and M&A Report." Reports are available at https://mercomcapital.com/clean-energy-reports.
8. Mercom, "2021 Q4 and Annual Funding"; Mercom, "Annual and Q4 Solar Funding."
9. Tom Fanning, Kevin Fitzgerald, and Tom Flaherty, "Innovation–Investment Nexus, Part II," *Public Utilities Fortnightly*, May 2020, https://www.fortnightly.com/fortnightly/2020/05/innovation-%E2%80%93-investment-nexus-part-ii.

CHAPTER 5

1. U.S. Department of Energy, "Brief History of the Department of Energy," accessed September 27, 2022, https://www.energy.gov/lm/doe-history/brief-history-department-energy.

2. U.S. Department of Energy, "The Institutional Origins of the Department of Energy," October 20, 2011, https://www.energy.gov/sites/default/files/Origins-of-the-Department-of-Energy.pdf.

3. U.S. Department of Energy Office of Science, "About the Office of Science," accessed September 27, 2022, https://www.energy.gov/science/about-office-science.

4. Paul Dabbar, phone interview by the author, April 29, 2022.

5. White House, "Fact Sheet: President Biden Announces Support for the Bipartisan Infrastructure Framework," June 24, 2021, https://www.whitehouse.gov/briefing-room/statements-releases/2021/06/24/fact-sheet-president-biden-announces-support-for-the-bipartisan-infrastructure-framework/.

6. White House, "Fact Sheet: The Bipartisan Infrastructure Deal," November 6, 2021, https://www.whitehouse.gov/briefing-room/statements-releases/2021/11/06/fact-sheet-the-bipartisan-infrastructure-deal/.

7. U.S. Department of Energy, "DOE Establishes New Office of Clean Energy Demonstrations under the Bipartisan Infrastructure Law," December 21, 2021, https://www.energy.gov/articles/doe-establishes-new-office-clean-energy-demonstrations-under-bipartisan-infrastructure-law.

8. "Nuclear Supporting Infrastructure Becomes U.S. Law," *World Nuclear News*, November 16, 2021, https://www.world-nuclear-news.org/Articles/Nuclear-supporting-infrastructure-bill-becomes-US.

9. U.S. Department of Energy, "Organization Chart," March 2022, https://www.energy.gov/organization-chart; U.S. Department of Energy, "About Us," accessed September 27, 2022, https://www.energy.gov/about-us.

10. U.S. Department of Energy, "FY 2022 Budget Justification," May 28, 2021, https://www.energy.gov/cfo/articles/fy-2022-budget-justification.

11. U.S. Department of Energy, "FY 2022 Budget Justification."

12. U.S. Department of Energy, "FY 2022 Budget Justification"; U.S. Department of Energy, "FY 2011 Budget Justification," February 1, 2010, https://www.energy.gov/cfo/downloads/fy-2011-budget-justification.

13. Dabbar, phone interview by the author.

14. U.S. Department of Energy Office of Policy, "Energy Earthshots Initiative," November 5, 2021, https://www.energy.gov/policy/energy-earthshots-initiative.

15. U.S. Department of Energy, "Hydrogen and Fuel Cells R&D FY 2021 FOA Selections," July 7, 2021, https://www.energy.gov/eere/fuelcells/articles/hydrogen-and-fuel-cells-rd-fy-2021-foa-selections.

16. U.S. Department of Energy, "The State of the DOE National Laboratories, 2020 Edition," January 2021, https://www.energy.gov/sites/default/files/2021/01/f82/DOE%20National%20Labs%20Report%20FINAL.pdf.

17. U.S. Department of Energy, "The State of the DOE National Laboratories."

18. U.S. Department of Energy, "National Incubator Initiative for Clean Energy (NIICE)," accessed September 27, 2022, https://www.energy.gov/eere/technology-to-market/national-incubator-initiative-clean-energy-niice-0.

19. U.S. Department of Energy, "National Incubator Initiative."

20. U.S. Department of Energy, "DOE Announces New $2.5 Million Prize to Support Diversity in Innovation," September 30, 2021, https://www.energy.gov/articles/doe-announces-new-25-million-prize-support-diversity-innovation.

21. U.S. Department of Energy, "DOE Awards $9.5 Million to Support Clean Energy Innovation and Commercialization Across America," June 4, 2021, https://www.energy.gov/articles/doe-awards-95-million-support-clean-energy-innovation-and-commercialization-across-america.

22. U.S. Department of Energy, "DOE Awards $9.5 Million."

23. U.S. Department of Energy, "Technology Readiness Assessment Guide," September 15, 2011, https://www2.lbl.gov/dir/assets/docs/TRL%20guide.pdf.

24. ARPA-E, "SCALEUP 2019," accessed September 27, 2022, https://arpa-e.energy.gov/technologies/scaleup/scaleup-2019.

25. ARPA-E, "SCALEUP2019."

26. ARPA-E, "Our Impact," accessed September 27, 2022, https://arpa-e.energy.gov/about/our-impact.

27. ARPA-E, "Our Impact."

28. ARPA-E, "Fiscal Year Budget Request," 2009–2022, https://arpa-e.energy.gov/about/budget-requests.

29. Lane Genatowski, phone interview by the author, April 26, 2022.

30. ARPA-E, "ARPA-E Energy Innovation Summit: The Future Needs to Be Now," accessed September 27, 2022, https://www.arpae-summit.com.

31. ARPA-E, "OPEN 2021," September 27, 2022, https://arpa-e.energy.gov/open-2021.

32. ARPA-E, "OPEN 21."

33. EPRI, "Overview," provided to author, February 2022.

34. EPRI, "Overview"; "Interview with Arshad Mansoor," *EPRI Journal*, March 2002.

35. Arshad Mansoor, phone interview by the author, March 11, 2022.

36. "Interview with Arshad Mansoor."

37. Drew McGuire, "Rethinking Resistance: The Underground Option," July 19, 2022, p. 3, https://arpa-e.energy.gov/sites/default/files/03%20Drew%20McGuire%20EPRI%20APRA-E%20Workshop%20McGuire.pdf.

38. McGuire, "Rethinking Resistance."

39. McGuire, "Rethinking Resistance."

40. Arshad Mansoor, phone interview by the author, March 14, 2022.

41. McGuire, "Rethinking Resistance."

42. McGuire, "Rethinking Resistance."

43. McGuire, "Rethinking Resistance."

44. "EPRI's Greatest Achievements," *EPRI Journal*, January–February 1993, pp. 34–40, http://eprijournal.com/wp-content/uploads/2016/01/1993-Journal-No.-1.pdf; "Milestones of Science and Technology: 25 Years of Powering Progress," *EPRI Journal*, January–February 1998, pp. 4–15, http://eprijournal.com/wp-content/uploads/2016/02/1998-Journal-No.-1.pdf.

45. EPRI, "Developing a Framework for Integrated Energy Network Planning (IEN-P): Executive Summary—10 Key Challenges for Future Electric System Resource Planning," 2018, http://mydocs.epri.com/docs/PublicMeetingMaterials/ee/000000003002014154.pdf.

46. EPRI, "Developing a Framework."

47. Anda Ray, "Eyes Wide Open: The Digital Utility," presentation at the Western Area NARUC Conference, May 23, 2017.

48. "Milestones of Science and Technology."

49. EPRI Incubate Energy, "Contributions by Incubatenergy Staff," May 2022, internal document.

50. "Milestones of Science and Technology."

51. Incubatenergy Labs, "Welcome to Incubatenergy Labs," accessed October 24, 2022, https://labs.incubatenergy.org.

52. EPRI Incubate Energy, "Contributions by Incubatenergy Staff."

53. GTI Energy, "GTI and EPRI Low-Carbon Resources Initiative Surpasses 50 Global Partners to Advance Net-Zero Solutions," February 14, 2022, https://www.gti.energy/gti-and-epri-low-carbon-resources-initiative-surpasses-50-global-partners-to-advance-net-zero-solutions; "EPRI, GTI Research Vision Identifies R&D Priorities to Accelerate Energy System Decarbonization," *PR Newswire*, April 19, 2021, https://www.prnewswire.com/news-releases/epri-gti-research-vision-identifies-rd-priorities-to-accelerate-energy-system-decarbonization-301271519.html.

54. "EPRI, GTI Research Vision Identifies R&D Priorities."

55. Mansoor, phone interview by the author, May 11, 2022.

56. EPRI, "Strategies and Actions for Achieving a 50% Reduction in U.S. Greenhouse Gases by 2030," November 19, 2021, http://mydocs.epri.com/docs/public/EPRI-Whitepaper-Strategies-and-Actions-for-US-GHG-Reduction.pdf.

57. EPRI, "Strategies and Actions."

58. EPRI, "Technology Innovation Prospectus, 2020–2021: Pathways to a Decarbonized Future," August 13, 2020, https://www.epri.com/research/products/000000003002019513.

59. Mansoor, phone interview by the author, May 11, 2022.

60. EPRI, "Technology Innovation Prospectus."

61. EPRI, "Technology Innovation Prospectus."

62. EPRI, "Technology Innovation Prospectus."

63. EPRI, "Technology Innovation Prospectus."

64. EPRI, "2022 Research Portfolio: Driving Toward a Clean Energy Future," June 15, 2021, https://www.epri.com/research/products/000000003002020301.

65. Mansoor, phone interview by the author, May 11, 2022.

66. EPRI, "2022 Research Portfolio."

67. EPRI, "2022 Research Portfolio."

68. EPRI, "2022 Research Portfolio."

69. Edison Electric Institute, "About EEI," accessed September 27, 2022, https://www.eei.org/about-eei/About.

70. Statement provided via email to the author by EEI on behalf of Tom Kuhn, May 2022.

71. Edison Electric Institute and American Gas Association, "EG/Sustainability Template, Version 3," 2021, https://www.eei.org/en/issues-and-policy/esg-sustainability.

72. Edison Electric Institute and American Gas Association, "EG/Sustainability Template."

73. Carbon-Free Technology Initiative, "About the Carbon-Free Technology Initiative," February 7, 2022, https://www.carbonfreetech.org/-/media/Files/CarbonFree/documents/CFTI-Overview.pdf.

74. Carbon-Free Technology Initiative, "About the Carbon-Free Technology Initiative."

75. Carbon-Free Technology Initiative, "About the Carbon-Free Technology Initiative."

76. EPRI, "LCRI Research Vision: Executive Summary," May 20, 2022, https://lcri-vision.epri.com/summary/.

77. EPRI, "LCRI Research Vision."

78. Edison Foundation Institute for Electric Innovation, "2022 Year Ahead," 2022, https://www.edisonfoundation.net/-/media/Files/IEI/about/IEI_Year-Ahead_2022.pdf.

79. Edison Electric Institute, "Emerging Technologies to Bridge the Gap to Net Zero: Clean Energy Transition Hybrid Forum," October 2021.

80. Edison Electric Institute, "Emerging Technologies."

81. Richard McMahon, phone interview by the author, May 2022.

82. Guggenheim Securities, "Investing in Advanced Nuclear: A Catalyst for Our Clean Energy Future," April 2022.

83. Statement provided via email to the author by EEI on behalf of Tom Kuhn, May 2022.

84. Edison Electric Institute, "Delivering America's Resilient Clean Energy: Electric Power Industry Outlook," February 9, 2022, https://www.eei.org/-/media/Project/EEI/Documents/Issues-and-Policy/Finance-And-Tax/WSB-Prepared-Remarks.pdf.

85. Energy Impact Partners, "Get in Touch with Us," accessed September 27, 2022, https://www.energyimpactpartners.com/how-to-reach-us/.

86. Energy Impact Partners, "Platform Overview," April 2022, internal document.

87. Statement provided via email to the author by EIP on behalf of Hans Kobler, May 2022.

88. Mark Lantrip, interview by the author, Atlanta, GA, May 2022.

89. Energy Impact Partners, "Platform Overview."

90. Energy Impact Partners, "Platform Overview."

91. Energy Impact Partners, "Platform Overview."

92. Energy Impact Partners, "Get in Touch with Us."

93. Energy Impact Partners, "Management Information," June 2022, internal document.

94. Energy Impact Partners, "Platform Overview."

95. Kevin Fitzgerald, phone interview by the author, San Diego, CA, May 2022.

96. Energy Impact Partners, "Management Information."

97. Energy Impact Partners, "Get in Touch with Us."

98. Energy Impact Partners, "Get in Touch with Us."

99. Energy Impact Partners, "Platform Overview."

100. Energy Impact Partners, "Platform Overview."

101. Energy Impact Partners, "Get in Touch with Us."

102. Statement provided via email to the author by EIP on behalf of Hans Kobler, May 2022.

103. Energy Impact Partners, "Platform Overview."

104. Statement provided via email to the author by EIP on behalf of Hans Kobler, May 2022.

105. CLT Joules, "Strategy Advance," February 17, 2016, internal document.

106. CLT Joules, "Strategy Advance."

107. CLT Joules, "Strategy Advance."

108. Bob Irvin, phone interview by the author, March 14, 2022.

109. Joules Accelerator, "Partner Engagement: Decarbonization through Innovation," Quarter 1, 2022, internal document.

110. Joules Accelerator, "Partner Engagement."

111. Joules Accelerator, "Partner Engagement."

112. Joules Accelerator, "Partner Engagement."

113. Irvin, phone interview by the author.

114. Joules Accelerator, "Partner Engagement."

115. Joules Accelerator, "Partner Engagement."

116. Joules Accelerator, "Partner Engagement."

117. Joules Accelerator, "Partner Engagement."

118. Irvin, phone interview by the author.

CHAPTER 6

1. Ameren, "2014 Point of View Update: Full Report," internal document, August 14, 2014.

2. Cortex Innovation Community, "About," accessed September 30, 2022, https://www.cortexstl.org/about.

3. University of Illinois Urbana-Champaign, "Ameren Innovation Center Opens at the University of Illinois Research Park," February 10, 2015, https://researchpark.illinois.edu/article/ameren-innovation-center-opens-at-the-university-of-illinois-research-park.

4. Ameren, "Technology Application Center and Innovation Summary," 2022, internal document.

5. Mark Fronmuller, interview by the author, St. Louis, MO, April 21, 2022.

6. Warner Baxter, interview by the author, St. Louis, MO, April 21, 2022.

7. Ameren, "Mission, Values, Vision, Strategies," 2015, internal document.

8. University of Illinois Urbana-Champaign, "Success Stories—Ameren Innovation Center," accessed September 30, 2022, https://researchpark.illinois.edu/impact/success-stories/ameren.

9. Ameren, "New Member On-Boarding Packet," 2015, internal document.

10. Fronmuller, interview by the author.

11. Ameren, "Innovation Categories," 2021, internal document.

12. Fronmuller, interview by the author.

13. Ameren, "Crowdsourcing Event Summary," 2022, internal document.

14. Steve Mitnick, Gui Maia, Tracy West, and Kevin Schwain, "Fortnightly Smartest Utility Projects, 2020," *Fortnightly Magazine*, September 2020, https://www.fortnightly.com/fortnightly/2020/09/fortnightly-smartest-utility-projects-2020.

15. Energy Impact Partners, "Platform Overview," April 2022, internal document.

16. Cultivation Capital, "Midwest Seed Stage," accessed October 24, 2022, https://cultivationcapital.com/strategies/midwest-seed-stage; Nathan Rubbelke, "What Pandemic? Spirit of St. Louis Fund Boosts Startup Portfolio by 44% since March," *St. Louis Business Journal*, September 15, 2020, https://www.bizjournals.com/stlouis/news/2020/09/15/what-pandemic-spirit-of-st-louis-fund-boosts-sta.html.

17. Fronmuller, interview by the author.

18. Ameren, "Summary Energy Foundry Fund," May 2022, internal document.

19. Ameren, "Start-Up Companies Selected for the Ameren Accelerator," *PR Newswire*, July 28, 2017, https://www.prnewswire.com/news-releases/startup-companies-selected-for-the-ameren-accelerator-300495869.html.

20. Ameren, "Six Start-Up Companies from around the World Selected to Participate in the 2018 Ameren Accelerator," *PR Newswire*, June 22, 2018, https://www.prnewswire.com/news-releases/six-startup-companies-from-around-the-world-selected-to-participate-in-the-2018-ameren-accelerator-300670638.html; Ameren, "Six Start-Ups Showcase Sustainable Technologies and Innovations at Ameren Accelerator Demo Day," *PR Newswire*, November 4, 2019, https://www.prnewswire.com/news-releases/six-energy-startups-showcase-sustainable-technologies-and-innovations-at-ameren-accelerator-demo-day-300950773.html.

21. Fronmuller, interview by the author.

22. Baxter, interview by the author.

23. Ed Schlect, "Innovation Background Notes," Avista, March 11, 2022, internal document in.

24. Schlect, "Innovation Background Notes."

25. Avista, "Avista's History of Innovation," March 2022, internal document; Schlect, "Innovation Background Notes."

26. Avista, "130 Years of Innovation," 2022; Curt Kirkeby, "Innovation Timeline—Technology Milestones," April 8, 2022, internal document.

27. Scott Morris, phone interview by the author, April 18, 2022.

28. Heather Rosentrater and Ed Schlect, interview by the author, Spokane, WA, April 15, 2022.

29. Rosentrater and Schlect, interview by the author.

30. Urbanova, "Fact Sheet," December 2019, https://urbanova.org/wp-content/uploads/2019/12/Urbanova-Fact-Sheet.pdf.

31. Avista, "Avista's Legacy of Innovation," April 2022, internal document.

32. Avista, "Innovation Station: Connecting Ideas and Filling the Gaps," 2019, internal document.

33. Morris, phone interview by the author.

34. Rosentrater and Schlect, interview by the author; Latisha Hill, interview by the author, Spokane, WA, April 15, 2022.

35. Latisha Hill, "Community Recognition for Pedestrian Bridge and Progress Notes," Avista, October 25, 2019, internal document.

36. Living Future, "South Landing at University District," 2019, internal document.

37. John Gibson and Curt Kirkeby, interview by the author, April 15, 2022.

38. Morris, phone interview by the author.

39. Energy Capital Ventures, "Providing a Platform for Innovation," accessed October 3, 2022, https://www.energycapitalventures.com/about.

40. Rosentrater and Schlect, interview by the author.

41. Dennis Vermillion, interview by the author, Spokane, WA, April 15, 2022.

42. Vermillion, interview by the author.

43. Wolfe Research, "Utilities and Power: What Bear Market: AGA Conference Takeaways," May 19, 2022, internal document.

44. Duke Energy, "Earnings Review and Business Update: Q4, 2021," February 10, 2022, p. 10, https://desitecoreprod-cd.azureedge.net/_/media/pdfs/our-company/investors/news-and-events/2021/4qresults/q4-2021-earnings-presentation-reg-g.pdf.

45. Duke Energy, "Innovation Research and Development," 1997, internal document.

46. H. B. Wolf, "Duke Energy Company Innovation," 1986, internal document.

47. Wolf, "Duke Energy Company Innovation."

48. Duke Energy, "ETO Evaluation Process and Technology Roadmaps," 2012, internal document.

49. Duke Energy, "ETO Evaluation Process."

50. Lynn Good, interview by the author, Charlotte, NC, March 15, 2022.

51. Duke Energy, "Innovation Overview: Energy Technology Innovation and Training Center," February 28, 2022, internal document.

52. Duke Energy, "Duke Energy's Industry Leading Carbon Calculator Tool: Enabling Sustainability," March 2022, internal document; Duke Energy, "Customer Prototype Lab Transforming Customer Experience through the Power of Collective . . . ," March 2022, internal document; Duke Energy, "Innovation at Its Finest: Customer Solutions Teammates Invent the Smart Cord," March 2022, internal document; eTransEnergy,

"Streamlined Fleet Electrification," accessed October 3, 2022, https://www
.etransenergy.com; John Downey, "Duke Proposes 'Cutting Edge' Electric
Vehicle Pilot Program," *Charlotte Inno*, February 16, 2022, https://www
.bizjournals.com/charlotte/inno/stories/news/2022/02/16/duke-energy
-proposes-flat-fee-car-charging-pilot.html; Duke Energy, "First-of-a-
Kind Innovation," March 2022, internal document.

53. Tom Fenimore, "Emerging Technology Innovation and Training Center:
    Initiatives Overview," February 28, 2022, internal document; Duke Energy,
    "2021 Duke Energy Annual Report and Form 10-K: Powering the Clean
    Energy Transformation," February 24, 2022, https://desitecoreprod-cd
    .azureedge.net/annual-report/_/media/pdfs/our-company/investors/
    de-annual-reports/2021/2021-duke-energy-annual-report.pdf.

54. Brian Savoy, interview by the author, Charlotte, NC, April 14, 2022.

55. Brad Wood, "Energy Evolution Crowdsourcing Challenge Notes,"
    March 24, 2022, internal document.

56. Wood, "Energy Evolution Crowdsourcing Challenge."

57. Wood, "Energy Evolution Crowdsourcing Challenge."

58. Duke Energy, "The Businesses We're In," accessed October 3, 2022,
    https://www.duke-energy.com/our-company/about-us/businesses.

59. Duke Energy, "The Businesses We're In."

60. Duke Energy, "The Businesses We're In."

61. Duke Energy, "The Businesses We're In."

62. Good, interview by the author.

63. National Grid Partners, "About," accessed October 3, 2022,
    https://ngpartners.com/about.

64. National Grid USA, "NGUSA Innovation Report: FY22 Mid-Year,"
    September 2022, internal document.

65. National Grid USA, "NGUSA Innovation Report."

66. John Pettigrew, video interview by the author, April 20, 2022.

67. John Pettigrew, Ben Wilson, and Steve Woerner, phone interview by the
    author, April 2022.

68. Steve Woerner, interview by the author, May 2022; Edison Electric
    Institute, "National Grid Becomes First Major Utility to Join EV 100,"
    June 2021, https://www.eei.org/delivering-the-future/Articles/
    National-Grid-Becomes-First-Major-Electric-Company-to-Join-EV100;
    Jonathan Glass, interview by the author, April 2022; Jonathan Greig,
    "IBM and Boston Dynamics Partner for National Grid Project Involving
    Robotic Dog," *ZD Net*, October 29, 2021, https://www.zdnet.com/article/
    ibm-and-boston-dynamics-partner-for-national-grid-project-involving
    -robot-dog/; National Grid, "Collaboration Brings World-First Kerbside

Charging to London," January 30, 2019, https://www.nationalgrid
.com/uk/stories-journey-to-net-zero/collaboration-brings-world
-first-kerbside-charging-london; Zero Carbon Humber, "Capture for
Growth: A Roadmap for the World's First Zero Carbon Industrial
Cluster," 2019, https://www.zerocarbonhumber.co.uk/wp-content/
uploads/2019/11/Capture-for-Growth-Zero-Carbon-Humber-V4.9
-Digital.pdf; National Grid, "National Grid Builds World's First T-Pylon
in Somerset," September 13, 2021, https://www.nationalgrid.com/
national-grid-build-worlds-first-t-pylon-somerset; National Grid, "North
Sea Link: Connecting the UK to Clean, Reliable Energy," May 11, 2022,
https://www.nationalgrid.com/national-grid-ventures/interconnectors
-connecting-cleaner-future/north-sea-link; National Grid, "National Grid
and Hitachi Energy Announce World's First Collaboration to Replace
Existing SF6 in High-Voltage Equipment," December 9, 2021, https://
www.nationalgrid.com/national-grid-and-hitachi-energy-announce
-world-first-collaboration-replace-sf6-existing-high.

69. Lisa Lambert, "NextGrid Alliance: Change Is Coming—Time for a
Conversation," accessed October 24, 2022, https://ngalliance.energy/page/
about-the-nextgrid-alliance; see also NextGrid Alliance, "Investing in the
Potential of Energy," accessed October 24, 2022, https://ngalliance.energy/
page/about-national-grid-partners.

70. National Grid, "Strategy Briefing: Shaping Our Future," July 26, 2016,
internal document.

71. National Grid, "Strategy Briefing: Shaping Our Future."

72. National Grid, "Strategy Briefing: Shaping Our Future."

73. National Grid, "Strategy Briefing: Shaping Our Future."

74. National Grid, "A Message from Andi Karaboutis: Digital," October 3,
2019, internal document.

75. Ben Wilson, video interview by the author, April 20, 2022.

76. National Grid, "Strategy Briefing: NG Digital Strategy," January 29, 2019,
internal document.

77. National Grid, "Strategy Briefing: Scaling Digital," 2021, internal
document.

78. National Grid, "Strategy Briefing: Scaling Digital."

79. David Smith, phone interview by author, May 10, 2022.

80. BCG Digital Ventures, "National Grid Hack-a-Future: Embed
Handbook," October 2019, internal document.

81. Smith, phone interview by the author.

82. Chris Kelly, interview by the author, March 9, 2022.

83. National Grid, "Strategy Briefing: Scaling Digital."

84. National Grid, "Strategy Briefing: Scaling Digital."

85.   Pettigrew, video interview by the author.
86.   National Grid USA, "NGUSA Innovation Report."
87.   National Grid Partners, "About."
88.   National Grid Partners, "About."
89.   National Grid Partners, "About."
90.   National Grid Partners, "About."
91.   Sam Heys, *Innovative Solutions: A History of R&D at Southern Company* (Atlanta: Southern Company, 2013).
92.   Heys, *Innovative Solutions*.
93.   Heys, *Innovative Solutions*.
94.   Heys, *Innovative Solutions*.
95.   Heys, *Innovative Solutions*.
96.   Heys, *Innovative Solutions*.
97.   Heys, *Innovative Solutions*.
98.   Heys, *Innovative Solutions*.
99.   Heys, *Innovative Solutions*.
100. Southern Company, "50 Year Anniversary Stories: Research and Development," 2019, internal document.
101. Southern Company, "Innovation," accessed October 7, 2022, https://www.southerncompany.com/innovation.html.
102. Southern Company, "Research Portfolio," accessed October 7, 2022, https://www.southerncompany.com/innovation/research-and -development/research-portfolio.html.
103. Southern Company, "Innovation."
104. Southern Company, "Innovation."
105. Tom Fanning, interview by the author, Atlanta, GA, March 30, 2022.
106. Southern Company, "SO Prize: Meeting with Tom Fanning," April 2014, internal document.
107. Southern Company, "A Message from Tom," April 1, 2015, internal document.
108. Southern Company, "SO Prize: Idea Inventory Tracker," June 2014, internal document.
109. Southern Company, "SO Prize: Inventing Southern Company's Future— Commemorative Edition," 2014, https://www.southerncompany .com/content/dam/southern-company/pdf/public/SO_Prize_2014_ commemorative_book.pdf.
110. Southern Company, "SO Prize: Inventing Southern Company's Future."
111. Southern Company, "SO Prize: Inventing Southern Company's Future."
112. Southern Company, "Energy Innovation Center," December 14, 2018, internal document.
113. Southern Company, "Energy Innovation Center."

114. Southern Company, "Energy Innovation Center."

115. Mark Lantrip, interview by the author, Atlanta, GA, March 30, 2022.

116. Energy Impact Partners, "Private Placement Memorandum: Energy Impact Fund LP," May 2017, internal document.

117. Energy Impact Partners, "Platform Overview," April 2022, internal document.

118. Fanning, interview by the author.

119. John Gurda, *Path of a Pioneer: A Centennial History of the Wisconsin Electric Power Company* (Milwaukee: Wisconsin Energy Company, 1996).

120. Gale Klappa, phone interview by the author, April 18, 2022.

121. Gurda, *Path of a Pioneer*, 199–257.

122. Klappa, phone interview by the author.

123. Gurda, *Path of a Pioneer*.

124. Gurda, *Path of a Pioneer*.

125. Gurda, *Path of a Pioneer*.

126. We Energies, "Power the Future," 2012, internal document.

127. We Energies, "Power the Future."

128. WEC Energy, "Our 'ESG' Progress Plan: Investing in Efficiency, Sustainability and Growth," May 2022, https://s22.q4cdn.com/994559668/files/doc_presentations/2022/05/05-2022-May.pdf.

129. We Energies, "Power the Future."

130. WEC Energy, "Our 'ESG' Progress Plan"; U.S. Department of Energy Office of Fossil Energy and Carbon Management, "Milestone Project Demonstrates Innovative Mercury Emissions Reduction Technology," January 12, 2010, https://www.energy.gov/fecm/articles/milestone-project-demonstrates-innovative-mercury-emissions; "Pleasant Prairie Chilled Ammonia Project Shows 90% Carbon Capture, Companies Say," *Power*, October 14, 2009, https://www.powermag.com/pleasant-prairie-chilled-ammonia-pilot-shows-90-carbon-capture-companies-say; Edison Electric Institute, "Wisconsin Energy Wins Prestigious Edison Award for Innovative Combustion Products Program," June 8, 2004; "Oak Creek Power Plant Upgrades Cooling Water System," *Power*, March 1, 2009, https://www.powermag.com/oak-creek-power-plant-upgrades-cooling-water-system.

131. WEC Energy, "WEC Energy Group Announces Hydrogen Power Pilot Program," *PR Newswire*, January 25, 2022, https://www.prnewswire.com/news-releases/wec-energy-group-announces-hydrogen-power-pilot-program-301467367.html.

132. Klappa, interview by the author.

133. Energize Ventures, "About," accessed October 7, 2022, https://www.energize.vc/about.

134. Helen A.S. Popkin, Alan Ohnsman, and Kenrick Cai, "The AI 50, 2022," *Forbes*, May 9, 2022, https://www.forbes.com/lists/ai50/?sh=1c919e39290f.

135. Dan Krueger, phone interview by the author, April 2022.

CHAPTER 9

1. Energy Information Administration, "Electricity Residential Retail Choice Participation Has Declined since 2014 Peak," November 8, 2018, https://www.eia.gov/todayinenergy/detail.php?id=37452#.

About the Author

THOMAS J. FLAHERTY, a former senior partner at Strategy&, has enjoyed a global consulting career that has spanned more than 45 years, leading utilities consulting practices at several top-tier firms. Focusing on all sectors of the utilities industry, he specializes in corporate strategy, mergers and acquisitions, business models, organization architecture, and innovation. He is currently a senior advisor to EY-Parthenon, focusing on these areas.

Starting in 2013, Flaherty assisted numerous utilities in identifying market trends that would drive reshaping industry market position; evaluating emerging technologies and use cases that could benefit grid and network performance, flexibility, and insight; and supporting the introduction of utility innovation models, design and conduct of crowdsourcing events, evaluation of potential partnerships, stand-up of focused innovation centers, and adoption of potential methods to embed a culture of innovation within the business.

He is also the author of *Roll-Up: The Past, Present, and Future of Utilities Consolidation*, a look at how industry consolidation developed and was executed through the modern era of utility mergers and acquisitions.